BRITAIN, AMERICA, AND THE VIETNAM WAR

Recent Titles in International History

BRITAIN, AMERICA, AND THE VIETNAM WAR

Sylvia Ellis

International History

Erik Goldstein, William R. Keylor, and Cathal J. Nolan, Series Editors

Westport, Connecticut
London

Library of Congress Cataloging-in-Publication Data

Ellis, Sylvia.
    Britain, America, and the Vietnam War / Sylvia Ellis.
        p.   cm. — (International history)
    Includes bibliographical references and index.
    ISBN 0–275–97381–6 (alk. paper)
        1. Vietnamese Conflict, 1961–1975. 2. Vietnamese Conflict, 1961–1975—Great
    Britain. 3. Vietnamese Conflict, 1961–1975—United States. I. Title. II. Series.
    DS557.7.E474   2004
    959.704'3341—dc22   2004000291

British Library Cataloguing in Publication Data is available.

Library of Congress Catalog Card Number: 2004000291
ISBN: 0–275–97381–6
ISSN: 1527–2230

First published in 2004

Praeger Publishers, 88 Post Road West, Westport, CT 06881
An imprint of Greenwood Publishing Group, Inc.
www.praeger.com

Printed in the United States of America

The paper used in this book complies with the
Permanent Paper Standard issued by the National
Information Standards Organization (Z39.48–1984).

10 9 8 7 6 5 4 3 2 1

For my parents, Harold and Elaine

Contents

Series Foreword

Erik Goldstein, William R. Keylor, and Cathal J. Nolan

This series furthers historical writing that is genuinely international in scope and multi-archival in methodology. It publishes different types of works in the field of international history: scholarly monographs which elucidate important but hitherto unexplored or underexplored topics; more general works which incorporate the results of specialized studies and present them to a wider public; and edited volumes which bring together distinguished scholars to address salient issues in international history.

The series promotes scholarship in traditional sub-fields of international history such as the political, military, diplomatic, and economic relations among states. But it also welcomes studies which address topics of nonstate history and of more recent interest, such as the role of international nongovernmental organizations in promoting new policies, cultural relations among societies, and the history of private international economic activity.

In short, while this series happily embraces traditional diplomatic history, it does not operate on the assumption that the state is an autonomous actor in international relations and that the job of the international historian is done solely by consulting the official records left behind by various foreign offices. Instead, it encourages scholarly work which also probes the broader forces within society that influence the formulation and execution of foreign policies, social tensions, religious and ethnic conflict, economic competition, environmental concerns, scientific technology issues, and international cultural relations.

On the other hand, the series eschews works which concentrate exclusively on the foreign policy of any single nation. Hence, notwithstanding the central role played by the United States in international affairs since World War II, or of Great Britain in the nineteenth century, history written according to "the view from Washington" or "the view from London" does not satisfy the editors' criteria for international history, in the proper sense of that term. The books in this series do not assume a parochial perspective. In addition to reviewing the domestic context of any one country's foreign policies, they also accord appropriate consideration to the consequences of those policies abroad and the reciprocal relationship between the country of primary interest and other countries (and actors) with which it comes into contact.

The vast majority of recent publications in international history, in both book and article form, deal with the period since the end of the Second World War. The Cold War in particular has generated an impressive and constantly expanding body of historical scholarship. While this series also publishes works which treat this recent historical period, overall it takes a long view of international history. It is deeply interested in scholarship dealing with much earlier, even classical, eras of world history. The prospect of obtaining access to newly declassified documentary records (from Western governments and especially from the former members of the Warsaw Pact Organization) is an exciting one and will doubtless lead to the publication of important works which deepen our understanding of the recent past. But historians must not be dissuaded from investigating periods in the more distant past. Although most of the pertinent archives for such periods have been available for some time and have already been perused by scholars, renewed interpretations and assessments of earlier historical developments are essential to any ongoing understanding of the roots of the contemporary world.

The editors of this series hold appointments in departments of history, political science, and international relations. They are, therefore, deeply committed to an interdisciplinary approach to international history and welcome submissions from scholars in all these separate, but interrelated, disciplines. But that eclectic, humanistic approach should not be misconstrued to mean that any political science or international relations work will be of interest to the series, or its readers. Scholars from any discipline who locate their research and writing in the classical tradition of intellectual inquiry, that which examines the historical antecedents of international conflict and cooperation in order to understand contemporary affairs, are welcome to submit works for consideration. Such scholars are not interested in constructing abstract, and abstruse, theoretical models which have little relation to historical reality, and possess no explanatory power for contemporary affairs, either. Instead, they share the conviction that a careful, scrupulous, deeply scholarly examination of historical evidence is a prerequisite to understanding the past, living in the present, and preparing for the future. And most fundamentally, although they may disagree on the precise meaning of this or that past event or decision, they reject the fashionable but ultimately intellectually and morally sterile assertion that historical truth is entirely relative, and therefore that all interpretations of past events are equally valid, or equally squalid, as they merely reflect the whims and prejudices of individual historians. This group of scholars, the natural clientele of this series, instead believes that it is the principal obligation of scholarship to ferret out real and lasting truths. Furthermore, they believe that having done so, the results of scholarly investigation must be conveyed with clarity and precision to a more general audience, in jargon-free, unpretentious language which any intelligent reader may readily comprehend.

Acknowledgments

In the process of exploring British involvement in the Vietnam War I have incurred many debts. Generous financial support was provided by the British Academy and the University of Northumbria for the completion of the project. Several colleagues read and commented on parts of this book, including Donald MacRaild, John Dumbrell, Bernard Porter, Patrick Salmon, and Brian Ward, and many others encouraged me along the way. I also owe thanks to associates who provided me with useful guidance, research materials, or both, including Clive Ponting, Colin Holmes, John Thompson, and John Ramsden. Special thanks also go to those politicians and diplomats on both sides of the Atlantic who agreed to be interviewed by me, often at short notice. I was also aided by the efficiency and guidance of librarians and archivists at the John F. Kennedy Library, the Lyndon Baines Johnson Library, the Public Record Office, and the Virginia Historical Society.

My family supported this project from start to finish. My parents are my inspiration in life and have always loved, supported, and believed in me. I dedicate this book to them. My sister Denise and brother-in-law Jeremy have done more than their fair share of duties as godparents of my children, and always with a smile. The arrival of my two beautiful daughters, Cara and Aisling, delayed production of this volume but provided a reason to continue with it. They have tolerated my absences, both physical and mental, and have proved a welcome distraction at times of frustration. Most of all my thanks go to my husband, Anthony, whose own love of the United States meant that family vacations often dovetailed research trips and who alone knows how much I value his patience, help, and understanding.

Introduction

In 1971, George Ball, former U.S. undersecretary of state in the Johnson administration, famously admitted that Vietnam "made it very hard to get attention on anything else, that judgments tended to be colored by the Vietnamese situation...we were getting things totally distorted....In fact, I once drew a map for Dean Rusk and said, '[T]his is your map of the world.' I had a tiny United States with an enormous Vietnam lying right off the coast." As an example of this obsession Ball mentioned that the Johnson administration "pressed the British so hard to stay in line on Vietnam" that he was "sure we were willing to pay some costs for it we wouldn't have paid otherwise."[1] The need for allied support in its Vietnam crusade was extremely important to the United States, and this work will consider the pressure U.S. leaders put on the United Kingdom to remain loyal on Vietnam and what price they were willing to pay to ensure this. The United States, strong militarily and economically, was unable to convince its European allies to give direct aid to the American fight in Vietnam, having to settle instead for verbal, diplomatic approval of its actions. The value of British support, as will be shown, was extremely important to the Johnson administration's efforts in Southeast Asia, even if that support was limited, and political rather than military.

This book examines three interrelated themes. First, it seeks to further understanding of the Vietnam War by focusing on the bilateral relationship between the United States and one of its key allies, the United Kingdom, during the years in which the war escalated. It will also continue the process of providing a broader context to the study of the war in particular, and of American foreign relations in general, in that relatively little attention has been paid to the international environment in which the United States made its decisions on Vietnam or to the impact of its policies on the wider world.[2] Yet external as well as internal factors clearly shaped American policy on Vietnam. Despite its

weakening economic and military position, Britain was still an important and
respected actor on the world scene; even President Johnson referred to the
country, however disingenuously at times, as America's most important ally.
The American public agreed with their president's assessment. A Gallup opinion poll in March 1965 found that respondents judged Britain the United
States' most reliable ally and ranked it as the fourth most important country in
the world after the United States, the USSR, and China.[3] A study of
Anglo–American relations during the Vietnam War highlights America's difficulties in persuading Great Britain to cooperate on this issue and will explore
why, unlike in the Korean War that preceded it (and the subsequent wars in the
Gulf), the United States was forced to fight without the military support of its
closest ally. It is also necessary to ask whether the British government can be
criticized for failing to challenge the Johnson administration over its involvement in Vietnam or to offer alternatives to its policies there. Due to the British
30-year rule, historical assessments of the effects of the Vietnam War on
Anglo–American relations have until recently been constrained by the dearth
of authoritative sources. As a result, most analysis of Britain and the Vietnam
War has been found within the context of broader studies of the Anglo–
American relationship or the Vietnam War.[4] The main object of this study,
then, is to provide the first detailed account of the impact of the Vietnam War
on the transatlantic relationship.

It is in this context that one must examine Clive Ponting's claim in *Breach of
Promise* that 1965 saw President Johnson and Harold Wilson negotiate a series
of "understandings" that tied American financial support to a British commitment not to devalue the pound and to retain a military presence East of Suez.
The position of sterling, Britain's defense commitments, and the war in Vietnam were issues that could never be separated, and indeed the complex inter-
play between the three burdens is a key feature of Anglo–American relations in
the mid- to late sixties. Ponting's claim is now widely supported by most scholars in the field, although its exact nature is open to dispute.[5] Ponting also
claimed that by the spring of 1965 Wilson and Johnson had come to a "general
understanding" on the part the United Kingdom should play in Vietnam. The
British would provide no direct military assistance to the United States but
would support American action in Vietnam; the Americans committed themselves to keeping their transatlantic ally well informed of their policy in Vietnam and "reluctantly accepted" that Britain should use its role as cochair of the
1954 Geneva Conference to seek peace.[6] This work will describe the evolution
of British policy in Vietnam through the "understandings" and will show how
the Labour government avoided a direct confrontation with the Johnson administration through these secret agreements. It will consider, in particular,
what part Vietnam played in the later controversial understanding that linked
American support for sterling with the maintenance of Britain's worldwide
role.

The second aim of this book is to shed light on the nature and workings of the "special relationship" during what was undoubtedly a difficult period for both countries. The United States faced domestic and international criticism of its war in Vietnam; at the same time the country was riven with racial and other social unrest. If, as Ernest May and Gregory Treverton have claimed, the special relationship amounts to "a sense of company in a confusing, unfriendly world," then America clearly needed all the friends it could get during one of its most troubled periods.[7] Equally, Great Britain faced major economic turmoil and a concomitant readjustment to its world role; it too needed all the help it could get. Unlike most studies of Anglo–American relations, this study does not primarily examine the inequality of power between the nations, although much of the debate over Vietnam was predicated on the knowledge of this fact. It also concedes that Anglo–American relations during the 1960s were predicated on national interest, and thus it worked best where there was a convergence of objectives. However, this study will show how other factors—domestic politics, public opinion, and personality—affected the special relationship, focusing on how quite serious disagreements between Great Britain and the United States over Vietnam were handled and to some extent accommodated within the framework of the special, if unequal, relationship.

Case studies of the Anglo–American relationship have focused on short-term crises such as Suez, the Skybolt affair, and the Falklands War; a study of Anglo–American relations and the Vietnam War affords an opportunity to study how the relationship fared during a prolonged period of tension.[8] Richard Neustadt argued in *Alliance Politics* that misunderstandings are much more likely between countries with an intimate and close relationship; differences are magnified because more is expected of each other. At no time was this more apparent than during the Vietnam War. The Johnson administration hoped and expected, and at times almost demanded, loyalty and support from Britain on Vietnam. However, a brief consideration of the history of Anglo–American relations in Asia should have made the leadership in Washington well aware that Britain was unlikely to toe the line completely in this area. Usually agreeing on their aims in relation to Southeast Asia, since the Second World War Britain and America had, on several occasions, disagreed over the methods necessary to achieve their ends. The relationship was also characterized by a lack of frankness on Southeast Asia, with attendant mutual suspicions over the other's true position and motives. Most notably, tensions surfaced over Britain's willingness to recognize communist China and over the United States' failure to consult its key ally during the Korean War.[9] A cursory examination of British domestic politics should also have told the Johnson administration that there would be definite limits to the Labour government's support for U.S. actions in Vietnam. Britain would remain a reluctant and unconvinced ally on Vietnam.

Despite this relevant history, an analysis of Anglo–American relations and Vietnam in the mid-1960s shows that the White House and the State Department seemed to be operating a practice of doublethink where Britain and Vietnam were concerned. Although they acknowledged the reasons that the Wilson government could not commit troops to Vietnam, this acknowledgment did not overcome Washington's gut feeling that the British were not doing enough to help. The rhetoric and reality of the special relationship contributed greatly to this confusion in Washington and in London, for it is clear that the British government was also torn on how to behave "correctly"—according to conflicting criteria—regarding Vietnam. Should they be true friends by revealing their own misgivings about the Vietnam War, or should they support their closest ally come what may? In other words, to understand the mixture of intimacy and rancor that characterized Anglo–American relations in the mid-1960s, one needs to recognize that there was not only a divergence of national interest over Vietnam, but also a difference in perception between London and Washington over the role of a true ally.

Third, this work explores the relationship between personality and politics. It has long been considered true that relations between Harold Wilson and Lyndon Johnson were not merely cool but positively icy, especially when compared to the image of warm intimacy associated with John Kennedy and Harold Macmillan.[10] A great deal has been written about the part played by personal relationships in the smooth functioning of the special relationship, and though scholars agree that Anglo–American relations are, first and foremost, interest-led, there is still a lack of unanimity on the part played by personal chemistry.[11] It is generally acknowledged that a warm personal relationship between the leaders of Britain and America provides excellent public relations material for both countries and the individual heads of state involved and can foster a more cooperative working environment. The extent to which personal relations influence policy making is much less certain. It is hard to deny, however, the personal significance of the Vietnam War to President Lyndon Baines Johnson and many of his key advisors. For that reason, it has to be asked whether LBJ's obsession with Vietnam, mixed with his already volatile personality, decisively influenced U.S. relations with Great Britain. On the other side of the Atlantic, was Harold Wilson so impressed by, and fearful of, LBJ as a world leader and personality that his judgment was impaired on the issue of Vietnam? Was Britain, as Fredrik Logevall has suggested, too timid in its dealing with the Johnson administration on Vietnam?[12] Was this partly caused by uncertainty about the reaction Britain might face from an increasingly paranoid, possibly mentally unstable president? Could Britain have played a part—along with other critics of the U.S. military intervention in Vietnam—in preventing the Americanization of the Vietnam War by challenging the Johnson administration's premise for such action in the months leading up to July 1965? And, once the United States was committed to war, did Britain have any influence on the course of events in Southeast Asia?

The major sources of materials for this book were the Public Record Office, Kew (PRO), and the Lyndon Baines Johnson Library (LBJL) in Austin, Texas.[13]

Most files, and documents within files, have now been declassified. British government documents are often written in formal language that is largely dispassionate and considered. Fortunately, Harold Wilson often wrote his immediate thoughts and reactions on the documents, giving the historian some sense of the prime minister's personal stamp on events. President Johnson's presence is, however, noticeably absent in the papers contained in the Johnson Library. Reflecting his preference for verbal communication, particularly via the telephone, he rarely put his thoughts down on paper and only occasionally scribbled his responses on memoranda and letters.[14] Consequently, LBJ's opinions and feelings are gauged largely through his actions and through second and third parties such as advisors, ambassadors, and journalists. Fortunately, the secret White House tapes of the president's telephone conversations are now being released and allow invaluable insights into LBJ's thoughts. The relatively few conversations between Wilson and Johnson are not yet available. However, notes and transcripts of some key conversations do exist. The great benefit of the holdings in the LBJ Library is the inclusion of personal papers as well as official ones. These papers, particularly those of Johnson's key national security advisors, McGeorge Bundy and Walt W. Rostow, tend to be less formal than the State Department papers, although even these are more relaxed and open than British Foreign Office minutes. The Rostow and Bundy papers, along with the cable exchanges between the British ambassador in Washington and the Foreign Office, and the U.S. ambassador and the State Department, are crucial in understanding the behind-the-scenes activity that took place over Vietnam.

The papers contained in the LBJ Library and the PRO were buttressed by published sources such as the *Pentagon Papers*, the U.S. State Department's *Foreign Relations of the United States* series, and *Hansard*. Such official and semiofficial documents were supplemented by the private papers of key actors and by the many diaries, memoirs, and political autobiographies of the period. Though generally less reliable due to the possibility of self-aggrandizement on the part of the authors, they do provide either contemporary or retrospective explanations and justifications of British and American actions. The David Bruce diaries were particularly useful in ascertaining the day-to-day unfolding of events. Additional minor sources include newspapers and oral interviews with key politicians and diplomats. Many of these interviews were conducted on a confidential basis on the grounds that the interviewee could be more candid. In general, however, these interviews served only to confirm analysis based on consideration of available documentary evidence.

The book is divided into five major chapters, organized around the development and unraveling of the understandings between the White House and Downing Street on Vietnam. The chronological structure reveals both the oscillating nature of Anglo–American relations during the period and the processes by which policy was formulated and implemented. The chapters necessarily cover different lengths of time, dependent on the degree and frequency of activity between Britain and America on Vietnam. Chapter 1 discusses the background to and development of the Wilson government's thinking on Vietnam, focusing in particular on the first few months in office and the first summit meeting with President Johnson in December 1964. Chapter 2 examines how, as the war in Vietnam escalated, the British and the Americans increasingly occupied contested space on the issue of peace negotiations and recognized that a breach between the nations could be prevented only through an informal but real understanding on the issue. This understanding was reached by April 1965. Chapter 3 goes on to show that during the remainder of 1965 Washington and London sought to establish a wider understanding that encompassed Vietnam, East of Suez, and sterling. Chapters 4 and 5 show how, once the two nations reached that understanding, Prime Minister Wilson gradually reneged on those understandings during Johnson's remaining time in office. Ultimately, this work demonstrates that Vietnam was a constant and damaging undercurrent in relations between Washington and London between 1964 and 1968.

NOTES

1. Transcript, George Ball oral history interview by Paige E. Mulhollan, interview 2, tape 1, July 9, 1971, 17, Lyndon B. Johnson Library, Austin, Texas (henceforth LBJL).

2. The most important work in this area is Fredrik Logevall, *Choosing War: The Lost Chance for Peace and the Escalation of War in Vietnam* (Berkeley: University of California Press, 1999). Several recent conference and doctoral dissertations suggest that the international context of the war is a flourishing area of study.

3. C. J. Bartlett, *'The Special Relationship': A Political History in Anglo-American Relations since 1945* (London: Longman, 1992), 109.

4. To date, the only major examination is Caroline Page's doctoral thesis, "The Strategic Manipulation of American Official Propaganda during the Vietnam War, 1965–6 and British Opinion on the War." Based largely on unofficial sources and examining a brief time span, Page's study focused mainly on the effectiveness of American propaganda in retaining the support of the British press, public, and government. John Dumbrell's article "The Johnson Administration and the British Labour Government: Vietnam, the Pound and East of Suez," *Journal of American Studies* 30, part 2 (August 1996): 211–31, examined Anglo–American relations from the American viewpoint. Peter Busch, *All the Way with JFK? Britain, the U.S., and the Vietnam War* (Oxford: Oxford University Press, 2003) covers the period 1960–63.

5. Clive Ponting, *Breach of Promise: Labour in Power 1964–1970* (London: Penguin, 1990). Ponting's views are supported by scholars of Anglo–American relations and the Labour government, such as Alan P. Dobson, *Anglo-American Relations in the Twentieth Century* (London: Routledge, 1995); Bartlett, *'The Special Relationship'*; Ben Pimlott, *Harold Wilson* (London: Harper Collins, 1992); Philip Zeigler, *Wilson: The Authorized Life of Lord Wilson of Rievaulx* (London: Weidenfeld and Nicolson, 1993); Dumbrell, "The Johnson Administration and the British Labour Government"; and Saki

Dockrill, *Britain's Retreat from East of Suez: The Choice between Europe and the World?* (Basingstoke: Palgrave, 2002). The main challenge to this view can be found in Jeremy Fielding, "Coping with Decline: U.S. Policy towards the British Defence Reviews of 1966," *Diplomatic History* 23, no. 4 (Fall 1999): 633–56.

6. Ponting, *Breach of Promise*, 148.

7. Ernest R. May and Gregory F. Treverton, "Defence Relationships: American Perspectives," in William Roger Louis and Hedley Bull (eds.), *The Special Relationship: Anglo-American Relations since 1945* (Oxford: Oxford University Press, 1986), 181.

8. Richard Neustadt, *Alliance Politics* (London: Columbia University Press, 1970); Louise Richardson, *When Allies Differ: Anglo-American Relations during the Suez and Falklands Crisis* (New York: St. Martin's Press, 1996). The 1956 crisis over Suez was by far the most serious in terms of the international consequences; Skybolt was very much an intra-alliance crisis; and disagreements over the Falklands showed how the interests of Britain, the weaker power, conflicted with the interests of the stronger. However, in between the Skybolt crisis of 1962 and the Falklands crisis of 1982 was another important area of conflict: the Vietnam War.

9. Victor S. Kaufman, *Confronting Communism: U.S. and British Policies toward China* (Columbia: University of Missouri Press, 2001).

10. Scholars of Anglo–American relations characterize the relationship as cool. See Dobson, *Anglo-American Relations*; Bartlett, *'The Special Relationship'*; David Dimbleby and David Reynolds, *An Ocean Apart: The Relationship between Britain and America in the Twentieth Century* (London: Weidenfeld and Nicolson, 1988). Only Ziegler, *Wilson*, portrays the relationship as, on the whole, warm.

11. Esmond Wright, "The Special Relationship," *History Today* (April 1991), 53–57.

12. Logevall, *Choosing War*, 336, 403.

13. The files most consulted at the Public Record Office, Kew (henceforth PRO) were the Foreign Office (FO371), the Prime Minister's Office file (PREM), and the cabinet Minutes (CAB). In April 2003 the Public Record Office joined with the Historical Manuscripts Commission to become the National Archives of England, Wales, and the United Kingdom.

14. David C. Humphrey, "Searching for LBJ at the Johnson Library," *SHAFR* (Society for Historians of American Foreign Relations) *Newsletter* 20, June 1989, 1–17.

Chapter 1

The Labour Government's Position on Vietnam

In the 1950s and 1960s the British government placed Anglo–American relations at the center of its foreign policy, recognizing the need for an ally that
could be a key provider of manpower and resources in areas where Britain still
retained interests. This has been described as wanting "power-by-proxy."[1] With
decolonization well under way, the Foreign Office anticipated a reduced military burden combined with a continuance of British influence and interests in
its former colonial areas. By 1962, the Minister of Defense could state that
Britain's military strength was "no longer a concept of British forces dispersed
around the world in small pockets but a concentration on three main bases ...
Britain, Aden and Singapore."[2] Although its role had been reduced, Britain's
military commitments overseas still included major deployments in Europe,
the Middle East, and the Far East and as such were important in world affairs.
But as Jones has noted, Anglo–American relations faced a paradox in the 1960s.
Just as Great Britain was disengaging "from its old colonial commitments and
tried to refashion its international position according to its limited resources,
pressure from Washington to maintain a global role was actually on the increase."[3]

WASHINGTON'S SEARCH FOR ALLIES

Throughout the Kennedy and Johnson years, the U.S. government was alert
to the propaganda benefits of making its involvement in Southeast Asia appear
part of an allied crusade to prevent communist domination of the area. As early
as 1954, at the Geneva Conference, the American government had looked into

the likelihood of British military involvement as part of "united action" to prevent a French defeat in Vietnam. Britain refused, partly because further military action in the region would have been difficult to sell to the public in light
of the recent experience in Korea, but mainly on the grounds that any attempt
to internationalize the conflict might antagonize the Chinese and thereby cause
further instability in the region.[4] With the advent of the Kennedy administration and as America's own intervention in Vietnamese affairs intensified, even
more exhaustive inquiries into the possibility of allied contributions began. The
discussion of "Task Force Vietnam" inevitably encompassed the idea of inter-
nationalizing the problem. Along with the possibility of United Nations assistance (as ground observers) and the consideration of U.S. involvement under
the SEATO (South East Asia Treaty Organization) umbrella, the Kennedy advisors were particularly keen to get the British committed politically to the defense of South Vietnam.[5] One aide admitted that "others should share with us
the responsibility for Viet-Nam" and that British participation would "maximize the political benefits to be obtained within the western alliance by sharing
responsibility for this difficult problem."[6]

At this stage, the British government was supportive of U.S. attempts to find
a military solution to the conflict, believing firmly that communist domination
of the area was unacceptable, although harboring doubts, in private, about the
political leadership of President Diem.[7] In July 1961 this resulted in a private,
bilateral agreement between the British government and the government of
South Vietnam (GVN) to establish the British Advisory Group in South Vietnam, or British Advisory Mission (BRIAM), as it became known.[8] The purpose
of this mission was revealed to the House in a written answer on October 23,
1961, when Edward Heath answered questions on behalf of the government on
the circumstances surrounding the mission:

The Government of the Republic of Vietnam, one of whose major problems is the lack
of a sufficient number of trained administrators, requested Her Majesty's Government
to provide expert assistance in the field of administrative co-ordination and police matters. Her Majesty's Government agreed to dispatch an Advisory Mission to Saigon for
this purpose. The British Advisory Mission to Vietnam, which arrived in Saigon at the
end of September, consists of three officers and a small administrative staff led by Mr.
R.G.K. Thompson.[9]

The three officers were former members of the Malayan Civil Service and were
attached to the U.S. counterinsurgency team in Saigon. Robert Thompson had
demonstrated his credentials in counterinsurgency during the 12-year-long
Malayan emergency.[10] The costs of this mission were expected to total £110,000
per year, and the mission was not expected to issue reports on its work to the government. This angered many opposition members of Parliament (M.P.s), who felt
that Parliament should closely monitor the mission. While the British government denied that BRIAM was involved in the planning of specific operations, the
mission's role remained suspect throughout 1962 and 1963. Still, in October 1963

the government advised Parliament that the mission's life was to be extended to March 1965.[11] Its role was to advise on counterinsurgency techniques the British had mastered during the Malayan emergency in the 1950s. The strategic hamlets program that became a cornerstone of the U.S. policy of pacification was "the child of the British Advisory Mission."[12] It is now clear that the mission helped plan the clearing of Communists from the Mekong delta.[13]

Closely associated with BRIAM was a British-sponsored Jungle Warfare Training School in Jahore, Malaysia, where American and South Vietnamese soldiers were trained in guerrilla tactics.[14] Other assistance to the U.S. struggle in Southeast Asia included Royal Navy training exercises with the South Vietnamese navy and the passing on to the Americans of any Vietnamese radio traffic intercepted by the British signals intelligence outstation in Hong Kong.[15]

Still, this limited military and nonmilitary aid was not enough to assuage the Americans. In November 1961 Kennedy was advised by his aides in a memorandum discussing, among other things, the "problem of allied support" that he should "get as much backing as possible from Allies" and that "this means a strong line with [the] British."[16] The need for "multilateral participation from...allies and other friendly nations" was made clear to ambassadors in Washington on November 17 and 18, 1961, when such nations were formally asked for "public support and economic and military contributions."[17]

In late November 1961 Edward Heath, in his position as Lord Privy Seal, declined during House of Commons questions to "give an assurance that no British troops will be used or stationed in Vietnam."[18] David Bruce, U.S. ambassador to Great Britain, remarked to Washington that this was "most significant," indicating that at this point the situation regarding a British troop contribution was still fluid.[19] And, indeed, Busch's recent work indicates the Macmillan government could have been persuaded to contribute troops under the SEATO banner, albeit reluctantly.[20] However, the fact that the Labour opposition regularly called on the Conservative government to recommend the reconvening of the Geneva Conference to discuss the deteriorating situation in Vietnam and questioned the civilian status of the British Advisory Mission may have led the government to question the political wisdom of a British military involvement in Vietnam, especially given that the British public was not convinced that a British interest was at stake. In March 1962 Harold Wilson, then chairman of the opposition Labour Party, was one of many M.P.s to urge the government, as cochair of the Geneva Conference, to reconvene the conference to stabilize the situation in Vietnam. He also made the point that "this situation would perhaps have been eased if all of us had carried out our commitments with regard to the holding of free elections in Vietnam."[21] This implied criticism of both the British and American governments was not repeated after Wilson became prime minister. However, it is indicative of the future prime minister's personal feelings on the matter.

Despite mounting Parliamentary concern, the Conservative government continued to defend U.S. policy in Vietnam, disfavored a negotiated settlement on the model of the Laos one in 1962, but stopped short of sending British troops. Nevertheless, in 1963 and 1964 the Conservative Foreign Secretary, R. A. Butler, was facing numerous inquiries on Vietnam from backbenchers of all three main political parties. He was questioned persistently by one M.P. in particular, left-wing Labour backbencher William Warbey, who warned of the dangers of American and British involvement in what was essentially a civil war. Parliamentary opinion over U.S. handling of events in Southeast Asia would become an increasingly important factor in British policy on Vietnam.

Just as the United States put pressure on Britain to step up its involvement in Vietnam, Britain faced its own crisis in the same region of the world. Although the Foreign Office had expected a reduced overseas military burden as a result of having fewer colonies to defend, in the short term the British government felt forced to commit large numbers of troops in Malaysia. The Malaysian Federation had been established in September 1963 and was made up of Malaya, Sabah, Sarawak (former British colonies), and Singapore (which seceded from the federation in August 1965). It was hoped that "here...would be a colonial successor state, closely aligned with Britain, offering base facilities in return for the promise of strategic protection if it became necessary, altogether a powerful bastion of British and Western influence in a politically volatile region."[22] Britain was soon called on to honor its commitment. The Republic of Indonesia, under the leadership of Achmed Sukarno and backed by the Communist bloc, opposed the union and announced a "state of confrontation" with Malaysia aimed at ending British influence in the area. Britain, Australia, and New Zealand gave military support to Malaysia in its attempts to defend itself against Indonesia, whose guerrillas fought intermittently between 1963 and the end of the confrontation in August 1966. The British took a firm stance on Malaysia, refusing to make concessions to Jakarta, and, after the United States made it clear that it would not help out militarily, committed large numbers of troops to the effort. Thirty thousand British servicemen were stationed in Malaysia at the peak of the conflict (out of a total of 54,000 on duty in Southeast Asia)—the largest commitment of British troops to any one area since the Second World War.[23] The Americans gave Britain verbal support in its campaign in Malaysia but did not offer any military assistance. Instead, the United States tried to mediate between the parties involved, hoping a diplomatic solution could be found before Indonesia turned to communism.[24] Britain's defense of Western interests in Malaysia—Singapore was a key base in the effort to contain Chinese communism—meant that the Macmillan, Douglas-Home, and Wilson governments could emphasize their own efforts in the Cold War battle and thus avoid a commitment to Vietnam. However, the British lack of military restraint in Malaysia meant that it would appear hypocritical to Washington's ears to receive criticism of its own actions in Vietnam.

The Kennedy administration had sought and gained limited free world assistance for South Vietnam, but it was the Johnson administration that adopted an official policy in order to gain additional support for its Vietnam policy. The "more flags" program launched by President Johnson at a press conference in late April 1964 was formalized as U.S. policy when Dean Rusk, secretary of state, cabled U.S. embassies around the world seeking help. At this stage, the program had two main objectives—one overt, the other covert. The main, public goal was to obtain nonmilitary aid from as many free-world countries as possible.[25] Washington insisted that this practical and material support receive much press attention in order to demonstrate international approval of U.S. action and to encourage other nations to commit to the "more flags" program. This was because of the second aim that Rusk spelled out. "The nature and amount of contributions being sought are not for the present as significant as the fact of their being made. The basic objective is to have Free World Governments display their flags in Viet Nam and indicate their recognition of the fundamental nature of the struggle there."[26] In other words, though it was important that the South Vietnamese government receive as much outside help as it needed, what was more important to Washington was that the U.S. government receive as much support as possible for its own stand in Vietnam. Contained in Rusk's message was a table listing the countries providing assistance to South Vietnam and a brief description of the kinds of nonmilitary assistance being given. At this stage Australia, Canada, France, West Germany, Japan, Malaya, New Zealand, South Korea, and the United Kingdom were included in the table. The United Kingdom's contribution included the "Advisory mission on counterinsurgency and police operations; loans; equipment for medical, mining, and engineering schools; [and] English language teachers." So, in the case of Britain, the Johnson administration already had a "flag," but not one that was big enough or prominent enough for its liking. Consequently, the "more flags" policy entailed gaining not only more supporters of U.S. policy in Vietnam but also more visible support from key allies. Britain's position became more important when the response to Rusk's first request for nonmilitary aid was lukewarm to say the least. By the middle of June Rusk could only report to Johnson that 11 free-world nations were participating in the "more flags" program and only 3 countries (Taiwan, Thailand, and the Philippines) were new. Although by December—after personal pleas from the president—the number of countries sending assistance to South Vietnam had increased to 15, only 6 of these were judged to be offering significant rather than token help (South Korea, Australia, New Zealand, the Philippines, Thailand, and Taiwan). President Johnson began considering changing the emphasis of his program. In a cable to Henry Cabot Lodge, the U.S. ambassador to South Vietnam, Johnson said: "We propose to seek the military and political co-operation of the governments of Thailand, the Philippines, Australia, New Zealand, and the United Kingdom."[27] The original purpose of the "more flags" program—the humanitarian goal of more nonmilitary aid for South Vietnam—would have only secondary importance. Now, to prevent the image of the United States acting unilaterally in Vietnam, the acquisition of military aid *and* combat troops from a handful of America's friends and allies would become

Johnson's goal. Recognizing that few nations would commit troops voluntarily (only Australia and New Zealand did this), the Johnson administration had to find another way of ensuring international support.[28] Understanding that a military involvement necessarily involved greater economic and political costs, the State Department announced on December 15, 1964, that it was willing to pay all costs involved in any third-country commitment to South Vietnam. As Blackburn puts it, "If Lyndon Johnson, using ideological arguments and diplomatic pressures, could not convince other countries to adopt America's Vietnam policy as their own, he would now attempt to bribe them into doing so."[29] Despite this financial inducement, no new countries chose to contribute to the program. Although Dean Rusk attempted to persuade Johnson that the program was working by stating in May 1965 that 29 nations were sending aid to South Vietnam, it is clear that at least 10 of these were sending relief assistance due to monsoon flooding. The first stage of Johnson's "more flags" program could be deemed only a limited success. After March 9, 1965, and the introduction of U.S. combat troops, the second stage began in earnest. The "more flags" program began to concentrate on recruiting troop commitments from third countries. The addition of extra trained manpower—from whatever source—would have helped ease the demand for American soldiers. However, as many military strategists argued, the logistical and language problems inherent in multinational armed forces meant that the main benefits of third-party support remained psychological and political. As Ambassador Lodge warned in his mission to South Vietnam in April 1964, "[P]sychologically it is most important that others share with us the casualties of the U.S. effort here."[30] In the "zero-sum" atmosphere of the Cold War, the Americans would have liked to have had as many world powers as possible lining up on their side in Vietnam. The United States understood that its ability to win the war, especially the propaganda war, would be enhanced if Vietnam could be turned into an allied crusade, thereby invoking images of the Second World War and Korea. The policy also fitted neatly into the internationalist perspective of most of the White House advisors, a view that had meant that the collective security policy had been an important principle of U.S. foreign policy since 1945.[31] In the end, South Korea, the Philippines, and Thailand received financial aid in exchange for their deployment of substantial numbers of combat troops.[32]

As we shall see, despite early indications to the contrary, Britain remained a key target of the "more flags" campaign throughout the Johnson years. It is easy to see why. Having Britain on board was of particular importance because of its roles within the Western Alliance, the UN Security Council, and SEATO. Britain was also a leading social democracy whose example counted; any condemnation or ambivalence on its part would be seized upon by North Vietnam and its supporters as proof of the weakness of America's cause. William Bundy, assistant secretary of state for Far East affairs, later argued that a British troop commitment would also have had an impact on the U.S. domestic scene, believing it "would have made a considerable psychological difference...particularly in liberal circles, which was where the main criticism of the war came from."[33] Wilson recalled LBJ saying, in their July 1966 Washington meeting, that "a platoon of bagpipers would be sufficient, it was the British flag that was needed."[34] Or as Dean Rusk put it to the journalist Louis Heren: "All we needed was a regiment. The Black Watch would have done."[35] The prospect of a new government in Great Britain was consequently of great importance in Washington as the White House sought, at the very least, to maintain the current level of support for the war in Vietnam, and, at best, to significantly increase it.

THE JOHNSON ADMINISTRATION AND LABOUR IN OPPOSITION, JANUARY–OCTOBER 1964

The Labour government that came to power in October 1964 inherited an established policy on Vietnam that was part of a wider foreign policy in Southeast Asia. The British government, under the Tories, had throughout the 1950s and early 1960s supported the American aim of containing communism in Vietnam and as a loyal ally did so openly. But as the Americans put it, London had decided that it "must help quietly because of its peacekeeping role under the agreements of 1954."[36] Moreover, the British refused to become directly involved in the conflict, consistently turning down American requests for troops.

But if, as Busch suggests, the British government did nothing between 1961 and 1963 to stop the United States on its path to tragedy in Vietnam, the new Labour government could, of course, have changed direction on this issue. A sizable part of the left wing of the Labour Party was traditionally anti-American— some advocated a "third force" in the Cold War—and many within the party were concerned about the route being taken by the United States in Vietnam. Indeed, Wilson's own views on the Anglo–American relationship and on Vietnam changed over time. During the 1950s Wilson had spoken out against American foreign policy in the area. In a speech in Coventry in February 1952, Wilson stated that "it must be the duty of the British Parliament, and the British Labour Movement in particular, to make it clear that if any section of American opinion sought to extend the area of fighting in Asia they could not expect us to support it."[37] And in 1954, at May Day celebrations in Liverpool, Wilson argued, "Not a man, not a gun must be sent to defend the French in Indo-China. We must not join with nor in any way encourage the anti-Communist crusade in Asia, whether it is under the leadership of the Americans or anyone else."[38] In even stronger language, during a speech on the same day in Manchester, Wilson said, "[T]he Government should not further subordinate British policy to America. A settlement in Asia is imperilled by the lunatic fringe in the American Senate who want a holy crusade against Communism.... Asia is in revolution and Britain must learn to march on the side of the peoples in that revolution and not on the side of their oppressors."[39]

Such speeches by Wilson occurred during his brief left-wing period—the Bevanite phase.[40] From the mid-1950s until the early 1960s Wilson, as shadow chancellor, became engrossed in domestic and economic issues and "much of his former antagonism to American foreign policy was transferred to American penetration of the British economy."[41] When Wilson became shadow Foreign Secretary in November 1961, he had the opportunity to visit the United States more often and to meet its leaders. With the election of John F. Kennedy it appears Wilson saw America in a new light. In an interview after Kennedy's death, Wilson admitted that Kennedy's youth and dynamism had influenced him greatly, leading Wilson to believe he could work with a Democratic administration.[42] Perhaps Kennedy's election also coincided with Wilson's growing realization of the vital importance of the United States to the United Kingdom, both in defense policy terms and economically. Either way, by the time Wilson became leader of the Opposition in 1963, anti-American statements were no longer part of his speeches, although he did criticize the Tories mildly for their staunch support of American policy in Vietnam. For instance, in the lead-up to the 1964 general election, Wilson asked a number of questions on Vietnam in the House of Commons. In June he asked Prime Minister Douglas-Home to confirm that "we would not support any extension of the war into North Vietnam."[43] Douglas-Home did not do this and, as it turned out, Wilson was the prime minister who received much condemnation for his decision to acquiesce to the continuous American bombing of North Vietnam in March 1965.

For almost a year before the Labour government took office, the British shadow cabinet and the Johnson administration anticipated working together. The Labour Party, and Wilson in particular, had reacted with sadness and genuine grief at President Kennedy's assassination but soon felt comfortable with the prospect of working with the former vice president, Lyndon Johnson, not only because of his obvious dynamism but also because they saw him as progressive on social justice. It is now clear, however, that the Labour leadership did not fully understand the new president's personality or his politics and consequently had unrealistic expectations for the future of Anglo–American relations. The Wilson government faced a complex president who, after his July 1965 decision to send large numbers of U.S. ground troops to South Vietnam, was increasingly obsessed by events in Southeast Asia and the consequences of those events back home. If the Wilson government was not involved in this all-important foreign affair, then Anglo–American relations inevitably would be strained during the Johnson administration. Moreover, given LBJ's views on loyalty and his growing paranoia that anyone who did not support him on Vietnam was against him in all things, the Anglo–American alliance would be threatened if the United Kingdom was not cooperative on this matter.

In 1964 the State Department was continuing to assess third-party contributions: assistance from countries other than the United States and South Vietnam. Given left-wing opinion on the war and Wilson's question in the House, Washington was keen to assess the possibility that a Labour government might prove a less loyal ally than the Conservatives on the issue. Thus a change in government in the United Kingdom could prove significant. Equally, Wilson and his colleagues were faced with a president who, in terms of political style and personality, was very different from his predecessor.

Anxious to be on good working terms with the Americans, members of the shadow cabinet visited Washington throughout 1964. In February, shadow Foreign Secretary Patrick Gordon Walker met several senior members of the Johnson administration, partly to lay the groundwork for Wilson's planned visit to the United States early the following month and partly to meet with their prospective opposition numbers in the U.S. cabinet. Denis Healey, Labour's spokesman on defense, also visited Washington in late March. Vietnam was a major topic of discussion during all three visits, and it is clear that at this stage both parties were probing each other's intentions on the issue. The Americans wished to reassure themselves that a Labour government would broadly continue Tory policy on Southeast Asia and, as America contemplated further escalating its involvement in Vietnam, to investigate the possibility of an increased British contribution (although given Britain's previous reluctance to deploy troops to Southeast Asia, the Americans were under no illusions as to the likelihood of a change in this position). The Labour shadow cabinet was of course keen to explore American plans in Vietnam and to gauge how far they might be pushed on this and other issues.

Lengthy discussions on Southeast Asia took place during the Gordon Walker visit in February 1964. This came shortly after Prime Minister Douglas-Home's visit to Washington, during which he assured the Johnson administration of continuing support of Vietnam in light of the Tonkin Gulf resolution and the subsequent decision to begin air strikes. In a morning-long talk with Walt W. Rostow, a senior State Department official and well-known hawk, one of the main subjects was Vietnam. Rostow judged that "it was clear that he [Gordon Walker] was still getting the facts and making up his mind" but "did not seem to have ruled out of his thinking some kind of negotiated settlement." Gordon Walker argued "from his Moscow conversations, that the USSR at least partially shared our interest in stopping the extension of ChiCom power in southeast Asia." The belief that Britain, along with the Russians, could mediate between the United States and North Vietnam seems therefore to have been a part of Labour's thinking before the election. Military strategy was also discussed. Gordon Walker asked Rostow if they were "prepared to put in the 'large numbers of troops' which would be required to win the war." Rostow was not exactly candid on this issue and recorded that Gordon Walker had "obviously not given much thought to the possibility of other kinds of escalation, except for covert raids on the North Vietnamese coastline."[44]

Harold Wilson's first serious meeting with President Johnson and his advisors came at the beginning of March 1964. This was Wilson's third trip to the United States since becoming Labour leader. Wilson had met with Kennedy in April 1963 and according to the Americans had "invited himself to Washington for the funeral in November," where he met Lyndon Johnson briefly.[45] The Americans accurately surmised that Wilson's reason for the March visit was "to become acquainted with you [Johnson] and your ideas, to enhance his *public image* in Britain, and to reassure you regarding his *reliability* as an ally."[46] Washington awaited the visit "with considerable interest,"[47] and Johnson's officials made in-depth and often accurate appraisals of the leader of Her Majesty's Opposition.

During Wilson's periods in office (1964–70 and 1974–76)—and for many years afterward—the man and his governments were criticized for their shallowness, lack of achievement, and superficiality. Wilson himself was invariably portrayed as a scurrilous, self-serving character with a distinct lack of genuine political beliefs and a dark private side, involving a possible sexual relationship with his personal secretary, Marcia Williams, and dubious links with several business tycoons.[48] Wilson's career and personality have, however, experienced a recent reappraisal.[49] The Wilson who emerges from the latest scholarship is more of a pragmatic, intelligent leader who, while ascribing to no particular political philosophy, had some well-intentioned ideas. Despite this rehabilitation, some of Wilson's less impressive personal characteristics rightly remain intact, particularly his susceptibility to the fantasy world Andrew Roth referred to when he called Wilson a "Yorkshire Walter Mitty."[50] Wilson did have delusions of grandeur when it came to his international role.

In an assessment of Wilson for the president prior to the Labour leader's visit, Rusk argued that Wilson was "not a man of strong political convictions himself, he now probably reflects the consensus of Labor Party opinion. He has succeeded in getting the warring factions of the Party to present a public image of unity in face of the common need to win the election." The secretary of state went on to assert that "somehow, he does not inspire a feeling of trust in many people. This is his greatest political hardship. It has led some to say that in the next election, the British are faced with a choice between 'smart aleck and dumb Alec.' "[51]

The day before the president's first official meeting with Wilson, McGeorge Bundy, special assistant for national security affairs at the White House, also summed up the Labour leader. "I think you will find Wilson interesting, affable, persuasive, and seemingly sincere (although he is widely accused of opportunistic insincerity). His detractors say that he has a photographic memory and can 'spout names, dates, and quotations like a champion quiz kid.' He is a cold man. . . . He enjoys talking." In relation to the Americans, Bundy concluded that Wilson's "political line is friendly to the United States except for reservations appropriate for a Socialist leader and a defender of British national prestige. He insists publicly and privately that Labor will be a more reliable political partner for the United States than the Tories have been."[52] A later CIA biographic statement confirmed this opinion, stating that "although he has 'flirted' with the left, Wilson is not a doctrinaire socialist. He is above all a pragmatist, well aware of the realities of power. His commitment to Anglo–U.S. relations is not based solely on sentiment." Commenting on his reputation as "a cold fish" with "no close political friends," the CIA noted that "it is said that he trusts no one completely and vice versa."[53]

Although this was a largely accurate picture of the Labour leader, some of the less flattering comments may have persuaded LBJ that Wilson was a difficult, devious man who was not to be trusted. To get to know Wilson better and perhaps to impress him, the Americans laid on special treatment for the opposition leader during his visit to Washington, including a packed, high-profile official schedule. Wilson had meetings with the president, the secretary of state, and the secretary of defense, a lineup usually reserved for heads of state. Wilson was accorded the same amount of media coverage as Prime Minister Douglas-Home had received during his visit to Washington the previous month. As *The Times*'s American editor, Louis Heren, suggested, this equanimity not only emphasized the importance attached to relations with Britain but also revealed "the eagerness to get to know the man who could be Prime Minister before the end of the year," especially given that Wilson had been in charge of the Labour Party for only just over a year.[54] Moreover, in recent months the Johnson administration had recognized that on some issues the Labour Party appeared closer to *its* position than the Conservative government. During Patrick Gordon Walker's visit a few weeks earlier, U.S. secretary of defense Robert McNamara had found Gordon Walker's views on defense similar to his own. In the lead-up to the general election the Conservatives had stressed their commitment to an "independent" nuclear deterrent. In doing so, the Tory leadership had also argued that this deterrent allowed them a certain amount of independence from the United States. Labour had seized on this opportunity. "Here was a chance of appearing to be the party most closely aligned with the United States by arguing for the abandonment of nuclear weapons (a call much loved by the Labour Left) and relying instead on closer relations with the Americans."[55] Labour began to argue against the nuclear deterrent and for a buildup of more traditional conventional forces. This position was much closer to McNamara's request that the Europeans provide conventional forces for his "flexible response strategy."[56] Not surprisingly, the Johnson administration was eager to further assess such possibilities.

Wilson arrived in Washington on March 1 for his two-day visit. The Johnson administration impressed upon Wilson similar issues to those emphasized to Prime Minister Douglas-Home. In particular, the administration was keen to discuss the multilateral nuclear force (MLF), the American proposal for a mixed-man (i.e., mixed-nationality) nuclear fleet that had been formulated to deal with German interest in joining the nuclear club. Although the Conservative government had shown some interest in this plan, the Labour Party was totally opposed to it. Vietnam was also brought up during a discussion on Southeast Asia. At this point, the Johnson administration merely talked of the current political and military situation in Vietnam. This was not a time for requests for help or firm commitments from a prospective Labour government.[57]

This visit was much more important in terms of the personal relationships. Both Wilson and Johnson trusted in their interpersonal skills and hoped to be able to persuade the other on certain issues. Wilson had a 50-minute meeting with the president at the White House. The leader of the Opposition reportedly said shortly afterward that he had got on "all right" with Johnson and that the conversation had been "very enjoyable and very frank. There had been no difference of communication or any waste of words."[58] Back home Wilson's recollection of this first meeting with Johnson was more glowing. Many of his political colleagues in Britain were left with an extremely favorable impression of events. Postmaster General Tony Benn's diary entry of the time states that Wilson "had got on excellently with President Johnson" and added that he thought they were "both highly political animals" who "understand each other well."[59] The press, however, picked up on some confusion arising out of the Wilson visit. In his endeavor to demonstrate his desire, should he become prime minister, to strengthen Anglo–American relations, Wilson apparently voiced his opposition to continued moves toward European unity, seeing Britain's future in strong Anglo–American ties in cooperation with the Commonwealth.[60] Such views were looked upon with suspicion by an administration that still felt European unity was the best way to prevent political instability on the European continent. Overall, however, Wilson's opinions were warmly received, particularly his commitment that under Labour Britain would continue its world role. Despite this, the president was less than glowing in his appraisal of Her Majesty's leader of the Opposition. In a telephone conversation with Senator William Fulbright, Johnson said that he "liked him pretty good...I think it was all right...he's a little big...I'm not sure I want him more than Home."[61]

Still, the following months saw the Labour Party congratulate itself on the prospect of close relations with the Americans. Tommy Balogh, a close advisor to Harold Wilson, visited the White House in April 1964 and reported back that "the White House is passionately committed to a Labour victory in Britain— more so than when 'that Eastern aristocrat, Kennedy was in charge.' "[62] Despite the outwardly positive outcome of Wilson's first meeting with the Johnson administration, it was soon apparent to Labour Party observers that the Anglo–American relationship still had its downside, particularly in relation to events in Southeast Asia. By August 1964 Benn wryly noted Wilson's reaction to the Tonkin Gulf crisis in Vietnam: "[W]e are terrified of saying anything that might upset the Americans...The British Government needs American support against Sukarno, who is attacking Malaysia and Wilson is particularly anxious not to upset Johnson at this stage."[63] In any case, Gordon Walker as shadow Foreign Secretary had by August come to the conclusion that a Labour government "must back [the] US in SE Asia—tho' working slowly for a solution by leaving things to people of the area."[64]

During the long lead-up to the British general election, David Bruce, the U.S. ambassador in London, continued to keep the Johnson administration informed about the potential new prime minister and relevant Labour policies. On July 20, 1964, Bruce described Wilson as "exceptional in ability, brilliant in debate."[65] Richard E. Neustadt, a Harvard professor and special consultant to the president during 1964–66, spent time in London during June and July, largely to gauge prospective Labour policy regarding the MLF. He was clear that Wilson, if elected, would have his own "recollections of the Anglo–American relationship" based on his experiences during and shortly after the Second World War and "hopes for his own personal relationship which are quite different from perceptions of reality held by many American officials."[66] Johnson had no particular fondness for the British, despite the rhetoric, and obviously did not have the same recollection of his meeting with Wilson. Neustadt therefore felt that "numbers of things can be done to avoid shocking his sensibilities."[67] And indeed, as we shall see, during Wilson's first two years in office, the Johnson administration attempted to shield the prime minister from the president's true feelings about him in order to maintain Wilson's morale at home and his commitment to Anglo–American relations.

THE LABOUR GOVERNMENT AND ANGLO–AMERICAN RELATIONS

On October 16, 1964, the Labour Party was declared the winner of the British general election and asked to form Her Majesty's Government with an overall majority of just six M.P.s in the House of Commons. On the day of Labour's election victory, Bruce wired Rusk to "speculate about his [Wilson's] possible attitude toward Anglo–American negotiations." The U.S. ambassador's positive appraisal of Wilson continued as he agreed with the charge that Labour's election campaign had been a "One Man Band." "As a politician, Mr. Wilson clearly demonstrated his superiority, in intellectual ability, adroitness, and persuasiveness, over his associates." Bruce therefore judged that "Wilson's first cabinet will be nothing to brag about in terms either of intellect or of experience. He is aware of this and means to take all key decisions into his own hands. He wants not merely to make ultimate decisions but to pass issues through his own mind early, sitting at the centre of a brains-trusts, with himself as first brains-truster on the model, he says, of JFK." He expected Wilson to take a key role in foreign affairs and felt that the United States should expect "a greater degree of high level negotiation with the British than has been our previous experience."[68] This analysis proved correct; Wilson's foreign secretaries complained about his constant interference in foreign affairs.

President Johnson took Wilson's election as prime minister in stride. Bruce noted that the president "viewed the results with no surprise, as was his habit whenever anyone came into office who had been previously in opposition" and "extended...rather quickly an invitation to Mr. Wilson to meet him."[69] Also, according to William P. Bundy, "[N]o outstanding foreign issues were involved.... So far as American official feelings were concerned, Harold Wilson had made a generally good impression over the year and a half since the death of Hugh Gaitskell, and the change was greeted calmly and with every expectation that the close ties between Britain and the United States would continue."[70] Bruce anticipated problems over the proposed MLF—to which Labour was opposed—and British entry into the Common Market, but he acknowledged America's strength in any such negotiations: "We will find Mr. Wilson a resourceful, tough, realistic, opinionated bargainer, but solely our own lack of equal resourcefulness and determination would enable him to profit at the expense of our more powerful position."[71]

The president helped prepare his own country for the change in British government in his foreign policy address to the nation on October 18, just one day after Labour's electoral victory, when he said that "the British Labor Party is the same party that held power when the Atlantic Alliance was founded; when British and American pilots flew the Berlin airlift together; when Englishmen joined us in Korea...It is a party of freedom, of democracy, and of good faith. Today it has the confidence of the British people. It also has ours."[72] The change was also accepted uncritically by most of the American press. A *Washington Post* editorial stated that the president's "remarks on Great Britain's change of government were timely and felicitous. The United States and Great Britain have a working relationship that is a party issue in neither country and that is not likely to be disturbed by the outcome of any election." The *New York Herald Tribune* expected slight differences in policies: "To the extent that objective realities have determined British policy, they will probably continue to do so, but in details—which could add up to very considerable changes—the United States must be prepared for new adjustments." Other newspapers, such as the *Baltimore Sun*, were encouraged by the appointment of Patrick Gordon Walker as Foreign Secretary, describing him as "a man of moderation and a friend of the United States."[73]

The Johnson administration, certainly within the cabinet, felt little apprehension at working with a nominally socialist Labour government.[74] Wilson's hostility to American foreign policy was well in the past, and his visits to Washington since becoming leader of the Labour Party had convinced most of Washington that his socialist statements were largely for public consumption. Many of those within the Johnson administration knew senior Labour politicians well. Walt Rostow knew Harold Wilson and Denis Healey, the new defense secretary, from his time as a Rhodes scholar at Oxford. Dean Rusk also knew Healey and was described by David Bruce as having "a warm feeling for him."[75] Harlan Cleveland, U.S. assistant secretary of state for international organizations, had been one of Wilson's students at University College, Oxford, and most senior British cabinet members had met with officials in the Johnson administration prior to the 1964 election. A healthy working relationship was also facilitated by the continuing strong ties between personnel within the American administration and the British civil service. Sir Patrick Dean, British ambassador to the United States, was admired by Johnson. Sir Michael Palliser, the prime minister's assistant for foreign affairs, and Walt Rostow, the president's national security advisor, were old friends from Oxford who enjoyed working together at their respective stations.

At this stage there was little to suggest that Anglo–American relations would falter so much over the coming years. However, two related problems dominated the first Wilson government's time in office: the position of sterling and British defense commitments East of Suez. The Labour government inherited an economic position that would shape its time in office and have consequences for the wider financial world. It inherited an £800 million balance of payments deficit that threatened sterling and Britain's defense programs.[76] This parlous situation was made clear the day after Labour's electoral victory in a treasury brief that showed that, despite an apparently healthy economy, imports were rising rapidly and the growth rate lagged behind that of much of the Western world. The new government took the decision not to devalue the pound and to avoid descent into protectionism. Wilson's part in the previous Labour government's decision to devalue in 1949 played a part in this decision—the prime minister and his colleagues wanted to avoid Labour being forever linked with devaluation in the minds of the electorate.[77] Instead, the government initiated a defense review and placed a 15 percent import surcharge on all goods excluding food, tobacco, and raw materials; raised the bank rate by 2 percent; and secured a loan from Western banks of $3 billion.[78] None of these acts avoided a sense of crisis for sterling, which faced its first speculative attack in November 1964. From this point on the pound was under constant attack, and Britain faced serious sterling crises in July 1965, July 1966, and the autumn of 1967.

In his first budget, chancellor of the exchequer James Callaghan announced that defense costs for the years 1964–69 would be reduced from £2,400 million to £2,000 million. Partly this was related to the Labour government's domestic commitments on health, welfare, and education, but it was also a response to the worsening balance-of-payments problem linked to Britain's high and escalating defense expenditure. At the same time, however, the prime minister said he was committed to continuing Britain's global role, including its position East of Suez, indeed declaring in 1965 that Britain's "frontiers were on the Himalayas."[79]

The first phase of the defense review lasted from October 1964 to January 1966 and concerned itself with determining how to achieve economies through its equipment program rather than questioning Britain's existing defense commitments. This resulted in the cancellation of three aircraft projects (TSR-2, HS-681, and P-1154). The Defence White Paper of 1966 admitted to some limitations in the future scope of British military operations. Despite this, British ministers were adamant that the British still be committed East of Suez.[80] In the summer of 1966 another sterling crisis prompted a second defense review and in July 1967 the government concluded that a reduction in forces outside

Europe was necessary and that withdrawal of forces from Malaysia and Singapore would be required by around 1975.[81] Following yet another deterioration in the balance-of-payments situation in the autumn of 1967, resulting in the devaluation of the pound, the government announced a further review of public expenditure. The "Statement on Public Expenditure 1968–9 and 1969–70" contained the historic East of Suez decision, which called for an acceleration of the withdrawal from Singapore and Malaysia, to be completed by the end of 1971 rather than 1975; undertaking to withdraw from the Gulf by the same date; and an acknowledgment that Britain no longer planned "to maintain a special military capability for use in this area."[82]

The sterling crises and the uncertainty over Britain's global defense commitments were important factors in the British government's decision making over Vietnam. Inevitably, given the Johnson administration's driving desire to find allies in the field, the temptation to link all three in a formal agreement was a possibility that Washington could not fail to explore.

PRIME MINISTER WILSON'S VISIT TO WASHINGTON, DECEMBER 1964

With preliminary examinations of one another out of the way, the realities of working together began. Just 10 days after Labour's victory at the polls the new Foreign Secretary, Patrick Gordon Walker, "an old and esteemed friend" of the United States, visited the White House at the invitation of Dean Rusk.[83] The Johnson administration wanted to use this opportunity to make sure the Labour government had "a clear concept" of U.S. objectives and policies on key foreign policy issues "before its own positions solidify."[84] This was particularly the case in relation to defense matters, especially MLF and Polaris. Rusk told Johnson the main reason for the visit was to "assure you that the United Kingdom does not plan any radical foreign policy initiatives embarrassing to the United States." A visit so soon after the election would also demonstrate to the British that "the United States continues to value its association with Britain now that Labor is in control."[85]

At this point Rusk showed measured optimism about the new British government. "This could be a turning point in Atlantic affairs comparable, in some ways, to the period 1947–50, when the United States and a previous Labor Government launched other great ventures to strengthen the Atlantic partnership."[86] In the post–Second World War period, the Labour government had aligned itself closely to Truman's Democratic administration on such issues as monetary policy, nuclear bases, and the H-bomb, largely due to vehement anti-communism of the Foreign Secretary, Ernest Bevin. Perhaps the Americans felt that the new British Labour government, in an attempt to downplay some of the party's anti-Americanism and to demonstrate its credibility as a close friend of the Americans, might be equally cooperative. The weakening position of the pound might also have encouraged the feeling that the British would be more susceptible to American pressure.

The Americans therefore intended to push on with Atlantic policy issues such as the Kennedy round of financial talks, MLF, and improved political consultation. At this stage MLF was without doubt the most vital issue for the Atlantic Alliance. The Americans, particularly McNamara, felt that MLF (by this stage including a Polaris-armed surface fleet, staffed by a mixed-nationality crew) was the best way to satisfy German nuclear aspirations and to prevent the proliferation of independent nuclear deterrents in Europe. The Labour government intended to maintain its opposition to MLF on the grounds that a mixed-man fleet would be extremely unpopular "in Europe, not least in Britain" because of "any suggestion, however indirect, of a German finger even influencing the nuclear trigger."[87] Moreover, Wilson and Healey felt the MLF would further antagonize the Soviets, who were alarmed at the prospect of further nuclear proliferation in Europe. The importance of MLF was conveyed to Wilson via Walker at the White House meetings. However, it was agreed that "detailed discussion of certain specific questions, such as the MLF and the Polaris Sales Agreement, should be left for a later meeting with Prime Minister Harold Wilson."[88] Nevertheless, Rusk was well aware of Wilson's small working majority and was prepared to take account of it in the coming months. "We should...not say anything at this time which might be taken as serving notice on the British that we intend to move ahead with them if they are willing, but without them if necessary. Our position should be one of calm reaffirmation of our commitment to the development of the Atlantic partnership without any overtone of pressure at this stage."[89] Any strong pressure at this time might have led Wilson to submit to backbench pressure and openly come out against MLF. In the meantime, Wilson and his defense secretary, Denis Healey, worked on an alternative to the MLF that might satisfy American objectives: an Atlantic nuclear force (ANF). This proposal envisaged British and U.S. nuclear submarines, as well as mixed-man land-based Minuteman missiles in the United States and V-bomber squadrons, being incorporated into a new command structure of participants under the umbrella of the existing North Atlantic Treaty Organization (NATO). For the British, ANF avoided the increased costs of establishing a new surface fleet, offering "the Allies equality of status, not by everyone trading up to British levels but by the British trading down to everyone else's level except the American."[90]

Interestingly, on Vietnam, the Johnson administration expected "no change...in...position" because "the British have firmly supported us in Vietnam, in part as a quid pro quo for support of their effort in Malaysia."[91] In the minds of the Americans these two issues were inextricably linked. Moreover, despite Labour's criticism of Tory policy on Vietnam and its nominally socialist status, the Americans did not expect the new government to withdraw British diplomatic support from their actions or to be any more sympathetic to North Vietnam. Indeed, William Bundy remembers that "on the most crucial East

Asian matter in which Britain was involved, Wilson at once made clear his intent to maintain and if necessary strengthen British help to Malaysia against the Indonesian 'confrontation;' there, British forces had been strengthened in September, and during October and November were further increased."[92]

Harold Wilson's first visit to Washington as prime minister, in December 1964, was important on a number of fronts. Although preparatory work had been carried out during the previous month and a half, this visit would see the proper beginning of the relationship between Wilson and Johnson and would witness the formulation of new policies and the consolidation of old ones. On Vietnam, Johnson was at this stage unsure of how to proceed with his "more flags" policy.

Importantly, during this trip Wilson elaborated on his grand ideas about the future of Anglo–American relations. In his reply to Johnson's welcoming address on December 7, Wilson was careful in his use of words in describing his hopes for a continued strong relationship with the United States:

In the changed circumstances of the sixties, we seek still a closer relationship based on common purposes and common aims, on consideration for the interest of Great Britain's partners within the Commonwealth and of our allies in Europe and elsewhere. The theme of these talks, as I conceive them, Mr. President, whether for the strength of our alliance or for our wider approach to the fight for a constructive peace is expressed in the on word "interdependence"—truly as among men so among nations we are all members one of another.[93]

Later that day during his toast at the formal dinner, Wilson talked about the responsibilities of friendship:

We have our differences. There are always differences between friends. We are good enough friends to speak frankly to one another, but there will never be anything peevish or spiteful. If we ever have differences, we will look you straight in the eye—and we will expect you to look us straight in the eye—and say what you would expect we can do as friends and only what we can do as friends.

Wilson continued in his speech by talking of his own up-to-date assessment of Anglo–American relations:

We hear arguments. I have heard this often enough about whether there is a special relationship between the United States and Great Britain. Some of those who talk of the special relationship, I think, are looking backwards and not looking forward. They talk about the nostalgia of our imperial age. We regard our relation with you not as a *special* relationship but as a *close* relationship, governed by the only things that matter, unity of purpose, and unity in our objectives. We don't come to you at any time on the basis of our past grandeur or of any faded thoughts of what the grandeur was . . . we have, and we always shall have, a close relationship.[94]

What exactly did Wilson mean by a "close" relationship with the United States? In practical terms, how distinct was Wilson's concept of a "close" relationship from traditional interpretations of the "special relationship"?

Despite there being no specific mention of British relations with the United States in Labour's election manifesto, Wilson had by the time of the general election decided to reinvigorate the Anglo–American relationship. Anglo–American relations would remain at the center of British foreign policy, along with ties to the Commonwealth, but would be reenergized. Wilson's vision of the future of the relationship had two aspects. Clearly, Wilson hoped to establish an approach that differed from those of his predecessors. In spring 1964, Wilson had sketched out his hopes for the Anglo–American relationship at a private gathering of press and politicians. According to Tony Benn, Wilson believed "a Labour government would be able to establish a much more informal relationship with the American President than Home" had been able to accomplish and "imagines that he can telephone and fly over as and when necessary, without the usual fuss of top level meetings. . . . As soon as the Election is over, he and his top colleagues will fly to Washington to renegotiate the whole basis of Anglo–American relations in the field of defence and foreign affairs."[95] A more informal relationship, taking advantage of the benefits of speedy transatlantic flights and modern communications and based on regular face-to-face meetings and frequent telephone conversations, would ensure that the two leaders remained up-to-date on each other's thinking. This would help to ensure the greatest levels of cooperation between the two countries and maximize Britain's influence on a global basis. Wilson expanded on this aspect of the special relationship at a press conference after his first formal meeting with Johnson in Washington, D.C., in December:

It is first a relationship at all levels. President-Prime Minister meetings are essential and should be frequent. There is a good deal to be said for the growing informality which has been developed, so that they tend to be routine and not symbolising any great crisis or dramatic turn of events. It means an equally close relationship between senior British ministers and senior American cabinet officials, particularly Secretary of State, Secretary of Defence, and Secretary to the Treasury.[96]

Wilson's ideas about an informal working relationship between Britain and America had been shaped after his meeting with President Kennedy. Invigorated by the president's youth and dynamism and believing that he had established a personal rapport with JFK based on their shared intellectual qualities, Wilson began to think that Anglo–American relations could be more modern and purposive. At one stage, Wilson even envisaged appointing an ambassador to Washington who would have cabinet rank and thus attend meetings of the National Security Council.[97]

As well as hoping for a change in the style and conduct of Anglo–American relations, Wilson desired a change in content. The prime minister's emphasis on "close" rather than "special" relations suggested he envisaged a relationship based on a realistic assessment of Britain's current position in the world: that Britain was no longer a leading world power and was declining in strength year by year. Moreover, Wilson and the Foreign Office were well aware that Britain was dependent on the U.S. nuclear shield.[98] Though he hoped for a period of co-operation between the nations, similar to the last time a Labour government had worked with a Democratic administration, this time a close working relationship would not be founded on the notion of an "English-speaking alliance" policing and leading the world but would see Britain playing a central role in international peacekeeping. The Labour government would abandon vain "nuclear posturing" and instead be more committed to NATO in conventional terms. Thus Labour's "new approach" to defense would mean a renegotiation of the Nassau agreement to buy Polaris missiles from the United States and "the strengthening of our conventional regular forces so that we can contribute our share to Nato defence and also fulfil our peace-keeping commitments to the Commonwealth and the United Nations."[99] And, clearly, Wilson hoped to maintain some independence from the United States. Somewhat like Ernest Bevin's "third force" concept, Wilson hoped to find a middle way between the two superpowers by exploiting his own connections in the Soviet Union.

Once in Downing Street, and faced with the true extent of Britain's financial difficulties, the new prime minister was probably relieved to find the Americans were as opposed to the devaluation of sterling as he was and would help to avoid this by providing massive loans to the British. As Paul Foot later put it, "American loans and promises of loans strengthened what used to be called 'the special relationship.' "[100]

However, there were problems with Wilson's hopes for a "close" Anglo–American relationship, particularly its place in the wider international scene. In the summer of 1964, Richard Neustadt had warned the Johnson administration about the dangers of Labour's "Dreams of Glory (retrospective)." "Their vision of the place and power in the world which they hope to assume as HM Government has rather more to do with 1951 than 1964, judging by the overtones when they discuss their prospects. Many of the educative shocks which Tories and officials have encountered in the interim do not seem to have registered in full on these outsiders."[101] In Wilson's case, Neustadt felt that this would manifest itself in "dreams of a role as honest broker in East-West relations (shades of 1945). Currently he is 'the man who knows Krushchev.' "[102] Neustadt was correct in sensing Wilson's hope that Wilson could mediate between Washington and Moscow. This belief was very much grounded in the prime minister's sense of his own talents and experience.[103] In addition to his faith in his interpersonal skills, Wilson also believed in his reputation as a leading authority on the Soviet bloc. Wilson had first visited Moscow in 1947 as part of a British trade delegation and had continued to travel there to develop East–West trade in the 1950s as an employee of the timber importer Montague Meyer. During these trips Wilson increased his knowledge of the Soviet Union and its leaders.[104] If the Wilson government could establish a strong relationship with the Americans, it could help make the Cold War world more peaceful.

The difficulty with Wilson's notion of himself as go-between was Britain's declining importance in world affairs: Britain simply did not have the strategic or military significance to bring either of the superpowers to heel. In the absence of this political muscle, the only way for Wilson to play the powerful role he so desired was to establish an intimate working and personal relationship with President Johnson. This was also problematical in that Johnson displayed a lack of enthusiasm about working with the Europeans. The president did not want a close working alliance with Britain, or with any other European nation, for that matter.[105] Although Europe remained the first priority for U.S. foreign policy and presidential commitment to NATO was as strong as ever, Johnson had no new initiatives on Europe. Indeed, George Ball admits that he took the lead on European policy and in general did not get much interference or guidance from Johnson in this.[106] Johnson clearly felt more at home with Latin American and Asian nations.[107] His presidential visits reflected this preference; overseas trips concentrated largely on the Western Hemisphere and the Far East. So, although Johnson recognized the unique nature of Anglo–American relations in terms of language, culture, and tradition, he did not see them as "special" in any real sense, due to Britain's decline as a great power and the rise in importance of other European nations, particularly West Germany. He was also suspicious of the East Coast foreign policy establishment's Anglophilia, describing some of his advisors as "dangerously sympathetic to the UK."[108]

This lack of concern for or empathy with the British could be explained by Johnson's personal sense of geography. William McChesney Martin, while chairman of the Federal Reserve Board, recalled to journalist Henry Brandon what he thought were Johnson's true feelings toward England. "First of all you have to know that he does not consider easterners . . . as real Americans. To him they look too much to Europe. Secondly, the line of Texas, Missouri, Minnesota to him is the real America. Those Texans who have gone to live in California are in his mind Texans who weren't able to make a go of it in Texas. In this picture, England figures about as large as North Dakota."[109]

The main problem Wilson faced in trying to effect changes in the Anglo–American relationship was Johnson himself. How likely was it that the two leaders could develop a close working and personal relationship? When Wilson had met Johnson in March 1964, Tony Benn concluded, "Johnson is an old style, folksy, warm-hearted New Dealer with much more in common with Wilson than Kennedy had or than he (Johnson) has with Home. All that is very encouraging."[110] Clearly the two leaders' most notable shared personal characteristic was their total absorption in politics, and that is why they had a great deal of respect for one another as professional politicians. And perhaps Johnson also felt that Wilson was, like himself, not a part of his country's ruling establishment.[111] The two men certainly had relatively humble origins: Johnson's comfortable rural background in Texas hill country and Wilson's lower-middle-class upbringing in northern England meant that both had no more than a middling social status. However, Johnson's high school education stood in marked contrast to Wilson's academic success as an Oxford don, and although they both came from modest backgrounds, they had not had similar life experiences, and apart from politics, they had no shared interests. But Benn's conclusion may also have been a misreading of Johnson and his politics, something of which Wilson was also guilty. As Henry Brandon noted, "Like other Labour leaders, he was under the mistaken impression that there was little difference between a New Dealer and a British socialist. To him the Great Society was another way of talking about Labour's kind of socialism when in effect Johnson's approach to the welfare state did not prevent his being closer to business than to the labor unions."[112] Wilson may therefore have assumed a closer political affinity than was in fact the case.

Moreover, Johnson would increasingly judge his friends by their loyalty on Vietnam. It is no coincidence that of all the world's leaders, Johnson had the greatest respect for Australia's premier, Harold Holt. To the president, Holt had admirably supported the Americans and had honored his nation's SEATO alliance obligations by sending combat troops to Vietnam.

Johnson's international priorities and personal demands were not entirely clear to the British in December 1964. At this stage, the prime minister's plan for closer relations between Britain and the United States was still intact. And given that the personal dimension was an important forerunner to such a development, it was crucial that Wilson's first meeting with Johnson as prime minister go well. The Americans were also worried about this aspect of the Wilson talks, although perhaps for different reasons. On November 25, Richard Neustadt was sent to London to ensure that both sides were fully prepared for Wilson's forthcoming visit to Washington and to make it transparent "that the success of the talks would depend on the acceptance of MLF."[113] George Ball, undersecretary of state, reiterated this during a visit to London. Ball met with Wilson with the purpose of ascertaining the prime minister's views on an Atlantic nuclear force.

However, it is clear that Neustadt also wanted to stress the importance of the "personal equation" in the forthcoming talks between the president and the prime minister. Wilson was reluctant to see Neustadt, fearing that such a meeting would mean "letting the Americans have a clear insight" into British views ahead of time.[114] Derek Mitchell, the prime minister's principal private secretary, also met with Neustadt and recorded afterward that Neustadt "repeated the warning already given by him to the Prime Minister and others that the Prime Minister should not bank on everything going his way when he got face to face with the President." He added that "the President was not looking forward to the talks with anything approaching the same eagerness as the Prime Minister because he had other problems on his mind, for example South-East Asia and a number of personnel matters. Thus preoccupied he looked forward to next weekend as more of a chore than a major act of policy." All this indicates that even at this early stage misunderstandings were already evident in the relationship between the prime minister and the president. Neustadt made this clear when he explained that "it was known that the Prime Minister had received a strong impression from his personal meeting with the President which he had when he was Leader of the Opposition; and that he had been moved by the warmth of the message which was sent to him when he took up office. But the President himself had not the same recollection of the earlier meeting and the warm message of greeting was not more than the result of an instruction to officials to draft a warm message of greeting."[115] Derek Mitchell thought this assessment was a "little one-sided" and moved on the offensive by explaining that

it was a fact that the Prime Minister assumed he had a personal affinity with the President and if he were disabused of this in too rude or unfeeling a way he might take it very hard. I said that I hoped that he would not look at this problem exclusively as one of conditioning the Prime Minister to the President. The opposite approach, difficult as it might be for Professor Neustadt and his colleagues in Washington, might pay handsome dividends.

This advice may have been taken to heart, especially when one considers the lavish attention paid to Wilson on his visit to Washington. Mitchell summed up the conversation by saying that throughout the talk Neustadt's "emphasis was on the importance of the personal relationship and of making sure that there was no misfire or recoil as a result of the confrontation."[116]

Wilson undoubtedly received a great deal of advice—from a variety of sources—on his forthcoming visit to Washington. Apart from the Foreign Office and private secretaries, the prime minister was also overwhelmed with correspondence from members of his cabinet and party and received indirect advice from editors and journalists. In his political memoirs, Wilson records that an "ominous note" came from a British newspaper editor who had been told by Johnson during a meeting in Washington that "he would never trust a British Prime Minister again, because all his experience showed their Washington visits to be concerned mainly with domestic electioneering."[117] This may have been partly due to Johnson's disagreement with Prime Minister Douglas-Home during his visit to Washington in February of that year. Johnson had been furious after Douglas-Home's visit when the prime minister had by accident led the press to believe that he had acted firmly in response to American criticism about British trade with Cuba, particularly the sale of Leyland buses. The president was livid at the imputation that he had allowed an allied leader of diminishing international significance to speak to him in such a manner, and apparently Johnson never spoke to Douglas-Home again. No such mistakes would be made with Wilson. Throughout the Wilson–Johnson years, the Americans were particularly careful to monitor the prime minister's public statements and actively sought to influence them.

In addition, Johnson apparently took a moral stand against Wilson and examined the question of his being a security risk after being furnished with intelligence reports during the British general election telling of Wilson's supposed affair with his secretary, Marcia Williams. These reports appear to have originated in Britain and were picked up by the FBI's London office.

Charles Bates, the FBI legal attaché in London at the time, asserts that information surrounding Wilson's supposed liaison with his secretary were received by FBI chief J. Edgar Hoover and duly passed on to President Johnson.[118] The same rumors were passed on to McGeorge Bundy via Richard Helms, the CIA's deputy director of plans.[119] In an Oval Office meeting with the president and his advisors shortly before Wilson's December visit, David Bruce also noted that such gossip was in circulation:

The President made no allusion to what I had been confidently told was his prejudice against the Prime Minister, founded largely on gossip that the latter had conducted an irregular sexual connection with his secretary. This allegation had been muttered in certain circles during the campaign; Al Irving queried the Chief Whip—now Lord Bowden on the subject. He received the assurance that the lady's husband would not bring a suit against Wilson, naming as co-respondent, since the husband had been divorced, remarried, and was the father of a child of his second venture. Johnson is said to be puritanical in his views about such affairs, and heartily to disapprove of them.[120]

Given the rumors of Johnson's own marital infidelities, the hypocrisy of such a judgment is striking. Nevertheless, there can be no doubt that Johnson would have felt more confident in the knowledge that he had such information at his fingertips, especially given his axiom "I never trust a man unless I have his pecker in my pocket."[121] Johnson was also well aware of James Jesus Angleton's concern that Wilson was a Soviet agent, and although the president does not appear to have taken this intelligence too seriously (the CIA continued to pass information on Wilson to the president and his closest advisors, particularly regarding his relationship with the Russians), such poison may partly explain why the president's attitude toward Wilson changed periodically.[122]

In any case, Johnson was not prepared to have Williams accompany the prime minister to Washington and there was certainly some controversy over this issue. George Ball remembers that "on Wilson's first visit to President Johnson in Washington...relations got off to a bad start over the Prime Minister's insistence that his assistant, Marcia Williams, attend highly restricted meetings; she did not, in Johnson's view, have the rank to justify it."[123] Williams herself remembers the event somewhat differently. "The reason I was not taken on that first visit was mainly that the Principal Private Secretary had worries because never before had anybody political been taken abroad with the Prime Minister. It is difficult to tell if this view was accurate. But for another visit Derek Mitchell did helpfully suggest that I might have been able to go on the plane in the capacity of a 'maid' if Mrs Wilson was on the trip."[124] As it turned out, Wilson was accompanied to Washington by the Foreign Secretary, Patrick Gordon Walker; Defense Secretary Denis Healey; the secretary of the cabinet, Burke Trend; and senior Foreign Office and defense officials. The visit took place from Sunday, December 6, to Wednesday, December 9, and on the surface, "with Sir Winston Churchill day just over, good will for Britain" was "running high."[125] Privately, however, the difficulties in planning and preparation for the trip meant that uneasiness surrounded Wilson's first visit to Washington as prime minister.

On Wilson's arrival at the White House on December 7, President Johnson gave his traditional remarks of welcome on the south lawn. Wilson responded in much greater detail, and as John Freeman noted in the *New Statesman*, the prime minister's long-windedness was perhaps a danger to the future of Anglo–American relations:

There was a brief moment on Monday morning in the pale icy sunshine of the White House garden, when it seemed as if a new and unexpected objective of British policy was being revealed. To kill the President of the United States by exposure. The Prime Minister had been given the full red-carpet treatment: a 19-gun salute, a presidential reception, guards of honour, and a briefly graceful speech of welcome from President Lyndon Johnson, who faced the near-freezing atmosphere coatless. Harold Wilson, in a heavy greatcoat, stepped to the microphones and plunged into a portentous address about the purpose of his mission. It lasted nearly 10 minutes. Well before the end the assembled dignitaries were discreetly shuffling to restore their circulation. The President looked stoically blue with cold. And a little peeved. It seemed an ill-starred beginning to such important talks with such a sensitive man.[126]

Wilson—new to office—may well have been demonstrating his liking for the world stage, but given Johnson's undoubted ultrasensitivity, Freeman was probably correct.

It is worth examining Prime Minister Wilson's first private talk with President Johnson in some detail, not least because the dynamics of the personal relationship and the working relationship between the men were established on this occasion. In Wilson's account of the visit, he notes that during their first private meeting, which lasted from 11:30 A.M. to 1 P.M., the president started by repeating "that after his previous experience he had come to the conclusion that he would never trust a British Prime Minister again." Wilson said that he understood what Johnson meant—Alec Douglas-Home and the Cuban buses statement—and that he personally would "say nothing outside the White House that I had not said to him inside."[127] The president remembered that he had said that while Douglas-Home had caused problems on the steps of the White House, Wilson "had given him trouble ten days before the visit."[128] Wilson apparently apologized, saying that he had meant only to give a general discussion of ANF. Interestingly, Johnson later recalled that his warning to Wilson came after their discussion of the pound and Atlantic nuclear defense.[129] Either way, the fact that the president raised the Cuban bus incident is clear evidence of Johnson's intimidating style. Wilson was immediately put on the defensive.

Their discussion went on to their respective domestic political problems. Wilson felt that the president did not fully understand the British political system, especially the problem of governing with a small majority:

His political reputation had been built up by his success as Senate majority leader with, at times a small, and always unreliable, majority, so he felt that he understood the problems facing our parliamentary leadership. It was harder for him to see that while failure to carry a vote in the Senate did not mean the end of a presidency, which was secure for a four-year period, a serious parliamentary defeat might mean the end of the Government, or at least an immediate general election.[130]

This confusion over the differences between the British and U.S. political systems may account for Johnson's later inability to comprehend fully Wilson's difficulties in dealing with backbench dissent over Vietnam. Nevertheless, Johnson's interpretation of this discussion of domestic politics was somewhat different from Wilson's, again suggesting some problems with communication. In a debriefing of the conversation Johnson conveyed the following to McGeorge Bundy:

The President pointed out to the Prime Minister that there were a lot of problems which did not show in the U.S. returns, especially with respect to international affairs. He said that our folks were damned tired of being told that it was their business to solve all the world's problems and do so mainly alone and that he was very wary of taking any tall dives that might get him into the situation Roosevelt got into in 1937.[131]

There was no mention of Wilson's parliamentary difficulties. Such Wilsonian concerns did not register as important to Johnson when compared to his own foreign policy anxieties. Nevertheless, Wilson and Johnson undoubtedly enjoyed talking to each other about the management of politics.

Getting down to business, Wilson and Johnson then moved the discussion on to three major problems facing Anglo–American relations at that time: the proposed Atlantic nuclear force, sterling, and Vietnam. They started with a discussion of the pound. Again, Johnson remembered that he had spoken "frankly but kindly to the Prime Minister about the troubles which the latter had already given the President." He explained to the prime minister that the British budget had created great difficulties for him: "[I]ts heavy emphasis on social security, and the pressures created against the pound had combined to make [his] . . . own budgeting process very difficult." Johnson said he had originally thought of a budget in the region of $107–$108 billion but was now forced to think in terms of $102, "which would make it very difficult to carry out the programs he wanted."[132] As well as introducing a 15 percent surcharge within days of coming to office, the Wilson government had increased the bank rate by 2 percent on November 23. Johnson's own budget had been affected by British demands for help with sterling, and the administration acknowledged that "problems for the pound would also be problems for the dollar."[133] Consequently the president was blunt in his analysis of the dangers of a British devaluation but kind about the problems sterling caused the prime minister. After further lecturing the prime minister on British monetary action and the dangers of continuing British economic difficulties, the president talked to Wilson about problems that his speech in the House of Commons on Atlantic nuclear defense had created. According to Johnson, by this time "the Prime Minister was almost on the ropes."[134] Wilson explained that, contrary to the impression given during his statement in the House, he had "not said no to the MLF but only to a force without a U.S. veto."[135]

Later in the afternoon a full meeting between the prime minister; the president; and their respective senior colleagues, advisors, and note takers took place in the cabinet room of the White House. At this full-scale meeting Vietnam was discussed seriously for the first time. The Americans had, however, put much thought into the subject before the visit. Preempting the Wilson visit, McGeorge Bundy indicated to the British that the president had a "deep personal concern" about Vietnam and that he would discuss it with the prime minister.[136] Indeed, the British, New Zealand, and Australian embassies had been informed that the prospect of more serious decisions made it more vital than ever that the United States have increased third country contributions. It was suggested that the United Kingdom increase its number of police advisors.[137]

Prior to Wilson's visit, the CIA had advised the special assistant to the president for national security affairs, McGeorge Bundy, on the British and Vietnam. The assistant deputy director of intelligence felt that three points should be borne in mind when dealing with the British on Vietnam. First, the British were "already participating in a helpful, if quiet, way on the Vietnam problem through their British Military Mission." There was a concern, however, that the British were showing "signs of restlessness about this operation" and might end the missions once Robert Thompson's tour of duty had been completed. The CIA judged BRIAM to have "played a variety of useful functions" and argued that the British should be encouraged to continue this role after Thompson departed. Second, the CIA expected the British to play the Malaysia card. The British were "heavily committed in Malaysia and with the best will in the world are unlikely to be able to make much of an additional military commitment in Vietnam." It was likely, therefore, that the British would require "a quid pro quo with respect to Malaysia" and the United States could "wind up undertaking a bigger commitment (both military and political) in Malaysia than we would like—a commitment which would, in the event, outweigh the usefulness of an increased British role in Vietnam." Third, the CIA judged that "more important than a large number of flags flying at military headquarters in Saigon is a meaningful contribution by forces that can be assigned by MACV [Military Assistance Command, Vietnam]. Under the circumstances this would obviously include a British contingent, but for the reasons mentioned above, we should not press for this or ask for much more than is already being done by HMG [Her Majesty's Government]. In any case, I would think that part of the President's purpose could be served by providing greater publicity to the existing British effort in Vietnam." It was concluded that "since we will be putting a fair amount of heat on the Prime Minister re the MLF issue and perhaps others as well...the President should seek no more than to obtain Wilson's sympathetic understanding of our problem in Vietnam, U.K. support in the UN and in other forums, Wilson's agreement to maintain at least the present British commitment in Vietnam, and a readiness to take on the burdens of Co-

Chairman of a Geneva Conference and follow a policy in that capacity that is consistent with our own objectives in Indochina."[138]

Bundy assessed the CIA's information and outlined his own conclusions in a memo to Johnson the following day, including the difficulties surrounding the issue of "the British and Vietnam." He told the president that "the British will find it very, very difficult indeed to increase their commitment in Vietnam right now" because of a lack of political support for any such action. He went on to point out that in a sense it was now too late to start expecting serious support from the British, because

[f]or 10 years we have accepted a situation in which the British give political support, but avoid any major commitment on the ground of their other interests and their position as Co-Chairman of the Geneva Agreements of 1954.... It is hard to treat a thing as our problem for 10 years and then try to get people to take a share of it, just because it is getting worse (though we choose not to say so).

Bundy still felt it was worth hitting the British "hard" while in Washington but recognized that a "definite and affirmative answer" was unlikely. He also acknowledged that at present

the most that Wilson could possibly do...would be a slight enlargement of the Thompson advisory mission and of their police training effort, with perhaps a green light to a few bold British officers to get themselves in the line of fire as our men do. All this he would have to do quietly.... You might press him to go from the current level of 7 Britishers to about a hundred, but we would be lucky to get 50 in this first phase.

In relation to a possible second phase of the conflict entailing the need "to land a mixed force of U.S. and other troops," Bundy felt that "we might conceivably get a small British contingent along with larger ones from Australia and New Zealand." He judged that this request might succeed because "our own commitment would have gone up and there would be a better case for asking the British to join in." However, Bundy was clearly aware of the ambivalent position of the British due to their role as cochair of the Geneva Conference and the dangers inherent in any commitments on their part: "[I]f the British Co-Chairman send troops in, that might be the trigger, or at least the excuse, for the Soviet Co-Chairman to help Hanoi in a similar manner."[139] Consequently, the Americans decided to push the British gently on Vietnam, something the Labour government could only have dreamed of.

According to the official British record of the meeting, the president introduced Vietnam in connection with the importance of Britain's worldwide role. He suggested that "there were...places where a United Kingdom military presence, on however a limited scale, might have a significant effect. A few soldiers in British uniforms in South Vietnam, for example, would have a great psychological and political significance."[140] Wilson notes in his memoirs that the president's request for a token British force in South Vietnam was made "without excessive enthusiasm."[141] Cabinet minutes also record that "there was no real United States pressure for a United Kingdom presence on the ground in South Viet-Nam, apart from an initial suggestion that we should contribute a token force of 100 men."[142] The prime minister responded by acknowledging the parallels between the U.S. problem in Vietnam and the British problem in Malaysia and emphasizing the existing British help in Vietnam, which included the Thompson mission, the training of Vietnamese troops in jungle warfare, and the provision of police officers in Saigon. He explained that the British could not offer a troop contribution because they were the "cochairman of the Geneva conference, under the Agreements of 1954 and 1962, and would have a role to play in seeking a way to peace." He "stressed the fact also, which seemed new to him, that we had as many as fifty-four thousand troops in Malaysia."[143]

These two main arguments against the sending of British troops to Vietnam— that the British were already overstretched in the Far East through their commitment of troops to the Malaysian struggle against Indonesia and that the British position as cochair of the Geneva Conference precluded any active military involvement in South Vietnam—would continue to be Wilson's main line of defense against the Johnson administration's requests for allied help. In themselves, the arguments were reason enough not to get involved and provided a convenient mask behind which Wilson could hide his own feelings of apprehension about U.S. involvement in Vietnam.[144] The Johnson administration was not convinced by either argument. After the Soviet Union began supplying arms and aircraft to the North Vietnamese in 1965, Washington could not see why Britain continued to remain so sensitive about its role as cochair. If the Wilson government believed in the wisdom of America's objectives in Vietnam, then the Americans could not see how a small troop deployment could add significantly to the British military burden around the world. In addition to such practical reasoning against British involvement in Vietnam, a domestic political issue would soon become equally important, if not more so: the unpopularity of the war in Britain, particularly within Wilson's own party. Even if the prime minister had wanted to send a token force to Vietnam, his party would not have allowed it. Wilson therefore "accepted no new commitment apart from offering to do a little more training in Malaysia" and instead pursued the possibility of a British role in the initiation of peace negotiations. William Bundy recorded that the Americans discussed such issues with "great frankness."[145]

That evening at a state dinner in the White House, President Johnson delivered a toast to the prime minister. Things were sufficiently relaxed for LBJ to deliver one of his famous jokes alluding to the wiliness of the British at such summit talks:

Mr. Prime Minister, I want you to know that I am really enjoying them, although sometimes diplomatic negotiations recall Mark Twain's story of his visit to a friend up in New Hampshire.

Mark Twain was walking along the road and he asked a farmer, "How far is it to Henderson's place?"

"About a mile and a half," the farmer answered.

He walked awhile longer and he met another farmer and he asked the same question, "How far is it to Henderson's place?" The farmer answered, "About a mile and a half."

Mark Twain walked a little farther and he met a third farmer and he again asked, "How far is it to Henderson's place?"

"About a mile and a half," the farmer answered. "Well," said Twain, "Thank God I am holding my own."[146]

He continued with another of his humorous anecdotes:

We have many difficult problems. I am sure the traditional British ability to find reasoned solution will ultimately prevail. During World War II the British Minister in Algeria was called upon to mediate a dispute between British and American officers. The American officers wanted drinks served before their meals. The British wanted their drinks served after their meals. He came up with this answer: "In deference to the British," he said, "we will all drink after meals and in deference to the Americans, we will all drink before the meal." This kind of British genius has solved a great many problems.[147]

The sound recording of this event indicates much laughter at this point.[148] Despite the inauspicious start and Wilson's refusal to send troops to Vietnam, the relationship between the two leaders and their respective administrations appears to have been relaxed. Basking in his landslide victory in the 1964 presidential election by the biggest margin to that point in U.S. history, Johnson was confident and self-assured in December 1964. Working hard on his plans for a "Great Society," he was in his element, using his dynamism and enthusiasm to good effect. At this point, Vietnam was still a troubling problem but had not yet overwhelmed the president's every thought and deed.

At the final meeting between the president and the prime minister, with the secretary of state, the Foreign Secretary, and the secretaries of defense in attendance, Vietnam was discussed in further detail. Rusk talked about assistance from other countries "both for its practical effect as well as for the political impact, to demonstrate to Saigon and Hanoi the degree of free world solidarity." He then expressed the U.S. government's hope that the United Kingdom would "put people into the countryside. Engineers, technicians, and military were needed . . . Showing the flag was important." Rusk did not just want a small contingent of British advisors, as with the Thompson mission, but "a significant number of people."[149] The British contingent repeated its support for the American policy in Vietnam but again reminded the Americans of Britain's efforts against communism in Malaysia and said that the U.S. problem in Vietnam and the British one in Malaysia were essentially the same. Obviously responding to Rusk's comments about the display of the British flag, Gordon Walker admitted that publicizing British efforts, such as training Vietnamese troops in jungle warfare and providing medics, "would in fact step up the British commitment." The British concluded the discussion on Vietnam by reminding the Americans that they needed to be "consulted about steps contemplated in Vietnam so that they could support U.S. efforts effectively."[150]

The British left Washington feeling moderately pleased with themselves. Not only had Wilson managed to successfully put forward his alternative to MLF, the ANF, but he had also secured some sympathy and understanding on sterling and had avoided any major commitment on Vietnam. The prime minister's conviction that a strong, forward-looking Anglo–American relationship was central to British interests remained intact.

EARLY DEALS AND UNDERSTANDINGS?

This idea of an understanding was, in one form or another, in common circulation at the time.[151] Some Labour members, especially Foreign Secretary George Brown, believed Wilson came to some sort of an agreement with Johnson during his December 1964 visit to Washington. Barbara Castle records in her diary that Brown, not too drunk, complained,

We've got to break with America, devalue and go into Europe...[but] He [Wilson] can't budge...Because he is too deeply committed to Johnson. God knows what he said to him. Back in 1964 he stopped me going to Washington. He went himself. What did he pledge?
I don't know: that we wouldn't devalue and full support in the Far East? But both those have got to go. We've got to turn down their money and pull out the troops: all of them...I want them out of East of Suez. This is the decision we have got to make: break the commitment to America. I've been sickened by what I've had to do to defend America at the dispatch box.[152]

In fact, as this book will demonstrate, in many respects Ponting's use of the word "understanding" to describe Anglo–American policy making on these crucial areas seems more apposite than Brown's evocation of shady bargains. Castle herself doubted that Wilson made any specific deal, believing that "Harold wasn't Machiavellian in the way of sitting down and working out little deals...with people."[153] In his memoirs, James Callaghan, chancellor of the exchequer during the Wilson years, also vehemently denies any deal involving Vietnam. "Emphatically I must record that I encountered nothing said or implied to this effect."[154] And yet, while it is extremely unlikely that any formal deals were made between Wilson and the Americans, this does not mean that the prime minister was not aware of American thinking on the issue; as we shall see, he repeatedly made statements, initiatives, and decisions with regard to Vietnam in the expectation of certain responses from America toward Britain and its interests. As Castle notes, Wilson "would have a kind of understanding and it would be unwritten and almost unarticulated...done by instinctive reactions."[155] Wilson himself later recognized that in one sense the United Kingdom's hands were tied over Vietnam. Richard Crossman points out in his diaries how Wilson contradicted himself on this issue at a cabinet meeting on defense in February 1966:

First he repeated time after time that the Americans had never made any connection between the financial support they gave us and our support for them in Vietnam. Then about ten minutes later he was saying, "Nevertheless, don't let's fail to realize that their financial support is not unrelated to the way we behave in the Far East: any direct announcement of our withdrawal [from East of Suez]...could not fail to have a profound effect on my personal relations with L.B.J. and the way the Americans treat us."[156]

There is no substantive evidence that any deal or understanding was reached at this first meeting between the British and American governments linking American financial support of the pound, a British commitment to remain East of Suez, and a wider deal involving Vietnam. However, two other possible arrangements could have been made. The first may have related to MLF. In managing to persuade Johnson to consider abandoning the unpopular MLF, Wilson may have agreed to a quid pro quo that tied the British to the United States on Vietnam.[157] Wilson's chief whip, Edward Short, endorses this theory. Short argues that Wilson "paid a price—a high price" for American acceptance of Wilson's ANF.[158] Certainly as early as July 1964 Neustadt discussed Southeast Asia as a place "where the US might be threatened or the UK rewarded in the course of bargaining over MLF."[159] It is clear, however, that Wilson's "success" over MLF was not as great a personal victory as it first appeared. Prior to the December visit, McGeorge Bundy spelled out in a memo to Dean Rusk, Robert McNamara, and George Ball his reservations about the cost of success on MLF, including "a deeply reluctant and essentially unpersuaded Great Britain" and a "protracted and difficult Congressional struggle in which we would be largely deprived of one decisive argument—that this arrangement is what our major European partners really want." Moreover, Bundy also revealed that from his own conversations with the president, he was sure that "he does not feel the kind of personal Presidential engagement in the MLF itself which would make it difficult for him to strike out on a new course if we can find one which seems better. I believe we can."[160]

It would appear, therefore, that although Wilson may have felt victorious over the likely scrapping of MLF, it was a smaller sacrifice for Johnson than the prime minister realized. And, though Wilson may have received much favorable publicity over this, Johnson may have felt it was worth it if it made Wilson obliged to him, especially on Vietnam. Johnson certainly felt he had been good to Wilson over this. "I didn't shove him on MLF, all my advisers said I ought to demand that he move right then and there, but he only had a three-man majority and I tried to treat him like I'd like to be treated if I was in the same situation."[161]

The second "arrangement" could have been a continuation of U.S. support for the British in Malaysia in return for continued British assistance in Vietnam.[162] According to Roger Hilsman, with regard to Indonesia Johnson had "sided too heavily with the British. Of course, it was linked to Vietnam. He wanted British support on Vietnam, you see."[163] In many ways, this was a continuation of established policy. As early as February 1964 the link between the situations in Malaysia and Vietnam had been established. O. G. Forster, a diplomat at the British embassy in Washington, explained in July of 1964 that

the link is not in the form of "if you will help us in Malaysia, we will help you in Laos and Vietnam," . . . Rather it is in the self-evident parallel between the two situations. It is very difficult for the Americans to urge us not to indulge in mild escalation in Eastern Malaysia, when they are seeking to persuade us that this is the correct policy in Laos and Vietnam; it is very difficult for them to argue that we should not take the Malaysian question to the United Nations, when this has been under consideration for Vietnam and Laos for the very same reasons; it is very difficult for them to urge that a Conference of the countries concerned will solve everything, when they are resisting another Geneva Conference for the same purpose.[164]

Or, as Charles Baldwin, U.S. ambassador to Malaysia (1961–64), put it: "There was a kind of tacit understanding—really an unwritten agreement—that the United States was carrying all the burden with respect to Southeast Asia that we should carry at the time, and that Britain would consider the protection of the Malaysia area a British responsibility. That was clearly understood in London, Washington, and in Kuala Lumpar."[165] In a briefing paper for Wilson's December visit to Washington, the Foreign Office wrote of an "element of reciprocity in the support extended by each Government to the policies of the other." This support was, according to the Foreign Office, "implicit in the communiqué issued on February 13, 1964, after Sir Alec Douglas-Home's visit to President Johnson," the relevant passage being "the Prime Minister re-emphasized the United Kingdom support for United States policy in South Viet-Nam. The President re-affirmed the support of the United States for the peaceful national independence of Malaysia."[166] This section of the communiqué had been inserted only after careful consideration. In the McGeorge Bundy memo of two days before the Wilson visit, the president had been advised that "the reciprocal price" of any British force in Vietnam "would be stronger support on our side for Malaysia and perhaps closer participation in naval and air deployment designed to cool off Sukarno. This kind of bargain in this part of the world makes a good deal of sense, and Rusk and McNamara will be ready to go forward with the British in detailed discussion on this basis."[167]

However, though an agreement may have been implied to support each other in Southeast Asia, William Bundy casts doubt on the direct nature of any agreement. "There is no truth whatever, I am sure, in the idea that the Johnson Administration agreed at any time with any British government for a kind of sharing of the military burden—no American forces in Malaysia (never for a moment contemplated in any case) and no British forces in Vietnam."[168] Before the Wilson visit, the CIA advised the White House that given the United Kingdom's heavy commitment in Malaysia, "should they be pressed to increase their participation [in Vietnam], they will probably insist on a quid pro quo with respect to Malaysia . . . we will end up undertaking a bigger commitment (both military and political) in Malaysia than we would like—a commitment which would, in the event, outweigh the usefulness of an increased British role in Vietnam." British visibility in Vietnam would, according to this assessment, be most usefully gained by publicizing the work of the British advisory mission.[169] McGeorge Bundy, Rusk, McNamara, and the president disagreed with the assessment, instead believing that a slightly increased U.S. role in Malaysia might be a cost worth paying for a more substantial U.K. presence in Vietnam.

Although Rusk raised the possibility of a "joint venture" between the United States and the United Kingdom in Malaysia and Vietnam, Wilson and Gordon Walker did not bite. So, in a sense, the December meeting saw an agreement between the United States and the United Kingdom that each country would give the other only limited support in their respective Southeast Asian problems. And, most likely, negotiations about the pound, MLF, and Malaysia all played a part in the British decision to pledge limited support for U.S. policy on Vietnam. Certainly these issues, explicitly or implicitly, were part of the context in which Wilson suppressed his reservations about the wisdom of the U.S. fight in Southeast Asia.

Johnson's interpretation of his first meeting with Wilson is indicative of the dominant position U.S. leaders now felt in relation to the British. When a diplomatic correspondent asked the president how his meeting with Wilson had gone, he replied that handling Wilson was like approaching a girl the first time you date her—first you cuddle up a bit and then commence feeling around to test her response.[170] Clearly this was how Johnson approached Wilson on Vietnam. William Bundy states that as late as November 30, in a draft position paper, he had suggested that the president not ask for any additional British contribution "in view of the British role in Malaysia." Bundy argued against such pressure "when the 'confrontation' situation was at its height." Nevertheless, as Bundy outlines "in the final version of the Paper, the limitation was removed."[171] Though the administration did not have realistic expectations of a British troop deployment in Vietnam, it would appear that Johnson himself could not resist the opportunity to make his English ally squirm a little.

William Bundy summed up the discussions on Vietnam as "important initial explorations of what was to become a crucial subject" but "generally speaking... Wilson's reaction was one of support. There did not appear to be any significant change in the British view of Asia, through the transition from Lord Home's to that of Wilson."[172]

This first meeting between Wilson and Johnson was, according to Wilson's personal and political secretary, Marcia Williams, "the most important and successful" of all the prime minister's visits. Before his departure from Washington, Wilson said the talks "have been what I hoped for, not only friendly but practical, getting down to cases and tackling each problem factually and frankly without frills; no time-wasting, no set speeches, no theology, but a fascinating, urgent and down-to-earth approach to everything we discussed."[173] This assessment is undoubtedly correct. The trip established an apparently pleasant tone in the personal relationship, and Wilson's success in persuading the Americans to reject MLF was the high point of Wilson's diplomatic efforts in Washington. Wilson conveyed his positive feelings about his Washington visit to his colleagues and the country. The day after he returned from Washington he reported back to the cabinet. The meeting was recorded not only by the cabinet secretary but also by Richard Crossman, minister for housing. Essentially their notes convey the same detail, but the Crossman diary is couched in less diplomatic language and reveals some interesting asides. According to Crossman, and not mentioned in cabinet records, Wilson "started by stating there were two conferences, one which took place and one which the British press reported." He denied press reports that "a pistol had been put to his head on Vietnam."[174] Wilson himself felt that he had been in a stronger position, personally and politically, than was portrayed. Cabinet records note that the prime minister said his trip to Washington had been "a successful visit, conducted in a very friendly and relaxed atmosphere. It established our main purpose of making clear our basic defence policy and preparing the ground for further, more detailed, discussions." The Americans had emphasized the importance of Britain's world role and stressed their desire that this continue, particularly East of Suez. They did, however, appreciate "the burden on our economy which this entailed." According to Wilson's notes for the cabinet, the British "emphasised our determination to reduce defence expenditure and to get the economy going again. Very useful and understanding talk with L.B.J., Dillon and Martin—'the talk which never happened'—about the pressure on sterling and our need for time to allow our long-term measures to take effect. They endorsed both what we had done and what we had decided not to do."[175]

In an unpublicized meeting to discuss the British economy, Wilson got the impression that Johnson was extremely understanding. According to Crossman's recollection of Wilson's cabinet report, Johnson had "virtually promised us all aid short of war."[176] If the Crossman notes are the more accurate, it suggests either Wilson's tendency for embellishment or Johnson's for hyperbole. Either way, it again illustrates problems in communication.

On Vietnam, Crossman points out that Wilson was eager to point out that the final communiqué had emphasized continuing discussions at all levels. Wilson believed that this meant "they want us with them . . . They want our new constructive ideas after the epoch of sterility. We are now in a position to influence events more than ever before for the last ten years."[177]

At the end of 1964 Anglo–American relations appeared to be sound, and Vietnam was not as yet a substantial issue between the two nations. Although unhappy with Wilson's refusal to provide troops for the Vietnam War, the Johnson administration was not surprised at this decision. Still, the prime minister's lack of real support on Vietnam would be used as a source of criticism in future discussions regarding support of the pound and the maintenance of Britain's military role East of Suez. At the same time, however, the growing U.S. desire for "more flags" in Vietnam meant that Wilson could use U.S. hopes of a deeper

British commitment, or at least continuing loyal diplomatic support, to good effect. The fact that Wilson was unable to deliver anything of substance on Vietnam and his own hope for a close relationship with the United States, and Johnson in particular, may have meant that the Americans could reap dividends in other areas. In the foreign policy world of national interests, the Americans, and Johnson especially, were tempted to indulge in moral blackmail.

Wilson left Washington convinced that he had a growing personal relationship with LBJ and a sound basis for a stronger relationship with the United States.

NOTES

1. Kevin Ruane, "Containing America: Aspects of British Foreign Policy and the Cold War in South-East Asia, 1951–54," *Diplomacy and Statecraft* 7, part 1 (1966): 150.

2. Ibid., 148.

3. Matthew Jones, *Conflict and Confrontation in South East Asia, 1961–65* (Cambridge: Cambridge University Press, 2001), 304.

4. Ruane, "Containing America, 142."

5. Bob Komer to Walt Rostow, May 3, 1961, box 193, country file (henceforth CF), Vietnam, national security file (henceforth NSF), John F. Kennedy Library, Boston (henceforth JFKL); telegram from Nolting to Secretary of State, "Task Force Viet Nam," July 18, 1961, South-East Asia, Rostow Memos Viet-Nam, 7/21/61, box 231, NSF, JFKL.

6. "A Program of Action: To Prevent Communist Domination of South Vietnam," May 1, 1961, Task Force Vietnam, 1/61–7/61, NSF, JFKL.

7. For a full discussion of British policy during this period, see Peter Busch, *All the Way with JFK? Britain, the U.S., and the Vietnam War* (Oxford: Oxford University Press, 2003).

8. For a detailed discussion of BRIAM see Ian F. W. Beckett, "Robert Thompson and the British Advisory Mission to South Vietnam, 1961–1965," *Small Wars and Insurgencies* 8, no. 3 (Winter 1997): 41–63.

9. *Hansard*, October 23, 1961, vol. 646, col. 13.

10. Thompson led BRIAM until 1965. Even after this date presidents Johnson and Nixon continued to consult Thompson. See Sir Robert Thompson, *Make for the Hills* (London: Leo Cooper, 1989), and Richard Clutterbuck, "Sir Robert Thompson: A Lifetime of Counter-Insurgency," *Army Quarterly and Defence Journal* 120, part 2 (1990): 140–43.

11. *Hansard*, Written Answer, October 24, 1963, vol. 684, col. 235.

12. Report, "Developments in Viet-Nam between General Taylor's Visits—October 1961–October 1962," CF, Vietnam, box 197, 10/1/62–6/30/63, NSF, JFKL, 3.

13. Foreign Office Minute, February 23, 1961, FO371/166726, PRO.

14. Between January 1964 and November 1967, the British government trained 240 U.S. troops and 1,035 South Vietnamese troops at the school. The cost for the train-

ing of South Vietnamese troops alone was £132,364. *Times* (London), November 7, 1967.

15. British Embassy, Saigon to Right Hon. the Earl of Home, August 22, 1962, FO371/166753, PRO; Duncan Campbell, *The Unsinkable Aircraft Carrier* (London: Michael Joseph, 1986), 142.

16. Memo for the President, November 15, 1962, Subject: Notes for Talk with Rusk—November 15, box 195, CF, Vietnam, General, 11/14/61–11/15/61, NSF, JFKL.

17. Department of State telegram, box 195, CF, Vietnam, General 11/18/61–11/20/61, NSF, JFKL; Memo from Dean Rusk to McGeorge Bundy, Top Secret, November 20, 1961, Subject: Status of Actions with Respect to South Viet-Nam, box 195, Vietnam, General, Memos and Reports, 11/17/61–11/31/61, NSF, JFKL; State Cable to Multiple Embassies, November 19, 1961, box 197, CF, Vietnam, NSF, JFKL.

18. Telegram from Bruce to Rusk, Washington, December 2, 1961, CF, Vietnam, General, 12/1/61–12/2/61, box 195, NSF, JFKL.

19. Ibid.

20. Busch, *All the Way with JFK?*

21. *Hansard,* Oral Answer, March 14, 1962, vol. 676, col. 1318.

22. Ibid.

23. Harold Wilson, *The Labour Government, 1964–68: A Personal Record* (London: Weidenfeld and Nicolson, 1971), 23, 67–68.

24. Derek McDougall, "The Malayan Emergency and Confrontation," in *Munich to Vietnam: Australia's Relations with Britain and the United States since the 1930s,* edited by Carl Bridge (Melbourne: Melbourne University Press, 1992).

25. Requests for allied help under the "more flags" program actually came from Washington despite the State Department's illusion that they originated in Saigon. South Vietnam was in fact reluctant to seek free-world aid, and direct requests for aid really began only in 1965 after Washington insisted that they ask for it.

26. Message, Dean Rusk to American Embassies, 5/1/64, Vietnam Memos, vol. 8, 5/64, Item no. 110, 3, box 6, CF, Vietnam, NSF, LBJL; in Robert M. Blackburn, *Mercenaries and Lyndon Johnson's "More Flags": The Hiring of Korean, Filipino and Thai Soldiers in the Vietnam War* (Jefferson, N.C.: McFarland, 1994).

27. Quoted in Blackburn, *Mercenaries,* 22.

28. Eventually Australia sent 8,000 troops to Vietnam; New Zealand sent 550.

29. Quoted in Blackburn, *Mercenaries,* 24.

30. Patrick Lloyd Hatcher, *Suicide of an Elite: American Internationalists and Vietnam* (Stanford, Calif.: Stanford University Press, 1990), 58.

31. Ibid., 53–57. To avoid another Germany or Japan, security pacts and bilateral alliances would form a security arc around the Soviet Union and communism in general.

32. Blackburn, *Mercenaries,* 143.

33. David Dimbleby, BBC1 interview with William Bundy in David Dimbleby and David Reynolds, *An Ocean Apart: The Relationship between Britain and America in the Twentieth Century* (London: Harper and Row, 1988), 252.

34. Wilson, *Labour Government,* 341.

35. Louis Heren, *No Hail, No Farewell* (London: Harper and Row, 1970), 231.

36. Memorandum for the Record by Bundy, February 13, 1964, in *Foreign Relations of the United States 1964–68*, vol. 1, Vietnam 1964 (Washington, D.C.: U.S. Government Printing Office, 1995) (henceforth FRUS), 69–70.

37. *Daily Telegraph* (London), February 18, 1952, in Paul Foot, *The Politics of Harold Wilson* (Harmondsworth: Penguin, 1968), 203.

38. Liverpool *Daily Post*, May 3, 1954, in Foot, *Politics of Harold Wilson*, 203.

39. *Daily Telegraph* (London), May 3, 1954, in Foot, *Politics of Harold Wilson*, 204.

40. In April 1951 Wilson, then president of the Board of Trade, followed Aneuran Bevan, minister of labour, in resigning in opposition to the Labour government's plans for defense rearmament and the planned introduction of charges for NHS (National Health Service) dentures and eyeglasses. Under the influence of Bevan—the only credible left-wing leadership contender—over the next four years Wilson developed his radical instincts. Wilson condemned American foreign policy, particularly arms spending and U.S. accumulation of the world's raw materials. By 1954 Bevan's chance of challenging for the leadership of the Labour Party had diminished, and Wilson began to drift to the center of Labour politics.

41. Foot, *Politics of Harold Wilson*, 205.

42. Richard Neustadt, oral history interview quoted in Ben Pimlott, *Harold Wilson* (London: Harper Collins, 1992), 284.

43. *Hansard*, House of Commons Debates, 5th series, June 30, 1964, vol. 697, cols. 1134–35.

44. Memo from Walt Rostow to Mr. Tyler, February 17, 1964, Subject: Talk with Patrick Gordon Walker, File: UK, Meetings with Walker, 2/64, box 213, CF, UK, NSF, LBJL.

45. Memo from McGeorge Bundy to the President, March 1, 1964, File: UK, Meetings with Wilson, 3/2/64, CF, UK, NSF, LBJL.

46. Memo, Dean Rusk to the President, February 28, 1964, File: UK, Meetings with Wilson, 3/2/64, CF, UK, NSF, LBJL.

47. *Times* (London), February 28, 1964, 10.

48. See in particular Foot, *Politics of Harold Wilson*, and Andrew Roth, *Sir Harold Wilson: Yorkshire Walter Mitty* (London: Macdonald and Jane's, 1977). Accusations about Wilson's questionable liaisons with his secretary and business associates are now considered groundless.

49. Pimlott, *Harold Wilson*; Philip Ziegler, *Wilson: The Authorised Life of Lord Wilson of Rievaulx* (London: Weidenfeld and Nicolson, 1993); R. Coopey, S. Fielding, and N. Tiratsoo, *The Wilson Governments 1964–1970* (London: Pinter, 1993).

50. Roth, *Sir Harold Wilson*.

51. Memo, Dean Rusk to the President, February 28, 1964, File: UK, Meetings with Wilson, 3/2/64, CF, UK, NSF, LBJL.

52. Memo from McGeorge Bundy to the President, March 1, 1964, File: UK, Meetings with Wilson, 3/2/64, CF, UK, NSF, LBJL.

53. CIA Biographic Statement on Harold Wilson, File: UK, Wilson Visit Briefing Book, 12/64, CF, UK, box 213, NSF, LBJL.

54. *Times* (London), February 28, 1964, 10.

55. John Baylis, *Anglo-American Defence Relations 1939–1980: The Special Relationship* (Basingstoke: Macmillan, 1981), 81.

56. Ibid.

57. Memorandum of Conversation, Harold Wilson and Robert S. McNamara, March 5, 1964, File: UK, Meetings with Wilson, 3/2/64, CF, UK, NSF, LBJL.

58. *Times* (London), March 3, 1964, 8.

59. Tony Benn, *Out of the Wilderness: Diaries 1963–1967* (London: Arrow Books, 1989), March 4, 1964, 97. Benn became a cabinet member in October 1964 as postmaster general and continued to keep a diary. His comments are generally reliable and often extraordinarily perceptive, but, in keeping with all the diaries from this diary-rich government, they are also personal. They do, however, give scholars a good sense of how the Wilson–Johnson relationship was perceived at the time. In Benn's case, his belief in the strength of the prime minister's relationship with the president may well be related to his own closeness to Wilson at this time. Later comments which are more critical of Wilson's friendship with Johnson, again, perhaps reflect Benn's growing disdain for Wilson.

60. *Times* (London), March 4, 1964, 19.

61. Transcript, March 2, 1964, 2320a–2321a, Records and Transcripts of Telephone Conversations and Meetings, WH Series, box 3, LBJL.

62. Benn, *Out of the Wilderness,* April 27, 1964, 106.

63. Ibid., August 10, 1964, 135.

64. Papers of Patrick Gordon Walker, GNWR 314 1964 Foreign Policy, "Thoughts on Foreign Policy August 1964," Churchill Archives, Cambridge.

65. Telegram from David Bruce to George Ball, July 20, 1964, David Bruce diaries, Virginia Historical Society, Richmond (henceforth Bruce diaries).

66. Memorandum on the British Labour Party and the MLF, prepared by Richard E. Neustadt, July 6, 1964, published in *New Left Review* 51 (1968): 11–21.

67. Ibid.

68. Telegram from David Bruce to Dean Rusk, October 16, 1964, Bruce diaries.

69. Transcript, David Bruce oral history interview by Thomas H. Baker, December 9, 1971, tape 1, 9, LBJL.

70. Papers of William P. Bundy, box 1, chapter 16, 2, LBJL.

71. Telegram from David Bruce to Dean Rusk, October 16, 1964, Bruce diaries.

72. Radio and Television Report to the American People of Recent Events in Russia, China, and Great Britain, October 18, 1964 (686), *Public Papers of the Presidents, Lyndon B. Johnson,* vol. 2, *1964* (Washington, D.C.: U.S. Government Printing Office, 1966), 1379.

73. "Change in British Government," American Opinion Summary, Department of State, October 23, 1964, File: UK, Walker Briefing Book 10/26–27/64, CF, UK, NSF, LBJL.

74. It appears the U.S. intelligence community was worried that the Labour Party was headed by a leader who had links to the Eastern Communist bloc, notably the Soviet Union, a country Wilson had visited on numerous occasions. Although these trips were made largely on private business, suspicion remained that Wilson was a Soviet mole. James Jesus Angleton, head of the CIA's counterintelligence unit, firmly believed

that the Soviets had assassinated Wilson's predecessor, Hugh Gaitskell, in order to get "their man" in 10 Downing Street. Consequently, the CIA had a file, code-named Oatsheaf, on Wilson that remained open throughout his time in office. At the CIA's prompting, MI5 (the British Security Service) also monitored the prime minister's activities and investigated his friends and associates in a file named "Henry Worthington." See in particular Peter Wright, *Spycatcher* (Victoria, Australia: William Heinemann, 1987); Stephen Dorril and Robin Ramsay, *Smear! Wilson and the Secret State* (London: Grafton, 1992); David Leigh, *The Wilson Plot: How the Spycatchers and Their American Allies Tried to Overthrow the British Government* (New York: Pantheon, 1988).

75. Bruce diaries, April 14, 1962.

76. Alan P. Dobson, *Anglo-American Relations in the Twentieth Century* (London: Routledge, 1995), 131.

77. It has been argued that prior to 1964 Wilson and Callaghan were so concerned that they not be forced into devaluation by the nervous city of London that they sought and received an indication from the New York Federal Reserve Bank that they would receive financial backing should the pound come under attack upon Labour's electoral victory. See Dorril and Ramsay, *Smear*.

78. Dobson, *Anglo-American Relations*, 132.

79. Harold Wilson quoted in Darwin, "Britain's Withdrawal from East of Suez," 150.

80. Peter Catterall, (ed.), "Witness Seminar: The East of Suez Decision," *Contemporary Record* 7, no. 3 (Winter 1993): 612–13.

81. Ibid., 613.

82. Catterall, "East of Suez Decision," 614.

83. Suggested Points for Toast, Secretary's Dinner for Patrick Gordon Walker, October 27, 1964, File: UK, Walker Visit Briefing Book 10/26–27/64, CF, UK, NSF, LBJL.

84. Memo for the President, October 24, 1964, File: UK, Walker Visit Briefing Book, 10/26–27/64, box 213, CF, UK, NSF, LBJL.

85. Ibid.

86. Ibid.

87. Wilson, *Labour Government*, 71.

88. Memo for the President, October 24, 1964, File: UK, Walker Visit Briefing Book, 10/26–27/64, box 213, CF, UK, NSF, LBJL.

89. Ibid.

90. Note from Oliver Wright to the Prime Minister, "Strategy for Washington," December 2, 1964, PREM 13/103, PRO.

91. Talking Points Paper on the Far East, File: UK, Walker Visit Briefing Book, 10/26–27/64, CF, UK, NSF, LBJL.

92. Papers of William P. Bundy, box 1, chapter 16, 2, LBJL.

93. Remarks at the Welcome at the White House to the New Prime Minister of Great Britain, December 7, 1964, *Public Papers of the Presidents*, 1644.

94. Toasts of the President and Prime Minister Harold Wilson, December 7, 1964, *Public Papers of the Presidents*, 1648.

95. Benn, *Out of the Wilderness,* May 5, 1964, 108.

96. Ian S. McDonald, *Anglo-American Relations since the Second World War* (New York: St. Martin's Press, 1974), 219.

97. See Saki Dockrill, *Britain's Retreat From East of Suez: The Choice between Europe and the World?* (Basingstoke: Palgrave, 2002), 44.

98. Wilson, *Labour Government,* 87.

99. Labour Party Manifesto 1964—"Let's Go with Labour for the New Britain."

100. Foot, *Politics of Harold Wilson,* 212.

101. Memorandum on the British Labour Party and the MLF, 11–21.

102. Ibid.

103. Wilson had visited the Soviet Union numerous times since the 1940s, sometimes in an official capacity but also to establish trading links for the timber importer Montague Meyer.

104. See Ben Pimlott, *Harold Wilson,* 180–81, and Ziegler, *Wilson: The Authorised Life,* 57–58, 90–91. Wilson's regular trips to the Soviet Union led to allegations by U.S. intelligence services that he was a Soviet agent. There is no evidence, however, that Wilson had any sympathy with communism, despite the occasional radical statement made during his Bevanite phase suggesting that Britain maintain some distance from the United States in economic terms.

105. Frank Costigliola, "LBJ, Germany, and the 'End of the Cold War,' " in Warren I. Cohen and Nancy Bernkopf Tucker (eds.), *Lyndon Johnson Confronts the World: American Foreign Policy 1963–1968* (Cambridge: Cambridge University Press, 1994), 174.

106. Transcript, George W. Ball oral history interview by Paige E. Mulhollan, July 7, 1971, tape 2, 17, LBJL.

107. Some have attributed this to Johnson's personal experience as a teacher of young, poor Mexican Americans, which led him to feel he understood the problems of underdeveloped nations.

108. Memorandum for the Record, March 31, 1965, NSF, Files of McGeorge Bundy, box 18, LBJL.

109. Henry Brandon, *Special Relationships: A Foreign Correspondent's Memoirs from Roosevelt to Reagan* (London: Macmillan, 1988), 204.

110. Benn, *Out of the Wilderness,* April 27, 1964.

111. Stewart Alsop, "The Interesting Mr. Wilson," *Economist,* December 1964, 14.

112. Brandon, *Special Relationship,* 209.

113. Wilson, *Labour Government,* 75.

114. Jo Wright to J. N. Henderson, November 12, 1964, PREM 13/108, PRO.

115. Note of a Conversation with Professor Neustadt and D. Mitchell, Prime Minister's Visit to Washington, Top Secret, PREM 13/193, PRO.

116. Ibid.

117. Wilson, *Labour Government,* 76.

118. Leigh, *Wilson Plot,* 69.

119. Dorril and Ramsay, *Smear,* 56.

120. Bruce diaries, December 5, 1964.

121. Denis Healey, *The Time of My Life* (London: Penguin, 1989), 319.

122. See Wright, *Spycatcher,* and Dorril and Ramsay, *Smear.*

123. George W. Ball, *The Past Has Another Pattern: Memoirs* (New York: W. W. Norton and Company, 1982), 336.

124. Marcia Williams, *Inside No. 10* (London: Weidenfeld and Nicolson, 1972), 40.

125. *Times* (London), December 7, 1964, 10.

126. John Freeman, *New Statesman,* December 11, 1964, 916.

127. Wilson, *Labour Government,* 77.

128. McGeorge Bundy, Memorandum for the Record, December 7, 1964, Files of McGeorge Bundy, Memos for the Record 1964, box 18, NSF, LBJL.

129. Ibid.

130. Wilson, *Labour Government,* 78.

131. Memo for the Record, December 7, 1964, Files of McGeorge Bundy, Memos for the Record 1964, box 18, NSF, LBJL.

132. McGeorge Bundy, Memorandum for the Record, December 7, 1964, Files of McGeorge Bundy, Memos for the Record, 1964, box 18, NSF, LBJL.

133. Ibid.

134. Ibid.

135. Ibid.

136. Ibid.

137. Telegram from Rusk to U.S. Embassies in London, Canberra, and Wellington, December 4, 1964, LBJL, in Gareth Porter, *Vietnam: A History in Documents* (New York: New American Library, 1981), 289–90.

138. Memo from the Assistant Deputy Director (Intelligence) to McGeorge Bundy, "The British and Vietnam," December 4, 1964, PM Wilson Visit (1), 12/7–8/64, box 214, CF, UK, NSF, LBJL.

139. Memo to the President from McGeorge Bundy, Subject: "The British and Vietnam," December 5, 1964, box 214, PM Wilson Visit (1), 12/7–8/64, CF, UK, NSF, LBJL.

140. The Prime Minister's Visit to the United States and Canada, December 6–10, 1964, Top Secret, PREM 13/104, PRO.

141. Wilson, *Labour Government,* 79.

142. North American Visit, Notes for Cabinet, PREM 13/104, PRO.

143. Wilson, *Labour Government,* 79.

144. Johnson described Wilson's argument that he could not send troops to Vietnam without jeopardizing the British position as Geneva cochair as a "fig-leaf." Briefing Book 7/29/66, box 215/6, CF, UK, NSF, LBJL.

145. Papers of William P. Bundy, box 1, chapter 19, 21–22, LBJL.

146. Toasts of the President and Prime Minister, Harold Wilson, December 7, 1964, *Public Papers of the Presidents, Lyndon B. Johnson,* 1645.

147. Ibid.

148. Audiocassette, "The Humor of LBJ: 25th Anniversary Edition," LBJ Museum Store Production, Austin, Texas, 1989.

149. Record of a Meeting Held at the White House on Tuesday, December 8, 1964, at 3:45 P.M., the Prime Minister's Visit to the United States and Canada, December 6–10, 1964, PREM 13/104, PRO.

150. Memorandum of a Conversation, White House, Washington, December 8, 1964, 4 P.M., in FRUS 1964, 985.

151. See also P. Toynbee, "Dictators, Demagogues or Prigs?" *New Statesman*, January 5, 1965, in Kingsley Amis (ed.), *Harold's Years: Impressions from the New Statesman and the Spectator* (London: Quartet Books, 1977), 57; "Vietnam—What's Wilson Waiting For?" (editorial). *New Statesman*, March 12, 1965, 1.

152. Barbara Castle, *The Barbara Castle Diaries 1964–76* (London, Papermac, 1990), July 18, 1966, 76.

153. Interview with author, April 28, 1993.

154. James Callaghan, *Time and Chance* (London: Collins, 1987), 176.

155. Interview with author, April 28, 1993.

156. Richard Crossman, *The Crossman Diaries: Selections from the Diaries of a Cabinet Minister 1964–70* (London: Mandarin, 1991), February 14, 1966, 180.

157. See Saki Dockrill, "Forging the Anglo-American Global Defence Partnership: Harold Wilson, Lyndon Johnson and the Washington Summit, December 1964," *Journal of Strategic Studies* 23, no. 4 (December 2000): 107–29.

158. Edward Short, *Whip to Wilson* (London: Macdonald and Co., 1989), 96.

159. Memo on British Labour Party and the MLF, July 6, 1964.

160. Memo, Bundy to Rusk, McNamara, and Ball, November 25, 1964, McGeorge Bundy, 10/1–12/31/64 folder, box 2, Memos to the President, LBJL, in Paul Y. Hammond, *LBJ and the Presidential Management of Foreign Relations* (Austin: University of Texas, 1992).

161. Telephone Conversation between Lyndon Johnson and Robert Spivak, WH6504.06, side B, April 29, 1965, 12:43 P.M., LBJL.

162. See Matthew Jones, "U.S. Relations with Indonesia, the Kennedy-Johnson Transition, and the Vietnam Connection, 1963–1965," *Diplomatic History* 26, no. 2 (Spring 2002): 249–81, and Matthew Jones, *Conflict and Confrontation in South East Asia, 1961–65* (Cambridge: Cambridge University Press, 2001).

163. Transcript, Roger Hilsman oral history interview by David Nunnerley, January 26, 1970, JFKL.

164. O. G. Forster, British Embassy, Washington D.C., to J. E. Cable, Southeast Asia Department, Foreign Office, July 7, 1964, FO371/75063, PRO.

165. Transcript, Charles Baldwin oral history interview by Dennis J. O'Brien, March 14, 1969, JFKL.

166. Memorandum by J. E. Cable, "Malaysia and Vietnam. British and American Commitments and Undertakings," FO 371/175095/D1077/10, PRO.

167. Memorandum to the President from McGeorge Bundy, December 5, 1964, box 214, Prime Minister Wilson Visit (1) 12/7–8/64, CF, UK, NSF, LBJL.

168. Papers of William P. Bundy, box 1, chapter 19, 22A, LBJL.

169. Memo from Assistant Deputy Director (Intelligence) to McGeorge Bundy, December 4, 1964, "The British and Vietnam."

170. Frank Cormier, *The Way He Was* (New York: Doubleday and Co., 1977), 181.

171. Papers of William P. Bundy, box 1, chapter 19, 22–22A, LBJL.

172. Ibid.

173. *Times* (London), December 10, 1964, 12.

174. Crossman, *Crossman Diaries,* December 11, 1964, 53.

175. North American Visit: Notes for Cabinet, PREM 13/104, PRO.

176. Crossman, *Crossman Diaries,* December 11, 1964, 53.

177. Ibid., 54.

Chapter 2

The Search for an Understanding on Vietnam: January–April 1965

In the early part of 1965 the Johnson administration began laying the foundation for a major commitment to the war in Vietnam. The president and his advisors—military and civilian—discussed at length the avenues available to them as the situation in South Vietnam became increasingly unstable. The options at this stage centered mainly on military action, although negotiations had not been completely ruled out. In relation to its allies, America was keen to secure more solid support. Events in the United States meant that the British government faced new demands from Washington at the same time that it faced increasing domestic pressure to initiate peace talks in Indochina. Specifically, this led to calls for the renewal of the Geneva Conference. As the Wilson government pursued this and other options, the United States became increasingly irritated at Britain's mounting interference with regard to Vietnam without any significant military or material commitment to the conflict. Anglo–American relations therefore began to suffer as a result of tensions over the war. In particular, Britain was concerned about "creeping escalation" and a lack of adequate consultation, whereas America questioned Britain's reliability as an ally. Problems in the personal relationship between the two leaders exacerbated the growing rift between their two countries with regard to Southeast Asia. Consequently, by late March there was a serious need to find a practical, working solution to the difficulties Vietnam raised for the Anglo–American relationship.

ANGLO–AMERICAN RELATIONS AT THE BEGINNING OF 1965

At the end of 1964 Anglo–American relations appeared to be sound. In his annual review of the United States in 1964, Lord Harlech, British ambassador to the United States, informed Foreign Secretary Patrick Gordon Walker that "Anglo–American relations remained close and cordial." However, he recognized that in the coming years the "special relationship" would be tested by the force of "realpolitik." "We shall be increasingly treated on our merits and shall be regarded not so much for who we are as for how we perform. Above all our influence will depend upon our ability to solve our own economic problems and to bring an end to what seems to the Americans to be a position of chronic insolvency." Although Harlech felt the United Kingdom still possessed "a unique capability of influencing American policy," he warned that "this will be a wasting asset unless we handle our own affairs with considerable skill and attention to the correct priorities."[1]

Due to his apparent success during his December visit to Washington, Wilson believed he was the man for the job. He was convinced that he had made a strong impact on Johnson; had demonstrated the Labour government's loyalty and integrity as an ally; and had paved the way for yet closer relations between the United States and the United Kingdom, which would ultimately protect British security in Europe.[2] To capitalize on this, the prime minister planned another trip to Washington for early 1965.

Lyndon Johnson also planned to visit Britain for the first time as president. This almost happened sooner than anticipated when Winston Churchill died on January 24. The president, who greatly admired the wartime leader, very much wanted to attend the funeral but was unable to do so because he was recovering from a bad cold that had resulted in a three-day stay in Bethesda Naval Hospital. To the British, the visit would have been a welcome chance to get to know the Texan better. Many in the Foreign Office and in British political circles knew very little about the president, and just as importantly they felt that Johnson neither knew nor cared much about Britain. As it was, Johnson planned to send three official mourners in his place: Secretary of State Dean Rusk; Chief Justice Earl Warren; and the American ambassador to Great Britain, David Bruce. Unfortunately Rusk also pulled out of the funeral because of flu, leaving, to British eyes, two virtual unknowns at the funeral of the first "honorary American." Although a bad cold was potentially serious in a man who had had a heart attack, Johnson could not openly acknowledge his condition, and many viewed his decision not to go to Britain for Churchill's funeral as his choice rather than a medical necessity. Not surprisingly, LBJ received complaints from the public and the media on both sides of the Atlantic for not attending.[3] The president's inability to attend Churchill's funeral also meant that later in the year considerable effort would be put into attempting to secure a visit to Britain by both the president and the vice president, Hubert Humphrey, because, as Paul Gore-Booth, permanent undersecretary at the Foreign Office, admitted, "[I]t would be a good thing for the President to acquire some first-hand knowledge of Britain before his administration is much older."[4] Clearly, however, this mishandling of the arrangements for Churchill's funeral had done short-term damage to Anglo–American relations and was not a good omen for Anglo–American relations in 1965.

ESCALATION BEGINS

In January Walt Rostow, a senior State Department official, was sent to London to discuss the possibility of the selective bombing of North Vietnam. Though the Americans were not seeking advice as such, they clearly wanted to keep the British abreast of some of their thinking, to gauge the limits of the Labour government's support, and to assess possible international reaction to the bombing. Apparently Wilson gave Rostow "no encouragement" for such a move.[5]

When McGeorge Bundy announced he was going to visit Vietnam February 4–7, the Foreign Office commented that "the moment of truth approaches."[6] Wilson felt, and the cabinet agreed on January 28, that he should be in Washington at this crucial juncture, if only to ascertain whether the United States saw any role for the Geneva cochairs.[7] When the prime minister met with Dean Rusk at 10 Downing Street the following day he made it clear that although the United Kingdom would continue its support of American policy, he could not sanction U.S. policy ahead of time.[8] Although this was, of course, a sensible approach for the leader of a sovereign nation to take, Wilson was also leaving himself room to maneuver.

The Foreign Office considered Britain's position more fully when Alexei Kosygin, the chairman of ministers of the Soviet Union, visited North Vietnam at the beginning of February. The possibility existed that this visit might signal the beginning of a proposal from the Russians for a negotiated settlement in Vietnam. The time seemed ripe for Britain to "offer her services."[9] After further deliberation, the Foreign Office decided this would be a mistake given that the United States had already invested "too much effort, too many lives, too much money and, above all, too much prestige" in South Vietnam "to welcome such cold detachment" from an outsider. "We could do grave harm to Anglo–American relations by rushing in with unpalatable proposals. If failure comes in Vietnam, it is bound to cause profound dismay and recrimination in the United States. There will be a general search for someone to blame and British intervention at the present stage could all too easily make us the principal scapegoat."[10] For the time being, therefore, the British government decided to keep its opinions to itself, and the prime minister's plans for a visit to Washington were abandoned.

The Johnson administration's deliberations over air strikes ended on February 6 when an army advisors' barracks at Pleiku was attacked by the Vietcong, leaving nine Americans dead and over a hundred injured. The National Security Council advised the president to retaliate immediately. Johnson duly authorized Operation Flaming Dart, tit-for-tat bombing raids on North Vietnam. The Americans attempted to give Wilson and Michael Stewart, the new British Foreign Secretary, advance notice of this action but could reach only the permanent undersecretary, Harold Caccia, at the Foreign Office.[11] Regardless, the British government rushed to approve U.S. action, and as the Labour Party's left-wing journal *Tribune* noted: "Significantly enough, these reprisals were supported at the United Nations by only two nations—Great Britain and Formosa."[12]

The rapid escalation in U.S. military involvement in Vietnam, and the accompanying increase in world tension, led to British parliamentary unease. Stewart, in his first appearance at the Dispatch Box as secretary of state for foreign affairs, faced several questions on the issue. Stewart's appointment had proved pleasing to Washington in that he was seen as a longtime loyal friend to the United States, and his stout defense of U.S. policy in Vietnam began during his first series of questions in the House. As *The Times* reported the next day, "[I]f diplomacy is the art of remaining firm while giving the least offence to all sides, then Michael Stewart, the new Foreign Secretary, made a most impressive debut in the House of Commons.... Dealing with the situation in Vietnam, he displayed a smooth blend of tact and authority."[13] The Foreign Secretary rejected calls for the reconvening of the Geneva Conference on the grounds that "he doubted...whether sufficient agreement existed to justify such a conference."[14] This diplomacy endeared Stewart to the Americans but inflamed Labour's left wing and resulted in them tabling a peace motion in the Commons the following day. Fifty Labour M.P.s signed the motion, putting pressure on the British government to take an initiative to bring about a cease-fire and political settlement in Vietnam.

Given the Labour government's small majority in the House, this largely left-wing pressure was not taken lightly by the prime minister, especially given that he had also received private requests for "British diplomacy" on the issue. An old colleague and Labour M.P., David Ennals, had known Wilson for many years in his capacity as International Secretary of the Labour Party, and he used their personal friendship to try to influence the prime minister. He wrote to Wilson on February 9 arguing that "our co-Chairmanship of the 1954 conference does give us an opportunity and a responsibility" to act. He also suggested that "those forces in the USA who recognize...that negotiation is necessary would welcome British assistance to get them off the peg." Ennals therefore suggested that "without delay Michael Stewart should fly to Washington and then, if possible, to Moscow...It would dramatize our concerns, emphasize our sense of responsibility and would...be warmly welcomed throughout the country."[15]

These public and private requests for British action go some way toward explaining the most infamous exchange between Harold Wilson and Lyndon Johnson: the prime minister's late-night telephone call to the president. As the Foreign Office later put it, neither at home nor abroad could Wilson appear to be "standing idly by while events moved dangerously in Vietnam."[16] On the evening of February 10 Wilson received news of a Vietcong attack on the U.S. barracks at Qui Nhon in which 30 American servicemen lost their lives. He responded to this news with a proposal to fly to Washington to have a "personal discussion" with Johnson on the dangers of overreacting to the present crisis, particularly the risk of nuclear war.[17] The prime minister's vision of an informal "closeness" with the president was about to be put to the test. Unfortunately, as David Bruce put it, "[T]he President made short shrift of this project."[18]

Harlech informed the prime minister that the White House "was very strongly against a visit...at this time" but suggested that Wilson first contact the president by telephone before making up his mind.[19] McGeorge Bundy tried to delay such a call, suggesting that the prime minister ring the following morning.[20] Wilson was not willing to take this advice, however, because he knew he would have to face the House of Commons later in the day and meet with his cabinet at lunchtime on Thursday. The president agreed to receive the call, which took place on an open line between 3:15 and 3:30 A.M. British time (February 11) and between 10:15 and 10:30 P.M. Washington time (February 10).[21]

Unfortunately, this conversation does not appear to have been recorded or saved by Johnson. Nevertheless, the British transcript of this telephone call, most of which is declassified, reveals how Wilson was a recipient of the Johnson treatment. Johnson dominated the conversation and was easily able to put the prime minister on the defensive by letting "fly in an outburst of Texan temper," as Wilson so aptly put it.[22] McGeorge Bundy made notes on the president's side of the conversation, and his record does not contradict either the official British record or Wilson's recollection of the conversation contained in his memoirs.[23] The president appears to have regularly cut Wilson off midsentence and had ready, forceful, and often brusque replies to the prime minister's pleas and questions. Although Wilson often got close to offering advice and even hinted at criticism, Johnson interrupted him before it could be delivered.

Wilson began the conversation by outlining British concerns about a possible escalation in U.S. action in Vietnam and repeated his proposal to fly to Washington to discuss matters further.

Our problem is that every nation in the world is making a statement. India and France have taken the initiative. The U.S.S.R. were saying last week they would be accepting responsibility as Chairmen. It is very difficult here for us to be saying nothing at all except that whatever the U.S. decides to do we shall go along with of course. The feeling is that we tag along afterwards.... The feeling is that I should come over as quickly as possible.

Johnson thought such a visit would be "a serious mistake," that Wilson should "not get upset, keep a normal pulse" and in his position he "would wait until I was called upon to do something and consider it on the merits." The language here is particularly telling; already Johnson was letting Wilson know his place. Johnson nevertheless reassured Wilson that U.S. action would "be very measured and very reasonable action."

Clearly annoyed by Wilson's presumptuousness, the president reminded the prime minister that *he* was not constantly offering advice about Malaysia. "A trip, Mr. Prime Minister, on this situation would be very misunderstood and I don't think any good would flow from it. If one of us jumps across the Atlantic every time there is a critical situation, next week I shall be flying over when Sukarno jumps on you and I will be giving you advice." When Wilson countered, "We do not want to dash over. We just want to talk," Johnson replied, "We have got telephones!"

The president's suspicion that Wilson's proposal to fly over was part of the British prime minister's use of the "special relationship" for domestic political purposes is also apparent.

Johnson: Let me send you the exact situation as I view it on a classified cable. You could show this cable to your colleagues and then you could cable back to me with whatever suggestions you have.

PM: I cannot show it to the House of Commons, that is my trouble.

Johnson: You would not want to use me as an instrument to deal with the House of Commons.[24]

Eventually, the president's limited patience ran out. Wilson records in his memoirs that in relation to "an earlier reference to Clem Attlee's visit to President Truman over the danger of Korean escalation in December 1950, he [Johnson] pointed out that we had troops in Korea, not in Vietnam."[25] Although there is no specific mention of Korea in the transcript, Johnson evidently resented Wilson's interference, considering the lack of British troops in Vietnam. He pointed out that "as far as my problem in Vietnam we have asked everyone to share it with us. They were willing to share advice but not responsibility." He then delivered his most telling point. "I won't tell you how to run Malaysia and you don't tell us how to run Vietnam.... If you want to help us some in Vietnam send us some men and send us some folks to deal with these guerillas. And announce to the press that you are going to help us. Now if you don't feel like doing that, go on with your Malaysian problem."[26]

When, later in the conversation, Wilson made the mistake of saying the only thing he would be able to say to his critics at home was that there had been a call in the middle of the night, Bundy recorded that "the President replied with some sharpness that it was the Prime Minister and not he who placed the call in the middle of the night. The President was just answering it."[27]

Although this conversation consisted of more than a discussion of the situation in Vietnam, it is particularly notable that Malaysia was brought up in this context. The president clearly saw the limited U.S. involvement in Malaysia as parallel to Britain's limited involvement in Vietnam. Given that responsibility was not shared in these respects, advice should be sought and not forced on one another. Interestingly, LBJ also raised MLF during this argument, suggesting that he had compromised on this issue and had taken a backseat role, something Wilson should do on Vietnam. "I tried to be very co-operative on the MLF when you were here.... I tried to hold my real views until you had talked to the Germans. I had very strong views on that and I did not want to be domineering."[28]

By the end of the conversation Wilson had been exposed to many sides of Johnson's character: one minute ranting at the prime minister, the next expressing his understanding of Wilson's domestic difficulties; one minute playing the martyr or wounded soldier, the next bullying once more. Wilson was completely disarmed. Not only did he fail to get the president's approval to visit Washington, he also did not manage to put over any substantive points on Vietnam. Instead he was reduced to stressing British loyalty on Vietnam and promised that this would "be the position tomorrow."[29] Johnson expressed his appreciation.

This late-night conversation proved a turning point in the Wilson–Johnson relationship and does seem to turn on their personal chemistries. The call demonstrates Johnson's impatience with Wilson, and there is little sign of intimacy between the two leaders. In the midst of a growing crisis in Vietnam, Johnson was extremely annoyed by Wilson's apparent impertinence in thinking he had the right to put his views across in person. The call also provides another example of the darker side of Johnson's psyche. George Reedy, Johnson's press secretary throughout the 1950s and for much of the presidency, speaks of LBJ's "tendency to fly into rages for reasons totally inadequate to the degree of ferocity which he would display" and of his tendency to be a bully who "would exercise merciless sarcasm on people who could not fight back but could only take it."[30] Wilson did not yet fully understand Johnson's personality or comprehend the limits of his personal relationship with the president. The relationship between the two leaders was still in its infancy, and at this stage the prime minister may have believed the glowing press and official reaction to his December visit to Washington, seriously overestimating his ability to influence the president. The phone call would not be forgotten by the president. When rumors about the poor state of the relationship between Wilson and Johnson surfaced the next month, including the suggestion that the prime minister was not welcome in Washington, McGeorge Bundy told the president that "none of it takes account of the very great damage which Wilson did to himself by his outrageous phone call to you."[31] Although Wilson and Johnson would continue to exchange views, it was mainly by cable and letter and very infrequently by telephone. Johnson, a president who favored telephone communication, did not want to talk to Wilson unless it was absolutely necessary.

At the end of their conversation Johnson had agreed to send Wilson a cable outlining the situation in Vietnam and current U.S. plans. He would also brief Bruce, then in Washington, who would bring a personal message from the president to Wilson on his return to London. Within hours the cable was duly sent, via McGeorge Bundy, and included advance notice of U.S. plans to bomb an army barracks in North Vietnam. Wilson's call may have precipitated this advance warning; it certainly explains the timing of it. In the cable the president reminded the British prime minister how privileged and classified their communication was. He also repeated the request that in the future Wilson's suggestions should come via cable or telephone. The message was clear: the prime minister should stay at home.[32]

Wilson put the best possible gloss on this exchange when he informed the cabinet the next day that he had been "in personal touch" with the president and "had reaffirmed that we were ready, in our capacity as co-Chairman of the 1954 Geneva Conference on Vietnam, to put our good offices at the disposal of the parties." It was also noted tactfully that "the situation had not yet developed to the point at which the United States Government might wish to avail themselves of this offer."[33]

News of the late-night telephone call appeared in the British press on February 13. *The Guardian*'s Richard Scott reported that "Mr. Harold Wilson was contemplating flying to Washington at the beginning of this week to talk to President Johnson about the Vietnamese crisis."[34] The White House was furious at the apparent leak. George Reedy then confirmed in a press briefing that "there was a direct communication" between the prime minister and the president but did so only because there had been a leak in London. Given the president's request for secrecy surrounding their recent communications, the Foreign Office, at Wilson's request, sent an urgent cable to Washington to deny any involvement in the leak of specific details of the conversation, saying, "[T]he Prime Minister wishes the President to know that at this end we have kept strictly to the terms of the last sentence of your teleporter message to me of Wednesday 10 February: the rest is intelligent speculation."[35] Nonetheless, the leak—the first of many—added to the president's lingering doubts about Wilson's loyalty, and the personal relationship between the two was further soured.

On his return to London, Ambassador Bruce was put in an awkward position.[36] On February 16 he received a telegram from Washington annulling his previous instruction to brief Wilson; instead the ambassador was advised to "avoid seeing the Prime Minister, if this were possible, but if not, to confine" the conversation to "generalities."[37] The reason for this evasive action was that Washington was still carefully considering its options and had not finalized a timetable of action in Vietnam. Bruce met with Wilson and Stewart and informed them that he had been told to keep the prime minister "closely informed" on U.S. plans in Vietnam but that these plans were not formed.[38] The British were particularly anxious to know how the Americans saw the issue of the timing of a conference on Vietnam and on a possible cease-fire. Bruce could reply only that "the United States Government wanted a conference as soon as possible" but would have to continue its "program of retaliatory strikes" until a cease-fire had been agreed to.[39]

The next day, having received further instructions from the State Department, Bruce saw Wilson again. Unlike on the previous day, there was no talk of negotiations. Instead, Bruce reported that the United States would be continuing air and naval action against North Vietnam. Wilson commented that the "plan now appeared to be to step up military action without making proposals for a political solution" and "this was the pill without the jam." Furthermore, he believed that "this would make it very difficult for the outside world and in particular for the UK who would, of course, have to support the US without seeing a light at the end of the tunnel." He would personally "be in for a very rough reception" and there would be increased domestic pressure on him to act as a mediator. He also reminded Bruce of Johnson's earlier cable message saying he would get a "complete summary of proposed US action." He asked Bruce to report back to Washington that in his view "the question of entering into negotiations was a cardinal point of the package" and "without such negotiations" the United Kingdom would be put in a very difficult position as cochairman, particularly in view of renewed Soviet interest in that position.[40] Nevertheless, Wilson indicated that he "would solidly support" American action.[41] Surprisingly, the prime minister also asked the ambassador if he should try to contact Johnson directly over his concerns. Bruce remembers that he "tried as tactfully as I could to advise him [that] he not do so at the present time, but use as a channel his Embassy in Washington."[42] Obviously the president had communicated his annoyance at Wilson's late-night call to Bruce and his unwillingness to speak with Wilson at the present time. Either the prime minister did not recognize the extent of the breach in his relationship with the president, or he felt strongly enough about this issue that he felt it was worth pushing the president on it. Bruce, who had already earned the trust and respect of the president, would be increasingly relied on by the president to deal with the prime minister's regular questions.

Wilson was right to be concerned about the lack of talk of negotiations; the U.S. government was not keen on discussions at this stage. On February 17 the president met with former president Eisenhower, Secretary McNamara, General Wheeler, McGeorge Bundy, and General Goodpaster to listen to Eisenhower's thinking about the situation in South Vietnam. Johnson asked Eisenhower to comment on the message being sent to David Bruce as a basis for his discussions with Wilson, in which a major point was "we do not repeat not expect to touch upon readiness for talks or negotiations at this time." Eisenhower argued that the United States would do better to negotiate from strength rather than from weakness. "[N]egotiation from weakness is likely to lead only into deceit and vulnerability, which could be disastrous to us. On the other hand, if we can show a fine record of successes, or real and dramatic accomplishment, we would be in a good position to negotiate." Eisenhower commented that Wilson "had not had experience with this kind of problem. We, however, have learned that Munichs win nothing, therefore, his answer to the British would be 'Not now boys.' "[43] This was, in effect, what Johnson had instructed Bruce to say.

As well as forcing a parliamentary reaction, the U.S. air strike on North Vietnam also prompted the Foreign Office into a flurry of debate, and, as in the past, American and British diplomats differed over their approach to the problem of Vietnam. The head of the South East Asia department, J. E. Cable, assessed the problem of "seeking a solution in Vietnam" in an internal minute. Summarizing the American choice as being either "decision or drift," Cable felt that the British should "favour a deliberate American policy of cutting their losses in Viet-Nam, because this offers the best chance of avoiding the dangers of escalation while mitigating the adverse repercussions on Western influence and prestige. The question then arises whether we can afford to let the U.S. Government reach this conclusion themselves or whether we ought to or can attempt to influence their choice." He concluded that "it is probably premature to attempt to answer this question now. We know that the US Government are acutely sensitive on this subject and that advice from us would be resented."[44]

Cable's paper then progressed through the hierarchy of the Foreign Office, starting with E. H. Peck, head of the Far Eastern department. Peck felt Britain had "no option but to hear U.S. views in the hope they give us an opening to discuss, without rancour, an ultimate solution. Meanwhile we must support them in public, while getting down to a discussion of realities in private." The permanent undersecretary, Sir Harold Caccia, agreed with this summation.[45] Lord Walston, undersecretary of state for foreign affairs, felt Cable set "out admirably the unattractive choices facing the Americans" and suggested to Michael Stewart that, despite the Americans' sensitivity on this subject, "they should be pressed, with the utmost tact, to face the realities of the situation, to make up their minds, and to tell us what their choice is. The longer the choice is delayed, the harder it will be to make it objectively."[46]

Lord Walston further argued that "apart from the intrinsic importance of coming to a speedy decision on this matter, our continued apparent inactivity is giving the Russians and Chinese the opportunity of spreading it about that H.M.G. is no more than a lackey of U.S. Government policy and can take no stand on its own without the approval of its dollar masters."[47] Michael Stewart toyed with the idea of sending Cable's thoughts to the Americans, via the British ambassador, but as it was he asked Harlech to express his disappointment at American intentions in Vietnam to Rusk, stating, "[O]ur aim is not to make any unnecessary difficulties for the U.S. Government. But the point has come where they really must try to enable their friends to continue to back them wholeheartedly in public." Britain required "some indication of American readiness to do something other than responsive military action. In brief, what were the circumstances in which they would be ready to talk. This need not at this stage commit them to any particular forum."[48]

Bruce, apparently sympathetic to British arguments, said he would also do what he could to see that due weight was given them in Washington.[49] Wilson asked Bruce to let the Johnson administration know that he hoped "the British would be kept in a position to reply to critics that it had been fully informed in advance—he would prefer to say consulted—on proposed American tactics."[50]

By the end of the week that started with the U.S. air strikes on North Vietnam, Wilson, the Foreign Secretary, and the Foreign Office had all arrived at the same conclusion: the best way forward for the British was to bide their time in the hope that an opportunity would arise when they would either be invited to give their advice or could give it at a time when the Americans would be more open to it. The lesson to be drawn from Wilson's offer to fly to Washington was that LBJ could not be lobbied at times of crisis, particularly if the prime minister's motives were too political in nature. Johnson had received Wilson's approach as personal criticism, and the president had instantly gone on the defensive. Moreover, the lack of direct British involvement in Vietnam severely limited London's ability to contribute to the debate that was taking place in Washington over tactics.

As well as deciding to play a waiting game with the Americans—hoping to find a way of quietly and gently persuading the Americans as to the error of their ways in Vietnam—the Wilson government had decided to try to maintain some independence, and give the impression of activity, via a series of peace initiatives. Co-opting the Russians into action would be a good start.

THE RUSSIANS AND THE GENEVA CONFERENCE

While Washington deliberated over its reactions to the Pleiku and Qui Nhon attacks, the British began to pursue, more seriously, the possibility of revitalizing the cochairmanship of the Geneva Conference. George Thomson, minister of state for foreign affairs, flew to Moscow on February 12, ostensibly to sign a new Anglo–Soviet cultural agreement. However, the British press rightly surmised that the Thomson visit would foster diplomatic exchanges over Vietnam, especially if negotiations were to develop.[51] Up to this point the Soviets had been cool toward the prospect of using the Geneva conference to gain peace in Vietnam. However, by the time of Thomson's visit their attitude had changed. Sir Humphrey Trevelyan, the British ambassador in Moscow, felt that this was "the result of pressure on Mr. Kosygin from the North Viet Nam Government" and was probably a result of the deteriorating situation in Vietnam.[52] The Soviets were certainly alarmed by the American bombing of North Vietnam and verbally condemned it, not least because Premier Kosygin had been in the country at the time.

After tentatively courting the Soviets on the Geneva Conference through Thomson's visit, the British kept up the pressure through diplomatic exchanges at the embassy level. Lord Harlech was engaged in close consultation with Dean Rusk on this matter and reported back to the Foreign Office that although the Americans "were convinced that the time was not right for the US to take an initiative pointing in the direction of negotiation," there would be an advantage in getting the Russians to take some responsibility as Geneva cochairs because "if they were prepared to play this role they would be acting more as mediators than advocates for one side in the quarrel."[53] With domestic demands on the British to act on Vietnam, Harlech conveyed his wish that the activities of the cochairs be made public. Implicitly acknowledging Wilson's political difficulties, the Americans agreed to this request.[54]

Trevelyan met with Sergei G. Lapin, the Soviet deputy foreign minister, on February 20 and proposed that, as Geneva cochairs, the United Kingdom and Soviet Union approach all members of the 1954 Geneva Conference and the governments represented on the International Control Commission, requesting "a statement on their views of the situation on Vietnam, in particular, on the circumstances in which they consider that a peaceful conclusion could be reached."[55]

There were problems with this peace gambit from the start. The Russians would have liked a stronger proposal—a conference—rather than the British proposal for consultation with other countries. They were also unimpressed by British requests that a public statement be issued announcing their approach to the Soviets. Lapin said that they "should discuss this question without publicity...if you were to announce your initiative, even without revealing its precise nature, it would make the Soviet Government look passive, the Soviet Government would consequently be obliged to make an immediate public statement of its position."[56]

Another major obstacle in the way of progress with the Soviets was the possibility of further air strikes on North Vietnam, which would, according to the British ambassador in Moscow, "doom the British initiative with the Soviets."[57] The British urged Washington to "hold off" bombing until the Soviet Union had replied to the proposal.[58]

British initiatives were also hampered by the fact that Britain was still in the dark about American plans in Southeast Asia. As happened many times during the 1950s and early 1960s, London expressed extreme concern about the lack of clarity on the part of the American government. It was noted at a meeting of the British cabinet on February 18 that "before there could be any question of our trying to turn this development to our advantage in relation to a negotiated settlement of the dispute, the United States Government would have to indicate the type of negotiation which they would be prepared to undertake and the prior conditions which they might seek to impose before embarking upon it."[59] The administration was indeed "completely silent...both publicly and privately."[60]

When Rusk argued that the Soviets might make the ending of U.S. air strikes a precondition to playing a role as cochair, parallels were again drawn with the British position in Malaysia. In a now familiar refrain, Rusk "assumed that the British would make sure that into the ensuing consideration there would also be the demand for North Vietnam to put an end to infiltration," just as the British in Malaysia "would envisage reaction against Indonesia in response to rather less provocation."[61] The United States did, however, temporarily postpone its retaliatory air strikes, during which time Stewart and Trevelyan pressed the Soviets for an answer to their proposal.

Just three days later, on February 24, the United States informed London of its plan to restart air strikes (in response to the capture of a North Vietnamese freighter carrying arms and ammunition intended for the Vietcong) on February 26. Harlech repeated to Ball, British "anxiety" that such action might "jeopardize the chances of a favourable response from the Russians" and emphasized that the British "had hoped that action could be held up at least until we had seen the Russian reply."[62] David Bruce summarized the U.S. attitude on the matter: "While we recognize their concern, and the possibility of some Soviet reaction, we cannot ever by implication get into a position of withholding a continuation of our air program."[63]

It was clear to Harlech that the Americans would not accept a unilateral cease-fire and that at this stage the image of U.S. military strength was more important than peace talks.[64] Partly because of adverse weather conditions and because South Vietnam was in the process of establishing a new government under the leadership of General Quat, the United States did not restart air strikes on North Vietnam until March 2. British protests were, however, certainly part of the explanation for the delay in bombing as the United States pondered the implications of increasing its military efforts despite calls for more negotiations.

Benjamin Read, special assistant to the secretary of state, later described attempts to reactivate the role of the cochairs as "more form and less hope...it was something you went through periodically just because if you succeeded you'd be better off. But you put very little hope into the process."[65] The United States on this occasion did little to help the process along.

THE BRITISH DOMESTIC POSITION ON VIETNAM

One of the factors fueling the intense behind-the-scenes diplomacy with the Soviets and the Americans was the growing debate within the Labour Party, and the wider Labour movement, on Vietnam. The first half of 1965 saw backbench pressure become increasingly vocal and active in condemnation of the government. Wilson had said at the Labour Party conference in Brighton on December 12, 1964, "[W]e now have a Government ready and able to take initiatives for peace."[66] Consequently, expectations had been raised that the Labour government would intervene in Vietnam. Very quickly the left wing of the Labour Party was criticizing the Wilson government for its apparent inactivity in this area. Labour's "independent" weekly newspaper, *Tribune*, questioned the prime minister's emphasis on "strengthening the alliance" with America, saying that "whatever that policy may involve, it surely does not imply the complete and abject sacrifice of our right to independent action and opinion."[67]

Centrists within the Parliamentary Labour Party were also beginning to stir and, given the government's small working majority in the House, Wilson had to take the threat of a backbench revolt ever more seriously. On February 17, a group of Labour M.P.s who had sent a letter to *The Times* calling for an "immediate British initiative to achieve a cease-fire and the reconvening of the Geneva Conference" met in private with American embassy officials to discuss the situation in Vietnam. Among these were two senior members of the Labour Party, Philip Noel-Baker and John Hynd, and a number of relatively new M.P.s, namely, Dick Taverne, Shirley Williams, Bernard Floud, Colin Jackson, Peter Shore, and David Ennals. This was by no means a left-wing group of M.P.s; indeed, the group made it clear that it did not wish to cause embarrassment to its own or to the American government "by associating themselves with the extreme anti-American and pro-DRV [Democratic Republic of Vietnam] view of [the] Warbey faction in [the] Labor Party." Nevertheless, embassy officials failed to convince them of the feasibility of American policy in Vietnam. The group remained skeptical about the prospect of a military solution in Vietnam and stressed the dangers of escalation. For the time being, however, they were willing to voice their objections to American and British policy without joining forces with the Labour Party's left wing.[68] One of these M.P.s, David Ennals, approached the prime minister for a second time, informally, via a personal letter. In the letter Ennals requested a meeting to discuss Vietnam because "unless something can be said to the contrary—publicly or privately—there will be trouble for the party." Ennals indicated that he was representing backbenchers who did not want "another left-wing initiative."[69]

In an attempt to appease these moderate M.P.s—and indeed the bulk of the Labour Party—Wilson issued the following statement to the House on February 23.

It is our hope that Her Majesty's Government can play an effective part in helping to resolve the present problems and to arrive at a basis for a peaceful settlement. To this end, we have been actively engaged in diplomatic consultations of a confidential nature. These consultations are still going on, and I hope the House will understand that it would be unwise to prejudice the results of much patient and discreet diplomacy by any premature public announcement. As soon as it is possible to do so, I will inform the House of the progress we have made and of the further action which we consider could most fruitfully lead to an end of the fighting and an eventual settlement.[70]

This sort of announcement hinting at secret, behind-the-scenes diplomacy was to be one of the key tactics the prime minister and the Foreign Secretary used in dispelling the notion of government inactivity on Vietnam. It also implied a degree of intimacy with the Americans, which helped justify their public show of support for U.S. policy in Vietnam. It was clear, however, that the Wilson government would soon have to provide Parliament with more details of their "consultations."

At this stage, before the resumption of air strikes, hope remained that the Russians would give a positive reply to the British proposal. The British explained to the Americans that they were under increasing pressure to report their efforts to help in Vietnam "both vis-a-vis British public, Parliament and also with friendly countries and public figures who either have direct interests in [the] matter or have raised Viet Nam question with [the] British." They therefore wanted to inform several other countries (India, Laos, Thailand, and France) as well as the United Nations secretary-general and the Pope about their approach to the Soviets and to make a further statement to the House on the same lines.

Rusk had no "serious problem" with the British informing the other countries as long as they were "carried out on [a] strictly confidential basis," but given Russian sensitivities, Rusk felt a public announcement, such as a statement to the House of Commons, "would seem…almost sure to kill any chances of Russians agreeing to proceed." It was hoped that the British would therefore refrain from such action until all hopes of an affirmative reply from the Russians had gone.[71] Consequently, Harlech reported that the official reaction from Rusk and Ball was that the British "approach to the Russians had been an extremely useful initiative which might eventually open up a way to a satisfactory solution of the Viet Nam problem. They would be very reluctant to see us give up the effort now and felt very strongly that the Russians should be given time to respond."[72] In that the British felt they must give a further statement in the House but hoped to avoid damaging the chances of a positive reply, they asked the Americans to "review" the prime minister's draft statement.

Before the Labour leadership and the Americans had time to formulate their plans on a statement, there was another leak. News of the cochair's initiative was noted in an Associated Press report from London on February 23. Dean Rusk was "naturally concerned" at the leak, especially as the press report contained a direct quotation from Lapin's recent discussion with Trevelyan in Moscow. He was worried that this publicity might lead to an adverse response from the Soviets. The British again denied that the leak had taken place in London and tried to reassure the secretary of state that the quotation from Lapin had come before Russian requests for secrecy and therefore should not affect the Russian response.[73] Rusk was nevertheless worried that Wilson's acknowledgment to the House that "we have been actively engaged in diplomatic consultations of a confidential nature" would be taken as confirmation of the soundings being taken by the cochairs.[74] Wilson pointed out that his written reply to a parliamentary question carefully avoided naming any specific government.[75]

It is unlikely that the Labour government's denial of responsibility for the leak did anything to comfort President Johnson, who was increasingly obsessed with secrecy and loyalty issues. He was particularly concerned that speculation about peace talks, especially ones that may well have not amounted to anything concrete, would raise public hopes. And, when the rumors on the peace front came to nothing, the Americans would be blamed. Or, even more worrying, Washington might be trapped into unreasonable terms by third parties misrepresenting U.S. views. The revelation of the cochair initiative therefore added to difficulties in the Anglo–American relationship. In public, the United States tried to play down the talk of negotiations, especially after U Thant, secretary-general of the United Nations, intimated at a press conference that the United States was keeping the truth about potential peace talks secret. George Reedy denied that Johnson had any proposals before him.[76] This reaction confirmed opinion in the British government and the press that the United States was annoyed by talk of peace moves. David Bruce admitted, "[P]ublic opinion in Great Britain is overwhelmingly in favour of negotiations, through reconvening the 1954 Geneva Conference, or otherwise. That does not suit our book, but the President is under great pressure at home to state US policy; it will only be credible abroad when presented by him."[77]

Once the story was out, the British government saw no need to deny its basic validity. On March 1, 1965, Michael Stewart added to the prime minister's statement of February 23, and to press speculation, when he announced to the House that "as part of our confidential diplomatic discussions, we have been in touch with the Soviet Government. I am awaiting their comments on certain views which our Ambassador in Moscow communicated to them on 20th February. I would not want to prejudice the prospects by going into detail about these conversations."[78]

The following day saw the beginning of Operation Rolling Thunder—the sustained bombing of North Vietnam. It came as no surprise to the British, or the Americans, when the Russians finally came back on March 18 with a negative reply to the British suggestion that the cochairs invite opinion from interested parties.

THE WILSON–JOHNSON PERSONAL RELATIONSHIP

Not surprisingly, given the clear evidence of transatlantic diplomatic activity, the press began to speculate on the relationship between Britain and America, and especially between President Johnson and Prime Minister Wilson over Vietnam. *The Times*'s American editor, Louis Heren, argued in an article on February 25 that the Johnson administration was "in no mood to listen" to anyone on the issue of Vietnam, not even old allies like Britain:

The consequences are not only exasperated comments on the efforts of friendly governments to find a basis for negotiation but the virtual severance of relations with those countries as far as the crisis is concerned. President Johnson has never favoured personal exchanges with ambassadors, but recently the most distinguished have come away empty-handed from the State Department. Special relations are of little account; the exclusion is complete, and the British Embassy is not much better placed than the Burundi Embassy . . . in spite of the general irritation here there are no objections to Britain consulting in Moscow as long as American intentions are not misunderstood. The lack of communication here, however, does not make this easy.[79]

Heren was right to point out that the "special relationship" did not necessarily mean a preferential relationship. The Americans had long since stopped treating Britain to any special favors on Southeast Asia. In that sense, demands by Wilson's critics for stronger British action on Vietnam failed to take account of the realities of Anglo–American relations in Asia. Wilson, representing the British, did not have, and could not have, as strong a profile in the White House or as strong an influence on the president as some thought. Indeed, many have questioned the extent to which anyone not directly involved in the conflict could have influenced the president on Vietnam.

By the beginning of March stories of a rift between Lyndon Johnson and Harold Wilson were rife. Bruce cabled Washington explaining that there had been a "build up, on what appears to be a narrow base of fact, a public appearance of friction between the President and the PM over Viet-Nam." *The Guardian* noted "signs of exasperation" in Washington against "being pushed too far and too fast by her friends" toward peace.[80] Explanations of Johnson's annoyance with Wilson's peace moves varied. Godfrey Hodgson in the *Observer* felt that the president did "not take seriously Mr. Wilson's claim that he is engaged in 'diplomatic consultations of a confidential nature' with the Russians to get negotiations going."[81] On February 24 *The Daily Telegraph*'s lead editorial argued that Wilson's "secret feelers towards negotiations have brought him only a snub from Washington." Nevertheless, the paper also noted that reports that "President Johnson had expressed through a spokesman his annoyance over Mr. Wilson's posing as 'honest broker' in the Viet Nam situation have caused surprise in Whitehall."[82]

When Patrick Gordon Walker, former Foreign Secretary, visited the United States in early March and met with Dean Rusk, he informed the secretary of state that the British were alarmed by "stories in Washington that the President was upset by HMG's attempts to get some kind of talks going on South Vietnam" and did not believe the British government had done anything "without close and continuous contact with them." Rusk, although apparently out of town at the time of the stories, assured Gordon Walker that such reports "had not been officially inspired" and that "Washington was in no way disturbed by our action."[83] Despite this private reassurance, in order to preserve the image of a strong and united Anglo–American relationship, it was felt necessary for a State Department official to issue a denial of the stories of a rift.[84]

Despite Rusk's comforting words, there *was* discontent in the White House concerning the British. As indicated, Washington did not particularly welcome the cochair initiative, although once it was under way, it was taken seriously. Moreover, Johnson was becoming even more concerned that he was being used by the British prime minister for domestic purposes, particularly after the previous month's late-night call from Wilson. The president obviously preferred not to see the prime minister if at all possible. By the end of February, Jack Valenti, LBJ's close aide at the White House, informed him that "Dean Rusk says there is no escape from seeing Prime Minister Wilson when he is here in April."[85]

Another sign of Johnson's growing exasperation with the British was the mix-up over the announcement of Wilson's next visit to Washington (scheduled for April 14–15), which was eventually made in Washington on March 9.[86] Johnson prevaricated over the date of the visit because he was reluctant to meet the prime minister so soon, lest it be perceived as an indicator that something was happening on the negotiation front. Wilson later commented to Bruce on the delay in announcing his visit that "surely, if the President wished...the visit to be dissociated in the public mind from any discussions of the Viet Nam situation then the earlier the announcement was made the better. If the Prime Minister wished to mediate over Viet Nam he would not say that he was coming to do so in six weeks' time. The arguing about the announcement could have made both countries look very stupid."[87] Of course, the president's reluctance to set a date may also have been due to his growing disdain for Wilson's meddling on the peace front. It appears this either did not occur to Wilson, or at least he did not want to discuss this possibility with the American ambassador. The press, however, was quick to pick up on this latest incident. On March 13 the *Daily Mail* said that Johnson was "far from enthusiastic when he was first approached about a meeting with Mr. Harold Wilson.... He even suggested that he might delegate Secretary of State Mr. Dean Rusk to confer with the PM. However, he has now accepted that such a move would constitute an inconceivable snub and the White House has announced that the President would be 'very happy' to see Mr. Wilson.... Mr. Johnson's initial frigid reaction was not so much directed against Mr. Wilson personally. It reflected his general reluctance to get involved in top level diplomatic negotiations in the midst of the Vietnam crisis. Above all he does not want to give the communists the impression that he is under pressure from America's allies to enter into negotiations."[88] Clearly there was some unwillingness on Johnson's part to waste time dealing with the British. Michael Stewart was due to visit Washington toward the end of the month and, although Rusk recommended that the president see him, Johnson was reluctant. McGeorge Bundy reminded the president, via Jack Valenti, why in his view the president should see Stewart, if only for a few minutes. "Amongst other things, it seems pertinent to note that this is Stewart's first trip to the United States as Foreign Secretary; a bit of red-carpet treatment at the outset of our relationship with this important man might be worth some dividends to us later."[89] Johnson eventually agreed to Stewart's visit, but after Wilson's visit to Washington in April, Johnson postponed a number of state visits to the White House by international dignitaries, including President Ayub Khan of Pakistan and Indian prime minister Shastri, announcing that he would not be traveling abroad in the foreseeable future because of Vietnam and his heavy legislative schedule.[90] The war was beginning to consume the president.

CONTINUING PRESSURES ON WILSON

By the beginning of March the British government was becoming increasingly frustrated with the Soviet delay in replying to the proposal to approach interested powers regarding Vietnam. As Bruce noted in his diary on March 6, "[T]he restiveness here, especially in the House of Commons, over the British Government not seeming to play a more active part in trying to induce negotiations over Vietnam, continues."[91] The previous day, one of the chief left-wing critics of the government, Frank Allaun, resigned as principal private secretary to the colonial secretary, as he wished to have "the greater independence" of an ordinary M.P. The Labour leadership was desperate to report a development on the negotiation front.

Wilson's problems were also compounded in the cabinet on March 4 when a discussion about the public position of the government regarding Vietnam elicited "some disquiet."[92] Barbara Castle, minister for overseas development, "once again" raised the problem of Vietnam, a subject that had by then "been discussed pretty often."[93] Cabinet records show that by this time the fear was that as long as the government "refrained from disclosing the initiative"[94] recently taken, the more parliamentary unease was likely to continue and grow. Fortunately for Wilson, he was easily able to control cabinet unrest as many of its members were still finding their feet in government. For instance, Richard Crossman, minister of housing and local government, had not yet spoken on foreign affairs.[95] Consequently, Wilson was well able to convince the cabinet that behind the scenes he was working hard on the issue and that "the best course for the time being would be to maintain...diplomatic pressure on the United States Government to agree to a conference of the Powers concerned."[96]

Wilson knew that he would face sterner questions on Vietnam in the House of Commons on March 9 and that he had to give some sort of reassurance, to his own party in particular, that he was not passive on the negotiation front. He would issue the prepared statement on the subject that he had suggested the Americans vet before delivery. The level of influence the United States had over the Wilson government is apparent when one examines the ensuing debate over the statement's content. Bruce's diary entry of March 7, 1965, notes that "State and the British Embassy, Washington, have attempted to concert language for suggested use by the Prime Minister this week when the Vietnam situation is debated in the House of Commons." The original suggested text was as follows: "I can assure the House that we are by no means neglecting our responsibilities as co-chairman of the Geneva Conferences. We have been in touch with the other co-chairman and with the United States and other governments. We are continuing these diplomatic discussions with a view to achieving a peaceful solution. It would not be in the national interest to make a further statement at this time."[97] The text then saw a series of revisions. The day before Wilson faced questions in the House, Rusk responded to the latest revised draft statement, telling Michael Stewart of the British embassy in Washington that "our first choice remained no statement at all by the Prime Minister" as he feared the prime minister's words "would be advertised as a call by the British for a ceasefire."[98] Intent on making some mention of the British position regarding peace talks, Wilson began to lose patience with American interference in what was essentially a domestic affair. After making further revisions to his text, the prime minister made it clear that he would "be answering questions in the House of Commons.... in the revised terms suggested but should not invite the State Department to comment further."[99]

Despite this response, just one hour before Wilson was scheduled to deliver his statement to Parliament, Rusk was still attempting to dictate the wording. The secretary of state sent a telegram to Philip Kaiser, the U.S. chargé d'affaires in London to say that "we appreciate British government has a Parliamentary problem and recognize some statement will probably be required," but that "any reference to 'hostilities' should make a clear distinction between aggression from the North and U.S. efforts to assist in meeting that aggression. We should not object if the Prime Minister would wish to remind the House that the United States had made it clear that American forces in Vietnam could come home if North Vietnam would leave its neighbours alone."[100] He was particularly concerned that "Hanoi, Peiping and Moscow be encouraged by any indication of lack of solidarity between United States and United Kingdom" and insisted that any statement be related to the U.K.'s special role as cochair of the two Geneva conferences.[101]

Furthermore, Rusk's increasing lack of patience with the British led him to tell Kaiser to inform Stewart "that if he has a political problem at home, so do we, but ours extends to South East Asia." He also made threats, suggesting that until the British understood the Americans' position on this issue, and therefore adopted their wording, he "would request that Michael Stewart's visit not be announced until we can arrange more propitious circumstances."[102] Rusk explained that

if the Prime Minister makes a statement tomorrow which cuts across [the] very clear and simple statements of United States policy and, on the same day, announces Michael Stewart is coming to see me at my invitation, I shall be faced with great difficulty in countering the suspicion that vague and alarming moves are in the wind which would signal both to our allies in the Pacific and to [the] Houses of Parliament that we are on the run.[103]

Although Bruce and others briefed Rusk fully on the extent of Wilson's domestic problems on Vietnam, on this occasion little sympathy was shown for his predicament. Wilson recalls in his memoirs that on arriving back from Europe on the afternoon of March 9, the day of the debate, he "had just five minutes before going to the chamber for my Question time, during which George Thomson, the Minister of State at the Foreign Office, with strong Foreign Office pressure behind him, tried to get me to take a much more committed pro American line on bombing in Vietnam."[104] In the end Wilson did reluctantly bend to American will. He acknowledged to Bruce a few days later that "in response to last minute representations" from Rusk he "had changed the text of his reply."[105] His main statement in response to several questions on Vietnam therefore included the words "aggression by the North" and read as follows:

[W]hat would stop the fighting would be a proper observance of the 1954 Geneva Agreements, thus putting an end to the aggression by the North against South Vietnam. As the House knows, we have in our traditional role as Co-Chairman been engaged in diplomatic consultations of a confidential nature. It is the view of Her Majesty's Government that if there is genuine cessation of hostilities, then talks in some form should be started. But for the moment the form is of less account than the basis of the talks. Our main diplomatic efforts have been directed to seeing if the basis exists. As I have already told the House, we have been in touch with the Soviet Government, who were given our views on this problem on 20th February . . . [106]

Having given in to barely disguised American threats, Wilson was able to announce to the Commons the Foreign Secretary's visit to Washington on March 22 and 23, "when Vietnam will be among the subjects discussed . . . Meanwhile, we will continue our diplomatic consultations with a view to achieving a peaceful solution which stands some chance of assuring a lasting genuine settlement. The House will not expect me to say more."[107]

In domestic political terms the most controversial answer from the prime minister came in response to a question by Konni Zilliacus, M.P., when the extent of change in Wilson's attitude on Vietnam was revealed. "A year ago, the general supposition was that the fighting in South Vietnam was a spontaneous, so-called nationalist rising on the part of the Viet Cong people. But now there is no attempt at all to deny the responsibility of North Vietnam who have said that they are fighting a war in South Vietnam. That makes a big difference, I think, in terms of our analysis of the problem."[108] This answer was the final straw for many on the Labour left who felt Wilson was now completely subservient to the Americans.

There is no doubt, however, that the whole episode further strained an already troubled Anglo–American relationship. This time it was the British prime minister who was annoyed. The Americans had intervened with a heavy hand in British domestic politics. Wilson struggled to maintain some independence on this sensitive issue and was, not surprisingly, annoyed at the American interference. In conversation with Bruce, the prime minister talked about "the invidious position" he was in. The ambassador acknowledged in his diary that "it is unquestionable that, amongst other things, he resents U.S. officials trying to dictate the terms of his remarks in the House of Commons."[109] Bruce himself found the incident an unpleasant reminder of Johnson's tendency to play the bully, and consequently undertook his duties in this connection reluctantly. Indeed, Bruce told Rusk that he found instructing a foreign head of government what to say to his own parliament "a tasteless proceeding."[110] Given LBJ's sensitivity over Harold Wilson's very tentative "advice" in his late-night phone call, it is, of course, enormously ironic that the president and his advisors wielded a sledgehammer to crack this particular nut. Although Wilson gave in to American demands, his statement did at least put further pressure on the Americans to consider negotiations. The following evening, Manny Shinwell, chairman of the Parliamentary Labour Party, along with Arthur Henderson, Philip Noel Baker, Frederick Bellenger, Michael Foot, and Sydney Silverman, tabled a motion on Vietnam, stating "that this House, noting the recent declaration made by the Secretary-General of the United Nations, U Thant, which is consistent with the views expressed by the Prime Minister, calls for the cessation of hostilities in Vietnam and a reference of the dispute in Vietnam to a conference of interested parties."[111] As *The Times*'s political correspondent noted, the motion had "much more domestic and international significance than the surface of the form of words suggests." The reason for its importance was that it had "the Government's full backing and almost certainly was initiated by Mr. Wilson himself."[112] Wilson's chief whip in the Commons, Edward Short, also thought Wilson was behind the motion, believing the prime minister looked for "some compensatory action, which he could take to neutralise the complaints, and hopefully the complainants."[113] *The Times* assumed two main purposes behind Wilson's involvement in the motion:

First, and most important, it is intended to remind President Johnson that the British Government have given America loyal support in their Vietnam actions but that there is anxiety in London that some attempt should be made now to achieve a cessation of hostilities. Secondly, the motion is intended to mark out ground on which virtually all members of the Parliamentary Labour Party can stand with Mr. Wilson at a time of delicacy and difficulty. From right to left, pro-American and anti-American, Labour M.P.s are expected to agree that U Thant's declaration calling for a cease-fire in Vietnam and a conference is the right line for the Government they are keeping in office on a bare overall majority.[114]

With the benefit of the released diplomatic exchanges over the statement, a third purpose can be added. The prime minister was attempting to reassert his authority in the domestic affairs of his own country.

FURTHER ESCALATION OF THE WAR AND MICHAEL STEWART'S VISIT TO WASHINGTON, MARCH 1965

On March 12 rumors began to circulate in the press that President Johnson had decided to prosecute the war in Vietnam with all necessary means. The prime minister brought this up at a meeting with David Bruce the same day, insisting that even if the story in *The Times* was not correct, U.S. policy "had changed in nature as well as degree." And although the British government "had agreed to support any American response that was measured and specifically related to the provocation," this was no longer the case and "the United States Government had made the change without consulting their most loyal ally." He added that this "would place Her Majesty's Government in an intolerable position; if it were allowed to continue we should soon be hearing stories about satellites and the 51st state."[115] Wilson was alarmed at the adverse press he was beginning to receive in relation to Vietnam. He referred to the leading article of that week's *New Statesman*, which carried the headline "Vietnam— What's Wilson Waiting For?" The article noted the prime minister's apparent "somersault on Vietnam," calling his change from describing the situation in South Vietnam as "a spontaneous so-called national rising" into an overt war of aggression by North Vietnam "sheer impudence." It argued that Wilson "should stop worrying about incurring American wrath and should take on the role of 'honest broker' much as Eden had at Geneva." The editorial further pointed out that when Wilson "referred vaguely to midnight telephone calls, to Mr Gromyko's visit to London and Mr. Stewart's plan to go to Washington [, t]his was not good enough. The understanding on which this journal (among others) gave qualified approval to the British government's general support for the American position in Vietnam, was that this was to be accompanied by a process of secret diplomacy, at the highest level, to bring about a conference of the powers involved."[116]

Not surprisingly, Wilson informed Bruce, and thereby the Johnson administration, that Her Majesty's Government could abide by the originally planned posture of the United States, "a stick in one hand and an olive branch in the other," but the lack of the latter was extremely dangerous to Anglo–American relations: "[I]f things went on as they were, they could well lead to the biggest difficulty between Britain and the United States for many years, possibly since Suez."[117]

Meanwhile the Foreign Office was still perplexed by rumors that Washington was annoyed with British attempts to foster peace talks. "Her Majesty's Government have kept in close touch with the US Government in London and Washington as far as immediate policy is concerned, and have at no stage opposed the policy being followed by the United States, but rather by suggesting minor changes in timing or presentation from time to time, have acquiesced in it."[118] Even Bruce recognized that Wilson's support of American policy was a "blank check endorsement" and explained to the president the difficulties the prime minister was having because of this.[119]

The British press again picked up on the tension between the United States and its allies, including Great Britain, from comments made by George Ball, undersecretary of state, during a State Department conference on March 16. According to *The Times*'s Washington correspondent, Ball criticized those allies who had urged the United States to negotiate a peaceful settlement in Vietnam. The trouble with most Western European nations, he said, was that they had little experience in exercising far-flung responsibility, except when defending empires. Now that those had gone, they should develop a whole new set of attitudes. "To play a useful and effective role on the world stage it is not enough for a nation simply to offer advice on all aspects of world affairs. It should be prepared to back that advice with resources.... When national positions are vigorously promoted without regard to their effect on the responsible common efforts of other states, free world interests may well be injured." *The Times* concluded that the sum of the speech was that European nations had no right to be concerned about the prospect of American bombings provoking Chinese intervention and another global conflict. This was another example of what it called the superpower complex: "While Western Europe remains a sub-tribal group of pygmies it must do as it is told or be quiet, and apparently only superpowers have a right to be heard."[120] If it was hoped that the rumblings of discontent between the United States and its closest ally would abate with the British Foreign Secretary's visit to Washington, events would later dash these hopes.

During the preparations for Stewart's formal visit to Washington in March and Wilson's informal visit in April, both Washington and London recognized that Vietnam would dominate these meetings. Some sort of "understanding" had to be reached between the two governments because neither felt the other fully comprehended its position, and the issue was threatening to cause a serious rift in the Anglo–American relationship. The South East Asia department of the Foreign Office felt that Stewart should pursue with Rusk the fundamental question of "whether American military policy in Vietnam is aimed at inducing the North-Vietnamese to negotiate or to capitulate."[121]

By the middle of March the Johnson administration had come to the conclusion that it would not actively seek formal negotiations on Vietnam until it was in a stronger military position from which to deal. In the meantime, it could keep "quiet channels" via the United Kingdom and other third parties "open for hopeful signs."[122] The White House was confident that it could call on the Geneva Conference as and when it wanted to. But because Rusk in particular wanted "to keep the British just happy enough to hold them aboard," the Johnson administration would encourage the British to pursue their fellow cochair on Vietnam.[123] The White House considered this position shortly before Stewart's planned talks on March 23 with Johnson and Rusk, mainly because it was apparent that "only one serious question" was likely to arise, "the political problem of the Wilson Government in holding to its present support for us in Vietnam."[124] McGeorge Bundy informed the president that the British position was "not tenable without some slight help from us" and suggested two possible options:

[O]ne course might be to let the...Labor Party struggle with its own political problems, on the ground that Wilson's troubles are of his own making, not ours. The difficulty with this course is that since Wilson prefers his own survival to solidarity with us, he would be mortally tempted to begin to make critical noises about us, thus appealing both to his own party and to the natural nationalism of many independent Englishmen.[125]

The other alternative was to work out what was the "least" Washington could offer "in return for continued solidarity in support of the essentials of our policy in Vietnam."[126] According to Bruce this could be as little as joining the British "in saying publicly that there is a full and continuous exchange of views and of information at all levels between our two Governments on this important issue." Additionally, the White House could "put on some parsley" about how glad they were to receive Stewart and how much they were looking forward to the Prime Minister's visit. "In return, the British should undertake not to advocate negotiations and not to go back on their existing announced approval of our present course of action. They should limit themselves to expressions of hope that a path to a peaceful settlement will come, plus expressions of alertness, as Co-Chairman of the Geneva Conference, to any opportunities... which may develop in the future."[127] The contempt for Wilson and his problems is apparent in this document. However, there is also an implied recognition that the United States did not really want to risk losing British support on Vietnam and that it was therefore willing to make at least some effort to help Wilson with his domestic problems if the British did not publicly pressurize them on the negotiation front.

Stewart's visit to Washington was to take on further significance as his arrival coincided with two important developments in Vietnam. On March 22 the U.S. Defense Department announced that in addition to the use of napalm bombs it was also using a type of gas in Vietnam. On the same day, Maxwell Taylor, U.S. ambassador in South Vietnam, made a statement admitting that "no limit existed to the potential escalation" of the war.[128] The threat of a ground war in Vietnam, with the attendant risks of Chinese intervention and the use of nuclear weapons, suddenly looked within the American purview. Not surprisingly, and justifiably, alarm bells rang in the House of Commons. Immediately, six senior members of the Parliamentary Labour Party, led by the chairman of the party's foreign affairs committee, Philip Noel-Baker, sent a telegram to Stewart in Washington urging him to express British "horror and indignation" at the latest events.[129] A protest resolution was also put on the order paper of the House of Commons. Michael Foot, M.P., wrote later that week that "the blaze of anger about... Vietnam which swept through the Parliamentary Labour Party this week was hotter than anything felt there for a long time."[130]

If Wilson's memoirs are to be believed, the prime minister was also personally shaken by these events. His response to them seems to confirm this recollection. When Stewart arrived in Washington a telegram was awaiting him warning him to make no public statement until the following day. In the meantime Wilson grappled with the wording of two emergency telegrams on "the issue itself and its handling" and "on the domestic political aspects."[131] Wilson spent the evening dictating and repeatedly strengthening their terms. He eventually suggested that Stewart raise two further issues, in addition to questioning the use of gas and Taylor's inflammatory remarks. First, he should mention the press suggestion that instead of the planned bombing missions—which had themselves escalated far beyond measured tit-for-tat raids—American pilots would soon be permitted to range freely, selecting their own targets. Second, he should assert that the British had it from an authoritative source that U.S. military authorities in Saigon had a plan for the next month involving continuing escalation.[132]

Wilson told Stewart that Rusk "should be left in no doubt about the strength of feeling here and about the difficulties which we are facing. There is a danger of widespread anti-Americanism and of America losing her moral position."[133] As the British press was quick to note, this latest action placed "the propaganda battle on a plate to the Communists." Wilson was therefore furious that "Her Majesty's Government were given no, repeat no, warning that these actions were contemplated."[134] The attacks on Wilson were beginning to worry the prime minister. "It is becoming harder and harder for us, if the facts seem to support the jibe I have already had to put up with that Her Majesty's Government is the tail-end Charlie in an American bomber and I hope that more thought will be given to the wider aspects of these questions."[135] Wilson assumed that Stewart would reply appropriately if President Johnson tried to link this question with support for the pound. The prime minister felt it would be "most unfortunate" if Britain's "financial weakness...be used as a means of forcing us to accept unpalatable policies or developments regardless of our thoughts." It would raise "very wide questions indeed about Anglo–American relationships."[136] Despite this unease at this latest crisis, Wilson told Stewart that Britain would "not depart from the general Viet Nam line which we have taken."[137]

According to Wilson, Stewart spoke to Rusk and Johnson "in the strongest terms."[138] The British record of the conversation between the British Foreign Secretary and the U.S. secretary of state on the morning of March 23 adds weight to this assertion. Indeed, Stewart repeated much of what Wilson dictated in his telegrams. When Rusk opened his talks with Stewart by saying the important question was what useful diplomatic step could be made next, the Foreign Secretary refused to be sidestepped and interrupted him, saying there was an "immediate" question that he must raise—the strong feelings felt in the United Kingdom and elsewhere about the use of gas and the prime minister's intention to inform the House of Commons, if asked, that he had not been consulted about it. In reply, Rusk played the innocent, saying he could tell the British government only what they themselves knew: that the U.S. government had not known about this particular use of gas, and his belief was that it was the kind used for riot control purposes. He acknowledged that the matter had been badly handled but "expressed regrets" that Noel-Baker had acted "so impetuously in sending his protest before the full facts were known. If the United States Government had operated in that way they would have landed themselves in a dozen world wars by this time."[139]

The Americans did not fully understand British concerns over the use of gas—Bundy called it a "stupid fuss."[140] Indeed, Rusk later pointed out to Stewart that it was nonlethal gas and had been used by the British themselves during civil disturbances.[141] Wilson and Stewart expressed concern about gas and napalm bombs inflicting "undue suffering" and argued that such methods were in any case of "limited military use."[142] And as Rusk acknowledged, the revelation of its use was a public relations disaster.

As to General Maxwell Taylor's comments about there being no limits to the escalation of the war in Vietnam, Rusk confirmed that the United States was unwilling to impose limits on its own action but repeated that escalation depended on what the other side did. However, he reassured Stewart that at present there were no plans to bomb the Hanoi area and Her Majesty's Government would be informed in advance if the United States was thinking of bombing there or making any major changes in U.S. policy.[143]

Stewart was scheduled to meet the president the same afternoon. However, on his return from Texas, Johnson postponed his meeting with the British Foreign Secretary until the next day. This meant that Stewart would meet with the president just half an hour before facing, as Bruce put it, the ordeal of a lunch and speech at the National Press Club. The ambassador met with Bundy to try to resolve this "ticklish matter." Bruce thought Johnson's reluctance to meet with Stewart was related to the fact that the president "has an antipathy for the Prime Minister. He regards attempts on the part of the British to insinuate themselves into Vietnamese affairs as irrelevant and unimportant. He believes Wilson, for his own domestic political purposes, wishes to capitalize on a supposed close relationship with Johnson that is non-existent."[144] Bruce and Bundy saw "eye to eye" on the situation, feeling that Wilson needed to at least be able to portray to his associates and the House of Commons "the appearance of an intimacy and a mutual confidence that, in the President's view, is not a reality." To Bruce there was "no room ... for lack of conventional courtesies between chiefs of allied states."[145] The same day, Rusk also pressed LBJ in a similar vein, this time recommending a lunchtime meeting between the president and the prime minister during the latter's forthcoming trip to Washington. "We have an excellent degree of understanding and cooperation in crucial foreign policy matters from the new Labor Government in Britain. Anything we can do to maintain this state of affairs is in our best interests."[146]

An approach to the president was "concocted" that would "preserve at least an outward harmony" in his meeting with Stewart. LBJ was scheduled to meet Stewart alone at 11:30 A.M. for about 15 minutes, after which the diplomatic entourage of advisors, press officers, and diplomats joined them. However, Johnson took a phone call from journalist Drew Pearson at 11:35 A.M. The call lasted over 15 minutes, and during the conversation LBJ rehearsed his argument on the American use of gas. Clearly Johnson was happy to keep Stewart waiting given that he was in no hurry to be given a lecture from the British on how to conduct the war.[147] Because both the president and the Foreign Secretary had strict engagement schedules, they received constant reminders from their aides of time limitations. Nevertheless, according to Bruce, the president was in "talkative form." He described it as "great theatre; he fed us oratorical sandwiches, with layers of gravity and levity. At one time, after he had enumerated the variety of criticisms to which he was daily subjected over Vietnam, he remarked 'sometimes I just get all hunkered up like a jackass in a hailstorm.' " Despite Johnson's garrulity, according to Bruce, "Stewart kept reverting to the uproar in Britain over the use of non-lethal gas by the South Vietnamese air force." This "attack" was easily handled by the president, who gave a rendition of Rusk's arguments about the gas being stocked and used by many countries for quelling riots. Johnson discoursed for more than an hour, "explaining his objectives, hopes and fears," including the "fierce domestic pressures on him." According to Bruce, the president was "power sublimated, like Niagara Falls...I think he impressed his audience by his grasp of the issues involved, and his own mastery over decisions, but must have puzzled the British by the alternation of his manner." After photographs, Bruce records that Stewart "was released, after ninety minutes of an experience he is never likely to forget." After the Foreign Secretary had left, LBJ said that Stewart "had not offered a single practical or helpful suggestion, nor had General de Gaulle, or any other foreigner."[148]

Notwithstanding the president's best efforts, after leaving the White House, Stewart went directly to the National Press Club, where he criticized the American use of gas in Vietnam. And, although Stewart had informed the president that he would repeat his concerns publicly, it was soon reported that Johnson was "furious" with Stewart and that his reaction had been "sulphurous."[149] The president discussed how to respond to the Foreign Secretary's comments on the telephone the next day. Johnson indicated two things quite clearly in this recorded conversation. First, he told Rusk that he was tired of foreign leaders "lecturing us" on Vietnam and was concerned about the effects on Congress and the American people of visits to Washington from such critics as Shastri; Lester Pearson; Wilson; and France's foreign minister, Couve de Murville. Johnson told Dean Rusk, "I just hate to see my allies destroy me, I'd rather my enemies do it and I think that all the investment that we've made hasn't paid off very well."[150] Johnson suggested it would be best if Wilson did not come to Washington. Second, nothing in this conversation indicates that Johnson and Rusk reflected on what had been said to them. Rusk was told to deal with overseas criticism over the use of gas by ridiculing the critics, arguing to the press that there had been a "panic," that the criticism was not well thought out, and that surely it was better to use "something that'd stop 'em for three minutes than using a machine gun."[151] Apparently the president considered sending a rebuke to Wilson but decided against it, something Bruce was glad of in that he considered it "undignified and unnecessary" to do so.[152]

Back in London, Wilson was delighted with Stewart's handling of the gas affair, which the press characterized as "the bluntest straight-talking Britain had indulged in Anglo-US relations since the war." He believed it not only "won the approval of Labour MPs" but also made a real impact on the president, which it clearly had, but not in the way Wilson might have hoped.[153]

Ultimately, the gas episode demonstrated to Washington that the Labour government was beginning to place limits on its diplomatic support of America's Vietnam policy. Indeed, some members of the White House began to voice their concerns over the president's handling of the British. The day after Stewart's inflammatory remarks and the president's angry response, a White House aide, David Klein, spelled out the realities of the situation as he saw it in a top-secret, sensitive memo to McGeorge Bundy. He argued that the "firmest public support from *any* government on our policy in Vietnam has come from the British. This, despite the fact that Vietnam is a difficult issue for any British Government, and especially a Labor Government.... I think I understand the reasons for some of the pique with the P.M. here. But I honestly doubt that this in itself is sufficient justification for the way we are handling the P.M." Klein went on to spell out the dangers of continuing with a hard-nosed policy regarding the British:

Admittedly, the British do not have many places to go. But they have a capacity for mischief-making, and I would not under-estimate the possibilities for joint mischief-making with Paris—if the British put their minds to it. Moreover, I doubt very much that the political lid could be held for very long, if it should become publicly clear that Wilson is less than personna grata. Translated into domestic British politics, this could produce the next election issue—and given British pride, the end result could be a strong public endorsement of Wilson with all that would imply for the next five years... Have we really faced up to the possible consequences of our present course—which could put us into a solitary corner with perhaps only a single supporter—of doubtful courage at that—the West Germans? Is this really where we want to come out? Would this best serve our national interests?

In a handwritten note on the memo, Bundy said he agreed with this and had "made this point with *some* effect for the time being."[154] Wilson and Stewart were beginning to discriminate between the means and the ends. In an attempt to balance their need to be a loyal ally to the Americans with the need to placate the left wing of the Labour Party, the British would support the U.S. aims in Vietnam but reserve the right to object to its methods of achieving success there.

THE NEW APPROACH—GOING IT ALONE
AS GENEVA COCHAIR

When the Russians replied negatively to the British proposal to consult with other Geneva powers on Vietnam, London and Washington began to consider the possibility of a new kind of initiative. Due to their domestic political difficulties, Wilson and Stewart knew they would have to be seen to be pushing hard on the negotiation front, especially given the intensification of the conflict. Consequently, by the time of Stewart's visit to Washington the British knew they would have to undertake a unilateral approach for peace. They proposed to ask the Geneva powers and members of the International Control Commission (ICC) to express their views on what they saw as the basis for negotiations. The White House was alarmed at the prospect of the British driving the search for negotiations.

Consequently, when Rusk discussed diplomatic initiatives with Stewart on March 23 he tried to stall the British government's next move. He told the Foreign Secretary that he was aware that many people "were willing to be a midwife to a conference" but said he had no objections to contacts being made to assess the possibilities. However, he thought the United States might address its own message to the Geneva cochairs and the members of the ICC, containing an "extensive, reasoned and dispassionate account of South Viet-Nam, Laos and perhaps Cambodia."[155] This would obviously be a more limited initiative. When Stewart pressed for further details on what such a statement might contain, Rusk said it would refer to the need to respect the 1954 and 1962 agreements. "It would deal with the activities of the North Vietnamese in crossing the frontier into South Viet-Nam...would express regret that there was no indication from the other side that they were yet ready to stop these incursions. But...would not spell out...pre-conditions for a conference because to do so would make everybody muscle-bound."[156] Stewart thought it would be "unfortunate" if the U.S. message made no reference to the possibility of holding a conference, at which point Rusk repeated his belief that he did not want a conference at any cost. He asked the British to postpone their own planned unilateral approach to the parties concerned until they had received a draft of the proposed U.S. message. Pointedly, Rusk repeated that he was "happy that Her Majesty's Government should continue as Co-Chairmen but...did not want to see them playing the role of referee."[157] In other words, the secretary of state was reminding London that as an ally, it could not be an impartial judge on Vietnam.

One week later the U.S. administration had still not produced any statement of policy on Vietnam, and the Foreign Office began planning British unilateral action on the lines of the earlier proposal to the Russians. Rather than trying to establish the basis on which negotiations might begin, they would merely seek the views of the Geneva powers. The Americans had in the intervening days thought more closely about how best to appear interested in peace as well as war. They eventually settled on a presidential statement.

On March 25, President Johnson delivered a speech on the war. In addition to the usual line on North Vietnamese aggression, he included two important points. First, he declared that the United States sought "no wider war," and second that he was "ready to go anywhere at any time, and meet with anyone wherever there is promise of progress toward an honorable peace."[158] This speech eased the pressure a little on the Wilson government, and the U.S. government intimated that a further high-level statement was on its way. And, as it had been decided to send Patrick Gordon Walker on a fact-finding mission to Vietnam, for the time being London no longer felt it necessary or desirable to continue with its plans for unilateral action. Johnson's speech of March 25 provided the government with useful ammunition; as *The Times* put it, "[T]he most obvious and likely advantage to the British Government is that, until Mr. Gordon Walker can report his impressions—during, that is, the next three or four weeks at least—criticism from the left-wing of the Labour Party will to some extent be disarmed."[159]

Former Foreign Secretary Patrick Gordon Walker planned to visit the Southeast Asian capitals of Saigon, Phnom Penh, Tokyo, Delhi, Vientiane, Rangoon, Bangkok, Kuala Lumpur, Hanoi, and Peking from mid-April until early May. At this point, it was hoped that he would be able to establish whether a basis for a peace settlement existed.[160] When the British government proposed Gordon Walker's fact-finding mission, Washington felt that it should neither approve nor disapprove this action. This was because, as William Bundy put it,

for us specifically to approve would indicate to many that he might be going on our behalf and that we were pressing for negotiations without any sign that the other side is interested in a peaceful settlement. On the other hand, we would not wish to disapprove an effort by our ally who carried on the trip we would expect to say that we were informed and that we understand the visit is connected with Britain's responsibilities as a Co-Chairman, as discussed by the Prime Minister in the House of Commons.[161]

The Americans did not attach much importance to the Gordon Walker visit, except in that it would help defuse the anger within the House of Commons.[162]

Wilson's intraparty difficulties were also eased when the U.S. embassy in Saigon was bombed, resulting in 13 killed and 183 wounded.[163] According to the Americans, this incident was "extensively and sensationally reported in the British press" and made a "profound impression" in the United Kingdom that "largely erased emotional reaction to US use of non-lethal gas."[164] After a debate on Vietnam in the House on March 30, Philip Kaiser at the U.S. embassy in London was able to report to the secretary of state that there was strong bipartisan support for U.S. policy in Vietnam and that although the hard-core left wing strongly attacked government policy "along familiar lines," the Labour backbenches "were not crowded and left-wingers made no attempt to dramatize their opposition." The atmosphere in the Commons was described as "quiet except for [the] ejection of two protesting youths from [the] public gallery at the debate's end."[165] He concluded by commenting that the Labour left wing had been "temporarily driven underground" and that the prime minister impressed as the "undisputed master in his own house."[166] The White House was pleased with Wilson's performance in the House. McGeorge Bundy told Oliver Wright that "the Prime Minister had handled matters very well in limiting himself to the statement that he knew we did not intend any war without limits."[167] The

Americans were happy with such general statements and could understand the need for them "in the light of the quotation attributed to General Taylor." They were not, however, prepared for Wilson to reveal any specific detail, especially in regard to any potential area that might or might not be attacked. Wright was reminded that Washington was being careful to use indefinite phrases such as "measured, fitting, and adequate," and it was hoped that the British would do the same. Wright concurred, but the prime minister still indicated that he would like to talk to the president later that evening. Johnson preferred not to talk until later in the week, after Kermit Gordon, director of the bureau of the budget, had visited the prime minister to discuss the situation with regard to sterling.[168]

Wilson believed that the British government's pressure on the United States for a public statement of its position regarding its hopes for peace was instrumental in forcing the Johnson administration's hand.[169] And, clearly, part of the reason for the president's statement was the fear in the White House and State Department that the British might start a momentum for peace that they were not ready for, or the Labour government might give away military information as a result of its initiatives. On March 31 McGeorge Bundy indicated to the British that the Johnson administration hoped that the Patrick Gordon Walker visit to the Far East and the statements already made by the British government "would remove the need for any public appeal by them to us for a statement of our position." He also indicated that the White House was "considering the value of making such a statement either by a note or by a high-level speech, but...no decision had been taken on the timing or method of the statement."[170]

WILSON'S VISIT TO WASHINGTON, APRIL 1965

On April 7 Johnson made another major statement on Vietnam that put the United States into the role of potential peacemaker. The Baltimore speech, as it became known, was made at Johns Hopkins University and broadcast live. It contained two important passages: one regarding peace negotiations, the other regarding future economic aid to Vietnam. Johnson listed the essential elements of a just peace: an independent South Vietnam that was "securely guaranteed and able to shape its own relationships to all others—free from outside interference—tied to no alliance—a military base for no other country." And, most crucially, Johnson said that the United States remained ready for "unconditional discussions." He went on to propose a billion-dollar American investment in Southeast Asia once peace had come to the region.[171]

The British welcomed Johnson's speech. In public, Wilson described it as a "statesmanlike and imaginative approach to the serious situation in Vietnam."[172] In private, it was praised for placing "equal emphasis on the stick and the carrot" and for introducing "a new and more hopeful element in the situation."[173] In some ways, the Baltimore speech temporarily eased Wilson's position in the House of Commons in that he could now quote the United States' readiness for talks. However, although the majority of backbenchers regarded the president's offer of "unconditional discussions" as conciliatory, and a major breakthrough in the search for peace in Vietnam, they also took some credit for the "change" in Washington policy. This belief in the success of their sustained pressure through parliamentary motions meant that they felt the prime minister should now "maintain and intensify British efforts" to persuade all those involved in Vietnam to achieve a cease-fire and begin talks.[174] So, in some ways, Johnson's speech made Wilson's domestic problems even more acute by creating an air of unjustified expectations about the British potential to influence U.S. policy.[175]

Sir Patrick Dean judged the purpose of the speech to be "primarily to strengthen the position of the United States vis a vis their allies and the non-aligned nations and to put the onus for continuation of the fighting in South Viet Nam on the Communists." He also advised against "putting forward a large list of alternative steps" too soon given that the Americans would want time to "test the response of the other side and to assess reaction world-wide." He suggested that the best way of "leading the Administration and in particular the President to consider seriously the possibilities" the British had in mind "would be for the Prime Minister himself to initiate the discussion when he sees the President on 15 April."[176]

London was, however, quick to see this latest development in Washington as an opportunity to follow up on a seemingly genuine proposal made by the Soviet government on April 3. The Russians had asked Britain to agree to a message sent by them, as cochairs, inviting the members of the 1954 Geneva Conference to take part in a new conference on Cambodia. The Chinese had agreed to take part. The British were willing to consider this, especially if it might prove an indirect route to discussing Vietnam. The trick was to persuade the Americans of the desirability of this approach.

During the week between Johnson's Baltimore speech and Wilson's visit to the United States, preparations were being made on both sides of the Atlantic for the ostensibly informal yet very important meeting. Wilson's two-day visit to New York and Washington, postponed from February, was intended to be a follow-up to Wilson's discussions with the president in December. The two main items on the agenda—both publicly and privately—were the British economic position and Vietnam. Wilson records that by the time of his visit to Washington, "President Johnson, in the course of now affable exchanges, appeared...most ready to discuss the Vietnam situation with me."[177] The American record does, of course, indicate that this was far from the case.

Once the president had helped assuage domestic and world opinion via the Johns Hopkins speech, and with future escalation in mind, the Johnson administration began to think in terms of a quid pro quo. On April 9 Sir Patrick Dean warned London that it was evident from recent conversations with senior officials in the White House and State Department that "the President is still very anxious to see a greater participation on the ground in South Viet Nam from America's Allies, including ourselves."[178] The arrival of South Korean troops in South Vietnam had been the most recent "more flags" development. Australian troops would also be dispatched very shortly. Contacts suggested that the Americans envisioned a number of British options from the "provision of . . . military advisors or transport pilots, to a medical team or an expert British team to help in the handling of the growing refugee problem, or again more police advisors."[179] Despite his own protestations about British commitments in Malaysia and the difficulties of recruitment, the British ambassador thought it "very possible" that either the president or the secretary of state would bring the subject up again during the prime minister's visit the next week, believing "a practical demonstration of further help from us however limited would be valuable."[180] Dean thought "a willingness to consider additional help might pay quite disproportionate dividends in terms of our ability to influence United States policies, and I hope that the Prime Minister would be willing to say that he is at least prepared to see what more we can do."[181]

Pressure on Wilson to consider increasing the British contribution in Vietnam also came from diplomats in Saigon. Gordon Etherington-Smith, the British ambassador in South Vietnam, advised the Foreign Office on April 12 that "a limited increase in our aid is desirable if we are to retain influence in this theatre with Americans as well as Vietnamese."[182] His reasoning was that other countries had recently increased their contributions while the British effort had appeared to have diminished. The British Advisory Mission in Vietnam had run into difficulties in that its advice to the Americans was no longer taken seriously.

Etherington-Smith evaluated the various possible ways Britain could help. He was "doubtful" about the wisdom of volunteering to help the Vietnamese refugee problem because this was a risky project: "It is quite possible that the refugee situation may present a major problem in the months to come and if we tried to help the Vietnamese we might well be blamed if things went wrong."[183] He also considered a material contribution to be "costly and, having regard to the immense American effort, would soon be forgotten." Therefore, the "only form of help . . . worth considering would be to send an expert or small qualified team here for a short time to advise the Vietnamese Government on handling the problem. It would be essential that any such advisers be assured of full American support and local cooperation," something that had been lacking with the British Advisory Mission. He concluded that "the field in which we can not only help most effectively but earn most American appreciation is that of police training. A substantial increase in [the] present BRIAM team would not only be valued by [the] Americans here but would also be a direct contribution to the development of an effective participation programme and hence to defeat of the Communists [sic] threat.[184]

The Foreign Office was right to be worried about London's credibility with the White House, especially the prime minister's. The secretary of state was defending the British record to the president, saying that the British govern-ment's support for U.S. policy in Vietnam had been "stronger than that of our other major allies" and had been "skillfully conducted and stoutly maintained by the Prime Minister." Rusk also advised the president that his Baltimore speech and Patrick Gordon Walker's mission had helped relieve the pressure on the prime minister. The president's face-to-face meeting with Wilson would have the same result.[185] Rusk therefore felt that during the prime minister's visit to Washington the president should indicate appreciation for his support on Vietnam.

London was also increasingly aware of Johnson's touchiness on Vietnam generally. An insight into the president's mood at this time, and his feeling to-ward Britain and Vietnam, was gained during the presentation of the creden-tials of Sir Patrick Dean, the new British ambassador to the United States on April 13.[186] This ceremony at the White House took place just two days before the prime minister was due in Washington and was described by Dean as "very interesting and to some extent embarrassing." Dean recorded that after a few preliminary remarks to the Chilean and Danish ambassadors, who were also being appointed that day, the president "plunged straight into a discussion with me about British affairs and policy." He spoke of the strong feelings in Con-gress and in the United States that America's friends should give them more support in Vietnam. In particular, he "strongly criticised the attitude of the Labour back bench in Parliament and said that although he was at all times ready to listen to what his allies had to say, he would not be deterred by purely negative opinion."[187] In what appears to have been a typical Johnson ranting session, according to Dean, the president protested that he was

not a murderer, nor did he seek to wage war. The bombing by American aircraft had been carried out against strictly military targets—against steel and concrete as he put it—not even against military factories, still less towns. No women or children had been killed and the sole purpose was to prevent the supply of arms to those who were attacking South Viet-Nam. These bombing attacks against only strictly defined military objectives con-trasted strongly with the bombing attacks carried out on the ground against people sleep-ing in barracks and still more against embassies. In these and other Communist bombing attacks innocent women and children had been killed, but no one seemed to mind that. All the complaints were against the American military bombing only.[188]

The President could not resist making a barbed attack on the British govern-ment regarding recent complaints about the American use of gas, which "was not poisonous gas anyway and which the British had used just as frequently. In any case, the British were forced to kill quite a few Indonesian infiltrators every day and he made no complaint. He said that his friends and allies should cer-tainly state their views, but they should not stab him in the back or slap him in the face." At this point the President "slapped his own face quite vigorously." Dean pointed out that however much the President "might resent some of the attacks from the extreme Left Wing on American policy, he had received and was receiving staunch support from the British government and people." Johnson admitted and acknowledged that he "equally resented some of the ill-informed criticism which he was receiving in his own country."[189]

Dean recognized that he had been subjected to an "impressive performance" by Johnson, who had known full well that the public nature of their meeting precluded any serious dissent from the new ambassador.[190] Dean's silence in the face of such verbal onslaughts may, however, explain why the president went on to develop a fondness for the British ambassador. Dean concluded his report of the ceremony by saying it had been "an invigorating experience and of peculiar interest. It revealed in a remarkable fashion how strongly the President feels about the situation in Viet-Nam and how extremely sensitive he is to any form of criticism, particularly that of a negative character even though he acknowledged that he was receiving more than satisfactory support from H.M.G."[191] The British were, therefore, well aware that Wilson would have to handle the subject of Vietnam with some delicacy.

The prime minister arrived in Washington in a confident mood after delivering a "robust" speech to the Economic Club at the Waldorf Astoria in New York.[192] He had also met with U Thant at the United Nations headquarters on the morning of April 14, when they discussed the situation in Vietnam, among other things. Wilson was met by Rusk at the airport and went straight into talks with the secretary of the Treasury, Henry Fowler, at 11:15 A.M. The prime minister then met with the president, who began their talks by commenting positively on Wilson's speech to the Economic Club and on Britain's economic position in general. Washington was pleased with Wilson's "evident determination" to defend the pound without devaluation and hopeful that the measures taken in Labour's latest budget would help put the British economy on a sounder footing.[193] It was acknowledged that world liquidity remained a problem, and this was discussed at some length. The conversation then moved on to Vietnam. According to Wilson's official record of the meeting, the president began by expressing his "very deep appreciation of the line [Britain] had taken on Vietnam." Yet again Wilson gave the president a "short account" of the political difficulties the British government faced on this issue, but he thought the president was already "in no doubt about the problems." The prime minister also acknowledged that "the position had been transformed both in a world sense and in the British political sense by his Baltimore speech" but felt it necessary to tell the president frankly that "there had been a real danger that America's image had been suffering."[194] Johnson replied by summarizing the "agonising decision he had had to take, the pressures he had been under" and said that "his line throughout had been a middle path between those who wanted to use Vietnam as a jumping-off ground for an all-out attack on China, and those who felt the United States should quit without conditions." The president said he was taking the "bomb-plus-olive-branch" line and that his speech at Johns Hopkins University had outlined his 3-D approach: "determination, discussions and development." Wilson urged the president to follow up on the discussion part of the equation and suggested that "immediate action best lie[s] in the Cambodian Conference."[195]

Wilson noted with some surprise that "there was not at any time any suggestion of our committing troops to Vietnam nor any reference to police, medical team and teams to handle the flow of refugees." It appears, however, that the prime minister preempted any request by referring to the Australian decision to commit a battalion to Vietnam. Wilson recalls that he said that the British government "welcomed this though it added to our Malaysian burdens since although the Australians were partners in Malaysia their contribution was much smaller than ours."[196] This was another way of reiterating that the British were already overstretched militarily.

In a luncheon meeting that followed the two men continued their discussion. Johnson was apparently in an "expansive mood" and Wilson went into further detail on the British domestic situation. Overall, Wilson felt that this "time our discussion on Vietnam was much more constructive," perhaps in comparison to their late-night telephone conversation of February 11.[197] This was probably because the Americans had come to the conclusion that there was a danger that the British might stray from the fold. If Wilson felt it was necessary to pursue peace unilaterally, he might do this and by implication join forces with the many other world leaders calling for negotiations, including De Gaulle and U Thant. And, given British objections over the use of gas and concerns over escalation, it was important to ensure that these criticisms remained private. A public divergence on Vietnam would be extremely damaging to the U.S. propaganda effort. It would be better to condone their ally's peace efforts than block them, if only to ensure that U.S. views were properly represented. Consequently, Wilson admits in his memoirs that an understanding on Vietnam was reached. "Apart from the occasional moment in future years when President Johnson revived the notion of a British military presence in Vietnam, these April talks set out a division of function which he more than once stressed publicly. The American Government would not be deflected from its military task; but, equally, he would give full backing to any British initiative which had any chance of getting peace-talks on the move."[198]

In the afternoon, there were more detailed discussions on Vietnam in a meeting with the secretary of state. The talk centered on the issue of a possible conference on Cambodia. Rusk was interested in such a conference but was "concerned to ensure that it should not fail. It would be better that it should not start than that it should fall flat on its face . . . a full scale conference which broke down without agreement would be an unqualified disaster."[199] Rusk reasoned that before accepting the Soviet proposal, they should consider a number of possibilities, including asking Patrick Gordon Walker to ask Prince Sihanouk of Cambodia what he would regard as an acceptable result of the conference. Consequently, the U.S. government would "need a little further time—perhaps no more than 24 hours—in which to co-ordinate their views."[200] By April 20 there was still a "fundamental conflict between British and American views on this proposal." Essentially, the United States desired a prior agreement on the documents to be signed at a conference on Cambodia, whereas the British felt "the longer the Cambodian conference lasts the better, because it will probably be some considerable time before the Communists are ready to discuss Viet Nam seriously." As it happened, Sihanouk refused the idea of a conference anyway, mainly because the rumor went around that it would be used as a pretext for talks on Vietnam. And although the British continued to pursue the idea, invitations to attend a conference were never issued.

Due to the brevity and informality of Wilson's visit, reaction to it was relatively muted. Publicly, the two leaders presented a united front at the obligatory press conference. The president termed his talks with Wilson "very interesting, very cordial, very fruitful" and expressed his high appreciation for "the friendship and support of our Allies, particularly that of the distinguished Prime Minister and the British people." *The Times* reported that the visit had been "most useful" and that "tentative agreements" had been reached on sterling and on Vietnam.[201] Nothing was said about the personal relationship. Overall, Wilson felt the meeting with the president had been "very cordial and friendly, pretty fast moving" and recorded that the meeting was "largely an exchange of views without seeking any new agreements."[202] Wilson stressed his loyalty to the president on the general aim of U.S. policy in Vietnam but warned that he could continue with this limited support only if he was allowed to deal with domestic criticism through an active role in the peace process. Even though it saw little hope on the negotiation front, the Johnson administration was now willing to allow Wilson to explore publicly the possibilities for peace. This was a price the White House was willing to pay to keep the British on board.

On his visit to Washington, Wilson gave the president two symbolic gifts: a bell from the ship *Resolute*—LBJ called it a "unique symbol of the truly close friendship that exists between our two countries"—and a rain-repellent raincoat (a Ganex mac). The coat was the wrong size and had to be replaced.[203] These gifts were more symbolic than originally intended. Although there was an enduring closeness between the two countries, in the short term the relationship required readjustments over Vietnam.

NOTES

1. United States: Annual Review of 1964, January 4, 1965, FO371/179557, PRO.

2. Hubert Humphrey wrote to Wilson of the "splendid relationship between you and the President" and the "excellent" press coverage of the visit, January 6, 1965, PREM 13, 682, PRO.

3. John Ramsden, "Churchill's Funeral and Anglo-American Relations," paper given at the Summer Conference of the Institute of Contemporary British History, Anglo-American Relations in the Twentieth Century, July 8, 1998.

4. Paul Gore-Booth to Sir Patrick Dean, Foreign Office Minute, "Possibility of a Visit to the UK by President Johnson and/or Vice-President Humphrey," July 12, 1965, FO371/179573, PRO. Sir Paul Gore-Booth took over from Sir Harold Caccia on May 10, 1965.

5. Harold Wilson, *The Labour Government 1964–1970* (Harmondsworth: Penguin, 1974), 115.

6. Minute for P.M. Harold Wilson, February 4, 1965, PREM 13/692, PRO.

7. Cabinet meeting, January 28, 1965, CAB 128/39, PRO.

8. Bruce diaries, January 29, 1965.

9. Briefing Paper: Prime Minister's Visit to Washington, February 2, 1965, FO371/180539/DV 103145/20, PRO.

10. Ibid.

11. Gordon Walker had lost his seat at Smethwick during the 1964 election and was replaced by Stewart in January 1965. Stewart served as Foreign Secretary until August 1966.

12. *Tribune* 29, no. 7 (February 12, 1965): 8.

13. *Times* (London), February 9, 1965.

14. *Hansard,* February 8, 1965, vol. 706, col. 38.

15. David Ennals to Harold Wilson, February 9, 1965, PREM 13/519, PRO.

16. "Vietnam," February 11, 1965, PREM 13/692, PRO.

17. Wilson, *Labour Government,* 116.

18. Bruce diaries, February 11, 1965.

19. Memorandum for the Record, Oliver Wright, February 11, 1965, PREM 13/692, PRO.

20. Memorandum of Telephone Conversation between President Johnson and Prime Minister Wilson, FRUS, 1964–68, vol. 2, 229.

21. Record of a Telephone Conversation between the Prime Minister and President Johnson on February 11, 1965, PREM 13/692, PRO; Wilson, *Labour Government,* 116.

22. Wilson, *Labour Government,* 116.

23. Memorandum of Telephone Conversation between President Johnson and Prime Minister Wilson, FRUS, 1964–68, vol. 2, 229.

24. Record of a Telephone Conversation between the Prime Minister and President Johnson, PREM 13/692, PRO.

25. Wilson, *Labour Government,* 116.

26. Ibid.

27. Memorandum of Telephone Conversation between President Johnson and Prime Minister Wilson, FRUS, 1964–68, vol. 2, 229.

28. Ibid., 2.

29. Ibid., 5.

30. George Reedy, *Lyndon Johnson: A Memoir* (New York: Andrews and McNeal, 1982), x, 56.

31. Memorandum from the President's Special Assistant for National Security Affairs (Bundy) to President Johnson, March 22, 1965, FRUS, 1964–68, vol. 2, 468.

32. Telegram from McGeorge Bundy to Oliver Wright for the Prime Minister, February 11, 1965, PREM 13/692, PRO.

33. Cabinet Minutes, February 11, 1965, CAB 128/39, PRO.

34. *Guardian* (London), February 13, 1965, in Telegram from Murray, Foreign Office, to Patrick Dean, Washington, no. 1119, February 13, 1965, PREM 13/692, PRO.

35. Telegram from Foreign Office to British Embassy, Washington, February 13, 1965, PREM 13/692, PRO.

36. The ambassador lamented in his diaries later that week that "each night of this week after midnight I have been called on the telephone about Vietnam."

37. Bruce diaries, February 16, 1965.

38. Record of Conversation between the Prime Minister and the U.S. Ambassador, David Bruce, February 16, 1965, PREM 13/692, PRO.

39. Ibid.

40. Record of Conversation between the Prime Minister and the U.S. Ambassador, Mr. David Bruce, at No. 10 Downing St. at 10:30 A.M. on Wednesday, February 17, 1965, PREM 13/692, PRO.

41. Memo for the President from McGeorge Bundy, "Wilson's Talk with Bruce Today," February 17, 1965, Memos to President, vol. 8, 1/1/65–2/28/65, NSF, LBJL.

42. Bruce diaries, February 17, 1965.

43. Memo of Meeting with President Johnson, General Eisenhower, Secretary McNamara, General Wheeler, McGeorge Bundy, and General Goodpaster, February 17, 1965, FRUS 1964–68, vol. 2, 298.

44. J. Cable, "Seeking a Solution in Viet-Nam," February 15, 1965, FO371/180580, PRO.

45. E. H. Peck, "Vietnam," February 15, 1965, FO371/180580, PRO.

46. Lord Walston to Stewart, February 17, 1965, FO371/180580, PRO.

47. Ibid.

48. Telegram from Michael Stewart to Harlech, February 18, 1965, FO371/180589, PRO.

49. Note by J. M. Henderson to W. J. Adams, February 18, 1965, FO371/180580; Telegram from Stewart to Rusk, February 18, 1965, "Vietnam," FO371/180580, PRO.

50. Ibid.

51. *Times* (London), February 13, 1965.

52. Cable from H. Trevelyan, Moscow to Foreign Office, no. 326, February 16, 1965, PREM 13/692, PRO.

53. Telegram from Harlech to Foreign Office, no. 401, February 18, 1965, PREM 13/692, PRO.

54. The British were told they could tell the Russians "we are confident that the US would respond to a request for their views." Telegram from Lord Harlech to the Foreign Office, no. 401, February 18, 1965, "South Vietnam," PREM 13, 692, PRO.

55. Telegram to Bangkok re "Proposed Initiative by Co-Chairman on Vietnam," February 20, 1965, PREM 13/692. This proposal to the Russians was considered the first

serious international initiative for peace. "Negotiation Attempts on Vietnam," NSF, CF, Vietnam, Vietnam 6C, 1961–68, Peace Initiatives: General International Initiatives (Retrospective Accounts), LBJL.

56. Sir H. Trevelyan, Moscow to Foreign Office, February 20, 1965, PREM 13/692, PRO.

57. Memo of Conversation, "Discussion with British Ambassador on Viet Nam," between Lord Harlech, Michael Stewart, and Secretary Rusk, February 21, 1965, box 207, CF, UK, NSF, LBJL.

58. Washington to Foreign Office, February 26, 1965, PREM 13/692, PRO.

59. Conclusions of Meeting of the Cabinet, February 18, 1965, CAB 128/39, part 1, PRO.

60. Telegram from Harlech to Foreign Office, February 24, 1965, FO371/180581, PRO.

61. Memorandum of Conversation between Lord Harlech, Michael Stewart, and Secretary Rusk, "Discussion with British Ambassador on Viet Nam," February 21, 1965, box 207, vol. 3, CF, UK, NSF, LBJL.

62. Telegram from Harlech to Foreign Office, February 24, 1965, FO371/180581, PRO.

63. Bruce diaries, February 25, 1965.

64. Telegram from Harlech to Foreign Office, February 24, 1965, FO371/180581, PRO.

65. Transcript, Benjamin Read oral history interview by Paige E. Mulhollan, March 1970, tape 2, 16, LBJL.

66. *Tribune* 29, no. 8 (February 19, 1965): 1.

67. Ibid., 1.

68. Telegram from Bruce to Rusk, February 17, 1965, box 203, CF, UK, NSF, LBJL.

69. David Ennals to Harold Wilson, March 3, 1965, PREM 13, 519, PRO.

70. *Hansard*, Written Answer, February 23, 1957, vol. 707, col. 69.

71. Department of State, Rusk to William Bundy, Telegram, March 5, 1965, Declassified Document, Library of Congress.

72. Telegram from Harlech to Foreign Office, March 6, 1965, FO371/180582/DV1075/56(B), PRO.

73. Telegram from Harlech to Foreign Office, February 23, 1965, "Vietnam," PREM 13, 692; Telegram from Foreign Office to Harlech, February 24, 1965, 13, PREM 13, 692, PRO.

74. Telegram from Harlech to Foreign Office, February 23, 1965, PREM 13, 692, PRO.

75. Telegram from Foreign Office to Harlech, February 24, 1965, PREM 13, 692, PRO.

76. *Times* (London), February 25, 1965, 10.

77. Bruce diaries, February 28, 1965.

78. *Hansard*, Written Answer, March 1, 1965, vol. 707, col. 166–67.

79. *Times* (London), February 25, 1965, 10.

80. *Guardian* (London), February 26, 1965, in Bruce to Secretary of State, March 2, 1965, File: UK, vol. 3, Cables, 2/65–4/65, box 207, CF, UK, NSF, LBJL.

81. *Observer* (London), March 2, 1965, in Bruce to Secretary of State, March 2, 1965, File: UK, vol. 3, Cables, 2/65–4/65, box 207, CF, UK, NSF, LBJL.

82. *Telegraph* (London), February 24, 1965, in Bruce to Secretary of State, March 2, 1965, File: UK, vol. 3, Cables, 2/65–4/65, box 207, CF, UK, NSF, LBJL.

83. Patrick Gordon Walker diary, March 6, 1965, Churchill College Archives.

84. Bruce diaries, March 12, 1965.

85. Valenti to Johnson, February 26, 1965, GEN CO, box 76, folder—CO305 UK, 1/1/65–7/1/65, LBJL.

86. Record of Conversation between Prime Minister and U.S. Ambassador, Mr. D. Bruce, at 12:15 P.M. at 10 Downing Street, March 12, 1965, PREM 13/693, PRO.

87. Ibid.

88. *Daily Mail* (London), March 13, 1965, quoted in Telegram from Bruce to Rusk, March 13, 1965, File: UK, vol. 3, Cables, 2/65–4/65, box 207, CF, UK, NSF, LBJL.

89. Memo from McGeorge Bundy to Jack Valenti, Subject: Appointment with the President—British Foreign Secretary Michael Stewart, March 15, 1965, UK: Michael Stewart Visit, 3/21/65, box 214, CF, UK, NSF, LBJL.

90. *Times* (London), April 17, 1965, 8.

91. Bruce diaries, March 6, 1965.

92. Cabinet Meeting, March 4, 1965, CAB 128/39, part 2, PRO.

93. Richard Crossman, *The Crossman Diaries: Selections from the Diaries of a Cabinet Minister, 1964–70* (London: Mandarin, 1991), March 4, 1965, 86.

94. Cabinet Meeting, Thursday, March 4, 1965, CAB 128/39, part 2, PRO.

95. Crossman, *Crossman Diaries*, March 4, 1965, 86.

96. Cabinet Meeting, Thursday, March 4, 1965, CAB 128/39, part 2, PRO.

97. Bruce diaries, March 7, 1965.

98. Telegram from Rusk to American Embassy, London, March 8, 1965, PREM 13/694, PRO.

99. Telegram from Foreign Office to Washington, Tele 1865, March 8, 1965, PREM 13/694, PRO.

100. Telegram from Dean Rusk to Philip Kaiser, March 9, 1965, FO371/180582/DV1075/60/G, PRO.

101. Ibid.

102. Ibid.

103. Ibid.

104. Wilson, *Labour Government*, 120.

105. Record of a Conversation between the Prime Minister and the U.S. Ambassador, David K. E. Bruce, 10 Downing Street, 12:15 P.M., March 12, 1965, PREM 13/693, PRO.

106. *Hansard*, March 9, 1965, vol. 708, col. 237.

107. Ibid.

108. Ibid., col. 238.

109. Bruce diaries, March 12, 1965.

110. Nelson D. Lankford, *The Last American Aristocrat: The Biography of David K. E. Bruce, 1898–1977* (Boston: Little, Brown and Co., 1996), 331.

111. *Times* (London), March 11, 1965, 12.

112. Ibid.

113. Edward Short, *Whip to Wilson* (London: Macdonald and Co., 1989), 120.

114. *Times* (London), March 11, 1965, 12.

115. Record of a Conversation between the Prime Minister and the U.S. Ambassador, Mr. David Bruce, at 12:15 P.M., 10 Downing Street, March 12, 1965, PREM 13/693, PRO.

116. *New Statesman*, March 12, 1965, 1.

117. Record of a Conversation between the Prime Minister and David K. E. Bruce, U.S. Ambassador, 10 Downing Street, March 12, 1965, PREM 13/693, PRO.

118. Minute, South East Asia Department, March 15, 1965, PREM 13/694, PRO.

119. Bruce diaries, March 20, 1965.

120. Telegram from Bruce to Rusk, March 17, 1965, File: UK, vol. 3, Cables, 2/65–4/65, box 207, CF, UK, NSF, LBJL.

121. Secretary of State's Visit to Washington and New York, March 21–24, Brief no. 12, March 19, 1965, FO371/180584, PRO.

122. Paper Prepared by the Assistant Secretary of Defense for International Security Affairs (McNaughton), March 10, 1965, FRUS, 1964–68, vol. 2, 427.

123. Memorandum from the President's Special Assistant for National Security Affairs (Bundy) to President Johnson, March 6, 1965, FRUS, 1964–68, vol. 2, 404.

124. Memorandum from the President's Special Assistant for National Security Affairs (Bundy) to President Johnson, March 22, 1965, in FRUS, 1964–68, vol. 2, 468.

125. Ibid.

126. Ibid.

127. Ibid., 469.

128. Wilson, *Labour Government*, 122.

129. Ibid., 123.

130. *Tribune* (London), March 26, 1965, 5.

131. Wilson, *Labour Government*, 122.

132. Personal Telegram from the Prime Minister to Foreign Secretary, Washington, March 23, 1965, PREM 13/693; Draft Telegram from the Prime Minister to the Foreign Secretary, PREM 13/693, PRO.

133. Draft Telegram from the Prime Minister to the Foreign Secretary, PREM 13/693, PRO.

134. Telegram 2328 Personal for the Foreign Secretary from the Prime Minister Emergency Confidential, March 23, 1965, PREM 13/693, PRO.

135. Ibid.

136. Draft Telegram from the Prime Minister to the Foreign Secretary, PREM 13/693, PRO.

137. Telegram 2328 Personal for the Foreign Secretary from the Prime Minister Emergency Confidential, March 23, 1965, PREM 13/693, PRO.

138. Wilson, *Labour Government*, 123.

139. Record of a Conversation between the Foreign Secretary and Mr. Dean Rusk, the U.S. Secretary of State, at the State Department, Washington, at 10:30 A.M., March 23, 1965, PREM 13/693, PRO.

140. Memo from Bundy to the President, March 22, 1965, FRUS, 1964–68, vol. 2, 469.

141. Cabinet Minutes, March 25, 1965, CAB 128/39 part 2, PRO.

142. Record of a Conversation between the Foreign Secretary and Mr. Dean Rusk, Washington, at 10:30 A.M., March 23, 1965, PREM 13/693, PRO.

143. Ibid.

144. Bruce diaries, March 22, 1965.

145. Ibid.

146. Memo from Rusk to the President, March 22, 1965, Wilson Visit, 4/15/65, CF, UK, NSF, LBJL.

147. Telephone Conversation between LBJ and Drew Pearson, WH6503.11, March 23, 1965, 11:35 A.M.

148. Bruce diaries, March 23, 1965.

149. *Daily Mail* (London), March 23, 1965, in Telegram from Kaiser to Rusk, "Vietnam: British Press," March 23, 1965, File: UK, vol. 3, Cables, 2/65–4/65, box 207, CF, UK, NSF, LBJL.

150. Telephone Conversation between LBJ and Dean Rusk, March 24, 1965, 11:20 A.M., citation no. 7144, tape no. WH 6503.11.

151. Telephone Conversation between LBJ and Dean Rusk, March 24, 1965, 11:20 A.M., citation no. 7144, tape no. WH 6503.11.

152. Bruce diaries, January–March 1965 in Editorial Notes, FRUS, 1964–68, vol. 2, 481.

153. Wilson, *Labour Government*, 123.

154. Memo from David Klein to McGeorge Bundy, March 23, 1965, vol. 3, Memos, 2/65–4/65, box 207, CF, UK, NSF, LBJL.

155. Record of a Conversation between the Foreign Secretary and Mr. Dean Rusk, the United States Secretary of State, at the State Department, Washington, at 10:30 A.M., March 23, 1965, PREM 13/693, PRO.

156. Ibid.

157. Ibid.

158. Statement by the President on Vietnam, March 25, 1965, *Public Papers of the President, Lyndon B. Johnson, 1965* (Washington, D.C.: U.S. Government Printing Office, 1966), 319.

159. *Times* (London), March 31, 1965, 12.

160. Brief no. 3, March 30, 1965, NATO Ministerial Discussions, March 31–April 1, Vietnam—Talking Points, FO371/180585, PRO.

161. Telegram from British Embassy, Washington to Foreign Office, March 28, 1965, "Mr. Gordon Walker's Visit to South East Asia," PREM 13/304, PRO.

162. Memorandum for the Record, March 31, 1965, Memos for the Record, 1964, Files of McGeorge Bundy, box 18, NSF, LBJL.

163. *Times* (London), March 31, 1965, 112.

164. Telegram from Kaiser to Rusk, April 2, 1965, File: UK, vol. 3, Cables, 2/65–4/65, box 207, CF, UK, NSF, LBJL.

165. Telegram from Kaiser to Rusk, April 1, 1965, File: UK, vol. 3, Cables, 2/65–4/65, box 207, CF, UK, NSF, LBJL.

166. Ibid.

167. Memorandum for the Record, March 31, 1965, Memos for the Record, 1964, Files of McGeorge Bundy, box 18, NSF, LBJL.

168. Ibid. Despite Wright's reassurances, Bruce later told Bundy that Wilson had been "indiscreet in stating an American decision to avoid attacking 'industrial installations.'"

169. Wilson, *Labour Government*, 123.

170. Memorandum for the Record, March 31, 1965, Memos for the Record, 1964, Files of McGeorge Bundy, box 18, NSF, LBJL.

171. Address at Johns Hopkins University: "Peace without Conquest," April 7, 1965, *Public Papers of the Presidents of the United States: Lyndon B. Johnson, vol. 1, 1965* (Washington, D.C.: U.S. Government Printing Office, 1965), 394–98.

172. Telegram from Bruce to Rusk, April 8, 1965, File: UK, vol. 3, Cables, 2/65–4/65, box 207, CF, UK, NSF, LBJL.

173. M. Stewart (U.K. Embassy, Washington) to E.H. Peck, April 9, 1965, FO371/180685/DV 1076/20; Cabinet Minutes, April 8, 1965, CAB 128/39 part 2, PRO.

174. Telegram from Bruce to Rusk, April 9, 1965, File: UK, vol. 3, Cables, 2/65–4/65, box 207, CF, UK, NSF, LBJL.

175. *Sun* (London) and *Guardian* (London), April 8, 1965, in Telegram from Bruce to Rusk, April 9, 1965, File: UK, vol. 3, Cables, 2/65–4/65, box 207, CF, UK, NSF, LBJL.

176. Telegram from Patrick Dean to Foreign Office, April 9, 1965, FO371/180585, PRO.

177. Wilson, *Labour Government*, 133.

178. Telegram from Patrick Dean to Foreign Office, April 9, 1965, Prime Minister's Visit: Vietnam, PREM 13/694, PRO.

179. Ibid.

180. Ibid.

181. Ibid.

182. Telegram from Etherington-Smith to Foreign Office, April 12, 1965, British Aid to Vietnam, PREM 13/694, PRO.

183. Ibid.

184. Ibid.

185. Memo for the President from Rusk, April 14, 1965, Memos to the President from Bundy, vol. 9, NSF, LBJL.

186. Dean went on to establish a close relationship with Johnson.

187. Condensed Record of a Meeting with President Johnson at the White House on April the 13th on Presentation of His Credentials by Sir Patrick Dean, PREM 13/694, PRO.

188. Ibid.

189. Ibid.

190. Ibid.

191. Condensed Record of a Meeting with President Johnson at the White House on April the 13th on Presentation of His Credentials by Sir Patrick Dean, PREM 13/694, PRO.

192. Wilson, *Labour Government*, 135.

193. Memo for the President, "Call by the British Prime Minister," April 14, 1965, Memos to President from Bundy, vol. 9, Mar–4/14/65, NSF, LBJL.

194. Record of a Meeting between the Prime Minister and President of the United States at the White House on Thursday, April 15, 1965, PREM 13/532, PRO.

195. Ibid.

196. Ibid.

197. Wilson, *Labour Government*, 135–36.

198. Ibid., 136.

199. Record of a Meeting at the White House at 2:30 P.M. on Thursday, April 15, 1965, PREM 13/532, PRO.

200. Ibid.

201. *Times* (London), April 17, 1965, 8.

202. Record of Meeting between the Prime Minister and President of the United States at the White House—Thursday, April 15, 1965, PREM 13/532, PRO.

203. Telegram from President to Prime Minister, White House Central Files, EXCO305, United Kingdom, 1/1/65, box 76, May 7, 1965.

Chapter 3

The Search for a Wider Understanding:
May–December 1965

With an understanding on Vietnam reached during Wilson's visit to Washington, Anglo–American relations appeared to have improved significantly since the "gas episode" of March 1965. However, during the second half of 1965 domestic developments in both Britain and the United States impinged upon Anglo–American relations and Vietnam. In the United Kingdom, problems with sterling and a deepening crisis in Rhodesia added to the Wilson government's dilemma over Vietnam. In the United States, these months witnessed growing domestic upheaval, including further racial unrest and increasing activity on the part of the antiwar movement.[1] More importantly, the sterling crisis forced Washington to consider the possibility of seeking a wider understanding that encompassed not only British support for U.S. policy in Vietnam in exchange for financial aid, but also a commitment to retain British forces East of Suez. As we shall see, the sterling crisis coincided with the Americanization of the war in Vietnam. In July the United States gave up the pretense of aiding the South Vietnamese government and took on the military battle themselves, agreeing to send an additional 50,000 troops to Southeast Asia. Despite the apparent understanding reached between Johnson and Wilson in the spring, the British Labour government was alarmed by the conflagration and found it ever more difficult to support the methods the United States employed in its efforts to secure an independent South Vietnam.

THE CONTINUING SEARCH FOR ALLIES

On April 20 McNamara chaired a meeting of senior military and civilian advisors in Honolulu to assess the U.S. position in Vietnam. At this stage the

Americans had 33,500 of their forces stationed in Vietnam; the president had also recently authorized a change in the Marine role from static defense of base facilities to active, mobile combat roles, although at this stage still in support of South Vietnamese forces.[2] The conferees recommended, and Johnson accepted, further U.S. troop deployments. Immediately, an extra 9,000 troops were sent to South Vietnam. On May 4, LBJ asked Congress to approve a supplemental appropriation of $700 million to meet the increased costs in Vietnam, and by the end of June the president had authorized General William Westmoreland to use his forces in combat "independently or in conjunction with" South Vietnamese forces.[3] At Honolulu, Secretary of Defense McNamara had also recommended that, if possible, allied troops be increased. Obviously, these troops would reduce the numbers of U.S. ground troops being asked for, as well as further the image of a multilateral effort. On April 29 Chester Cooper, a member of the National Security Council, outlined the existing Free World Assistance to Vietnam in a memorandum to McGeorge Bundy. So far only Australia, New Zealand, South Korea, the Philippines, and Taiwan had sent military contingents to Vietnam, and most of these troops were noncombatant.[4] The United States consequently explored further possible "third party" support. Although the existing contributors presented the best hope for large-scale troop commitments, the Johnson administration again pressured its other friends and allies to contribute "more flags."

One possible way of engaging the British military in Southeast Asia lay in asking the government of Vietnam formally to invoke the SEATO treaty. The 10th meeting of SEATO was due to open in London on May 3, and Washington hoped this might provide an opportunity to announce such a move. The first draft of the communiqué for this meeting was prepared in advance and outlined this option. Bruce soon informed the State Department that, in his view, there was "no chance of persuading HMG to provide its military forces to SEATO for use in South Vietnam."[5] The British again stressed their military commitment in Malaysia and their need to appear as impartial as possible in order to fulfill their role as Geneva cochair.[6] Undersecretary George Ball and William Bundy, assistant secretary of state for Far Eastern affairs, then met with Patrick Dean to suggest an alternative communiqué on Vietnam "aimed at trying to meet British problems." It read as follows:

The Government of the Republic of Viet-Nam requested the Council members to take action under the Treaty to meet the aggression from North Viet-Nam. In light of the Protocol to the Treaty which designates South Viet-Nam as a protected State, the Governments of Australia, New Zealand, the Philippines, Thailand, the United Kingdom and the United States agreed that, pursuant to their Treaty obligations and within their capabilities, including their commitments elsewhere, they will take concerted action under the Treaty to meet the Communist aggression in South Viet-Nam. For this purpose they will continue and, wherever possible, intensify actions of the type they have been taking.[7]

William Bundy argued that as the British government had made clear its support of the government of Vietnam in previous SEATO council statements, another strong statement "would not further infringe upon British impartiality."
George Ball agreed that last year's council communiqué had already committed
SEATO members to further action "in fulfilment of their obligations under the
Treaty" and that if the Vietnam problem was "not dealt with forthrightly" by
the council, the "public impression will be created that [the] US is fairly isolated on this issue." "We are not pressing for collective action by SEATO as an
organization but feel that for Congressional purposes it is essential that [the]
SEATO communiqué appear stronger than last year's, particularly in view of
[the] fact that in [the] intervening year several SEATO members have sent
troop contingents to Viet-Nam." The point was also made that if SEATO could
not meet the crisis in Vietnam the "question rises as to what purpose [the] organization serves."[8]

These arguments cut no ice back in London. Michael Stewart told Dean to inform Rusk that in his view "the amendment suggested...make[s] this proposal
more rather than less objectionable. The proposed last sentence, for instance,
would be read as meaning that Britain was urging the United States and South
Viet Nam to intensify the bombing of the North." He further instructed the
British ambassador to make it "quite clear" that he was "not prepared to consider anything on the lines of the present proposal" as his objections were to
the "substance of the proposal not merely to the wording."[9]

When the Australians and New Zealanders were consulted, they had no real
problem with the notion of invoking the SEATO treaty, and they agreed to
send combat troops. However, after consulting with London they advised the
Americans that they would not press the British hard in view of their estima-
tion of British domestic difficulties.[10] The Americans duly shelved the idea.
When the "white man's club"—the United States, Great Britain, New Zealand,
and Australia—met at a dinner the day before the SEATO meeting was due to
start, the U.S. proposal was not openly discussed.[11] After consultation among
the council members, the communiqué that was issued at the end of the SEATO
meeting nevertheless provided firm support for U.S. policy in Vietnam; indeed,
The Times felt the Americans "could hardly have hoped for a more unequivocal
diplomatic backing than this." It talked of "aggression against the Republic of
Vietnam—an aggression organized, directed, supplied and supported by the
communist regime in North Vietnam in contravention of the basic obligations
of international law and in flagrant violation of the Geneva Agreements of
1954 and 1962." It also noted "with grave concern the increasing infiltration of
arms and combat personnel from North Vietnam into South Vietnam." And, in
wording suggested by the British, it expressed "warm support for the policy of
the United States Government as outlined by President Johnson on April 7." It
finished by saying that "until the communist aggression is brought to an end,
resolute defensive action must be continued."[12] Although the U.S. administra-

tion had secured a line that would satisfy its congressional critics, it had failed in its latest attempt to extract firmer British support on Vietnam.

THE FIRST BOMBING PAUSE

It was at this time, late April and early May 1965, that the Johnson administration began to give serious consideration to a bombing pause in North Vietnam. Opponents of the air strikes felt that the North Vietnamese would not be persuaded to talk while such American provocation continued. Given the growing criticism LBJ was facing at home over the Rolling Thunder operation, it was felt that a break in bombing would "put the onus on Hanoi" as well as relieve domestic pressure. As with the president's recent offer of "unconditional discussions," this latest maneuver was not expected to lead to negotiations but was, as some historians have suggested, another "time-buying device."[13] Still, George Ball discussed the option of a bombing pause in conversation with Harold Wilson at Downing Street on May 5. Ball informed the prime minister that at this stage the length of a break in the air strikes was not decided upon, but the idea was "to create the impression that the present attacks were not systematic" and "try to get through signals to Hanoi in order to see whether they were prepared to talk." Wilson replied that a pause in the bombing would be "an excellent thing to do if the US felt able to do it," but he was not sure if the North Vietnamese would respond. In any case, "[I]f this proposal were carried out and if there were any response from the North, then, once again, the US government would be in a sound moral position."[14]

On May 10 the president finally decided to end the bombing of the north "for a limited period."[15] The following day the U.S. ambassador in Moscow, Foy Kohler, was instructed to see the Democratic Republic of Vietnam (DRV) ambassador to convey a message announcing the bombing pause with the request that it be transmitted to Hanoi. The message said there would be no air attacks on North Vietnam from Wednesday, May 12, at noon until the next week, and that this action was "in response to 'suggestions from various quarters, including public statements by Hanoi representatives' that there could be no progress toward peace while air attacks continued." Just to make clear its position, the United States said it was "well aware of the risk that a temporary suspension of these air attacks may be understood as an indication of weakness" and if it was so misunderstood "it would be necessary to demonstrate more clearly than ever...that the United States is determined not to accept aggression without reply."[16] The threat contained in this message was not revealed to the public until Hanoi Radio broadcast the text in December of that year.[17]

When both the North Vietnamese embassy and the Soviet embassy refused officially to receive a copy of the U.S. message (although both copies were delivered and retained), on May 14 the Americans asked the British if they could convey the message directly to their representative in Hanoi.[18] So on May 17 the British consul general duly delivered a copy of the message to the DRV. The message was again returned. According to the Americans, "[I]n view of the negative, indeed hostile, reception by Hanoi to our approach, it was decided to resume bombing at about 0800 hours Saigon time May 18."[19] The pause had been complete in the north and lasted five days and 20 hours from May 12 to May 18. Bombing of the south had continued unabated.[20] The following day the French reported to the United States that the North Vietnamese had told them that "Hanoi's four points were to be considered as working principles for negotiations rather than prior [U.S.] conditions."[21]

GROWING BRITISH DISSENT ON VIETNAM

Patrick Gordon Walker returned from his fact-finding tour of Southeast Asia on May 4. Three days later he presented his findings to Prime Minister Wilson in a lengthy report. In his considered opinion, the United States' general military strategy in Vietnam was right, but the British government could be "critical" of some of the U.S. tactics. He was aware that should America's bombing "policy fail and South Vietnamese morale collapse again, the Americans might be tempted to bomb Hanoi and other centres of population." Gordon Walker felt that "any such decision would be a great error. It would throw Asian and world opinion against the United States to such an extent as to outweigh any military advantage.... In my view we should let the United States know that if they bombed Hanoi... they could not count on our support."[22] While in Southeast Asia, Gordon Walker had taken every opportunity to let the American authorities know his views on this. Nevertheless, his overall conclusion was that Britain "must back the Americans in their present operations in Viet-Nam. Their military effort is the only possible policy. An American defeat would be disastrous, even if a victory in the normal sense is unattainable." He suggested, however, that Britain "should search for a policy which, while backing America loyally, allows us a certain more apparent independence of view." One way of doing this would be to "let it be known that our analysis of the situation differs somewhat from the Americans. We see more division amongst the Communist forces, less of a solid chain from Peking to the Viet Cong. We would find some support for this attitude in the State Department. We might also indicate what kind of ultimate settlement we envisage. We might, too, make more clear our opposition to the bombing of Hanoi."[23] He acknowledged, however, that "all this would be a very delicate operation" and "would probably depend upon America getting into a position of greater strength."[24]

Wilson thought Gordon Walker's report was "excellent... filling a lot of the gaps" and that the report, and therefore the tour, was "well worthwhile."[25] This did not mean, however, that the prime minister would act upon all of the aforementioned suggestions, despite the fact that at times during the second half of 1965 the United States did appear to improve its military position. Limits placed on British support of American actions in Vietnam still tended to be couched in terms of Labour's internal political difficulties, rather than any open disagreement with the United States on its understanding of the war.

By May, America's allies were increasingly uneasy about the lack of consultation they were receiving over Vietnam. Although U.S. officials appeared at times to be confiding in the British over Vietnam, thus giving the illusion of a fair degree of consultation, in fact the White House was revealing very little about the future direction of its Vietnam policy. Moreover, just as the Johnson administration was being criticized at home for the lack of clarity of its aims in Vietnam, similar doubts were being raised abroad.

On May 10 Michael Stewart met with George Ball to discuss a range of foreign policy issues. Again the undersecretary appeared to be privileging the British on Vietnam by insisting that certain parts of the meeting's record be kept on "a very restricted basis in view of the delicate position of the US Government in relation to the Government of South Viet-Nam, with whom a number of these points had not been raised."[26] But the ensuing lengthy and detailed discussion of the possible routes to peace negotiations failed to illuminate American thinking on the subject.

Two days later during a discussion on Southeast Asia at a restricted session of the NATO Ministerial Council held at Lancaster House, Stewart felt it necessary to tell Dean Rusk

that the friends and Allies of the United States ought to support American policy in Viet-Nam. But this would be much easier if the United States would ensure that her friends and allies were fully informed in advance of American actions in Viet-Nam, of the reasons for these actions and of changes in the American judgement of the situation in Viet-Nam. It was also very important that the objectives of American policy in Viet-Nam should be constantly and publicly repeated.[27]

The U.S. secretary of state "accepted the need for more explanation and exposition," noted the request from members of NATO for more information on American activities, and said he would do his best to provide this in the future.[28]

The British government, in particular, wanted the Americans to be more open on Vietnam, not only because it was helpful in its own foreign policy making, but also due to the growing dissent on Vietnam within and without Parliament. It was vital that Wilson and Stewart appeared to be well informed on Vietnam if they were to continue their policy of public support for the United States, coupled with their reassurance that their influence was being exerted in private. As the United States increased its military involvement in Vietnam, parliamentary pressure grew. Major foreign affairs debates centering on Vietnam took place on June 3 and July 19–20. On June 15 and July 5, William Warbey, M.P., also attempted to force an urgent debate on Vietnam. Although he failed in this it was yet another sign of the growing impatience of Labour backbenchers.

The British government was well aware that it was not only the Labour left wing who were upset by British policy on Vietnam, although these elements remained the most vocal in their opposition to it. Pressure on the government's Vietnam policy came in many forms. On May 11 the *Daily Mirror* reported an interview with the British police advisers in South Vietnam.[29] According to the *Mirror* journalist, the police said that they were sick of the tortures used by the people who employed them. Emrys Hughes, M.P., asked the secretary of state for foreign affairs if it was now time to bring the advisers home. Instead Mr. Padley, minister of state for foreign affairs, answering for Stewart, said the *Mirror* report would be investigated. The police admitted to being interviewed but dissociated themselves from the substance of the report. The interview had, however, already raised the question of police presence, so that Padley was forced to reiterate that it did not represent a British military involvement in Vietnam given that the police were in fact civilians.[30] This two-week saga was yet another embarrassment for the government.

Trade unions were also voicing their concerns in greater numbers. By May 11 the prime minister admitted to Parliament that he had received 170 resolutions on Vietnam from trade unions. In reply he referred them to his statements in the House. The vast majority of the unions expressed dissatisfaction with the action of the bombing in North Vietnam.[31] The Parliamentary Labour Party continued to turn against the Labour leadership on Vietnam. On May 26, Len Williams, the general secretary of the Labour Party, issued a statement on behalf of the National Executive Committee (NEC) that was extremely supportive of the government's Vietnam policy. It argued that "the purpose of the Government policy from the outset had been 'to try to get discussion started.' " It concluded, "[I]f success is achieved, it will be due in large measure to the patient and vigorous efforts undertaken behind the scenes by the British Government, efforts that would have been brought to naught if they had taken the advice which was strongly pressed on them, to content themselves with public declarations."[32] The *Tribune* felt this was a gross distortion of the truth, rightly pointing out that critics of the government were calling for deeds as well as words. The reconvening of the Geneva Conference and an end to all British aid to Vietnam were just two concrete suggestions put forward by opponents of the government's policy. William Warbey later recalled that in conversation with him, Wilson had quoted a phrase of Aneurin Bevan's "to the effect that emotional declarations were a form of 'public masturbation,' in which responsible statesmen and diplomats could not afford to indulge."[33] Wilson appeared to be losing touch with his party.

More moderate and intellectual circles were also openly challenging the British government on Vietnam. By the beginning of May, Wilson had been derided by the *New Statesman* as "President Johnson's Poodle." Although this was largely in response to Britain's support in the United Nations of U.S. action in the Dominican Republic, the prime minister's seemingly uncritical support of the president's Vietnam policy was also being questioned.[34] The Fabian Society began to criticize Britain's support of American policy in Vietnam in its journal, *Venture*. Editorials expressed disappointment at the new government.

"If even a Labour government cannot be influenced by the course of informed discussion, *Venture's* function becomes merely academic. We are not in business just to comment on the international scene, but to indicate to the Labour Party and to the Labour Government what areas of the world and what policies are due for reappraisal."[35] They also pointed out the moral and political dangers of continuing Britain's present policy on Vietnam.

Opposition to the Vietnam war is not just a left-wing revolt, as some would have us believe, but a major revulsion both in Parliament and in the country against the short-sightedness and brutality of American policy. For the first time since Suez, the roots of popular anti-Americanism have been revealed. This could have disastrous consequences for Labour's policy of Atlantic solidarity. Mr. Wilson's Vietnam policy is not wrong because it is unpopular, it is wrong because it is wrong.[36]

Venture also highlighted the danger of British policy on Vietnam threatening the Western Alliance. "If we continue to support the Americans over Vietnam, we shall simply confirm our image in Europe as an American stooge [and this] makes impossible any attempt at an independent foreign policy, and disqualifies us from adopting a more mediatory position in any quarrel in which the United States is involved."[37] This was a realistic fear. Most obviously, the French, particularly de Gaulle, could use British subservience to the United States over Vietnam to justify their rejection of future British applications to join the European Economic Community.

Other extra-Parliamentary unrest on Vietnam included the launch on May 19 of the British Council for Peace in Vietnam (BCPV).[38] Chaired by Labour peer Fenner Brockway, BCPV was conceived as an umbrella organization and attempted to pull together as many anti-Vietnam groups as possible through its national campaign committee. This group aimed for a negotiated settlement of the war and although communist-run, it immediately gained the support of M.P.s, university lecturers, teachers, journalists, and students and eventually established support from 29 organizations—political, religious, and labor groups.

As was occurring elsewhere in the world, students were also beginning to debate and demonstrate on this issue. The first major "teach-in" in Britain came at the London School of Economics and was followed shortly afterward by one at Oxford on June 17, 1965, and a national teach-in was held at Westminster on July 1, 1965. The Oxford teach-in was particularly noteworthy, not least because it was televised in full on the BBC and widely reported in the press. Organized by the Oxford Union, its former president, the Foreign Secretary, Michael Stewart, agreed on short notice to speak, as did the former American ambassador to South Vietnam, Henry Cabot Lodge. Other speakers during the seven-and-a-half-hour session included Professor Max Beloff; Christopher Hill; Ralph Miliband of the London School of Economics; Commander Edgar Young; William Warbey, M. P.; and Eldon Griffiths, M.P.[39] The political makeup of much of the audience and most of the speakers meant that Stewart and Lodge were in for a rough ride. Stewart gave a speech, penned by the Foreign

Office, which was followed by a rigorous question-and-answer session. The Foreign Secretary's performance confirmed Washington's opinion of him as a loyal ally and staunch public advocate of U.S. action in Vietnam, despite his private questioning of U.S. tactics.

Bruce sent an effusive cable to Rusk describing Stewart's defense of U.S. policy as "brilliant." According to the ambassador the Foreign Secretary

was thoroughly at home and prepared for [the] rigged and biased audience with which he had to deal. During the acrimonious question period he fielded a series of loaded and tendencious questions superbly countering hostile allegations with cool, factual replies shot out without hesitation and avoiding pitfalls with masterly skill. Throughout he gave the impression of having thought out his positions after careful study of the facts and arguments of his opponents. His opening speech was outstanding for its lucidity, moderation, fair-mindedness, command of fact, conciseness, logical structure and exactitude of phrase.

Ironically, Bruce was so impressed with Stewart's arguments that he sent the full text of the speech to the State Department in the belief that it "may find its argumentation useful."[40] Later the same day, Rusk sent a message of appreciation to Stewart, congratulating him on his "brilliant exposition of our mutual vital interests in South East Asia."[41]

The speech was indeed pro-American. When asked at the teach-in how far the British government would go in support of the U.S. policy of escalation, Stewart replied with what was in fact an exposition of Britain's newly formed policy in Vietnam: "We have thought it right to say that we thought the American Government were justified in what they have so far done in Vietnam (uproar) but that the British government reserves completely its right to form and express its own opinions on any future events."[42] The Foreign Secretary's cool performance in the face of constant interruptions contrasted with Ambassador Lodge's. Bruce told Rusk that of the 900 attendees packed into the Oxford Union Hall, according to Lodge, 80–90 percent were hostile to U.S. Vietnam policy and many were communist sympathizers.[43] As The Times noted, Lodge "was given a much rougher ride of moans, groans and hisses, having misjudged the nature of his audience completely with talk of lavish American aid and references to Sir Winston Churchill." When Lodge was faced with such vehement opposition, he eventually asked the chairman of the teach-in, Christopher Hill, to "keep order."[44] On this occasion, the British were more self-assured and confident in explaining what was happening in Vietnam than the Americans.

As indicated by the growing Labour and student protest against the war, the Wilson government was also facing a growing public interest in Vietnam. On June 30, Philip Noel-Baker, M.P., presented a petition signed by 100,000 U.K. citizens to Parliament who were "gravely disturbed by the mounting cruelty and destruction of the war in Vietnam" and "therefore pray that Her Majesty's Government may act as a mediator for peace."[45] Public opinion polls were also registering concern about U.S. action in Vietnam and British support of it. In

April, for the first time the polls indicated that a majority of the British public disapproved of American armed action in Vietnam.[46] By May, 71 percent believed that Britain's role in the conflict was to try to get peace talks started.[47] With his own party, the trade unions, British youth, the general public, and much of the media beginning to ask questions about British policy on Vietnam, Wilson was right to be alarmed about domestic opinion on Vietnam, especially given the tenuous nature of his hold on power.

The Labour leadership began to complain to the Americans. During talks on defense with Robert McNamara in London, Denis Healey explained how the White House could not expect a greater British contribution in the Far East when London felt it had "not been sufficiently consulted by the United States" in relation to either Vietnam or the Dominican Republic. Although McNamara said the White House "did intend to consult with them," Healey went on to say that Wilson had "gone out on a limb supporting U.S. policy" and got "browned off" because he could not reach President Johnson on the telephone. A particular grievance for Wilson had been the mere 12 hours' notice he got regarding the resumption of bombing. McNamara tried to reassure Healey that the United States would consult with the British if it was planning to bomb Hanoi and Haiphong. Healey warned that in that particular case Wilson would definitely want to fly to Washington.[48]

On June 3 McGeorge Bundy sent a rather blunt memorandum to the president on the subject of "the British and Vietnam." It indicated not only Johnson's feelings on the issue but also showed that his advisors felt he was overly sensitive about it.

On a number of occasions you have showed your skepticism when one or another of us has remarked that the British have been very solid and helpful on Vietnam. And of course you have recollections, which the rest of us only have at second hand...Moreover, you feel the wounds of what Home said about busses and what Michael Stewart said about gas, although everyone else has long since forgotten about those particular episodes.[49]

Bundy felt that the president should make an effort with the British, explaining the value of Labour support. "The support of the UK has been of real value internationally—and perhaps of even more value in limiting the howls of our own liberals. It is quite true, of course, that we would get this kind of backing more or less automatically from a Conservative government, but support from Labour is not only harder to get but somewhat more valuable in international terms."[50] Indeed, Bruce informed Rusk a month later that in his opinion British support on Vietnam was stronger under Labour than it would be under a Conservative government. He quoted Mr. Godber, minister of labour in the last Conservative government, who believed "responsibilities of office have obliged Labor leaders to approach [the] question more realistically and in [a] more statesmanlike manner than they would in opposition" and if the Conservatives were in power "their support for US policy would still be strong but if as he anticipated Labour in opposition followed [a] policy closer to that advocated by its left wing" then the result might compel the Tories to adopt a "less forthcoming British Government position." Bruce agreed that "a Conservative Government under fire from Labor opposition might find it more difficult to muster popular support for US policy on this issue."[51]

Bundy also felt it was necessary to defend Wilson personally. "It remains a fact that every experienced observer from David Bruce on down has been astonished by the overall strength and skill of Wilson's defense of our policy in Vietnam and his mastery of his own left wing in the process."[52] Bundy concluded that

the only price we have paid for this support is the price of keeping them reasonably well informed and fending off one ill-advised plan for travel. This is not a very great cost. Moreover, we have had no leaks from the British, and no *public* expression of worry about the length of the pause....

I see no advantage at all in putting them at arms length and thus increasing the risk that they will be tempted to criticize. You have taught us all a great deal about the advantages of Congressional consultation in the last year and a half—I myself believe the same rules apply in diplomatic consultation. After all, we are dealing with human beings in both cases.[53]

This memo provided clear evidence of the president's lack of faith in the British on Vietnam and of his growing impatience with the British need to be seen to be close to him on this. It may also go some way to explaining Johnson's slightly more tolerant position toward Wilson during the second half of the year.

THE COMMONWEALTH PEACE MISSION

Wilson's next peace gambit—or gimmick, as his critics called it—was the larger and grander Commonwealth peace mission. The prime minister was scheduled to chair the weeklong Commonwealth prime ministers' conference being held in London beginning June 17, and he sensed the opportunity to play world statesman.

According to Wilson, after breakfast at Chequers on Monday, June 14, and while pacing the terrace in the sun, he came up with the idea of a three-man Commonwealth mission. The benefits of such an endeavor were obvious. The Commonwealth conference represented a sixth of the total United Nations membership of 117 countries and almost a quarter of the world's population.[54] At that time there were 21 Commonwealth nations.[55] Another strength was that "every political philosophy was represented there, including a majority of non-aligned nations. On the Vietnam issue there were pro-Americans, anti-Americans and the totally uncommitted: a microcosm of the UN and of the world itself. A peace mission sponsored by so widely representative a conference should therefore be accepted—as an individual nation's initiative from any quarter could not be." After Wilson discussed it with Derek Mitchell, his principal private secretary, and Oliver Wright, his Foreign Office private secretary, the proposal was ironed out and explained to the Foreign Secretary by lunchtime the same day. Wilson would "put to the conference at its opening session a proposal to set up, with the authority of the whole Commonwealth, a mission of four prime ministers—or five, if this became necessary to secure balance—representing every point of view on the Vietnam issue. No party to the dispute could feel that the mission was in any way rigged in favour of some preconceived solution."[56] The mission would visit Washington, Peking, Moscow, Saigon, and Hanoi and would also meet with the three members of the International Control Commission (Poland, India, and Canada) and would begin its journey during the first part of July. Stewart approved of the idea, as did the Foreign Office, but felt the White House should be consulted "as a matter of urgency."[57]

The British also thought it essential to get the mission endorsed by the Australians. Sir Robert Menzies, Australian prime minister, approved of the idea during a dinner with the prime minister at the Australian High Commission that evening. At this point, the Australian and British ambassadors in Washington met with Dean Rusk and William Bundy at the State Department. Patrick Dean showed Rusk a written copy of the proposal, and after Rusk had read it Dean pointed out that "the British government did not expect formal approval from the U.S. to go ahead with this initiative but hoped at least to have U.S. acquiescence." He also explained that "the aim of the British and Australian governments was to be helpful to the U.S. It was hoped that by floating this proposal on the first day of the Commonwealth Prime Ministers Conference, the Conference discussion on Vietnam could be turned into constructive channels." It was also hoped that this initiative would "take some of the wind out of the sails of the forthcoming Algiers Conference."[58] This was the Afro–Asian conference planned for June 24 to July 3. This conference of "third world" nations included many communists and nonaligned nationals, and Britain and America feared it might become "an anti-Western rally" passing critical resolutions.[59] Premier Chou En-lai of China would be attending, along with 12 members of the Commonwealth.[60] Rusk said he would confer with the president before giving Dean the U.S. reaction to the planned mission.[61]

The prime minister also explained the initiative in more detail to Ambassador Bruce later that night. Bruce enthusiastically described it as "brilliant," "a terrific idea," and "something with great prospects." Although raising some difficulties with the plan, he agreed that "provided the project could be got off the ground there were bound to be benefits whether it succeeded in its object or not."[62] The prime minister was indeed realistic about the chances of his initiative leading to a conference on Vietnam. Although "not over-hopeful"[63] about this, he too stressed that "it was bound to be a winner whether or not the Mission succeeded."[64] As the Foreign Office recognized, one way it could be a success was by highlighting the seeming intransigence of the Communist nations. "Even if the Mission fails...either through the refusal of Peking or Hanoi to receive it or because these capitals take an utterly negative line, then nonetheless there will be considerable advantage for the Western position in identifying the Governments which are making a Conference impossible. On the worst assumption, namely if Peking and Hanoi refuse to · . .ve the Mission at all, this will be taken as a great snub to Afro-Asian opir:on."[65] In this way, Wilson hoped to ingratiate himself with the Americans.

Bruce and Derek Mitchell discussed whether there should be any direct contact between the prime minister and the president on the mission. Mitchell said that a telephone call initiated by Wilson had been advised against because of the only previous occasion when he had done so, when the experience had been "thoroughly unsatisfactory." Instead, he thought it would be useful if the president could call the prime minister, "confirming whatever reactio:, was coming back to us through the diplomatic channel."[66] Later that night Bruce sent a telegram to Washington giving further detail on the Commonwealth initiative and urging the president to call the prime minister, or at least to send a pleasant personal message to him. The following afternoon Bruce followed this up by telephoning McGeorge Bundy, who informed him that "the President had no liking for hot line conversations, but he might be persuaded to send Wilson a telegram."[67] Attempts continued to convince the president that the British were worth the effort. Johnson did not call Wilson but did send a cable outlining "the President's own thinking about Vietnam at this stage."[68] The president was apparently "keenly interested in the Prime Minister's imaginative proposal" and welcomed "the readiness of the Prime Ministers to make another try" at ending the intransigence in Hanoi and Peking. He also said that he fully agreed with the view that "even if the mission fails in its immediate purpose, it should succeed in showing just where the responsibility lies."[69]

Whether drafted by LBJ or an advisor, this cable reflected the sentiment in Washington regarding the mission. Dean informed 10 Downing Street that the prime minister's initiative had been "very well received in Washington" and "so far from presenting any real problems has been positively welcomed."[70] That evening Bruce met Wilson again to convey Washington's "warm approval" of the initiative and its relatively minor reservation on the route the mission might follow. The Americans preferred that the first and last visits not be to Washington.[71]

At the cabinet meeting on Tuesday, June 15, Wilson used his plan to relieve the mounting pressure from his government colleagues to take action on Vietnam. Barbara Castle admits she went along "determined to have a showdown about Vietnam" but was forestalled by the prime minister when he opened the meeting with "a reference to mysterious negotiations of which he had high hopes. He and the Foreign Secretary were in the middle of a very delicate operation and he asked us not to press for more details at this stage. I merely contented myself with asking whether Vietnam would be discussed at the Commonwealth PMS' conference. After trying to hedge for a moment, he replied, 'Undoubtedly.' "[72] So, before the Commonwealth conference had even started, the prime minister and the Foreign Office had already finalized a great deal of their plans for the proposed mission. It was decided a three-man mission would be best; the prime minister would chair it and the other two members would be chosen by the conference, one from an Asian nation, the other from an African nation. The mission would report back to the Commonwealth prime ministers collectively and also to the interested governments and to the world at large. The governments concerned would be asked immediately if they would receive the mission. Only at this point would the United States publicly respond to the initiative.[73]

Wilson was now faced with the task of getting the other 20 Commonwealth nations to agree to his plans. As the presidents and prime ministers arrived in London, Wilson saw them one by one, either at 10 Downing Street or at their hotels, to broach the subject. He could not be too specific about the details of the plan because of the danger of leaks. His idea was, however, initially welcomed by Lester Pearson of Canada; President Ayub Khan of Pakistan; President Kaunda of Zambia; and, it appeared, President Nyerere of Tanzania, who, according to Wilson, was "prepared to accept it, without question, though equally without enthusiasm."[74]

On the morning the conference began the British informed Bundy at the White House that the prime minister would "now go into battle . . . with good hopes of bringing off this coup."[75] His high hopes for the conference were also revealed to Barbara Castle the same morning. "Harold, coming in to answer his PQS [Parliamentary Questions], slipped in next to me on the bench. He was as excited as a schoolboy: said he had worked out his peace initiative on Vietnam, sounded out a number of Commonwealth PMS and was just off to put it to them. If all went well, he hoped to be able to interrupt parliamentary business at about 6 pm to make his statement. It was 'very big.' "[76]

The official opening of the conference took place at Marlborough House on the morning of Thursday, June 17. The first working session began at 3:30 P.M. when Wilson persuaded the conferees to meet in restricted session in the chairman's room.[77] Wilson put the proposition to the members, and it appears to have been "warmly endorsed" by most of them. However, despite his earlier apparent willingness to go along with the initiative, Julius Nyerere of Tanzania was now not happy with it. According to Wilson, Nyerere "felt that for us to put forward even the neutral posture of an independent mission would appear to condone 'American aggression' " and "was also deeply concerned about the reaction our proposal might have in China." And,

the longer the argument continued and the greater the number of Commonwealth countries who supported me, the sharper became his objections. . . . As the evening wore on he made very clear, what I had feared all along, that while he was quite willing to attend a Commonwealth conference and play an active part in it, he was concerned also to take no action which would prejudice the success of the conference which was immediately to follow ours, the second Afro-Asian "Third World" conference, in Algiers.[78]

Despite Nyerere's objections, Wilson was adamant that a decision be made that night. So by 8:30 P.M. the conference had agreed to issue a communiqué announcing the mission. Tanzania still objected but did so covertly due to the "long-established convention of unanimity at Commonwealth conferences."[79] The only changes to Wilson's original plan were in the mission's format. According to Bruce, after "a tremendous row amongst the Prime Ministers ... Wilson had to shift ground."[80] The conference decided to appoint five heads of government, and none of them were from Asian countries. Instead, after much discussion the leaders of Britain, Nigeria, Ghana, Ceylon, and Trinidad were chosen.[81]

The prime minister emerged from the talks to give a television interview. Together with Bob Menzies, he outlined briefly what had just taken place. After that, around midnight, when there was a break in parliamentary business, Wilson announced the initiative to the House, where it was generally well received. The press used words such as "original" and "bold and imaginative" to describe it.[82] Immediate reaction was not all favorable, however. Castle "was disappointed by the nature of Harold's 'very big' achievement" because "there was no statement of principles to suggest the basis of a solution." It struck her, among others, as "a gesture rather than conviction."[83]

Wilson's portrayal of Commonwealth unity on the initiative was soon shattered. Later that evening at Wilson's Commonwealth reception at No. 10 for foreign ministers, it emerged that Murumbi of Kenya was also upset by the initiative. According to Castle, he was "very disgruntled by Harold's initiative, said he had rushed the conference too much. Anyway, it was quite wrong that Harold should be chairman of the mission: he was too committed to the American line. 'We expected better things of a Labour Government.' "[84] Although the next day's press gave Wilson's plan a "glowing reception," as Barbara Castle put it, the prime minister still had to deal with the "rumbles of discontent" among some of the Commonwealth delegates.[85] Wilson's handling of the previous day's events was one problem. Apparently when Nyerere had asked Wilson how he could record his disagreement, the prime minister had said, "You can't." The next day Nyerere "came out categorically against it as putting China in the dock."[86] He argued during a BBC interview that "the Commonwealth as a group should not appear to be backing up Mr. Wilson or the United States on Vietnam. We must not appear to be aligned in any action we take. Already an attempt has been made by the British Government [the Gordon Walker mission] and the other side has said 'No.' What is it we are suggesting which will appear to the other side to be a new initiative!" Murumbi also publicly declared his problems with the mission. He said that although Kenya supported the initiative, "[I]t is opposed to Britain or any other country which has committed itself on the issue being a member of the proposed mission."[87] Another problem was the insistence by some of the Commonwealth representatives that the mission see the Vietcong. This was "especially distracting" but was solved "by agreement that if the Viet Cong turn up in Hanoi as part of the North Vietnamese governmental apparatus, they can express opinions."[88] In private, the British had already reassured Washington that the Vietcong would be seen only in Hanoi.

Despite some disagreement, the prime ministers of the British Commonwealth went ahead and issued a joint message on Friday, June 18, to the United Nations secretary-general and to the heads of government of the United States, USSR, the People's Republic of China, the Republic of Vietnam (South Vietnam), and the Democratic Republic of Vietnam (North Vietnam). It expressed "deep concern at the increasingly serious situation developing in Viet-Nam" and suggested that a mission "make contact with the Governments principally concerned with the problem of Viet-Nam in order to seek their views as to the circumstances in which a Conference on Viet-Nam might be held." They were also asked whether they could be prepared to receive the four leaders representing the Commonwealth some time in July.[89] The same day David Bruce recognized that "the Prime Minister's imaginative conception of a Commonwealth mission" was "in disorder" and felt it necessary to telephone George Ball in Washington to "caution him against anyone in our Government making premature plans in connection with what may finally eventuate here."[90]

To counteract the now numerous diversionary press briefings by disgruntled members of the conference, Wilson came up with the idea of the mission announcing a cease-fire "in order to maintain the momentum."[91] Although Washington was willing to receive the mission, it had already informed Wilson that it was reluctant to institute a pause during the duration of the mission's tour. So when by Saturday, June 19, the mission members had proceeded to preparatory work for the tour and issued a statement clarifying the situation, although Wilson would have liked it, the United States insisted no mention be made of a cease-fire during the duration of the mission. Still, the statement appealed "to all parties concerned to show the utmost restraint in military operations as a step towards the total cease-fire which the mission hopes will be established at the earliest possible opportunity."[92]

Very soon negative responses to the proposed mission emerged from Hanoi and Peking. Chou En-lai, Chinese prime minister, denounced the initiative on June 19 as "a manoeuvre in support of the U.S. 'peace talks' hoax" and predicted its "ignominious failure." On June 21 an article in the Chinese *People's Daily* described Wilson as a "nitwit" and said the mission was a "continuation of the British Labour Government's constant efforts to serve as an errand boy for the United States." Hanoi's leading newspaper, *Nhan Dan*, described the peace initiative as a "vicious scheme."[93] Nevertheless, Wilson retained a measure of optimism, feeling that the Soviets were the key to the whole operation, and that the North Vietnamese and the Chinese might change their minds. However, on June 23 the Soviets refused to receive the mission, followed by the Chinese two days later.

The Americans cabled the prime minister regarding press reports indicating the mission might still go to Washington.[94] On June 24 Bruce noted,

If it should turn out that visit will only be made to U Thant, President Johnson, and the Government in Saigon, our officials are apprehensive of a call at Washington, thinking the Afro-Asian representatives could make remarks so hostile to our own policy that it would accentuate seriously our public opinion and Congressional problems. We were therefore instructed to make clear to the PM and Foreign Minister our belief that a mission of this kind would make no contribution to a peaceful settlement, but would only seriously impair the U.S. position and cause great ill will at home.[95]

By June 27, Washington and Saigon had officially accepted the invitation to give their views to the mission, although not necessarily agreeing to receive it.

By the end of the conference a set of "instructions for the mission" had been established:

(i)   a suspension of all United States air attacks on North Vietnam;

(ii) a North Vietnamese undertaking to prevent the movement of military forces or assistance or material to South Vietnam;

(iii) a total cease-fire on all sides to enable a conference to be convened to seek a peaceful settlement;

(iv) the objectives of such a conference might be to:

    (a) end the war in Vietnam;
    (b) secure the withdrawal of all foreign military presence from Vietnam and the neutralization of the area;
    (c) establish, for a period, an international peace force, under the auspices of the Geneva Agreement, to safeguard peace in Vietnam;
    (d) establish principles for the eventual unification of the country through free and internationally supervised elections.

Wilson wrote later that getting this set of guidelines through a conference of 21 states was "no mean achievement."[96] However, the Americans were troubled by these guidelines in that they appeared to suggest that in return for ending the bombing, the Americans would accept an "assurance" from the Communist countries to cease their activities. Rusk was also annoyed that they appeared to suggest that a cease-fire would be a precondition for talks, something the Americans had no intention of agreeing to at that stage.[97]

Ultimately the Commonwealth peace mission failed. The tour did not get off the ground. It was, however, Wilson's most ambitious and most serious attempt to establish peace talks. For that reason there has been much speculation as to his motives in proposing it. Wilson justified it largely on humanitarian and strategic grounds: it was a genuine attempt to end a costly and risky war. Though this may have been Wilson's ultimate objective, he acknowledged that the mission was highly unlikely to succeed. The mission could, however, help him deal with more immediate problems. First, such a high-profile initiative would greatly ease his domestic political problems. Indeed, Richard Crossman, minister of housing and local government, immediately labeled it a "stunt," feeling it was "designed to calm the left-wing of the Party."[98]

A possible second reason that Wilson pressed so hard for the peace mission on the first day of the conference lay in the increasing tensions within the Commonwealth over Rhodesia. Crossman began to suspect this when the conference had finished and he managed to discuss the initiative with Wilson while walking through the corridors of the Houses of Parliament. Crossman expressed his anxiety that the prime minister would have been away for about a month had the mission gone ahead. Wilson replied that it would have been only a fortnight but added, "Anyway, I think we have got most of the value we can out of it already." Crossman interpreted these words as meaning Wilson had managed to prevent a breakup of the conference on the first day over Rhodesia. "Black Africa is now virtually at war with Rhodesia whereas the white Commonwealth is still trying to keep the peace. In order to postpone that row and create a better atmosphere, Harold needed a personal initiative on the first day and in this sense I have no doubt that the stunt was brilliantly successful."[99] Wilson did indeed manage to get the conference to focus constructively on Vietnam and avoided a major discussion on Rhodesia. The conference's final communiqué merely talked about the possibility of summoning a "constitutional conference" on white Rhodesia in due course.

Crossman rightly concluded that the Prime Minister "had pulled off a diplomatic coup which was popular with public opinion, eased the situation in his own Party and prevented a potential breakdown of the Commonwealth Conference. One can't be surprised if he is rather pleased with himself."[100] It is certainly illuminating to see how the mission proposal was received. The Fabian Society's journal, *Venture*, was effusive in its praise of Wilson and the Commonwealth mission on Vietnam, saying that it

may fail in its objectives, but in its initiation some useful modifications of attitude have been produced. Britain, Australia, New Zealand and Malaysia have participated in a demand for the cessation of US bombing raids. Two nations whose friendship China does not wish to lose, Tanzania and Pakistan, have joined the demand to North Vietnam to stop the transit of military men and goods to the South. Three Western governments closely identified with US policy in Vietnam have joined in saying that their mission must meet the Vietcong, thus giving public, if not quite "diplomatic", recognition—in defiance of the US...These modifications of attitude are useful in themselves and mark a breaking down of the rigid positions. The Commonwealth mission, whatever it achieves in Vietnam, has stimulated some fresh thought elsewhere.... If one of Mr. Wilson's objects in calling the Commonwealth conference was to help rally the British Labour movement behind him, we can only report that with us he has succeeded.[101]

In the short term the Commonwealth peace mission had other positive political consequences. It was recognized that through the initiative Wilson had gained a measure of independence from the United States on Vietnam. Bruce noted that Wilson "approves generally of our policy in Vietnam, believing we are trapped, but reserves the right to criticize—as witness his calls for a cessation of bombings."[102] Tony Benn also interpreted Wilson's efforts in this way:

The Commonwealth Conference has allowed him to put on a Commonwealth hat in the place of the NATO hat which the Foreign Office is always trying to screw on to him. He has disengaged himself from his previous commitment on Vietnam with enormous skill....The Commonwealth Prime Ministers' conference has made a big difference but I don't think it's permeated through to ordinary people on the Left yet that it has permitted Harold to disengage himself from a close alignment with the American position.[103]

Unfortunately for Wilson, although the Commonwealth peace mission did temporarily quiet dissent on the Labour backbench, it was soon seen by many as yet another of Wilson's gimmicks. It is doubtful, however, that Wilson viewed his initiatives in this way. Some of Wilson's key advisors suggest that Wilson's peace initiatives were not intended as peace gimmicks but that he managed to turn them into such by his behavior.[104] Whereas previous prime ministers had been praised for their peace gambits—Macmillan flying to Moscow during World War II, Eden at Geneva in 1954—Wilson's manner and reputation prevented him from receiving much credit for his efforts. When he announced this particular initiative to the House of Commons Wilson had been aware that he should not arouse expectations unduly and therefore was careful to stress that the chances of success were not great. However, in a sense Wilson had already oversold the initiative before it became public, inflating his proposal by describing it to colleagues as "big." In addition his television announcement of the plan appeared too flamboyant. Crossman described it in the following terms:

I...was just settling down to Michael Stewart's teach-in on Vietnam at Oxford when it was interrupted for a news bulletin. There was the Prime Minister announcing the Commonwealth mission to Vietnam and Bob Menzies clapping him on the back and saying, "I give this trip to you, old boy. Really it was your idea." The political matiness and gimmickry of the proceedings were in startling contrast with Stewart's performance which preceded and followed it (he was a brilliant television success and put the American case more competently than any American has ever put it).[105]

As Lester Pearson, the Canadian prime minister, said privately of the British prime minister after a Commonwealth conference, "Harold Wilson has been superb. He has managed to convey every human emotion, except sincerity—even when he was sincere."[106] Wilson's apparent concern with his own personal prestige, his playing of the role of the "honest broker," troubled many. For instance, if he really wanted the Commonwealth peace mission to succeed, he need not have insisted on leading the initiative himself. The fact that he did led the Communist powers to suspect, correctly, that he was not working entirely independently of the United States.

THE HAROLD DAVIES VISIT TO HANOI

Wilson's reputation for gimmicks grew even further when he sent Harold Davies, M.P., to Hanoi. Even Wilson's loyal chief whip, Edward Short, thought it "his most colourful move so far."[107]

Although the signs coming out of Moscow and Hanoi were not good, the nature of the replies from the Soviets and the North Vietnamese left Wilson with some hopes for the Commonwealth mission. He informed the cabinet on July 1 that the Soviets "had evaded a direct response by suggesting that the effective decision lay with the Government of North Vietnam; and the latter, who were clearly subject to conflicting pressures from the Chinese and Soviet Government, had so far maintained an ambiguous attitude."[108] Wilson was alluding to the lack of an official refusal from Hanoi to receive the mission, and by July 6 the prime minister was informing President Johnson that "nearly two weeks have passed without the North Vietnamese imitating the Chinese example of final and formal rejection. Hanoi is obviously receiving conflicting advice from Moscow and Peking and is temporising accordingly. This leaves the door slightly ajar."[109] Wilson was determined to use this gap to further pursue the idea of the mission.

Joint parliamentary secretary in the ministry of pensions and national insurance and close friend of the prime minister, Harold Davies had been a regular visitor to Hanoi, had met some of its leaders, and had written extensively on Ho Chi Minh. He was considered someone who might be able to establish a link to Hanoi in secret. At Wilson's prompting, Davies contacted North Vietnamese journalists in London who "constituted an unofficial North Vietnamese presence"[110] to see if it might be worth his visiting Hanoi again. An affirmative answer came back, and Davies was told a visa would await him in Phnom Penh. Donald Murray, a specialist on Vietnam at the Foreign Office, was to accompany him. The Americans were apparently happy for Davies to try to make contact with the North Vietnamese, but he had no authority to speak for them. Sir Paul Gore-Booth found that Bruce "seemed to be quite relaxed about this initiative, though not surprised by the difficulties and not optimistic about the upshot."[111]

As Wilson put it, "[U]nfortunately, whatever hopes the Davies visit might have justified were dashed by a serious, indeed disastrous, leak in London, while he was on the way."[112] It was rumored that the leak had come out of the Foreign Office. Whether true or not, British diplomats were extremely dismissive of this particular initiative. Gore-Booth later admitted that "one could but advise, with all the respect due to Mr. Harold Davies' personal qualities and knowledge of the area, that his mission also could only be a failure. There seemed at the moment nothing that we could do."[113] Another senior Foreign Office advisor thought it was "an absolutely ludicrous mission to Vietnam but it gave him [Wilson] a respite for about three weeks."[114]

Davies visited Hanoi between July 8 and 13. Possibly due to the leak, Davies was not allowed to meet Ho Chi Minh or Prime Minister Pham Van Dong, instead being allowed about seven hours with the secretariat of the Vietnam Fatherland Front Central Committee. Murray was not even allowed in the country. Davies's brief was straightforward. He should tell the North Vietnamese leaders that even if they believed their struggle was just and that they could achieve a military victory, they should "explore the possibility of negotiation" in order to save thousands of lives and prevent the risk of the war spreading.[115] Davies found, however, that Hanoi exuded great confidence in its conviction of imminent victory and showed no signs of responding to the Commonwealth mission.[116] Still, he returned to London arguing that his trip had been worthwhile because he believed his portrayal of British views on Vietnam would be gone through and "not be ignored by the North Vietnamese leaders."[117] He contended that his defense of the British position and the Commonwealth mission created intensive discussions and that "this was the first time that any detailed argument from the West had been heard in Hanoi."[118] Wilson admitted that there had been no progress as a result of the Davies mission but thought "it might have done something to shift the ice-pack."[119] This was wishful thinking. The Davies mission did, however, succeed in keeping the Labour backbenchers under control. During a two-day foreign affairs debate on July 19 and 20, which Wilson opened with an explanation of British support for the United States on Vietnam, the atmosphere in the Commons remained muted. According to Bruce, the prime minister "evidently feels that if Davies trip had limited international results, it had been very helpful domestically in calming his own backbenchers."[120]

The British Foreign Office decided it was now time to reassess Britain's position on Vietnam and negotiations. Never altogether happy with Wilson's initiatives, by the summer of 1965 an obvious tension had developed between the prime minister and much of the Foreign Office. Moreover, the Foreign Office itself was divided on the best way to deal with the Americans over Vietnam.

On July 12, James Cable, head of the South East Asia Department at the Foreign Office, argued in a key memorandum that "British efforts to promote negotiation have relied on the argument that a compromise settlement would be preferable to the risk of escalation entailed by the pursuit of outright victory by either side. This argument commands widespread sympathy at home and, among those not directly involved, also abroad. But we should not suppose that it is yet accepted by the actual contestants." Cable then outlined the current thinking in Washington, Saigon, Moscow, Peking, and Hanoi. Peking and Hanoi believed that the British peace initiative had been undertaken at the instigation of the U.S. government. Therefore, "[E]ach fresh initiative on our part will have reinforced ... the conviction that the Americans are desperate and are trying to save by negotiation what they now realize will be lost if the fighting continues."[121] According to Cable, all involved parties interpreted what happened at Geneva in 1954 differently, which meant a return to the Geneva conference was fraught with problems. He concluded, therefore, that "in these circumstances it is most unlikely that further efforts on our part will induce the Communists to change their minds and offer acceptable terms for negotiation. On the contrary, further British initiatives will probably do more harm than good, by reinforcing the Communist conviction that the Americans are on the run, and will capitulate completely if pressed sufficiently hard."[122] Cable was not optimistic about the prospects of the United States achieving much military success in Vietnam and argued that the British now had two alternatives, "to remain passive and hope that intensified American military activity will induce the Communists to negotiate" or "to persuade the U.S. Government to negotiate on terms acceptable to the Communists." Believing the first option "would involve unacceptable risk" and the second one presented a real danger to Anglo-American relations that would involve the United States abandoning its South Vietnamese allies and thereby risking America's credibility as an ally, Cable came up with his own alternative solution to the problem. He wondered if it would be possible for the Americans to withdraw from Vietnam on the proviso that the South Vietnamese leadership be offered "a fresh start outside South Viet-Nam." He went into more detail. "Supposing, for instance, that there are as many as a million irreconcilable anti-Communists in South Viet-Nam, could the U.S. Government undertake to evacuate them all and establish them on some Pacific Island? Formosa would obviously be unsuitable, but there are plenty of under-populated islands in the Philippines and there may well be possibilities in the Anglo-French Condominium of the New Hebrides or in other island colonies of the South Pacific."[123] This notion of "towing the 'loyal' Vietnamese out into the Pacific" received short shrift from Cable's superiors, not least because it was impractical.[124] The problem was beginning to look insoluble to some within the Foreign Office.

E. H. Peck, head of the Far Eastern department, agreed with Cable's ultimate suggestion that Britain "should abstain from further public initiatives," believing the government had "done enough to demonstrate our good will and to do more would be detrimental to our own prestige and future influence as well as, in all probability, actually to impair the chance of negotiations." Instead a public campaign against Communist intransigence should be mounted, coupled with a private warning to the Communists that "the Americans mean business."[125]

Lord Walston, undersecretary of state for foreign affairs, took a harder and more optimistic line than Cable. On August 2 he wrote to Stewart arguing that the only way Hanoi would come to the negotiating table was when it was convinced it could not win the war. To this end, Walston felt that "the immediate job of the West...is to convince them of this fact." He recognized that "the most obvious way of doing this is to step up the bombardment, even to the extent of, for instance, bombing the dykes and flooding much of the North's fertile rice-land before the crop can be harvested." However, Walston not only doubted the effectiveness of bombing—it could strengthen the will to resist rather than weaken it—but also recognized that due to the unpopularity of bombing, this action would make Britain's job of "holding the line" very much harder. Intensification of America's military effort through ground operations would have "none of these drawbacks," and he argued, therefore, and Michael Stewart agreed with him, that "the most useful thing that we can do at the present time vis-a-vis the Americans is to try to convince them of these facts.

They will find it unpalatable because their instinct is to look for quick results by massive air superiority; and also because plodding jungle warfare is not the trade to which their soldiers have been trained. Nevertheless I believe we should try whenever the opportunity presents itself."[126]

At the end of August Cable wrote another discursive memorandum entitled "the possibility of a negotiated solution of the conflict in Viet-Nam." This memo considered what was "practicable" rather than "desirable."[127] He admitted that this was crystal-ball gazing because Britain remained "distinctly uncertain about the real intentions in this matter of the U.S. Government."[128] He tried to work out why over the previous few months the United States sought negotiations and progressively relaxed the conditions on which they would enter into such negotiations. He concluded that since the fall of President Diem, the political stability of South Vietnam had deteriorated and the Vietcong insurrection, with ever increased support from North Vietnam, had made steady headway in the south. And the costs in money and lives of the American efforts in Vietnam had risen, so that "the United States have become increasingly and understandingly reluctant to continue indefinitely escalating their efforts in pursuit of an ever receding objective." He then asked how far the quest for negotiations implied an abandonment of the basic U.S. objective—an independent, non-Communist South Vietnam—and how far it was purely tactical. He came up with three possible interpretations:

(a)   The United States Government are tired of the endless conflict in Viet-Nam and want negotiations in the hope that these would produce a facesaving formula enabling the United States to extract themselves from Viet-Nam without major damage to their prestige, even if this entails a disguised or deferred abandonment of their basic objectives;

(b)   for the reasons suggested above, the United States want negotiations, but have not admitted even to themselves that such negotiations would be likely to entail a disguised or deferred abandonment of their basic objective;

(c)   the United States Government still maintain their basic objective, but are advocating negotiations as a propaganda device intended to improve their posture in the eyes of Western and uncommitted public opinion at the expense of the Communists, who could thus be represented as intransigent warmongers.

Cable surmised that (b) seemed the most likely interpretation but acknowledged that American thinking might contain elements of (a) and (c) as well. Nevertheless, Cable outlined the various negotiation scenarios dependent on U.S. military success, defeat, or stalemate. He admitted, however, that neither side would make major concessions as long as there was any prospect of avoiding this by early military victory. Either way, he did not expect the United States to succeed in permanently eradicating or reducing long-term the Communist threat: "[T]he most we can hope for is a settlement enabling the United States to withdraw from Viet-Nam without major damage to American prestige and offering the South Viet-Namese a slight chance of maintaining a non-

Communist independence for a period of years." He therefore wondered whether

it would be...worthwhile to give the Americans a suitably bowdlerised version of this memorandum. Hitherto we have rather tended to regard Viet-Nam as too delicate and embarrassing a subject for frank or far-reaching Anglo–American discussion, but I wonder whether it might not be in the interests of both Governments to break this tradition and exchange views with no holds barred. There might be some hurt feelings, but, once these had subsided, we should have a much better idea of American intentions and future Anglo–American cooperation might be facilitated.[129]

Cable's suggestion came at a time when the United States "appeared" to be increasing its chances of military success. Etherington-Smith, British ambassador in Saigon, was so optimistic about this that he felt that there might not even be a negotiation in the end. Peck too thought Cable too pessimistic, agreeing with Etherington-Smith that "it is true that US might is now beginning to bite on the Viet Cong and that we could see a US negotiation from strength." Not surprisingly, therefore, Peck felt Cable's paper might go to Dean in Washington, "inviting his comments on the desirability of discussing it with the State Department but without doing so at this stage."[130] Cable therefore wrote to the British embassy on September 6 to seek its opinion. The reaction from Washington did not come until the end of October and was extremely cool in relation to Cable's suggestion of "frank" discussions with the Americans on Vietnam. Nigel Trench of the British embassy in Washington wrote that "we do not believe that the time is yet ripe for a 'no holds barred' exchange of views." The reason that the British embassy "would advise strongly against" any such action was that it did not believe American

thinking has reached a point where either we or they would get the best out of frank talks. Indeed, at the working level there is remarkably little indication that their thinking is anywhere near a coherent policy, and the Australians have reached very much the same conclusion. You may think that this is a sign either of short-sightedness or of a basic reluctance to consider negotiations at all, now that the situation on the ground in South Vietnam has reached a slightly more hopeful stage, but I do not think that this is the case.[131]

It was also pointed out that "the State Department at least—and I believe also the political side of the Pentagon—are under no illusions as to the determination of the North Vietnamese."[132] Trench also conveyed that, apart from the question of timing,

H.M.G.'s chances of influencing negotiations in the direction we think desirable would be prejudiced if we tried to push the Americans into discussions on the basis of a British paper. In view of our position as Co-Chairman they will naturally want in due course to take us into their confidence, if only to ensure that we play the game in the way that they think most effective, but since they are bearing the brunt of the fighting and expense, they would probably wonder why we thought we had the right to tell them how to play the hand, and this could lessen our chances of influencing them in the right direction. We must not forget that both their position and ours have changed since 1954, although this does not mean the U.S. Government under-estimate the value of the support which their Vietnam policy has received from H.M.G.

Trench therefore suggested that the British embassy keep a very careful watch on the situation and inform London when the time was right for negotiations with the Johnson administration.[133] By December 1965 the Foreign Office concluded that "in the international field no further initiatives are being planned."[134]

THE JULY DECISION TO AMERICANIZE THE WAR

When General William Westmoreland, head of the U.S. Military Assistance Command, Vietnam (MACV) requested an additional 150,000 troops in late June 1965, members of the Johnson administration debated the utility of a major U.S. troop commitment in Vietnam. Their deliberations took five weeks, until July 28, when President Johnson made up his mind and committed the United States to a ground war in South Vietnam. He did not make this decision easily and knew the odds against achieving the goal of an independent, anti-Communist South Vietnam were great. But most of his advisors, military and civilian, felt that even though it would be a long war with little chance of the United States winning, the alternatives would be disastrous in terms of U.S. prestige and credibility. The president therefore announced his decision to send 50,000 troops to Vietnam immediately, bringing the total number of troops stationed there to 125,000. He also admitted that "additional forces will be needed later, and they will be sent as requested."[135]

After the December 1964 refusal by Wilson to send troops to Vietnam, the Americans were reluctant to ask Britain to reconsider, at least not directly. British involvement was still very much desired, however. In discussions of a British troop commitment, American hopes and desires varied widely. The fact that Rusk talked of a brigade and Bundy of a platoon or a battalion indicates that the request for military help was largely symbolic. A brigade would have been a substantial commitment on the part of Great Britain, perhaps involving up to 6,000 troops. A platoon, on the other hand, would have been a much smaller gesture, involving only 12 to 24 soldiers. The precise figures appear to have been irrelevant; the important thing was the conspicuous presence of the British flag.

In early July 1965, according to Australian Foreign Minister Hanluck, Dean Rusk told him that "whilst the US Government had not asked for any British contribution in Viet Nam and had no intention of making any such request, the British would be well advised to send a brigade to Viet Nam if they valued American public opinion. In Mr. Rusk's view any such British gesture would have an immense impact on the US."[136] And, shortly after Wilson's visit to

Washington in July 1965, Sir Patrick Dean cabled the prime minister and Foreign Secretary with the following information. "In speaking of Viet Nam Bundy volunteered to me with much emphasis that what the President wanted from us was a military contribution in the form of men on the ground. Two platoons were suggested or even less or a military field hospital. Bundy said that the result of such a contribution would be worth several hundred million dollars."[137]

Shortly before publicly announcing the Americanization of the Vietnam War, the president sent a message to 29 countries contributing assistance to Vietnam, including Great Britain. The message served two purposes. First, it served as a warning of the American decision to commit to a land war. Second, the president asked for further third-party help in the conflict. While reassuring the message recipients that in addition to this major additional military effort he would also continue to make every political and diplomatic effort to find peace, and that U.S. objectives would still be the same, he argued for a multilateral effort.

In this situation I must express to you my deep personal conviction that the prospect of peace in Vietnam will be greatly increased in the measure that the necessary efforts of the US are supported and shared by other nations which share our purposes and concerns. I know that your Government has already signalled its interest and concern by giving assistance. I now ask that you give most earnest consideration to increasing that assistance in ways which will give a clear signal to the world—and perhaps specifically to Hanoi—of the solidarity of international support for resistance to aggression in Vietnam and for a peaceful settlement in Vietnam.[138]

Unlike Australia, Canada, the Netherlands, and the Philippines, who immediately expressed a willingness to consider an additional effort, the British did not respond right away. Instead the Foreign Secretary and the prime minister discussed the message for four days before informing Patrick Dean on July 30 that "as there was no explicit request for a British military contribution" it was "better to say nothing about this" in the prime minister's reply. Instead, the Foreign Secretary instructed Dean to make clear to McGeorge Bundy orally or "in whatever way you think best" that "there is in fact no question of a British military contribution, no matter how small, to the war in Viet Nam. Not only do I want to forestall another and more explicit message to the PM but, the longer hopes of a British military contribution are cherished in Washington, the greater the risks of a leak and of Anglo–American disagreement becoming public knowledge." The task of straight talking was delegated to the ambassador, who was given a long list of arguments he could make use of.[139] He could stress, among other things, Britain's existing, and planned, civilian and surgical role in Vietnam; that a military contribution would be to the detriment of Britain's defense of Malaysia; the political repercussions of a British military role in Vietnam; and the British belief that an increased British role in Vietnam "might well compromise our position as Co-Chairman of the Geneva Conference."[140]

Given Stewart's open and heartfelt support of U.S. policy in Vietnam, it is surprising how strongly he felt about this latest request, although no doubt his position was delivered more diplomatically by the ambassador. Despite his own personal feelings on the issue, Stewart clearly recognized the political balancing act Wilson faced in trying to keep his own party behind him while remaining loyal to Britain's major ally. Considering that Britain was at the time delicately negotiating with the Americans regarding the latest sterling scare, the vehemence of Stewart's views, however indirectly expressed, reflected the fact that sticking to the "no troops" position was imperative if the Labour government wanted to ensure its own survival. Stewart outlined this in further detail for Dean, saying that the president,

himself such a master politician, will readily appreciate what an effort it has been, in terms of the British political situation, for Ministers to maintain as much support as they have of American policy in Viet Nam, not least at a time when economic difficulties have compelled them to follow domestic policies falling short of the hopes of their supporters. Ministers have only been able to maintain their Viet Nam policy, because they have been able to assure critics that Britain is at least not involved militarily. Our attitude has also been of great benefit to the United States Government in terms of international opinion, if our example has helped to restrain a number of European and Commonwealth countries from giving more vocal and forcible expression to their own apprehension about the course of American policy in Viet Nam. In many cases these other Governments are also under pressure from their Parliaments or public opinion.[141]

Wilson's official reply to Johnson on August 2 was nowhere near as blunt; on the contrary, it was extremely supportive verbally, at times even sycophantic. "I have followed with admiration the careful balance you have throughout maintained between determined resistance to aggression and a patient insistence on your readiness to negotiate an honourable settlement. . . . In the face of the persistent North Vietnamese refusal to negotiate, I can see no alternative to your policy of strengthening your forces in South Vietnam." Nevertheless, in relation to the request for additional practical help, Wilson did repeat Stewart's arguments.

I wish there was more we could do to help you, but I need not remind you how far our contribution to international peacekeeping has already overstrained our resources and our economy . . . Moreover, I should be loath in present circumstances to run the risk of spoiling any chances we may have of fulfilling the functions which were originally accepted as co-chairmen of the Geneva Conference and have more recently tried to develop afresh by means of the Commonwealth initiative.[142]

Dean delivered the prime minister's message to the president via McGeorge Bundy. At the time the president was in Texas, but Bundy thanked Dean on the president's behalf and described the prime minister's reply as "a help." He also said the president was "well aware of the very great difficulty in political terms of a British military contribution at the present time" but admitted that "the important thing from the President's point of view was to have made the request." Afterward, Dean reminded the Foreign Secretary that it would be "most helpful" if he could tell Bundy that progress was being made in providing police advisors and getting a civilian surgical team together.[143] Toward the end of September, a British medical project for Vietnam had been assembled, initially led by a physician from Great Ormond Street Hospital. On hearing the news of the successful arrangement of the medical team, Wilson commented to Oliver Wright, "I take it we are telling the Americans."[144]

This high-level approach on Vietnam was, however, only part of the picture. Britain's position on Vietnam was also being discussed fervently and in detail in relation to the latest sterling crisis and Britain's ongoing defense review.

THE FUTURE OF ANGLO–AMERICAN RELATIONS: VIETNAM, STERLING, AND EAST OF SUEZ

At the beginning of June, the Johnson administration began to consider its options should the British economy, and the pound in particular, run into difficulties before winter.[145] Considering the president's growing impatience with the British, particularly over Vietnam, it was felt increasingly necessary to explain the Labour government's problems to the president. David Klein, a White House aide, drafted a memo for the president outlining the shape of the trouble for Anglo–American relations. Britain's economic problems, particularly its balance-of-payments deficit, continued, and although Wilson had rejected devaluation and "tried to meet the problem through tight money, tight budget, import restrictions, controls on capital movements and 'persuasion' on the wage-price front," the Americans were worried that this might not keep the speculators quiet.[146]

In the face of another attack on sterling, it was thought that Wilson would have the choice of either dampening the economy even more and risking a full-blown recession, imposing full-fledged exchange controls, devaluing, or letting things slide until the speculators forced a devaluation. The result of the last two options would have serious consequences for the United States by producing "heavy and sustained pressure on the dollar" and the serious possibility that Britain would turn inward and would move "away from selective international responsibilities."[147]

Klein explained to the president, in some detail, British weariness of sterling difficulties:

[T]he strain of coping day by day compounds the trouble. Ministers, reportedly, have lost a lot of steam. So have senior civil servants on whom any British Government depends. Walking their economic tightrope soaks up energy, saps initiatives, and colors their approach to every policy, emphatically including their political commitments overseas. Not only must they now consider cutting back commitments, they are also hard put to conceive of adding anything. This adds to their difficulty in responding to you in Vietnam.

Klein also warned the president that "considering the mood in London, tired and beset, there is also need on our side for great care about the tone."[148] Moreover, he alerted Johnson to the increasingly negative image of the United States in Britain. "On Wilson's left and Home's right there is a considerable amount of latent anti-Americanism. Santo Domingo and Viet Nam are sources of native irritation to some parts of the public, the press and even the bureaucracy. Our hard sell on behalf of our own aircraft (and other weapons) in markets coveted by the Englishmen doesn't help."[149] If the British did retrench abroad and devalue at home, Klein considered the areas where this would impact on the United States. If the overseas cuts came they would occur in Europe, East of Suez, or both. If the British army on the Rhine (BAOR) was cut back unilaterally then the Germans "will make new demands on us, and certainly will make it hard for us to withdraw U.S. troops by mutual consent. (If British forces remain at present strength, we might be able to negotiate some reduction in the U.S. presence.)"[150] If the reductions were made East of Suez, this would not only be a serious problem for the United States financially and militarily but would also leave the United States in the position of lone world policeman in some areas. "It is useful for us to have their flag, not ours, 'out front' in the Indian Ocean and the Persian Gulf—in areas where they have long historical associations. For we might be very much better off to pay for part of their presence—if they really can not afford it—than finance our own." Klein believed that "as the summer advances we shall have to make our minds up on a lot of these, and also on our fundamental attitude toward Britain's role as our ally in Asia *and* in Europe." He therefore warned of the need for "interagency coordination both of substance and timing" as London undertook a variety of consultations and negotiations at the departmental level, with Treasury, Defense, and State.[151] A contingency group was therefore set up to coordinate a response should the British ask for further help with sterling. This group included George Ball (undersecretary of state), Henry Fowler (secretary of the Treasury), Henry Martin (Federal Reserve), McGeorge Bundy (White House aide), and Robert McNamara (secretary of defense).

It was expected that a British plea would come during the visit of James Callaghan, the British chancellor of the exchequer, to Washington at the end of June to meet with Fowler; McNamara; and Gardner Ackley, chairman of the economic advisors, and to visit the International Bank, International Monetary Fund, and the Federal Reserve Board. Wilson was aware that Washington was generally opposed to linking the fate of sterling with the dollar. Nevertheless, he still had hopes that during Callaghan's visit the U.S. government would publicly announce its intention to give full support to maintaining the position of sterling. Interestingly, Bruce noted in his diary that Wilson "is justified in expecting from us gratitude for his unvarying defense thus far of our policy in Vietnam. On the other hand, I doubt his awareness of how this is simply taken for granted at home."[152] When Wilson asked if the president would see Callaghan while he was in Washington, McGeorge Bundy anticipated this would be to discuss the pound. He told Johnson that he had discussed this issue with other advisors:

We had a full discussion on the British problem in Joe Fowler's office and we are all agreed that we should not make any deals with the British on the Pound. Any deals we make should be put together in terms of our overall interests—political and economic, as well as monetary. None of us expects this kind of deal can be made with Callaghan. It will have to be a bargain at a higher and broader level.[153]

In the end, very little was decided during Callaghan's visit, and, indeed, McNamara and Callaghan appear to have "spoken at cross-purposes." McNamara was "only interested in Britain maintaining her political commitment on the Rhine and East of Suez," while Callaghan felt that "his over-riding concern was finance and that he could only under-take to do what he could pay for."[154] The following week Gardner Ackley traveled to London with a team of economic advisors to meet with top civil servants and key members of the cabinet to discuss Britain's short- and long-term economic policies.[155] George Brown conveyed his anger at reports of Callaghan's visit to Washington. In his opinion, even before the British defense review, McNamara had been "laying down the law" as to what Britain could or could not do. Brown told Ackley that the government was reviewing its defense commitment, would not act unilaterally, and would talk to Washington in detail about the review once it was completed. During these talks, Ackley reported that Sir William Armstrong, head of the Treasury, had openly disagreed with George Brown, agreeing with the Americans that the United Kingdom had not done enough to restrict demand and slow down inflation. Brown was outraged when Ackley suggested that the British needed to create unemployment levels of at least 2 percent, saying that "not only would it be inhumane and politically impossible, but it would be self-defeating, because it would remove the pressures for efficiency and investment." In sum, Ackley reported back to Washington that there was "real internal conflict going on within the UK government on the need for additional measures." Though it was his guess that Callaghan might favor them, Brown was extremely reluctant to go along with new measures, although he might be persuaded in the end.[156]

As it happened, the July 28 decision to Americanize the war in Vietnam and Johnson's request for more aid from Britain coincided with another sterling crisis. In June British reserves had fallen by £24 million and by another £50 million in July. This was despite Britain's overseas borrowing facility. And although the balance-of-payments situation had improved, there was still a lack of confidence in the financial world in that the British economy appeared to be overheating. July therefore saw heavy exchange losses.[157] On both sides of the Atlantic there was a recognition that a full reassessment of Anglo-American relations now seemed in order.

Washington considered the matter urgent and began discussing its available options in more detail. The British soon got wind of this. When Bruce met with the prime minister and the Foreign Secretary on July 26, Wilson told the ambassador that in a recent discussion with Richard Neustadt, "[I]t had become very clear that every aspect of Anglo–United States relations, every question of policy that the Government had to decide, every point of view about the future shape of the world was part of the same problem." He concluded that Anglo–American relations could be at a "turning point."[158] Bruce agreed with Wilson that there was a need for a broader look at the "whole complex of problems," but when Wilson suggested it might be time to have another talk with the president, the ambassador recommended instead that Sir Burke Trend, secretary to the cabinet, should go to Washington right away and, while there, explore the possibilities of a top-level talk in September. Sensing a crisis might develop that week, the prime minister thought "this was going about things in too leisurely a fashion." In addition, the ongoing defense review was due to report by September and the British government wished to have "a preliminary run over the ground with the U.S. administration" before any decisions were made.[159]

Washington, however, had not yet formulated a response to events in Britain. There were open divisions within the Johnson administration on how to deal with the problem. Clearly, discussions over the pound were taking place in between discussions of the wisdom of the proposal to massively increase U.S. involvement in Vietnam. Not surprisingly, the two problems could not be kept apart in the minds of many within the White House, the State Department, and the Treasury.

At midday on July 26, Bruce cabled Rusk to advise him that the British cabinet would be meeting the next day to consider further deflationary measures proposed by Chancellor James Callaghan. Bruce warned that if these measures were not accepted, or if they proved ineffective in restoring confidence, then in his opinion "we will witness [an] almost immediate terrifying run on the pound, with presently incalculable consequences . . . we would probably be faced with alternatives of British devaluation or full support of [the] pound by ourselves."[160]

The same day McGeorge Bundy telephoned Derek Mitchell at 10 Downing Street to talk about "money matters." Bundy made it clear that Callaghan's intended plan "might not be adequate to protect sterling," instead advising stronger measures to "convince the speculators and bankers that the Wilson government is in earnest about saving the pound." Washington strongly recommended "action on the regulator, with respect to fuels and consumer durables; much higher minimum down payment and short maturities on hire purchase; quantification of expenditure cuts."[161]

In reply, Mitchell explained to Bundy that not only did British economists think it dangerous to compress demand further than Callaghan's planned measures intended, it would be "very difficult to swallow politically."[162] Regardless, Bundy also suggested a six-month wage-price freeze as a possible dramatic alternative and emphasized the need to stay in close touch about developments.

The next day the chancellor told the cabinet first and then the House that further deflationary measures were needed because demand was continuing to rise and exports were not rising enough. The key provisions of his statement included a drastic reduction in planned public expenditure: defense expenditure for the coming year would be reduced by £100 million; building plans for hospitals, schools, and houses were frozen; and local authority lending would be reduced by placing restrictions on mortgages. In addition, hire-purchase provisions were tightened and restrictions were placed on private investments.[163] Consequently the Americans were not overly impressed by Callaghan's statement, or his apparent spurning of their suggestions, which might explain the events of the next few days.

Burke Trend became a conduit of information and ideas between the British and American governments. The Treasury department noted that "a principal purpose of Trendex is for us to pump Trend about the PM's thinking on what he might do and want from us." However, it was acknowledged that "a more delicate part of the exercise has to do with what we say or don't say about our intentions. Both sides understand that the purpose is not to negotiate but to explore each other's thinking—central staff to central staff."[164]

Shortly before Trend visited Washington on July 29 and 30, the contingency group had a series of meetings and communications in preparation for it, and a protracted debate about the fate of sterling ensued. Bundy sent a memo to the president regarding their next day's meeting with Joe Fowler to discuss the prospects of an imminent sterling crisis and the "conditions" for rescue action. Bundy acknowledged that he wanted to attend the meeting because his opposite number in Britain, Trend, was coming for a meeting planned months ago.

[T]here is a sense of urgency in his coming just now which gives me a feeling that the Prime Minister is trying to set the stage for a private understanding with you. I already know enough to be tough with Trend on this, but I want to be sure to use this meeting to get the right message to the Prime Minister, so that when and if there is a crisis your bargaining position will be the way you want it.[165]

Bundy hoped that the Fowler meeting would be "a useful first stage in making sure that we all understand each other as well on sterling as we have come to do on Vietnam in the last seven days," during which time the Johnson administration had agreed to fight a ground war in Vietnam.[166] He recognized that Fowler and the Treasury would be most interested in emphasizing to the British that devaluation would be disastrous for both countries, but added that his own interests, and those of McNamara and Rusk,

are wider. We are concerned with the fact that the British are constantly trying to make narrow bargains on money while they cut back on their wider political and military responsibilities. We want to make sure that the British get it into their heads that it makes no sense for us to rescue the pound in a situation in which there is no British flag in Vietnam, and a threatened British thin-out in both east of Suez and in Germany.

He also admitted: "What I would like to say to Trend myself, is that a British Brigade in Vietnam would be worth a billion dollars at the moment of truth for sterling. But I don't want to say it unless you want it said."[167]

On Wednesday, July 28, Fowler, Ball, Martin, and McGeorge Bundy met to discuss further what advice to give the British on sterling. They concluded that the United Kingdom should be told that devaluation was "unthinkable" and that it could not be permitted. When Gardner Ackley heard this, he immediately penned a memo to the president, disagreeing with this apparent consensus in thinking. He informed Johnson that though he was "no advocate of devaluation," and hoped and thought it could be avoided, he saw "serious danger" in telling the British "that it cannot under any circumstances be permitted." Ackley felt that the United States might be committed indefinitely and unlimitedly to unilateral rescue operations and that this would be more dangerous in the long run than devaluation given that confidence could be lost in the dollar as well as the pound, especially if the United Kingdom "was failing to take the necessary measures to put its house in order."[168]

As it happened, after talking to Fowler on the morning of July 29, Ackley decided not to send the memo to the president. Fowler had tried to convince Ackley that the previous day's meeting had come to the same conclusion. Nevertheless, Ackley remained unsure that this was the case and said so to Bundy in a note later that day.

My basic point is that the *UK has to make its own decision* as to whether the costs are worth it. If they hold back because *we* ask them to, or demand it, it's not going to work and we will end up holding the bag. We can argue that devaluation is unnecessary; that it would be bad for them, for us, and the world. But if we can't *persuade* them, it won't work. Whatever we tell *them*, it's also important what we tell *ourselves*. If we say it's unthinkable, the end of the world, we'll get hung up with a unilateral rescue.[169]

Ball was well aware of this and was at pains to convince the rest of the administration. It appears that initially the president, McNamara, and McGeorge Bundy all favored at least asking the British for a brigade for Vietnam.[170] Ball argued that the British were in no position to send a brigade at the present time, and if they were asked to in connection with financial talks, their "play" would be to refuse: "They will say if this is the price they have to pay they will devalue... the British would say we were making Hessions [sic] out of their soldiers."[171] According to Fowler, McNamara also said he would give the British "an extra billion dollars for one brigade."[172] Ball and Fowler agreed this would in effect be making mercenaries out of British soldiers. Later that morning Ball attempted to convince Bundy that the British would say their troops were not for sale. He hoped McNamara would not bring up the question of a Vietnam brigade in the context of U.S. help for the balance-of-payments problem.[173]

Bundy was not convinced on either point, arguing that "if they really want to do business with Lyndon Johnson they have to take into account his basic problems." And as far as Bundy was concerned the basic premise of the Trend visit was that "it would not be in any one context," and although he agreed that the United States did not want to be "buying troops," he maintained that "it is equally important that we get it clear in the British heads," and he did not think it was "clear that Lyndon Johnson will even do a short run rescue operation."[174]

Ball differentiated between the short-term rescue of the pound, which would not allow room for political discussion, and "from the beginning we can insist on the maintenance of the British existing commitment around the world" and the more medium term. He recognized that the British had "two weapons— two levers." First, a "pullback from commitments around the world" would be popular domestically. And, "[I]f he were Wilson he would play this as his first card with the Americans because...it would be most costly to have to pick them up rather than a one-time bailout." The second lever was to say that "if they can get no help they will have no option but to devalue and devalue big."[175]

Bundy felt the British would not devalue, whereas Ball "thought it a question of a balance of risks from our point of view...and at the end of the day we may have to be prepared to do something which we don't want to do even though the British don't meet our own demands more than 50%." Bundy agreed and thought the problem was a "tactical one to get the maximum out of the situation...our side is pretty much stonewalled."[176] Overall he was adamant that the British "not be under the illusion they can come to the President through the Treasury and make a money deal without our getting certain satisfaction on some political points. There will be strings attached to any short term thing."[177]

At Ball's suggestion, Bundy agreed to mention to McNamara, "not to inject anything too explicitly because he [McNamara] is a little insensitive to the kinds of reaction he might get from these people."[178] Francis Bator agreed with Gardner Ackley about "thinking about the unthinkable." "Vietnam is our paramount problem and what they say and do about it is bound to influence Washington's view of Anglo–American relations. How concrete should we be on what we would like from them?"[179] Regarding the possibility of a British troop reduction East of Suez or in the BAOR, it was felt that "anything which could be regarded as even a partial British withdrawal from overseas responsibilities is bound to lead to an agonizing reappraisal here." The sterling link was made clear. "We have a hint from Dick Neustadt in London that, whereas Brown and presumably Callaghan have the point loud and clear, the PM might not realize that UK performance on overseas defense is tightly linked with what we might do for them on money. On the other hand, we will wish to avoid giving them a sense that a threat of 'disengagement or money' will give them the keys to Fort Knox."[180]

The British wanted an open-ended U.S. declaration of support for the pound. Bundy met with Trend on Thursday, July 29, and Friday, July 30, and "had a long and searching discussion." The Americans put the British on notice that devaluation "would be destructive to all concerned" and that a rescue package would have to be multilateral and therefore "accompanied by a package that can be sold to European bankers." But Bundy informed the president that "in accordance with your instructions, I kept the two subjects of the pound sterling and Vietnam completely separate."[181]

By August 6 the Americans decided that they should place two firm conditions on their support for the pound:

a. That the British agree to maintain fully their worldwide defense commitments; and

b. That they agree to take whatever additional internal measures are necessary to make possible multilateralizing a rescue effort.[182]

Ball recognized that if the British did not comply with these conditions and opted for devaluation, this would "almost certainly turn the UK away from support of US policies (including South Vietnam) and substantially increase anti-Americanism in Britain."[183] There were risks on both sides in this diplomatic game of blindman's bluff.

By September, an "understanding" had been reached. George Ball met with Foreign Secretary Michael Stewart in London on September 8 and with Prime Minister Wilson later that day and also on the 9th, to discuss Singapore and Malaysia and the quadripartite meeting convened by the British government as well as the "relation of this problem to UK current financial difficulties."[184] Bundy later informed the president that "it took two talks for Wilson to agree to the association between our defense of the pound and their overseas commitments."[185] This statement is supported by a telegram from Ball reporting "the essence of these conversations" back to Washington after his meeting with Wilson and Stewart. Ball noted that he had "vigorously pressed the argument that the U.S. regarded the maintenance of British commitments around the world as an essential element in the total Anglo–American relationship." Wilson apparently "insisted that no clear link could be made between the U.S. efforts to assist Sterling and a common approach to foreign policy."[186] Ball acknowledged in the cable back to the State Department that "to clear up the American position on the point" a private talk was arranged between him and Ambassador Bruce and the prime minister on the evening of September 9 following Wilson's meeting with Secretary Fowler. The meeting lasted "almost an hour," and according to Ball he and Bruce "made emphatically clear that the U.S. Government considered that the Anglo–American relationship must be regarded as a totality, in which each element of the relationship should be given weight and each related to the other." Ball's cable then gives the strongest proof that the Americans felt they had given the British sufficient warning about a possible reduction in Britain's worldwide commitments.

Thus it would be a great mistake if the United Kingdom failed to understand that the American effort to relieve Sterling was inextricably related to the commitment of the United Kingdom to maintain its commitments around the world. All of the U.S. Gov-

ernment activities in relation to Sterling or the economic problems of the United Kingdom were necessarily related to the commitment of the two Governments to engage together in a 5-year review of the United Kingdom's defense program.[187]

Crucially, Ball also records that the British prime minister "agreed to all of this,
noting that he had expressed his earlier qualifications merely to make the
record clear that the United Kingdom would not accept an additional demand
for a United Kingdom contribution to Vietnam as a quid pro quo for U.S. Government short-term assistance for Sterling."[188] Bundy also noted that "the one
thing which he was apparently trying to avoid was a liability in Vietnam, and
you will recall that it was your own wisdom that prevented us from making
any such connection in the summer, although I did once informally say to one
of the Prime Minister's people that a battalion would be worth a billion—a position which I explicitly changed later."[189] But Wilson had "readily admitted
that all aspects of the relationship of the two Governments must be considered
as a totality in any long-range review of the United Kingdom defense efforts."[190] It seems, however, that the British did not have the same recollection
of the conversation. Indeed, there was some confusion as to whether "strings"
had or had not been attached to American support of the pound. According to
the Foreign Office, on September 9, Ball had been "at pains to emphasise that
no specific price, in defence or foreign policy, was being extracted from H.M.G.
in exchange for American help over the pound." Apparently Ball had said "this
[i.e., support for sterling] did not necessarily imply that in any particular situation quid pro quos were involved."[191] The Foreign Office concern, however,
was that the implication of Ball's words was that "the U.S. Government assume
that they and H.M.G. have common general objectives to which H.M.G. are
expected to adhere. It might also carry the implication that in some situations
(nature undefined) the U.S. Government might feel entitled to ask for a *quid
pro quo*."[192]

Wilson apparently "turned the argument by asserting as axiomatic the fact
that we have 'world-wide responsibilities' like the US, that we want to carry
them out, but cannot of course do so unless we are freed from the pressure of
economic stringency."[193] T. W. Garvey of the Foreign Office read this to mean
that Britain intends "to continue to do the various things that we are doing
'East of Suez' and elsewhere; but that we rely on the Americans to bail us out
if we run out of money; or alternatively, reserve our right to alter our policies."[194] Garvey's worry was the extent to which HMG might be "inhibited by
the recent sterling support operation and its undertones from adopting policies
in particular which are uncongenial to the U.S. Government." He concluded by
asserting that "we are not, however, as a result of American support for sterling, ipso facto inhibited from pursuing our own interests where they and U.S.
interests conflict."[195]

Bundy, however, said "pretty categorically" to Sir Burke Trend that there was
a quid pro quo. One Foreign Office official surmised that "the difference may

only reflect the more diplomatic approach of the State Department; it may, however reflect a difference in policies between the White House and the State Department. If so, in this context, I think it would be wise to assume that White House policies would prevail." Others thought the discrepancy "more apparent than real" or that there was no basic discrepancy: "[B]oth said sterling and defence were linked; neither tied the linkage to any particular quid pro quo; both implied the need for consultation before any action affecting defence commitments."[196]

The British Foreign Office decided there was no clear "understanding" on sterling, and by the end of the year Michael Palliser and Burke Trend had decided it would be worthwhile commissioning a study on "the extent to which, in financial terms, the Americans might be partly dependent on us as well as we on them."[197]

DOMESTIC PRESSURE ON WILSON, AUGUST–DECEMBER 1965

By the time of the Labour Party conference beginning in late September, dissent over Vietnam was widespread within the Labour movement. Although the summer recess in Parliament had given the Labour leadership some relief from direct harassment, Wilson and Stewart were well aware of the dangers of the conference disintegrating over Vietnam. The National Executive Committee was again persuaded to include a favorable reference to Vietnam in its foreign policy statement, concentrating on the government's peacemaking efforts.[198] The fact that the Vietnam statement came within the wider foreign policy one that included sections on the United Nations and Overseas Aid meant that it would "appeal to Labour idealists" and was therefore unlikely to be defeated in a vote.[199]

In his speech to the conference, the Foreign Secretary expanded on the NEC's foreign policy report. The general debate that followed was dominated by questions and comments on Vietnam. In his foreign policy address, the prime minister boasted, "Britain counts again in world affairs" because "Britain's power, Britain's influence...depends...on a Government with ideas, a Government aligned and attuned to the 1965 world we are living in." Much of the speech was directed to Vietnam, and Wilson specifically answered the charge made in the earlier debate and elsewhere that the Government's policy was linked to U.S. economic aid, "even though we were being asked by the United States Government to put British troops in Vietnam...neither then nor at any other time was there an attempt to link the financial co-operation with any aspect whatsoever of foreign policy."[200] Given Wilson's recent "understanding" with the Americans over sterling and East of Suez, this was, of course, a distortion of the truth, to say the least.

Wilson also argued that British support for U.S. action in Vietnam "no more invalidates our ability to act as co-chairman and to bring the parties to the conference table than Russian support for Hanoi invalidates their ability to act in this way, because it was always understood from Geneva onwards that one chairman (and there are two) broadly represents the views of the west and the other the views of the east."[201] He also denied that the British position of support for the Americans on Vietnam meant that his government was servile. "Is it not realised how much of the pressure we have put on to bring the Americans to the conference table has been related to our position in these matters? We have spoken out frankly. The Foreign Secretary expressed what we felt about napalm and about the use of gas, but that does not invalidate our general position so far as the Americans in Vietnam are concerned."[202] There were also two composite motions. The first one asked the conference, among other things, to condemn American intervention in Vietnam and was defeated on a voice vote. The second, more moderate and more specific composite asked the conference to call upon the government to dissociate itself from American policies and military operations in Vietnam. This composite went to a card vote and was defeated by almost a two-to-one majority. Still, a large section of the conference was clearly unhappy with government policy on Vietnam.[203]

Early in September and before Parliament resumed, William Warbey resigned the Labour whip because of his disagreement with the government's Vietnam policy. Given the government's narrow majority, Wilson noted that this action "again underlined our vulnerable position."[204] Even the Foreign Office was increasingly concerned about the state of public opinion on Vietnam, believing the war's declining popularity could easily be explained. "While much is being done to counterbalance the highly publicised opposition to Her Majesty's Government's policy, we believe our efforts would be more effective if we had a more adequate knowledge of the factors influencing that opposition, especially as it is by no means confined to Communists, fellow-travellers and professional anti-Americans."[205] The Foreign Office therefore proposed, and the Foreign Secretary and prime minister agreed, that a "small but sophisticated" public opinion poll be carried out. As Murray Maclehose at the Foreign Office acknowledged, "[S]o far as the Foreign Office is concerned a poll of this kind would be an innovation: nominally, at least, we have no responsibility for public opinion in this country," but in breaking "fresh ground" the poll would "ascertain not only people's views on Viet-Nam but, above all, how they arrived at them."[206] The prime minister received the preliminary results on November 19 and the full report on December 14. Essentially, the majority of Britain's elites supported the government's policy on Vietnam, although more Conservatives did than Labourites.[207]

However, by the end of November Wilson reported to Robert McNamara that "Vietnam was no longer really a political problem in Britain."[208] At the December meeting, the prime minister told the president he had "taken some raps" on Vietnam, but his position had been "unshakeable" since the president's Baltimore speech.[209] Wilson knew that although his Vietnam policy continued to cause dissent within the Labour Party, Johnson's Baltimore speech and the rejection of the various peace moves by the North Vietnamese had helped secure the line that the Americans were willing to talk.[210] On December 2 Michael Stewart on a taped television appearance in Moscow had appealed for Soviet help in bringing peace to Vietnam, and on December 9 the United Kingdom issued a 12-nation appeal for an end to the fighting and a negotiated peace. On December 12 Hanoi said it "categorically rejects all British plans and proposals made under the pretense of peace."[211]

WILSON'S VISIT TO WASHINGTON, DECEMBER 1965

Despite the negative portrayal of the relationship between Harold Wilson and Lyndon Johnson in the press, the British prime minister maintained his belief that relations were close and friendly. This was because comments coming from Washington, from Patrick Dean in particular, carried more weight with him than journalistic gossip. In August 1965, Wilson got feedback from Dean suggesting that he had every reason to be confident in the apparent strength of his relationship with Johnson. The president had seated himself next to the British ambassador during an ambassadorial dinner on a boat sailing down the Potomac. Dean wrote to Stewart that the president "spoke in the highest terms of yourself and the Prime Minister and said that he realised only too well how difficult it had been for Her Majesty's Government to continue to support US policy in Vietnam with so small a majority in Parliament and in the face of much criticism from the press and other quarters."[212] The president apparently "spoke bitterly of the criticism to which he had been subjected in some of the British newspapers," and Dean thought this an "interesting confirmation of our existing impression that such a dominant and successful character as the President should be so extremely sensitive to personal criticism, particularly of the type of intimate, gossipy remarks which are exemplified in 'The Observer' articles."[213] Dean thought the final "interesting" thing that the president asked was to "convey to the Prime Minister his best wishes and to inform him that he was ready to help him in facing our current problems in any way he could." Dean also thought that the fact that the president had been willing to spend so much time talking to him

goes to show I think that the President and the Administration generally…really are anxious to continue the close co-operation with us in all possible fields and that, although at times they are irritated by press and other forms of criticism, they recognise that our continued support is of real value to them. In order to preserve it I think they are prepared to go quite a long way to help us in our current difficulties, provided that they remain satisfied that we are ready to continue to help ourselves and do our share in the world.[214]

Dean emphasized, however, that

although our position in this respect is fairly strong, we are definitely not in a position to exert undue pressure or influence on the Americans. They are willing to help us and to talk things over with us extremely frankly, partly because they realise that it is in their interests to do so; but if they were to lose confidence in either of these they would not, with their present resources, find it difficult, although they would regret it, to ignore us altogether and to go their own way. In these circumstances, we have obviously a good deal of room for manoeuvre and a reasonable chance of influencing them in the conduct of their affairs, and we should certainly do so, provided we use the right methods and speak frankly to them.[215]

Despite Dean's generally positive assessment of the climate in Washington, Wilson's visit in December was not expected to be easy. Lyndon Johnson was recovering from a gall bladder operation carried out on October 7 that had resulted in the president being hospitalized for two weeks in Bethesda Naval Hospital. Still recovering from surgery, the president was seeing Wilson in between two other state visits: president Ayub Khan of Pakistan was due to meet Johnson on December 14, Wilson on December 15 and 17, and Chancellor Erhard of West Germany on December 20. Consequently, the British expected the president to be stressed. This was confirmed by McGeorge Bundy, who informed them that, as the president was still convalescing, the best time for Wilson to talk to the president would be in the morning and early afternoon, because "after that he still gets tired and is not in very good form."[216] There were also alarming reports of the president's growing volatility. The decision to escalate U.S. involvement in the war had not been an easy one, and Johnson was aware that the war might jeopardize his entire presidency, but particularly his plans for the Great Society. According to his advisors, by the summer of 1965 the president was increasingly paranoid and his moods erratic.[217] Johnson, never comfortable with criticism, was reacting angrily to the growing number of opponents of the war, on the political right and left, and to those questioning his actions on the race issue.

If the president's physical and mental states were not already troublesome enough, the preparations for Wilson's visit had yet again further annoyed the president. Bruce noted on November 17 that the president appeared to be in need of further rest. This was the ambassador's way of saying that Johnson was in a bad mood. He also noted that "the President was irritated by the request made today by the PM for them to meet on December 17. He said he was tired of Wilson trying to commit him to such meetings through newspaper leaks."[218] Johnson complained to Arthur Goldberg that Wilson was "presumptuous" and "arrogant" in announcing his visits to Washington and hoped that Wilson would not behave like Canada's prime minister, Lester Pearson. In Johnson's eyes Pearson had denounced him on Vietnam during a speech in Philadelphia: "[T]hey come down and make a hell of a speech and denounce you and then come up and spend the night with you."[219]

The president would rather not have met with the prime minister, but Bundy advised that "if Wilson is in the country to address the United Nations, and asks to see you, there really isn't much choice." At that stage, the plan was to mini-mize the visit to "one serious talk at the Ranch, and leave it at that" and that "the real point of the visit is for you and Wilson to talk."[220] Bruce was also of this opinion, telling Rusk that in regard to the upcoming visit, "[t]he PM's chief preoccupation is over the brevity of time which will constrain him in making a round and persuasive presentation to the President. From his own standpoint, both personal and political, he probably envisages this visit as an excellent op-portunity to enlarge his own freedom of interchange of opinions with the Pres-ident and establish friendly compatibility with him."[221]

Accordingly, Michael Stewart told the prime minister he was "making the visit at a time when the President is reported not wholly to have recovered his strength and good humor. You might hit him on a bad day."[222] Stewart sug-gested that given the short time the prime minister would have with the pres-ident there was a "danger of the Americans generally, and of the President in particular, feeling that, in our own difficulties, we have too little consideration for the present troubles of the United States administration." Stewart felt, therefore, that in his talks with Johnson it would be advantageous if Wilson paid lip service to the problems of Vietnam and the U.S. budget difficulties.

If you did this at a fairly early stage it would pave the way to a better reception of our own demands on the United States, which are likely to be considerable,—concrete sup-port...over Rhodesia, understanding our insistence that we shall have in due course to leave Singapore, a proposal that the Americans should take over the main burden of the defence of Libya and contribute to installations in Australia and a general desire for fi-nancial support for sterling.[223]

The press rightly surmised that the main theme for the talks would be the British government's defense review.[224] A "defence week-end" had been held at 10 Downing Street on November 13–14, after which it was felt it was time for the prime minister to have a "personal discussion" with the U.S. president "about the global relationship between the United Kingdom and the United States." It was expected that the Foreign Secretary and defense secretary would visit early in 1966 to discuss matters in further detail.[225] The Americans, however, recognized that Rhodesia and Vietnam/Malaysia would also be at the top of Britain's Wash-ington agenda. They also knew it would be necessary to indulge Wilson a little. When planning the "cast of characters" for the president's working lunch with Wilson, McGeorge Bundy recommended keeping the group small, with just the major players involved—the president, Rusk, Bruce, and himself—as this would help "Wilson's own sense that he is getting businesslike treatment."[226]

Vietnam continued to cause tension between the two countries. Wilson started his trip to the United States by delivering a speech to the general assembly of the United Nations in New York. Rusk had told Bruce that "it was important for the Prime Minister in his speech to the UN on Wednesday of this week not to sur-prise us by embarrassing references to the Vietnamese war, indeed he would pre-fer no statement at all by the PM on the subject."[227] Bruce was uncomfortable with this degree of interference, describing it as "a somewhat difficult matter to handle," remarking that he was "not sure if President Johnson were making a speech to the UN he would welcome advice from the British as to what its contents should be." The ambassador spoke to Oliver Wright on the matter, who said he would pass the comment on to the prime minister.[228] Wright called Bruce the next day to say that the prime minister "would certainly say nothing of an embarrassing nature" about Vietnam in his speech.[229] He was good to his word. Although his speech ranged over the gamut of world problems, the United States was most keen to know what he had said on Vietnam and Rhodesia. Ball asked Arthur Goldberg whether Wilson had said anything about the possibility of U.S. bombing of petrol, oil, and lubricant storage facilities in Hanoi and Haiphong— he had not, instead giving the United States strong support on Vietnam.[230] The speech was memorable for another reason. Due to British reluctance to use force against the Rhodesian government (which had recently issued its unilateral declaration of independence), as soon as Wilson stood to speak, virtually all the African delegates walked out.[231]

THE DECEMBER BOMBING PAUSE

In the months leading up to Wilson's visit, the Johnson administration was considering another bombing pause. In late November, and after enduring particularly heavy U.S. casualties during a battle in the Ia Drang valley, William Westmoreland informed President Johnson that his estimate of the number of troops needed for 1966 needed to be revised upward by 200,000 men.[232] With the war going badly, McNamara reconsidered U.S. options, telling Johnson that the United States should either seek a compromise solution or pursue the war with the required number of troops. The president preferred the second course, but not McNamara's advice that it should be preceded by another bombing pause. McGeorge Bundy and Dean Rusk joined McNamara in trying to persuade the president that the domestic and international arguments for a pause were stronger than ever. One of Bundy's given reasons was that during talks with Secretary McNamara and Ball in London on November 27, Prime Minister Wilson had indicated, without elaborating, that he had "some new Vietnam gambit up his sleeve," as Bundy put it, and that the plan had a 1 in 10 chance of success.[233] Wilson intended to put it to the president during his December visit. The Americans surmised that the prime minister would say that the United Kingdom was willing to talk with the DRV and the Vietcong if this was attractive to the United States. As Bundy argued, "[W]e will spike his guns and those of everyone else like him if we have a pause in effect at the time of his visit."[234] As Johnson deliberated about the relative merits and demerits of a cessation in bombing, Bundy told him that the cutoff date for a decision would be the Wilson visit "because we don't want him proposing it to us, if we're going to do it we want to tell him rather than the other way round."[235]

McGeorge Bundy also advised the president that Wilson would be "very inquisitive about our future plans" in Vietnam, and that the president's frankness on this issue would "help to keep his flag nailed to our mast." Given that many of the administration's next decisions had not been finalized, it was also suggested that the president speak to Wilson "very privately," perhaps during one of their one-on-one talks.[236]

The prime minister met the president privately on both December 16 and 17, and in formal talks with their respective advisers once. They also talked during lunch on December 17. Because Rusk was not back in Washington until December 17, Vietnam was not discussed in any detail during the first day of talks. Instead, after a talk of almost one hour, Wilson and Johnson joined their advisers to discuss Rhodesia, nuclear sharing, and the British defense review. The Americans pledged to "reinforce and supplement" British actions on Rhodesia, which included an oil embargo and airlift for Zambia.[237] Wilson expressed his appreciation of American support on this. On the defense review the prime minister was more guarded, giving no specific details to the Americans apart from acknowledging that cuts were necessary East of Suez, and that Singapore was the most likely target. He did, however, reaffirm that Britain would maintain a world role and said no decision would be made until the Americans had had an opportunity to give their views on the matter. Bruce later noted that Wilson had been "careful in phrasing his remarks on the defense review to indicate a desire to have our comments while avoiding any commitment that British decisions would conform to our views."[238]

On the morning of December 17, the president discussed the visit of Prime Minister Wilson in a meeting with Rusk, McNamara, Ball, Bundy, and Jack Valenti. Rusk had just returned from attending the ministerial meeting of the North Atlantic Council in Paris (December 14–16) and was asked by the president if he had brought back any peace proposals. Rusk answered, "No. After moving around in NATO, I find Wilson is a paragon of courage. The rest are doing nothing. I really can't see why the British can't put in men to support the Australians." The president responded bitterly, saying, "Wilson is going to do nothing. He wants a DSC [Distinguished Service Cross] for fending off his enemies in Parliament."[239]

When Johnson and Wilson had a brief discussion on Vietnam before lunch that day, the prime minister again highlighted his problems back home by showing the president a letter he had received from 68 Labour M.P.s, "only a few of them traditionally concerned with the Vietnam question." According to Wilson, Johnson was sympathetic to his difficulties but nevertheless went on to describe his own internal problems.[240] At the lunch that followed, attended by the prime minister, the president, and Dean Rusk, very little of any consequence was said on Vietnam. All three agreed that the best role for Her Majesty's Government at present "was to pursue vigorously and by every means the possibility of opening negotiations."[241] Wilson did raise the issue of an extended bombing pause, which the Americans admitted they were seriously considering, and also indicated that any bombing of Hanoi or Haiphong "would create the most serious problems for him and his Government in determining what line they would be obliged to adopt."[242] The prime minister also agreed to increase the British contribution to the Asian Development Bank from $10 million to $30 million.[243]

Overall, the prime minister felt that "the talks could hardly have been more friendly, more open and more generally satisfactory and the Americans clearly welcomed the opportunity for a frank exchange of views."[244] He was once more particularly keen to emphasize the warmth of the personal relationships, telling his colleagues about the president and Mrs. Johnson's invitation to join them for the Christmas tree celebrations on the White House lawn. Wilson thought the visit had been "eminently successful." Bruce said that the prime minister had "every right to be pleased" by the visit, "for President Johnson has been favourably impressed by him, and their relationship will be more intimate than heretofore."[245] The president's own account of the meeting was indeed favorable; he commented that "the most important thing about the meeting was the feel of it, not the substance," saying, "[I]t was like two partners meeting each other after each of them had taken a business trip and reaching a conclusion that each thought the other did all right."[246] Rusk noted that "in sum, the President made it clear that this had been a most satisfactory and helpful discussion."[247]

The Americans noted that the Wilson visit "marked another step forward in the understanding and mutual respect between the British Government and our own.... The President and Prime Minister were able to understand each other quickly and easily on every issue they discussed, and both governments will now be able to move forward with confidence in a whole series of efforts which are of great concern to both of them."[248] Wilson also ended the year with talk of the "good atmosphere" created by his visit to Washington still prevalent. Bundy told Dean that "he thought this general feeling would begin to percolate widely since the President was letting everybody know how pleased he had been with his talks with you and how valuable they were likely to be as a foundation for the future."[249] Noticeably, Bruce told Washington that on Vietnam, "[T]he Prime Minister has harnessed himself to our chariot, and I hope and believe, will not break away."[250]

There can be little doubt that part of the reason for the temporary improvement in Anglo–American relations was the recent abstention by the British from peace initiatives. The December visit had seen very little discussion or movement on the issue of Vietnam, partly because the British focus had turned to Rhodesia.

NOTES

1. Members of the Johnson administration were surprised at the speed with which criticism of the war grew. Although they expected opposition to the war to a be factor if the conflict continued for three years or so, the White House was staggered to find that

by mid-1965 the leading antiwar group, Students for a Democratic Society (SDS), was organizing the growing agitation. Washington, D.C., began to see organized marches involving tens of thousands of critics of the war. Campus protests were regular occurrences. At this stage, however, the president was most concerned at congressional criticism of the war, particularly from its conservative element, led by Mississippi senator John Stennis, who was urging the administration to take stronger action. A rightwing backlash could jeopardize his entire domestic program. LBJ felt a personal sense of embattlement over all these developments.

2. Lyndon Johnson, *The Vantage Point: Perspectives of the Presidency, 1963–69* (New York: Holt, Rinehart and Winston, 1971), 141.

3. Ibid., 142–43.

4. McGeorge Bundy Teach-In, May–June 1965, Files of McGeorge Bundy, boxes 18 and 19, NSF, LBJL.

5. Telegram from Bruce to Rusk, April 27, 1965, File: UK, vol. 3, Cables, 2/65–4/65, box 207, CF, UK, NSF, LBJL.

6. Wilson apparently said, "In Malaysia, we are doing the fighting and the Americans are doing the negotiating... In Vietnam, it is the Americans who are doing the fighting and we who are doing the negotiating." Quoted in William Warbey, *Vietnam: The Truth* (London: Merlin Press, 1965), 122.

7. Telegram from Rusk to Bruce, SEATO: Council Treatment of Vietnam, April 29, 1965, File: UK, vol. 3, Cables, 2/65–4/65, box 207, CF, UK, NSF, LBJL.

8. Ibid.

9. Telegram from Michael Stewart to Patrick Dean, April 30, 1965, PREM 13/694, PRO.

10. Telegram from Bruce to State, May 1, 1965, File: UK, vol. 4, Cables, 5/65–6/65, box 207, CF, UK, NSF, LBJL.

11. George Ball was to attend for the United States in the place of Dean Rusk, who was busy in talks on the Dominican Republic crisis.

12. *Times* (London), May 6, 1965, 13.

13. Marilyn Young, *The Vietnam Wars, 1945–1990* (New York: HarperCollins Publishers, 1991), 155. See also Herring, *LBJ and Vietnam: A Different Kind of War* (Austin: University of Texas Press, 1994), 97.

14. Record of a Conversation between the Prime Minister and U.S. Undersecretary of State, George Ball, at 6:30 P.M. at 10 Downing Street, May 5, 1965, PREM 13/694, PRO.

15. Johnson, *Vantage Point*, 137.

16. Top Secret Report by William J. Jordan, Subject: The Five Day Bombing Pause (May 1965), File: Marigold-Sunflower, Files of Walt W. Rostow, box 9, NSF, LBJL; Young, *Vietnam Wars*, 155.

17. Young, *Vietnam Wars*, 155.

18. The Soviets appeared not to want to be middlemen in the peace effort at this stage.

19. Top Secret Report by William J. Jordan, Subject: The Five Day Bombing Pause (May 1965), File: Marigold-Sunflower, Files of Walt W. Rostow, box 9, NSF, LBJL.

20. Between 1965 and 1968, more than a million tons were dropped on South Vietnam, at least twice the tonnage dropped on the north. Kevin Ruane, *War and Revolution in Vietnam, 1930–1975* (London: UCL Press, 1998), 75.

21. Top Secret Report by William J. Jordan, Subject: The Five Day Pause (May 1965), File: Marigold-Sunflower, Files of Walt W. Rostow, box 9, NSF, LBJL.

22. Report by the Rt. Hon Patrick Gordon Walker on his Fact-Finding Tour of South East Asia as Special Representative of the Foreign Secretary, April 14–May 4, 1965, PREM 13/304, PRO.

23. Ibid.

24. Ibid.

25. Handwritten note on Report by the Rt. Hon Patrick Gordon Walker on his Fact-Finding Tour of South East Asia as Special Representative of the Foreign Secretary, April 14–May 4, 1965, PREM 13/304, PRO.

26. Record of Meeting between the Foreign Secretary and Mr. George Ball, 4 P.M., May 10, 1965, FO371/180586, PRO.

27. Record of a Discussion on South-East Asia in Restricted Session of the NATO Ministerial Council held at Lancaster House, May 12, 1965, FO371/180586, PRO.

28. Ibid.

29. *Hansard,* May 17, 1965, vol. 712, col. 1003.

30. *Daily Mirror* (London) in *Hansard,* Written Answer, May 17, 1965, vol. 712, cols. 1003–4; *Hansard,* May 31, 1965, vol. 713, col. 153. For a comprehensive coverage of British press reaction to the war, see Caroline Page, "The Strategic Manipulation of American Official Propaganda during the Vietnam War, 1965–1966, and British Opinion on the War," Ph.D. dissertation, University of Reading, England, 1989.

31. *Hansard,* May 11, 1965, vol. 712, cols. 261–62.

32. *Tribune* (London), June 4, 1965, 7.

33. Warbey, *Vietnam: The Truth,* 111.

34. *New Statesman,* Friday, May 7, 1965, 1.

35. *Venture,* editorial, April 1965, 2–4.

36. Ibid.

37. Ibid.

38. *Times* (London), May 20, 1965, 8.

39. *Times* (London), June 15, 1965, 12.

40. Telegram, Bruce to Rusk, June 17, 1965, NSF, CF, UK, box 207, File: UK, vol. 4, Cables, 5/65–6/65, LBJL.

41. Telegram, Bruce to Rusk, "Suggested Text for Message from Secretary to Foreign Minister Stewart," June 17, 1965, NSF, CF, UK, box 207, File: UK, vol. 4, Cables, 5/65–6/65, LBJL.

42. British Information Services, June 18, 1965, NSF, CF, UK, box 207, File: UK, vol. 4, Memos, 5/65–6/65, LBJL.

43. Telegram, Bruce to Rusk, June 17, 1965, NSF, CF, UK, box 207, File: UK, vol. 4, Cables, 5/65–6/65, LBJL.

44. *Times* (London), June 17, 1965, 12.

45. *Hansard,* Petitions, June 30, 1965, vol. 715, cols. 593–94.

46. 41 percent disapproved, 31 percent approved, 28 percent undecided; Gallup opinion poll.

47. Not surprisingly, therefore, July's Gallup poll showed a 65 percent approval rating for the prime minister's peace proposals. Gallup opinion poll.

48. John. T. McNaughton, Memorandum of Conversation, Subject: McNamara–Healey Conversation in London, May 30, 1965, Name File, Klein Memos, box 5, NSF, LBJL.

49. Memo for the President from McGeorge Bundy, June 3, 1965, vol. 5, Memos 6/65, box 208, CF, UK, NSF, LBJL.

50. Ibid.

51. Telegram from Bruce to Rusk, July 16, 1965, File: UK, vol. 3, Cables, 7/65–9/65, box 208, CF, UK, NSF, LBJL.

52. Memorandum for the President from McGeorge Bundy, June 3, 1965, vol. 5, Memos 6/65, box 208, CF, UK, NSF, LBJL.

53. Ibid.

54. Harold Wilson, *Labour Government 1964-1970* (Harmondsworth: Penguin, 1974), 150.

55. The following leaders represented their countries at the Commonwealth prime ministers' conference: Harold Wilson (Great Britain), Shri Lal Bahadur Shastri (India), President Ayub Khan (Pakistan), Tunku Abdul Rahman (Malaysia), F. Wijemanne (Ceylon), Robert Menzies (Australia), Keith Holyoake (New Zealand), Lester Pearson (Canada), Eric Williams (Trinidad), Donald Sangster (Jamaica), President Kaunda (Zambia), David Jawara (Gambia), President Nkrumah (Ghana), Abubaka Tafawa Balewa (Nigeria), Albert Margal (Sierra Leone), President Nyerere (Tanzania), Hastings Banda (Malawi), Joseph Murumbi (Kenya), Milton Obote (Uganda), Borg Olivier (Malta), and Spyros Kyprianou (Cyprus).

56. Wilson, *Labour Government*, 150.

57. Ibid., 151.

58. Memo of Conversation, "Commonwealth Initiative on Vietnam," W. Bundy, Thomas Judd, Pat Dean, Minister Stewart, and John Walker, June 15, 1965, File: UK, vol. 6, Memos 2 of 2, 7/65–9/65, box 208, CF, UK, NSF, LBJL.

59. Telegram from Rusk to Bruce, June 16, 1965, Declassified Documents Series, Library of Congress.

60. Ceylon, Cyprus, Ghana, India, Kenya, Malawi, Nigeria, Pakistan, Sierra Leone, Tanzania, Zambia, and Uganda.

61. Memo of Conversation between Dean Rusk, William Bundy, Patrick Dean, John Keith Walker, June 15, 1965, File: UK, vol. 4, Memos 2 of 2, 7/65–9/65, box 208, CF, UK, NSF, LBJL.

62. Derek Mitchell, Note for the Record, Midnight, June 15, 1965, Commonwealth Mission on Vietnam, PREM 13/660, PRO.

63. Ibid.

64. Telegram from Foreign Office to All Posts, June 16, 1965, "Vietnam," FO371/180566, PRO.

65. Ibid.

66. Derek Mitchell, Note for the Record, Midnight, June 15, 1965, Commonwealth Mission on Vietnam, PREM 13/660, PRO.

67. David Bruce diaries, June 16, 1965.

68. Telegram from Bundy to Bruce, June 16, 1965 in FRUS 1964–68, vol. 3, 11.

69. Ibid., 12.

70. Patrick Dean, Washington to Foreign Office, no. 1563, June 16, 1965, PREM 13/695, PRO.

71. Note of meeting at 10 Downing St. on Wednesday, June 16, 1965, at 7 P.M., The Prime Minister, American Ambassador, Mr. Reid, PREM 13/695, PRO.

72. Barbara Castle, *The Barbara Castle Diaries 1964–76* (London: Papermac, 1990), June 15, 1965, 20.

73. Telegram from Foreign Office to All Posts, June 16, 1965, "Vietnam," FO371/180566, PRO.

74. Wilson, *Labour Government*, 151–52.

75. Message to McGeorge Bundy, delivered 11:15 A.M., June 17, 1965, PREM 13/695, PRO.

76. Castle, *Barbara Castle Diaries*, June 17, 1965, 22.

77. Wilson, *Labour Government*, 152.

78. Ibid.

79. Ibid., 153.

80. Bruce diaries, June 17, 1965.

81. The following day the prime minister of Ceylon dropped out for reasons of health.

82. See Wilson, *Labour Government*, 154.

83. Castle, *Barbara Castle Diaries*, June 17, 1965, 22.

84. Ibid., 22.

85. Ibid., 22, June 18, 1965.

86. Ibid., 22, and Wilson, *Labour Government*, 154.

87. *Keesing's Contemporary Archives*, July 10–17, 1965, 20841.

88. Bruce diaries, June 19, 1965.

89. Commonwealth Prime Ministers' Conference, Draft Message, FO371/180567, PRO.

90. Bruce diaries, June 18, 1965.

91. Record of Events, Commonwealth Peace Mission, June 14–20, 1965, PREM 13/660, PRO.

92. *Times* (London), June 21, 1965, 8.

93. *Times* (London), June 22, 1965, 9, and *Keesing's Contemporary Archives*, July 10–17, 1965, 20841.

94. Hand Delivered to PM by Phil Kaiser. Rusk to Bruce, June 23, 1965, File: UK, vol. 5, Cables, 6/65, box 207, CF, UK, NSF, LBJL.

95. Bruce diaries, June 24, 1965.

96. Wilson, *Labour Government*, 162.

97. Memorandum of Conversation between Patrick Gordon Walker and Dean Rusk, Department of State, Washington, June 29, 1965, File: UK, vol. 6, Memos 2 of 2, 7/65–9/65, box 208, CF, UK, NSF, LBJL.

98. Richard Crossman, *The Crossman Diaries: Selections from the Diaries of a Cabinet Minister 1964–70* (London: Mandarin, 1991), June 17, 1965, 115, and June 18, 116.

99. Ibid., June 27, 1965, 117.

100. Ibid.

101. *Venture,* July–August 1965, editorial, 3–4.

102. Bruce diaries, June 26, 1965.

103. Tony Benn, *Out of the Wilderness: Diaries 1963–67* (London: Arrow Books, 1991), June 28, 1965, 281, and June 30, 1965, 283.

104. Off-the-record interviews with author.

105. Crossman, *Crossman Diaries,* June 17, 1965, 116.

106. Geoffrey Smith, *Reagan and Thatcher* (London: Bodley Head, 1990), 264.

107. Edward Short, *Whip to Wilson* (London: Macdonald and Co., 1989), 160.

108. Cabinet Meeting, July 1, 1965, CAB128/39 pt. 2, PRO.

109. Prime Minister to President, Confidential, July 6, 1965, PREM 13/1196, PRO.

110. Wilson, *Labour Government,* 167.

111. Foreign Office Minute by Sir Paul Gore-Booth, Talk with US Ambassador, July 9, July 12, 1965, FO371/179573, PRO.

112. Wilson, *Labour Government,* 167.

113. Paul Gore-Booth, *With Great Truth and Respect* (London: Constable, 1974), 336–37.

114. Confidential interview with author, April 27, 1993.

115. Foreign Office Memo, "Talking Points for Use in Hanoi," July 5, 1965, PREM 13/696, PRO.

116. Memorandum from W. Bundy, Negotiating and International Actions Concerning Vietnam, July 24, 1965, Declassified Documents Series, and J.E. Cable, Foreign Office Minutes, "Vietnam and Negotiations," July 12, 1965, FO371/180587, PRO.

117. Harold Davies Report to the Prime Minister of Visit to Hanoi from July 8–13, 1965, PREM 13/696, PRO.

118. Ibid.

119. Record of a Meeting in the Prime Minister's Room at the House of Commons, July 15, 1965, between the Prime Minister and Dr. Eric Williams, Prime Minister of Trinidad, PREM 13/696, PRO.

120. Telegram from Bruce to Rusk, July 19, 1965, File: UK, vol. 3, Cables, 7/65–9/65, box 208, CF, UK, NSF, LBJL.

121. J.E. Cable, Foreign Office Minute, "Viet-Nam and Negotiations," July 12, 1965, FO371/180587, PRO.

122. Ibid.

123. Ibid.

124. Handwritten Minute, E.H. Peck, August 24, 1965, "Future of South Vietnam," FO371/180588, PRO.

125. J.E. Cable, Foreign Office Minutes, "Vietnam and Negotiations," July 12, 1965, FO371/180587, PRO.

126. Walston to Michael Stewart, August 2, 1965 (with handwritten note by Michael Stewart), FO371/180587/DV1075/167, PRO.

127. J. E. Cable, Foreign Office Minutes, "The Possibility of a Negotiated Settlement of the Conflict in Vietnam," August 26, 1965, FO371/180588, PRO.

128. Letter from J. E. Cable to N. C. C. Trench, September 6, 1965, FO371/180588/ DV19075/187, PRO.

129. Minute by J. E. Cable, August 26, 1965, FO 371/180588, PRO.

130. Minute by E. H. Peck, September 6, 1965, FO371/180588, PRO.

131. Letter from N.C.C. Trench to J. E. Cable, October 26, 1965, FO371/180588/ DV1075/187 (F), PRO.

132. Ibid.

133. Ibid.

134. Foreign Office Minute, "Vietnam Negotiations," no date (December 1965), FO371/180589, PRO.

135. Young, *Vietnam Wars*, 160; Johnson, *Vantage Point*, 153; Larry Berman, *Planning a Tragedy: The Americanization of the War in Vietnam* (New York: W. W. Norton and Company, 1982), xii.

136. Telegram, Canberra to Mr. Kinber, Commonwealth Relations Officer, July 7, 1965, "Vietnam: British Involvement," PREM 13/696, PRO.

137. Cable from Sir Patrick Dean to Prime Minister and Foreign Secretary, July 25, 1965, FO 371/180542.

138. President to Prime Minister, July 26, 1965, PREM 13/697, PRO.

139. Telegram, Stewart to Dean, Washington, July 30, 1965, PREM 13/696, PRO.

140. Ibid.

141. Ibid.

142. Message from Prime Minister to President Johnson, August 2, 1965, PREM 13/696, PRO.

143. Telegram from Dean to Stewart, tel. no. 1984, August 2, 1965, PREM 13/696, PRO.

144. Memo from J. E. Rednall, Private Secretary, Minister of Overseas Development, to Oliver Wright, Medical Project for Vietnam, September, 20, 1965, with handwritten note by the prime minister, PREM 13/1271, PRO.

145. For further details on the debate taking place in Washington during this period see John Dumbrell, "The Johnson Administration and the British Labour Government: Vietnam, The Pound and East of Suez," *Journal of American Studies* 30, part 2 (August 1996): 211–31.

146. Draft Memorandum for the President from David Klein, June 1, 1965, File: UK, Trendex (Burke Trend), 4/65–8/65, box 215, CF, UK, NSF, LBJL.

147. Ibid.

148. Ibid.

149. Ibid.

150. Ibid.

151. Ibid.

152. Bruce diaries, June 24, 1965.

153. McGeorge Bundy to President, June 28, 1965, Memos for President from Bundy, vol. 2, June 1965, NSF, LBJL.

154. Record of a Meeting between the Prime Minister and the U.S. Ambassador at 7:30 P.M. at No. 10 Downing Street on July 26, 1965, PREM 13/572, PRO.

155. Heller, Kermit Gordon, Capron, and Brimmer.

156. Gardner Ackley, Report on Visit to the United Kingdom, July 10, 1965, UK, Memos, vol. 6 (1 of 2), 7/65–9/65, box 208, CF, UK, NSF, LBJL.

157. Nicholas Woodward, "Labour's Economic Performance, 1964–70," in R. Coopey, S. Fielding, and N. Tiratsoo (eds.), *The Wilson Governments 1964–1970* (London: Pinter, 1993), 170; Castle, *Barbara Castle Diaries*, 26.

158. Record of a Meeting between the Prime Minister and the United States Ambassador at 7:30 P.M. at No. 10 Downing Street, July 26, 1965, PREM 13/672, PRO.

159. Ibid.

160. Bruce to Rusk and Fowler, July 26, 1965, Re: Sterling, Declassified Documents Series, Library of Congress.

161. Memorandum for the Record, Subject: Bundy-Derek Mitchell Conversation, July 26, 9:05 P.M., Situation Room, July 28, 1965, Declassified Documents Series, Library of Congress.

162. Ibid.

163. *Hansard*, July 27, 1965, Balance of Payments: Government Measures, vol. 717, cols. 229–32.

164. Francis Bator, Preparation for Trend, 6:00 P.M., July 28, 1965, Declassified Documents Series, Library of Congress.

165. Memo for the President from McGeorge Bundy, July 28, 1965, Subject: Your Meeting with Joe Fowler at 12:30 Tomorrow, File: UK, Trendex (Burke Trend), 4/65–8/65, box 215, CF, UK, NSF, LBJL.

166. Ibid.

167. Ibid.

168. Draft memo to the President from Gardner Ackley, July 29, 1965, Subject: Advice to the UK, July 29, 1965, UK, Balance-of-Payments Crisis, 1965, CF, UK, NSF, LBJL.

169. Handwritten Note from Gardner Ackley to McGeorge Bundy, July 29, 1965, Subject: Advice to the UK, Balance-of-Payments Crisis, 1965, CF, UK, NSF, LBJL.

170. Fowler/Ball Telcon, July 29, 1965, 10:20 A.M., LBJL.

171. Ibid.

172. Ibid.

173. McGeorge Bundy/Ball Telecon, July 29, 1965, 11:15 A.M., LBJL.

174. Ibid.

175. Ibid.

176. Ibid.

177. Ibid.

178. Ibid.

179. Agenda, Preparation for Trend, July 28, 1965, by Francis Bator, Declassified Documents Series, Library of Congress.

180. Ibid.

181. Memo for the President from Bundy, Subject: News from the British Front, August 2, 1965, Memos to President from Bundy, vol. 13, August 1965, NSF, LBJL.

182. George Ball, British Sterling Crisis, August 6, 1965, Trendex (Burke Trend), CF, UK, NSF, LBJL.

183. Ibid.

184. Telegram from George Ball to State, September 9, 1965, Cables, vol. 6, 7/65–9/65, box 208, CF, UK, NSF, LBJL, doc. 21.

185. Memo for the President from Bundy, September 10, 1965, Memos to the President from Bundy, vol. 14, 9/1/–9/22/65, NSF, LBJL.

186. Telegram from George Ball to State, September 9, 1965, Cables, vol. 6, 7/65–9/65, box 208, CF, UK, NSF, LBJL, doc. 21.

187. Ibid.

188. Ibid.

189. Memo for the President from Bundy, September 10, 1965, Memos to the President from Bundy, vol. 14, 9/1/–9/22/65, CF, UK, NSF, LBJL.

190. Telegram from George Ball to State, September 9, 1965, Cables, vol. 6, 7/65–9/65, box 208, CF, UK, NSF, LBJL.

191. Foreign Office Minute, T. W. Garvey to Sir C. O'Neill, September 21, 1965, FO371/179587 AU1159/4, PRO.

192. Ibid.

193. Ibid.

194. Ibid.

195. Ibid.

196. G. C. Mayhew, Foreign Office Minute, October 13, 1965, FO371/179587 AU1559/4, PRO.

197. Letter from P. Rogers, Cabinet Office, to Michael Palliser, December 29, 1965, FO371/179587, PRO.

198. Foreign Policy Statement by the National Executive Committee Presented to the Annual Conference, September 27–October 1, 1965, Blackpool, NEC Minutes, May–December 1965, 681.

199. Craig Wilson, "Rhetoric, Reality and Dissent: The Vietnam Policy of the British Labour Government, 1964–1970," *Social Science Journal* 23, no. 1 (1986): 17–31.

200. Report of the 64th Annual Conference of the Labour Party, Blackpool, September 27–October 1, 1965 (Transport House, Smith Square, London SW1), 198.

201. Ibid.

202. Ibid.

203. Ibid.

204. Wilson, *Labour Government*, 185.

205. Letter from C.M. Maclehose, Foreign Office, to Oliver Wright, 10 Downing Street, September 8, 1965, PREM 13/689, PRO.

206. Ibid.

207. "Vietnam: British Elite Opinion," December 1965, PREM 13/689, PRO.

208. Extract from a Record of a Conversation between the Prime Minister and the United States Secretary of Defense, Mr. Robert McNamara, at luncheon at 10 Downing Street on Friday, November 26, 1965, PREM 13/1271, PRO.

209. Telegram from Rusk to Bruce, December 23, 1965, Cables (2 of 2), vol. 7, 10/65–1/66, box 209 (1 of 2), CF, UK, NSF, LBJL.

210. The president reported after his December meeting with Wilson that the prime minister "says his line has been steady since the Baltimore speech. Wilson tells his opposition to bring the Viet Cong to a conference table and he'll produce the President." FRUS, 1964–68, vol. 3, 645.

211. "Negotiation Attempts in Vietnam," NSF, CF, Vietnam, Vietnam 6C, 1961–68, Peace Initiatives: General, International Initiatives (Retrospective Accounts); "Some US Efforts to Achieve Peace in Vietnam," File: Pennsylvania, box 9, Files of Walt Rostow, NSF, LBJL.

212. Letter to Michael Stewart from Patrick Dean, British Embassy, Washington, August 12, 1965, FO371/179573, PRO.

213. Ibid.

214. Ibid.

215. Ibid.

216. Letter from Patrick Dean to Burke Trend, Cabinet Office, November 30, 1965, PREM 13/6, PRO.

217. Robert Dallek, *Flawed Giant: Lyndon Johnson and His Times 1961–1973* (Oxford: Oxford University Press, 1998), 281–84.

218. Bruce diaries, November 17, 1965.

219. Telephone Conversation between Lyndon Johnson and Arthur Goldberg, November 18, 1965, WH6511.07, LBJL.

220. Memo for the President from McGeorge Bundy, Subject: Visitors, File: UK, Wilson Visit 12/17/65, box 215, CF, UK, NSF, LBJL.

221. Cable, Bruce to Rusk, December 13, 1965, vol. 7, 10/65–1/66, box 209 (1 of 2), CF, UK, NSF, LBJL.

222. Michael Stewart to Prime Minister, "Your Visit to the U.S.," December 10, 1965, PREM 13/686, PRO.

223. Ibid.

224. Telegram from Bruce to Rusk, December 16, 1965, Subject: Press Comment on Defense Aspects of Johnson–Wilson Talks, File: UK, Cables, vol. 7, 10/65–1/66, box 209, CF, UK, NSF, LBJL.

225. Prime Minister's Visit to the United States and Canada, December 15–20, 1965. PREM 13/686, PRO; Telegram from Bruce to Rusk, December 16, 1965, Subject: Press Comment on Defense Aspects of Johnson–Wilson Talks, File: UK, Cables, vol. 7, 10/65–1/66, box 209, CF, UK, NSF, LBJL.

226. Memo to Mr. Bill Moyers from McGeorge Bundy, Subject: Cast of Characters for a Wilson Working Lunch, December 13, 1965, File: UK, Wilson Visit, 12/17/65, box 215, CF, UK, NSF, LBJL.

227. Bruce diaries, December 13, 1965.

228. Ibid.

229. Ibid., December 14, 1965.

230. Telephone Conversation between Ambassador Goldberg and George Ball, December 16, 1965, 12:50 P.M., Declassified Documents Series, Library of Congress.

231. Goldberg estimated about 35 delegations. Wilson thought it was around 20. UDI (Unilateral Declaration of Independence) declared on November 11, 1965.

232. The United States suffered 300 dead, the North Vietnamese 1,300. See Robert McNamara, James Blight, Robert Brigham, Thomas Biersteker, and Col. Herbert Schandler, *Argument without End: In Search of Answers to the Vietnam Tragedy* (New York: Public Affairs, 1999), 276–78.

233. Memo from McGeorge Bundy to the President, November 27, 1965, in FRUS, 1964–68, vol. 3, 583; "Wilson Visit," 12/17/65, File: UK, Wilson Visit, 12/17/65, box 215, CF, UK, NSF, LBJL.

234. Memo from McGeorge Bundy to the President, November 27, 1965, in FRUS, 1964–68, vol. 3, 583.

235. Tape WH6512.02, side B, Telephone Conversation between LBJ and McGeorge Bundy, December 11, 1965, 12:18 P.M.

236. Memo for the President from McGeorge Bundy, Subject: The Wilson Visit, December 16, 1965, File: UK, Wilson Visit, 12/17/65, box 215, CF, UK, NSF, LBJL.

237. Notes on President's Meeting with Prime Minister Wilson, December 17, 1965, Declassified Documents Series, Library of Congress.

238. Visit of Prime Minister Wilson, no date, File: UK, Memos, vol. 7, 10/65–1/66, box 209, CF, UK, NSF, LBJL.

239. Notes of a Meeting, December 17, 1965, in FRUS, 1965–68, vol. 3, 644.

240. Record of a Conversation between the Prime Minister and the President before Luncheon at the White House on Friday, December 17, 1965, PREM 13/686, PRO.

241. Record of a Conversation at Lunch at the White House on Friday, December 17, 1965, PREM 13/686, PRO.

242. Visit of Prime Minister Wilson, no date, File: UK, Memos, vol. 7, 10/65–1/66, box 209, CF, UK, NSF, LBJL.

243. Record of a Conversation at Lunch at the White House on Friday, December 17, 1965, PREM 13/686, PRO.

244. Telegram from Commonwealth Relations Office to Canberra, December 24, 1965, Washington Talks, PREM 13/686, PRO.

245. Bruce diaries, December 17, 1965.

246. Cable, Rusk to Bruce, December 23, 1965, File: UK, Cables (2 of 2), vol. 7, 10/65–1/66, box 209, CF, UK, NSF, LBJL.

247. Ibid.

248. Kaiser, December 20, 1965, File: Additional Backup for the Visit of Prime Minister Wilson of the United Kingdom, December 16–17, 1965; The President's Appoint File (Diary Backup), 12/6/65–12/31/65, box 26, LBJL.

249. Letter from Patrick Dean to Prime Minister, December 28, 1965, PREM 13/686, PRO.

250. Telegram from Bruce to Rusk, December 13, 1965, File: UK, Cables (2 of 2), vol. 7, 10/65–1/66, box 209, CF, UK, NSF, LBJL.

Chapter 4

The Understanding Tested: January–July 1966

With President Johnson's domestic difficulties mounting week by week, and with a military solution to the war in Vietnam proving illusory, Anglo–American relations were never likely to be a priority issue for the Johnson administration in 1966, particularly now that the British government had made clear its decision not to play a military role in Vietnam. But Vietnam remained the Wilson government's major day-to-day domestic political problem. As the war escalated still further, the prime minister was faced with the difficult task of attempting to distance himself from the Johnson administration on Vietnam without alienating himself from the president and damaging the wider special relationship. This would require delicate political footwork, not least because Britain still required American financial help for the pound.

However appreciative he was during his rational moments of Wilson's diplomatic support on Vietnam, Johnson was furious that Wilson was not absolutely loyal, and therefore compliant, on this all-important issue to his administration. Throughout 1966 the president's gut reaction toward Wilson and the British would challenge his logical understanding of the prime minister's domestic political problems. As the war continued to escalate and to appear increasingly intractable, so the absence of the British flag in Vietnam became more problematic. And after Wilson increased his parliamentary majority in the 1966 general election, the Johnson administration feared that the Labour government might begin to backtrack from the "understandings" reached in 1965.

ANGLO–AMERICAN RELATIONS, JANUARY 1966

On February 18, 1966, Patrick Dean delivered his annual review of the United States for 1965 to the British Foreign Secretary, Michael Stewart.

Anglo–American relations were characterized as "close and friendly but essentially business-like." Two particular issues stood out now that "the Johnson stamp" had become clearer.[1] First was the fact that America's European policies had suffered due to the prioritization of Pacific and Far Eastern affairs; second, the fact that Americans viewed any alliance in terms of its usefulness to them had been "brought out more brutally by President Johnson then [sic] by his predecessor."[2] Although Wilson's visit to Washington in December was described as "a notable diplomatic success," Dean stressed that "Mr. Johnson, like most Americans, believes that alliances are of little value unless they produce results. We are judged on what we can give to the free world and the stability and prosperity of the United States."[3] Britain would be judged on its ability to deal with its continuing economic difficulties, and any American help in that direction would come at a cost.[4] The only other noteworthy issue during 1965 was, of course, Vietnam. According to Dean, "British support for the American position in Viet-Nam was...warmly acknowledged throughout 1965, though criticism of British shipping in North Viet-Nam ports appeared fairly regularly at the end of the year."[5]

The Johnson administration had indeed continually pressed the British government to deal with the shipping issue. At the end of January 1966, Dean Rusk, secretary of state, again spoke to Stewart of congressional "resentment" of British-registered ships visiting Hanoi and, indeed, said that this affected congressional understanding of other British problems, including Rhodesia. He believed that if there were to be a vote it would go against the British, three to two.[6] In May 1966, after a presidential approach on the issue, Wilson replied that the British had done all they could to get their flag shipping out of North Vietnam, and indeed the problem had been "almost entirely reduced to Hong Kong registered British flag ships." The Americans concluded that "[we] do not feel there are any additional persuasive considerations which can be advanced to Wilson at this time."[7] It was nevertheless a festering sore in Anglo-–American relations in Southeast Asia and contributed to the sense that the British were not being entirely cooperative on Vietnam.

THE CHRISTMAS BOMBING PAUSE: DECEMBER 1965–JANUARY 1966

By the end of 1965 the U.S. air force had intensified and escalated its bombing program. On December 15, the United States bombed a major industrial target—a thermal power plant in the north—and was even bombing Laos in order to curb infiltration of South Vietnam via the Ho Chi Minh Trail.[8] Moreover, on November 23 Westmoreland requested an additional 200,000 troops for 1966, which would bring the total U.S. forces in Vietnam to 410,000. This was in contrast to his original estimate of 275,000. As McNamara later noted, this meant "a drastic—and arguably open-ended—increase in U.S. forces."[9]

The continued military buildup in South Vietnam added to the Wilson government's fears that the United States was still seeking a military solution to the war.

Yet, in the midst of this escalation, the United States had begun a peace offensive. Wilson later described the offensive as "beautifully orchestrated," especially as it had "strengthened his hand with his left wing" as he was able to tell them that when the M.P.s contacted William Fulbright, chairman of the Foreign Relations Committee (D.Ark) and a friend of Johnson, they should communicate with Hanoi as well.[10] Beginning on December 24, the United States and the National Liberation Front (NLF) agreed to a 30-hour Christmas truce. As part of this truce, the United States suspended its bombing of North Vietnam.[11]

The president was persuaded to extend the halt in bombing—mainly by Robert McNamara and against his own inclinations—in order to allow diplomatic exchanges to continue (either directly or indirectly through third parties), and to demonstrate the U.S. desire for peace to the growing number of opponents of the war.[12] To explore every possible diplomatic channel, and thus emphasize the seriousness of the U.S. endeavor for peace, President Johnson also wrote to 113 world capitals to discuss the route to negotiations. This correspondence included Rusk's "fourteen points," issued on December 29, that contained the elements Washington thought should be included in any settlement. This was, of course, partly aimed at countering the North Vietnamese's "four points." As well as the presidential approach to world leaders, Vice President Humphrey was sent to Asia to see the leaders of Japan, Korea, Formosa, and the Philippines in person, while UN ambassador Goldberg had conversations with UN secretary general U Thant, the Pope, General de Gaulle, Italian leaders, and Prime Minister Wilson.[13]

Wilson had, however, requested the briefing he received from Goldberg; it had not been volunteered.[14] As a result, throughout the prolonged bombing pause the United States kept in close touch with London. As part of the peace offensive, President Johnson cabled Harold Wilson on December 29, asking for his advice and for his suggestions about possible British action.[15] After some deliberation, Wilson replied on December 31. Not only did Wilson encourage the United States in its peace efforts, but he also offered British services. He suggested to the president that, as well as informing the North Vietnamese about the continued pause through the American ambassador in Rangoon[16] as the U.S. intended, the British could also approach them through their consul general in Hanoi and would also approach the Russians to persuade them of the sincerity of the American desire for peace.[17]

During the pause the Soviets sent a five-man mission to Hanoi headed by Alexander N. Shelepin, secretary of the central committee of the Soviet Communist Party.[18] Speculation was rife in London and Washington as to the purpose of this visit and to the possibility of talks developing from Shelepin's visit. The British suggested that Washington extend the bombing moratorium, at least until Shelepin returned from Hanoi. This was partly because Patrick Dean had informed the Foreign Office that "some of the President's less sophisticated advisers" were not "taking full account of the difficulties which the other side would have even if they wanted to change course."[19] The British worried that Washington would not give peace a chance.

Although the Americans may have agreed with the British that it was worth waiting for Shelepin to return home, they were not entirely confident that the British could be trusted with the delicate role of mediation. Rusk, in particular, felt the British were too anxious for peace and indeed told the president that they had to be watched as "they'd be inclined to give away too much. We don't want to lose cards we need to deal with. We must be clear with Britain."[20] This lack of trust in the British as intermediaries was, by now, a recurring theme in U.S. attitudes toward British peace efforts. On this occasion, the president thought that Wilson ought to understand the situation by now; that is, he should know the British could not speak for the United States without prior authorization and understand the necessity for secrecy in Moscow or anywhere else.

Although there was some evidence that Hanoi was probing the "fourteen points," after almost a month without bombing the Johnson administration's patience began to fail.[21] On January 24 the president gave Wilson "as one of those who have most strongly supported our peace effort" a full picture of American views on the suspension of bombing, informing him "that the pause had been successful everywhere except in Hanoi and Peking."[22] Worried about the adverse publicity a resumption of bombing would attract, the prime minister told the president, "[I]t is of course of vital importance to the American image in the world, as well as to us and your other friends who will wish to defend your actions, that everything possible should be done to bring home your case to world opinion." To this end, Wilson suggested making public "all the evidence you are able to release of the use which the North Vietnamese have made of the bombing pause and the two holiday truces to reinforce their own military and to inflict casualties on American and South Vietnamese troops and civilians."[23] Johnson listened to this advice as he was well aware that some of America's allies, including Japan, Canada, Poland, and Pakistan, were against a resumption of bombing at this time.[24] When bombing began again, the president knew it was crucial to "hold down statements from other nations" in order to prevent the escalation of domestic and international condemnation of the war.[25] However, Rusk admitted that the Americans were "a little thin about VC [Vietcong] activity on the ground" and that this might "cause some trouble" when they resumed bombing. The president nevertheless agreed to all diplomatic missions receiving a summary of enemy military activity during the pause. And as one of the United States' "special friends" Wilson received notice from Johnson on January 30 that bombing was about to be resumed, and Johnson told the prime minister that his firm support of this action was "another encouraging proof of the depth of our understanding."[26] The bombing of North

Vietnam resumed on January 31, 1966; the pause had lasted 36 days and 15 hours and was the longest of the war.

BRITISH DOMESTIC POLITICS: JANUARY–MARCH 1966

The death of Henry Solomons, Labour M.P. for Hull North, on November 7, 1965, reduced the Labour government's majority to one.[27] Hull North was a highly marginal seat, and the by-election that followed centered on the issue of Vietnam. Richard Gott of the Radical Alliance stood against the Labour candidate, Kevin McNamara. Although Labour increased its majority in the Hull North by-election on January 27 from 1,181 to 5,351, the by-election illustrated the growing importance of Vietnam in British domestic politics and highlighted the precariousness of Wilson's hold on power.[28]

The U.S. resumption of bombing in North Vietnam meant, as Wilson put it, that "suddenly, the Labour Party was deep in a new crisis over Vietnam."[29] Much of the outrage was caused by a statement issued by Michael Stewart on the day the bombing restarted which said that Britain "understood and supported" the action. This statement had in fact been written by the Foreign Office, which, according to Wilson, had been "falling over itself to get into line" and issued a statement that had not been submitted to him for approval. Despite later arguing that he would "not have agreed to a statement in those terms," Wilson had no choice but to tell his critics that the Foreign Secretary had acted with his full authorization and cabinet approval. Privately, Wilson was "fuming" about it.[30] By now there was a growing divergence of views between the upper echelons of the British Foreign Office and 10 Downing Street.

The response to the government's latest act of diplomatic support for U.S. policy in Vietnam was widespread and vociferous. On the same evening Stewart's statement was issued, 90 Labour M.P.s signed and sent a telegram condemning the action to William Fulbright, U.S. senator, chairman of the Foreign Relations Committee, and a growing critic of U.S. policy in Vietnam.[31] No doubt LBJ was infuriated by this action, not least because Fulbright was rapidly becoming the president's bête noire. Until he openly turned against the Vietnam War in the autumn of 1965, the senator had been a longtime friend of Johnson's. Fearing a confrontation with China or the Soviet Union, and believing the United States could not win where the French had lost, Fulbright was about to open Senate hearings on the war. Johnson would never forgive him for this betrayal. The Labour M.P.s could not have chosen a more telling target; by sending their concerns to Fulbright, they were aware they were fueling congressional criticism of the Johnson administration's conduct of the war.

Despite the victory in the Hull by-election, the media reported excitedly on a Labour split over Vietnam.[32] On February 2 Wilson faced these critics at a private meeting of the Parliamentary Labour Party (PLP).[33] In what Wilson characterized as a "major storm," he replied for 30 minutes on the subject of Vietnam.[34] As he later put it when telling Johnson of his actions, "the Foreign Secretary and I decided to meet the challenge head on whatever the risk."[35] With a general election in the offing, the prime minister was alarmed that Labour was "presenting the image of a badly split party."[36] One "high placed Labour Government source" leaked the details of this meeting to the Americans and confirmed that the prime minister had indeed laid down the law and the "political facts of life" and was "in most aggressive, uncompromising, and effective style, completely overwhelming critics."[37] According to the source, Wilson had let them know that he "could not continue to govern with this kind of sniping from party dissidents on so central an issue. Moreover, he implied that if dissidents persisted in open opposition, which only gave comfort to Tories and weakened Labor's public credit, his hand might be forced and he would have to consider whether [the] matter should be put to [the] country."[38] Wilson took particular pleasure in telling the president that he

got considerable mileage out of pointing out that during the 40 days bombing pause there was not a sound out of them commending the United States administration for the opportunities they had opened up for a peaceful settlement.... What I think was really damaging to the critics was my repeated jibe that none of them during this period had thought fit to send a telegram to Ho Chi Minh demanding now that he should respond in kind, or to demonstrate with "peace in Vietnam" banners outside the Chinese Embassy. This had the effect of detaching from the lobby all but the irreconcilables.[39]

This taunt was also repeated on February 8 when Wilson faced a further grilling in Parliament during a lengthy debate on South and Southeast Asia when Wilson also voiced his conviction that President Johnson was sincere in his desire to end the fighting in Vietnam.[40] As Bruce pointed out, the prime minister's emphasis on Hanoi's part in the conflict "did well in ridiculing in advance points dissident Labour MP's" were likely to make.[41] He was also happy to report that as a result of "the rout" in Parliament, a telegram was duly sent to Ho Chi Minh by some of the same individuals who had earlier sent a telegram to Fulbright. Wilson summed up the "operation" as a "total success" but reminded the president that the problem was not likely to go away. "We have got over a very awkward moment though it shows once again the difficulties I am bound to have from time to time when subject to group pressures with a parliamentary majority so much less than my real present majority in the country."[42] This emphasis on a small working majority, naturally ever present in the prime minister's mind, would soon come back to haunt Wilson in his dealings with the president over Vietnam.

The day after the prime minister's meeting with the PLP, February 3, a meeting of the cabinet took place that resulted in what Barbara Castle termed "the most spirited wrangle yet on Vietnam."[43] Although the cabinet minutes merely record that the discussion of the Foreign Office statement elicited "considerable disquiet," it is clear this meeting presented Wilson with yet another challenge to his authority. Castle recalls that as well as herself, Richard Crossman, minister of housing and local government; Frank Cousins, minister of technology; and Frederick Lee, minister of power, protested at Stewart's statement of support for the renewal of American bombing. Apparently even Wilson's loyal chief whip, Edward Short, was also "angry" about it, provoking Stewart to lose his temper with him.[44] Barbara Castle acknowledged that this had been Harold's "most stormy week over Vietnam" but that he had "succeeded in allaying some of the bitterness about Michael Stewart's statements" during the Parliamentary Party meeting.[45] However, many in the cabinet suggested that the government could have dissociated from the resumption of bombing while maintaining the official policy of support for American involvement in Vietnam. Wilson and Stewart defended their actions firmly, still maintaining that Britain could act best as a mediator by not criticizing the Americans publicly. Indeed, they argued that it was their "initiative which had originally persuaded the United States Government to institute a short bombing truce over Christmas and to extend it thereafter for a longer period than they had originally envisaged."[46] Wilson later repeated this opinion in his memoirs, saying that "[we] had pressed in Washington for the Christmas truce... to be extended. The President had agreed."[47] Although it could be argued that Wilson genuinely misjudged the extent of his influence on LBJ, this exaggeration of the truth was probably a case of retrospective self-aggrandizement by Wilson. The Johnson administration was under pressure from a number of countries to begin and then continue the bombing pause. However, external pressure was only one factor influencing the Johnson administration's actions. Domestic considerations were much more important. Rusk admitted to the U.S. ambassador in Vietnam on December 28 that "the prospect of large scale reinforcement in men and defense budget increases... requires solid preparation of [the] American public. A crucial element will be clear demonstration that we have explored fully every alternative but that [the] aggressor has left us no choice."[48] Rusk quoted the latest opinion polls showing that the American people overwhelmingly favored a renewed effort for a cease-fire and those same people would favor increased bombing if a pause or cease-fire failed to spark the interest of the enemy.[49] He further acknowledged that the administration had the same problem in Congress. So, on this occasion, international pressure to institute a bombing pause had been worrying for the United States, but it had not been a crucial factor in its decision; dissent at home was a much more urgent factor.

By February 9 Wilson was bemoaning to the president that "the Foreign Secretary and I have had over the past ten days to face by far the most dangerous attack from within the Parliamentary Party on the question of Vietnam."[50] The prime minister had proved adept at handling this crisis. It proved to be the last one that threatened his government's existence. On February 28 Wilson announced a general election for March 31. Unlike in the Hull by-election, Vietnam was not an important issue in the general election campaign and Labour won convincingly, increasing its overall majority to 97. This had important ramifications for the prime minister's relationship with the White House, in that Wilson could no longer justify his policy on Vietnam to President Johnson, as he had so often in the past, in terms of a small working majority. However, initially Wilson felt that with a majority of 97, rather than 3, it would be easier to cope with dissent on Vietnam.[51] In some ways this was true; the chances of a collapse of his government had diminished, but it would also mean the chances of an internal rebellion with regard to Vietnam were much greater. Dissenters would now have much more freedom to express publicly their opposition to Wilson's policy on Vietnam. Likewise, the prime minister also knew he would have more freedom to act in relation to the United States. With a comfortable majority, devaluation of the pound would also not necessarily threaten the very life of his government.

YET MORE PEACE INITIATIVES—WILSON'S VISIT TO MOSCOW, FEBRUARY 1966

On January 31, the day President Johnson announced the resumption of bombing, he also asked the United Nations Security Council to consider a draft resolution seeking an international conference to end the war in Vietnam and establish peace in Southeast Asia. Clearly this was part of the propaganda effort to persuade domestic U.S. opinion that despite the end of the pause the government was still seeking peace by all means possible. It also had the added bonus of helping to assuage British domestic opinion along the same lines.[52] On February 1 the Security Council met to discuss the resolution, but North Vietnam rejected any such action.[53]

During the bombing pause Wilson had also raised with the Americans the possibility of a new British initiative as Geneva cochair.[54] After the resumption of bombing the prime minister felt it more urgent than ever that he try some new approach during his trip to Moscow, planned for February 21–24. To this end, he cabled Johnson to say that he would attempt to persuade the Russians to call for the reconvening of the Geneva conference. He also had another idea. He would try to arrange a meeting between himself and a senior North Vietnamese representative "who might come from Hanoi for the purpose, but, failing that with their resident representative in Moscow."[55] If the meeting took place, Wilson told Washington he would "explain that the United States cannot be expected to accept the Four Points as they stand and that it is useless to suppose that your Government will be worn down by any military pressure North Vietnam can exert. I would then try to probe the North Vietnamese about possible ambiguities or loopholes...in their own proposals and would again offer to transmit any messages or proposals they may have."[56] Wilson saw two advantages to this approach. Even if it produced no tangible results it would still be "a further demonstration of our will to peace and determination to try every means" to achieve it. And further, if the North Vietnamese refused to meet with him, Wilson would "at least be able to tell the Russians, with added force and emphasis, that their cooperation in joint action by the co-chairmen is indispensable if there is to be any progress towards a peaceful settlement."[57] Johnson replied that he thought Wilson's proposal was a "good idea" and promised to furnish the prime minister with the latest communication from Hanoi, although reminding him of "the great sensitivity of this contact."[58]

Wilson's trip to Moscow proved fruitless on Vietnam. On his return the prime minister cabled Johnson to let him know that the British delegation "made, as expected, absolutely no progress at all."[59] It appeared the Russians felt they had little room to maneuver at this stage in that any move on their part to put pressure on Hanoi would be taken advantage of by the "militant Chinese."[60] Hanoi did not take Wilson up on the idea of a meeting of senior men, and instead a minister of state at the Foreign Office, Lord Chalfont, met with the North Vietnamese chargé d'affaires for a four-hour discussion. The prime minister reported to LBJ and to his cabinet that Chalfont also made no progress.[61] The private nature of this latest peace effort, not reported to Parliament or leaked to the media, indicates the prime minister's genuine desire to be of help in ending the war, although any resultant public diplomatic activity would, without doubt, have gained him plaudits at home.

THE END OF THE MALAYSIAN "CONFRONTATION"

On February 22 Defense Secretary Denis Healey's review of British defense policy was published. The white paper outlined sharp cuts in defense expenditure. The aim was to cap the defense budget at £2,000 million for the years 1967–70 by reducing it by £400 million. This would reduce the percentage of Britain's gross domestic product spent on defense from 7 percent to 6 percent. These economies would be achieved through, among other things, the withdrawal of British forces from Aden in 1968 and the cancellation of plans for a British aircraft carrier. American F-111 aircraft would instead provide a shore-based strike force role.[62] Although the review spoke of the maintenance of a number of worldwide commitments, including a presence East of Suez, it was clear on both sides of the Atlantic that it was only a matter of time before Britain's military responsibilities overseas would be scaled down even further. In the meantime, President Johnson and Secretary McNamara were adamant that Britain maintain its presence in the Far East. The Johnson administration also renewed its hopes for a more conspicuous, military role for Britain in Vietnam.

By early 1966 the United States began to realize that if the confrontation in Malaysia ended, Britain would have a substantial number of troops that could be made available for the fight in Vietnam. Consequently, another of Wilson's lines of defense against a troop commitment would have gone. Late in 1965 Sukarno was overthrown in a coup and replaced as president of Indonesia by

Suharto, who signed a peace agreement with Malaysia on August 11, 1966. It was apparent throughout the first half of 1966 that the Commonwealth forces were in a commanding military position and that the confrontation would shortly be resolved.[63]

Although the United States sensed an opportunity to put pressure on the British to commit more fully to Vietnam, Rusk was worried that the ending of the confrontation in Malaysia might instead signal a complete withdrawal of British forces from the Far East. In January 1966 he voiced his concerns to the British Foreign Secretary while he was in Washington. "It would be difficult for the United States if United Kingdom plans for reduction of forces were predicated solely on the ending of confrontation. It would be much better if the assumption were more general, such as a peaceful situation in the Far East."[64] As far as the British were concerned, a pullout East of Suez was certainly not imminent at this point but neither was a deeper commitment in Vietnam. Stewart, apparently in answer to a direct question, said that "even if confrontation [in Malaysia] ended, it would be extremely difficult for the United Kingdom to consider sending troops to Viet-Nam." Rusk then asked if anything could be done in terms of civil aid, pointing out that even Iran had just undertaken responsibility for medical work in one province of Vietnam. He further pointed out that "in the United States the tendency was to call the roll and see which of America's allies were in Viet-Nam. The Administration had used our Indonesian preoccupations in our defence, but in view of recent developments in Indonesia which most Americans considered favourable to us, this was wearing thin."[65] On this occasion Stewart did not respond to the implied criticism.

When the improved situation in Malaysia coincided with Labour's increased majority in the general election, the United States decided to act. In the middle of May one of the president's special assistants on Vietnam, Robert Komer, asked George Thomson, chancellor of the duchy of Lancaster, if Her Majesty's Government might be able to provide help on the "civil side" in Vietnam "from assets [the] UK might otherwise redeploy from Malaysia as a result of [the] easing of Indonesian confrontation policy." The Americans were interested in civil truck outfits or construction units, specifically requesting 200 trucks.[66] Thomson told Komer he had no idea about their availability but would look into it.[67]

In early June Dean Rusk met Stewart again at a NATO meeting and discussed the United Kingdom's contribution in Southeast Asia more fully. He repeated his earlier observation, speaking of "the great difficulty that would be caused for the Administration if the ending of confrontation resulted in large withdrawals of British manpower from Malaysia without any compensating contribution to the stability of South East Asia."[68] Recognizing that the British government faced severe political constraints on Vietnam, Rusk tried a different tack, suggesting the British had no parliamentary commitments in respect of Thailand, and asked Stewart to give "very serious consideration" to helping the military there. The Thais had asked the Americans for about 12 helicopters to help with the counterinsurgency in the northeast.[69] The Foreign Secretary said he would think over the request but admitted that "it would certainly cause Parliamentary difficulty...and moreover there was the financial aspect to be considered."[70] The British government would have to think carefully about these latest propositions, especially in light of the latest defense review.

With two American requests for material assistance already on the table— one for civil truck units for use in Vietnam, the other for military helicopters for use in Thailand—and with the prime minister due to meet Rusk on June 10, the British Foreign Office urgently considered the best response.

On May 17, under intense parliamentary pressure over Britain's Vietnam policy, Wilson had affirmed in the House of Commons that the British government "was not supplying arms directly or indirectly for the fighting in Vietnam."[71] Wilson had based this policy on the British position as cochair of the Geneva conference, although he was eager to emphasize that the Soviets had no such compunction as cochair and were "supplying arms on a very considerable scale for use in Vietnam."[72] Despite British claims of the moral high ground, we now know that the British government had considered selling weapons to the U.S. navy for use in Vietnam. According to a June 1965 memo of a conversation between Secretary of State Dean Rusk and the British ambassador, Sir Patrick Dean, "the British Ambassador said that the UK had received a request through Navy channels for certain bombs to be used in Vietnam. The UK was naturally only too happy to sell the bombs but preferred that in the future it not be said that they were to be used in Vietnam."[73]

The supply of trucks alone was a complicated matter that would require the British government to engage in yet another balancing act. Because Britain was a major ally, it was policy to sell military equipment to the United States. Admitting to selling arms for the war in Vietnam had been viewed as too sensitive, however, thus explaining the prime minister's statement on May 17. Consequently, to send trucks to Vietnam would be to go against this statement and Britain's decision not to become involved militarily. The Foreign Office acknowledged that in terms of "political considerations," to send truck units to Vietnam would be in effect to send troops there and would therefore also be "contrary to H.M.G.'s policy." Moreover, it could be the start of something bigger. "If truck units went to Vietnam we might soon be faced with the request for armed troops to guard them; and in any case, we could not ensure that they would be used for purely civilian purposes."[74] The Foreign Office also questioned the advantage the Americans "would gain by introducing new-type vehicles into Vietnam, with all the attendant difficulties of maintenance and spare parts." One Foreign Office diplomat acknowledged the truth of the matter, in a handwritten comment: "[T]hey want to be able to say we are helping."[75] The symbolic help such a commitment would have given was ultimately much more important than the practical help it would have provided.

The request for helicopters was even more difficult. Indeed, this would have been a "new departure," contrary to British policy of avoiding further military commitments on the Asian mainland, while also running afoul of the defense review's proposal to reduce costs. Unlike South Vietnam, which was only a protocol member of SEATO, Thailand was a full member. British army engineers were already there building a military airfield, in line with existing SEATO commitments. But as the Foreign Office acknowledged, "[T]o station an operational unit in Thailand for active counter-insurgency tasks is a very different matter from supplying engineer units for a SEATO constructional task which is almost completed."[76] This would be a military, combatant role that would be unacceptable politically to the British government.

The prime minister discussed this request with Rusk during a meeting in London on June 10. The secretary of state repeated his request for help in Thailand, expressing his hope that "H.M.G. could...draw some distinction between military aid for Vietnam and for Thailand."[77] Instead of refusing immediately, the prime minister detailed the nature of his domestic political problems over Vietnam, and also explained that the opposition to U.S. policy on Vietnam had now been "compounded by growing Parliamentary and political opposition to the whole of Britain's East of Suez policy. This was essentially an unnatural alliance between those who held extreme left-wing or pacifist views and others who wished Britain to centre all her efforts in Europe." He further explained that

though unnatural, this alliance was potentially dangerous, more particularly since its general approach was supported by sophisticated economists who argued that we could not afford an East of Suez policy. We could not ignore the danger that giving what would inevitably be very marginal help to Thailand to deal with the bandits would strengthen this movement of opposition (which included a number of people who were increasingly taking a strongly anti-American line as well) and thereby merely create more difficulties for H.M.G.'s policy of support for the United States in Vietnam.[78]

Wilson had already begun to signal to the Americans the likelihood that due to domestic pressure, rather than his own predilections, he might soon be forced to reconsider his position on the British presence East of Suez.

Denis Healey, also at the meeting, was more blunt. He suggested that Britain's "difficulties resulted from the underlying motive for the American request," which was "to commit H.M.G. publicly to a military presence further north within SEATO than hitherto." This wish was "politically very delicate in Britain." Rusk asked if the British people knew that Britain already had troops in Thailand, to which Healey replied they did not. Moreover, he believed there would "be real opposition to what Mr. Rusk was proposing, or indeed to anything like a further Thomson-type mission to Vietnam. We could get away with what was on the ground now; any addition would multiply our difficulties." In any case, Healey explained that Britain was actually "very short" of helicopters and crews, and these were the last kind of equipment they would wish to release for American use.[79]

The British record of this meeting also reveals a debate over whether the problem in Thailand was a legitimate issue for SEATO. If it was an internal security matter, a view Healey espoused, then it was not covered under the Manila pact; if it was an external problem, as Rusk believed, then it was covered by the SEATO agreement. A debate ensued on the part SEATO played in international politics, with Wilson arguing that it "certainly existed, but surely it was not at the centre of any of our policies." The United States had, of course, used its commitments under the SEATO treaty as a partial legal justification for its involvement in Vietnam and, therefore, the alliance was a more salient topic in the United States than in Great Britain. Healey, probably reflecting Wilson's views as well, had let slip his belief that the Vietnamese problem was a civil war and was not likely to be won by the Americans.[80]

After the meeting, the prime minister cabled the president, saying the talk with Rusk had been useful and that he wished "we could help you with a few helicopters in Thailand" and that he would "look carefully at this."[81] This was a stalling exercise. The British had no intention of being sucked into the Vietnam War via a military commitment to Thailand, and it was decided that Stewart should inform the SEATO meeting in Canberra, June 27–29, that the British government could not undertake any force commitment specifically to counter Communist subversion in Thailand.[82]

Denis Healey further confused the issue of arms sales by making a statement in the House on June 23, 1966, in which he attempted to refute newspaper allegations that Britain had agreed to supply British bombs and other weapons without imposing restrictions as to their use in Vietnam. He said that "the reports are totally inaccurate, and Her Majesty's Government have no intention of acceding to any such request." When pressed on the nature of the requests made by the United States, he informed Parliament that "a request for certain airborne weapons was received from the United States a year ago, and we were unable to accept it. A further request was received some weeks ago. We are considering it, but we are satisfied we shall be unable to accept that, either." Leader of the Opposition Edward Heath asked if the reason for the negative reply to these requests were "reasons of production, or because the weapons will be used in Vietnam."[83] Healey admitted, "[W]e shall be unable to meet it for reasons of production." After cries of "Ah" were heard in the House, Healey went on to say, "But, in any case, after looking into the matter . . . we are satisfied that it would not have been proper to meet this request."[84]

To ease parliamentary pressures, Healey even considered seeking cabinet approval for a government statement barring the sale of lethal weapons that might be used in Vietnam.[85] The Americans were extremely unhappy with these public statements and did not see Healey's proposal as much of an improvement, firmly believing that the United Kingdom, as a major ally of the United States, should assert its willingness to sell arms to them "without restriction as to [end] use."[86] Washington, and the president in particular, also viewed British prevarication as further evidence of the British distancing themselves from U.S. policy on Vietnam. Bruce advised Washington that "if the US wants the British to repudiate Wilson's and Healey's prior statements . . . the only chance of taking this up successfully would be at the personal level between the President and Prime Minister."[87] However, the ambassador recognized that if Washington took this line it would be "posing Wilson with a most sensitive domestic political problem" and that "if the President does communicate with [the] Prime Minister he may wish to consider proposing that [the] British take [a] position that they are willing to restrict arms sales for use [in] Viet Nam if Soviets do likewise."[88]

Before this issue was resolved the United States bombed oil installations near Hanoi and Haiphong, and priorities changed. Healey did, however, try to clarify the British government's position in a written answer on June 30, when he said:

Her Majesty's Government draw a distinction between the intentional supply of arms to Vietnam via a third country, which we would not allow, and the general supply of arms to allies, on which we do not normally place any restrictions. As I indicated in the House on 23rd June, Her Majesty's Government can and does ensure that arms exports are restricted, both by type and destination, to those which cannot be used in violation of its policies.[89]

The Americans were still far from impressed by this apparent arms embargo, describing Healey's comments as a "serious error."[90] However, after the Hanoi–Haiphong bombing, Bruce admitted to Washington that the issue of Vietnam was becoming "so acute" for the British government that the chances of getting a "substantially improved HMG statement on arms policy" was "becoming more remote."[91] Despite some additional parliamentary statements that attempted "to make amends," as Walt Rostow put it, the arms sales issue cast a long shadow over U.S. perceptions of Britain's trustworthiness as an ally.[92]

"HALF THE WAY WITH LBJ": BRITISH DISSOCIATION FROM THE BOMBING OF HANOI AND HAIPHONG, JUNE 29, 1965

In the weeks leading up to the bombing of Hanoi and Haiphong, the British and the Americans engaged in a protracted debate about the efficacy of such action. Much of this debate took place, by telegram, between the prime minister and the president.

On June 2, 1966, General Earle Wheeler, chairman of the Joint Chiefs of Staff, told General William Westmoreland, commander of the U.S. Military Assistance Command, Vietnam, that it was time to take a decision on expanding the air campaign against North Vietnam. For the previous six months Washington had been considering targeting two oil installations near Hanoi and Haiphong. In a cable to Wilson sent on May 27, 1966, the president explained, "I am coming to believe it is essential that we reduce their oil supply in light of the radical increase in the flow of men and material by truck to South Vietnam. For me the calculus is, simply, whether they shall have less oil or I shall have more casualties. But I am determined that their civilian casualties be low and minimal."[93] Well before this, at their Washington meeting the previous December, the prime minister had warned the United States that Britain would have no choice but to dissociate from any bombing of Hanoi and Haiphong, and on his return to London he had told the House of Commons that the government had "always made it clear that there are some escalations of the bombing which we could not support, including bombing of the major cities in North Vietnam."[94]

Colonel Rogers, a U.S. Army officer, was sent to London by Secretary McNamara on June 2 to brief the prime minister and the British Foreign Secretary on U.S. plans to bomb petrol, oil, and lubricant (POL) storage installations near Hanoi and Haiphong. Immediately after the meeting at 10 Downing Street, David Bruce cabled Washington to say that in his opinion, despite the fact that the prime minister understood the military arguments, his belief that the bombing would cause "unfavourable political repercussions in Britain and worldwide" would lead him to dissociate himself from it but reassert his general support for U.S. policy in Vietnam. Bruce based this view on the consistency of Wilson's remarks on the matter, including his statement in the House of Commons on February 8, 1966.[95] The prime minister cabled the president the next day with his response to the briefing. Although sympathetic to the president's "dilemma" over this decision, and aware of the great efforts to ensure that civilian casualties would be low, Wilson reiterated his view that

as seen from here, the possible military benefits that may result from this bombing do not appear to outweigh the political disadvantages that would seem the inevitable consequence. If you and the South Vietnamese Government were conducting a declared war on a conventional pattern...this operation would clearly be necessary and right. But since you have made it so abundantly clear—and you know how much we have welcomed and supported this—that your purpose is to achieve a negotiated settlement, and that you are not striving for total military victory in the field, I remain convinced that the bombing of these targets, without producing decisive military advantage, may only increase the difficulty of reaching an eventual settlement.

He then repeated his own intentions in this matter.

The last thing I wish is to add to your difficulties, but...if this action is taken we shall have to dissociate ourselves from it, and in doing so I should have to say that you had given me advance warning and that I had made my position clear to you.... Nevertheless I want to repeat...that our reservations about this operation will not affect our continuing support for your policy over Vietnam.[96]

Walt Rostow was not impressed with Wilson's argument, telling the president that the part about a "declared war" was "Oxford debating and unacceptable in my view."[97] Nevertheless, the decision to order the bombings was

delayed, in part, because the Americans wanted time to convince their closest
ally not to dissociate from this action.[98] Rusk arranged to see Wilson in London
and informed Washington that he would do his best to encourage the prime
minister to rethink his decision.[99] The meeting on the morning of June 10
lasted only 15 minutes, however, and as previously noted mainly consisted of a
discussion on British military assistance in Vietnam. Rusk was faced with a
prime minister who had obviously made up his mind on proposed POL bombings, and the secretary of state soon realized his task was now damage limitation. To this end, he told the prime minister that the president approved of, and
indeed hoped, Wilson would say he had been consulted on U.S. intentions prior
to the bombing. However, he also hoped that the British would reaffirm their
belief that Hanoi was the stumbling block over negotiations. The prime minister and the Foreign Secretary examined their draft statement that would be issued in the event of POL bombings and decided "the point was adequately
covered."[100]

Wilson did, however, elaborate on the rationale behind his deep concern over
the planned escalation in bombing. He argued that bombing Hanoi and
Haiphong would further jeopardize the chances of reconvening the Geneva
conference on either Cambodia or Vietnam, especially as there had recently
been evidence that the Russians were eager to have further talks with him on
Vietnam. Rusk appeared to be extremely interested in these latest developments and agreed that Wilson should discuss his ideas with President Johnson
before visiting Moscow again. Yet again Rusk encouraged Wilson to believe
that the United States was exhaustively exploring every peace hope, thus in-
dulging Wilson's belief that the U.S. believed in Britain's "private" peace initiatives.

Although Rusk explained to Wilson that the decision to bomb had not been
finalized, the prime minister came away from their meeting feeling it was "virtually inevitable."[101] British approval was desirable, but ultimately the military
and civilian strategists in Washington were prepared to go ahead without it.
Still, a series of terse exchanges between the president and the prime minister
began the same day. Wilson and Stewart were puzzled over the apparent inconsistencies in the American position. If Washington "thought there was some
chance of the Russians proving responsive to ideas of this kind," the decision to
bomb Hanoi and Haiphong was "even more incomprehensible."[102] Privately
the prime minister believed the bombing decision "was now necessary if only
for domestic reasons in the United States," referring to increased right-wing
pressure to win the war by escalation. He cabled Johnson to point out the effect
the decision to bomb would have on the prospects for reconvening the Geneva
conference: "I don't see how this can fail to affect the prospects of reconvening
a Cambodia conference or of suggesting a meeting at Geneva for those who
wish to come."[103]

At the same time that consultations over the POL bombings got under way,
Wilson raised the prospect of another visit to Washington. The prime minister

told Bruce on June 2 that there were a number of things he would like to discuss with the president, and it had been six months since their last meeting. Perhaps sensing presidential sensitivities over his visits, he assured the American ambassador that "part of one day" would be sufficient.[104] Although Bruce thought Wilson would not "go along" with the bombing "affair," he still felt "the pros of a meeting, so obviously desired by him outweighed the cons" and therefore recommended that the president see him because "in other policies of vital interest to us, I think he will be steadfast, and would be encouraged by direct contact with you."[105] It was proposed that the meeting be unofficial as this would "be conducive to an informal atmosphere."[106]

Bruce explained to Johnson that he and Wilson felt the problem of a meeting was its timing: a visit shortly before the bombing "might be construed as a last minute plea" for Johnson to abandon the plan; if it took place just after, it "might be interpreted in Britain as representing a summons from you to rake him over the coals for not having supported you in this respect."[107] At their meeting on June 10, Dean informed Wilson that Johnson had agreed that another visit would be useful. Later that day the prime minister cabled the president to elaborate on his ideas regarding the date of a visit. He said that he would prefer the visit to take place before he went to Moscow (a visit planned for July 9–10) "so that I am fully up to date on your thinking when I talk to the Russians" but recognized that this might not be possible, in which case he could visit after his return from Moscow "and would at least be able to give you a first hand account of their view." On the issue of the POL bombing, Wilson argued that he was sure "it is right for us not to meet too near the bombing. I should not wish to come before it. It would be a political mistake for both of us if people could say that I was making a trans-atlantic dash, with my shirt-tails flying, to put pressure on you."[108] Wilson then admitted the reason for his gentle pressure on the issue of a visit. He said he wanted to announce it publicly because "I have a tricky Parliamentary Party meeting on June 15 (though it is causing me no loss of sleep) and I think there is some slight advantage in letting it be known that we are to meet before rather than after this, simply because an announcement after may get a bit close to your own d-day." At this stage Wilson was prepared merely to announce that they had agreed, in light of the prime minister's "useful talk" with Dean Rusk, to have a further brief meeting, as they did at fairly regular intervals, and that this would probably take place at the end of June or early in July.[109] What is remarkable about this cable is Wilson's continuing disregard for Johnson's strong resentment about being continually used to deal with Wilson's domestic problems. The president's suspicions on this count were compounded by the lack of a specific agenda for such a meeting.

On June 14 Johnson tried the personal approach with Wilson over the British plan to dissociate. He cabled the prime minister, expressing his deep hope that Wilson could "find a way to maintain solidarity" with the United States, asking him to "give further thoughts" to British "interests and commitments in

Southeast Asia under the SEATO Treaty." The president's patience was obviously stretched on this point. "Dean tells me that, in his talk with you and your colleagues, several references were made to the 'revival [of] SEATO.' South Viet Nam and five signatories of SEATO are not talking about a revival but are committing troops to repel an armed attack from the north." He also let it be known that he now considered Britain's cochairmanship of the Geneva conference a convenient fig leaf behind which to hide. "Nor do I believe that your role as co-chairman means that Britain should stand aside; the other co-chairman is furnishing large quantities of sophisticated arms and other assistance to North Viet-Nam and is, therefore, an active partner in the effort to take over South Viet Nam by force."[110] Recognizing that his personal plea would probably be in vain, Johnson then virtually dictated Wilson's dissociation statement:

Quite frankly, I earnestly hope that you will not find it necessary to speak in terms of dissociation. But it would be important to us if you could include the following elements:

1. You were informed of the possibility that such an action would, in our minds, become necessary.

2. You expressed your own views to us in accordance with statements which you have already made in the House of Commons.

3. The particular step taken by U.S. forces was directed specifically to POL storage and not against civilian centers or installations.

4. Since Britain does not have troops engaged in the fighting, it is not easy or appropriate for Britain to determine the particular military action which may be necessary under different circumstances.

5. It is a great pity that Hanoi and Peiping have been so unresponsive to unprecedented efforts by the U.S. and others to bring this problem from the battlefield to the conference table.

6. Britain is satisfied that U.S. forces have no designs against civilian populations and are taking every possible precaution to avoid civilian casualties.

7. Britain as a member of SEATO fully understands and supports the determination of its fellow SEATO members to insure the safety and the self-determination of South Viet Nam.

I would hope that you could in this context affirm your support for the effort in Viet Nam and your understanding that it is Hanoi which is blocking the path to peace.[111]

The president also wrote that the timing of Wilson's visit to Washington was "somewhat complicated." He agreed that there should be "a good deal of blue sky" between the visit and POL bombings and therefore felt that any time in June was no good. Early July was also problematic as the two leaders' respective calendars were quite full. He therefore suggested mid- or late July if the prime minister felt a talk at that time "essential." Precise dates for the visit would be left "open for further determination."[112] Again, the suggestion was there that if Wilson did not comply with Johnson's wishes regarding the statement, a visit to Washington might not happen at all.

Not surprisingly, the president's cable worried London. Stewart sought Patrick Dean's advice on the president's reply, protesting that the cable was "disappointing in terms both of timetable and of substance." He found the president's emphasis on military action in relation to the POL bombings, without any mention of possible peace explorations with the Russians, and his comments on SEATO particularly "discouraging."[113] However, the Foreign Secretary advised Dean that although HMG would have to dissociate, "[W]e should not have too much difficulty in incorporating most of the elements mentioned by the President" in the dissociation statement, except for point 7. This point, linking Vietnam to SEATO, would cause "considerable difficulty" for Britain in that it was not "either in the interests of SEATO itself, or politically feasible for H.M.G." Regarding the timing of Wilson's visit to Washington, it was noted that the tone of the president's reply made a meeting in mid-July "all the more desirable," and indeed the "Prime Minister would prefer to visit Washington to clear the air fully with the President, before going to Moscow."[114]

Patrick Dean agreed with Stewart's summation, admitting that "apart from its content" he also found the tone "quite disturbing.... in its emphasis on military action, the possible implied link between satisfying the President's wish for public support and his agreement to a Washington visit, and his apparent lack of interest in the Moscow visit, [it] seems to indicate an unusually difficult frame of mind. This, unfortunately incalculable, consideration is perhaps the most important factor against which the desirability of a visit in mid-July should be measured."[115] Dean was probably well aware of the rumors circulating around Washington about Johnson's state of mind. From early 1965 reports emerged from the White House of the president's increasing paranoia regarding anything to do with the war. By the middle of 1966 the president's moods were increasingly unpredictable. As more and more people questioned his policy in Vietnam, including Robert McNamara—who was now privately expressing his view that a military solution was impossible—the more Johnson "hunkered down." LBJ felt a growing sense of frustration as he led his country into a deepening conflict in the knowledge that there was no immediate military or political solution in sight. He was tormented by the loss of life, regularly quoting the number of American "boys" lost each day. Moreover, the war on poverty and the Great Society programs were being damaged by the spiraling costs of the war. Congressional critics of the war, though still relatively small in number, were becoming increasing vociferous, especially senators Mike Mansfield and William J. Fulbright. The antiwar movement intensified its activities with sit-ins, mass marches, and teach-ins now commonplace. The chant of "Hey, hey, LBJ, how many kids did you kill today?" could be heard outside the White House. By the beginning of June public opinion polls revealed that 37 percent of the American public disapproved of the job the president was doing in Vietnam, with 41 percent approving.[116] The sentiment in the country appeared to be either win the war by escalating it or withdraw from it. By the end of June more people disapproved of the president's handling of the war (42%) than approved (40%).[117]

Johnson's image of his own presidency was crumbling before his eyes. Instead of rethinking the limited war strategy, in light of the lack of military progress and the growing domestic and international criticism of U.S. involvement, he increased his determination to plow on with the bombing and the war in general. Consequently 1966 saw a marked hardening of the president's attitude, accompanied by an increasingly stubborn cantankerousness toward critics and allies—especially ones who failed to toe every inch of the U.S. line—alike. By and large, his advisors fell into line with this tougher attitude. As Robert Dallek put it, by the middle of 1966 "the war now so engaged Johnson, Humphrey, and most other foreign and defence policy makers in the administration that they could no longer respond unemotionally to criticism of their actions . . . they had come too far to turn back. . . . There was a quality of illusion to everything they said and planned for Vietnam."[118]

All this may explain why the British ambassador in Washington asked HMG to reconsider its stance on SEATO.

The SEATO point is one on which, I must underline, the administration has become deeply committed in public not least in relation to its attempt to maintain support in Congress. . . . This is strongly reflected in the President's sour remark about "not talking about a revival of SEATO." This is of course for the Americans not a legalistic point, but goes to the very heart of the notion of collective security and their approach to Asian defence, which they see as being in our interests to share.[119]

As a compromise, Dean wondered if it would be possible "to go some way to meet the President's seventh point, which merely asks us to understand and support the determination of our fellow SEATO members, by reaffirming previous statements about Viet Nam made in the context of SEATO." He acknowledged, however, that he could not be sure if this would satisfy the president.[120]

Dean was equally concerned over the matter of another visit by the prime minister to Washington.

I cannot escape the impression that the President is trying to meet the Prime Minister's wish for an early announcement while in fact leaving himself free to call the visit off later on, on some pretext or other. This would be entirely consistent with his general policy of keeping himself uncommitted for as long as possible to specific engagements. In other words he would like to wait and see what the position is in general following the bombing. He cannot now foresee what complications and difficulties there might be and hence cannot decide at this stage whether a visit by the Prime Minister would be in his interests or an added embarrassment.[121]

Three factors might influence LBJ's decision—first, whether or not Wilson announced a visit to Moscow after the bombing; second, the prime minister's actual reaction to the bombing; and third, how congressional and public opinion shaped up in response to the prime minister's position on the bombing.[122] The ambassador therefore advised the prime minister to postpone any announcement of a possible visit in the hope that an amicable agreement could be reached with the president.

Before replying to the president, Stewart, on Wilson's suggestion, arranged to meet with American ambassador David Bruce for further guidance.[123] Bruce felt the prime minister "should not be put off by the apparently chilly phrase 'if you think it essential' " and should therefore go ahead with the visit in mid- to late July. He thought it particularly important that the personal relationship "be kept up by means of a further visit."[124] He was also "emphatic" that, once the meeting was arranged, the president would not cancel it but advised "very strongly against making an announcement before its terms and date had been cleared with the President." He apparently volunteered that the British "should not repeat that all the time the Prime Minister required would be a working lunch. It was just possible that this idea might be taken literally."[125] He advised not commenting on the content of Johnson's message.

Wilson listened to this advice and responded to the president's cable the next day, merely saying that he was grateful for Johnson's frankness, acknowledging that "each of us now fully understands the other's position about the bombing of the oil installations."[126] He did, however, note that the recent exchange had convinced him of the need for a short meeting and accepted the president's suggestion that they meet in mid- or late July. Because he suspected the bombing would start shortly, Wilson pressed for an announcement as soon as possible. Unusually for Johnson, who rarely put his thoughts down on paper, he scribbled his response to Wilson's acceptance of his suggested dates on the cable. He wrote, for Walt Rostow's reading, "OK if Rusk and you think necessary."[127] This was yet another clear indication of LBJ's indifference to the British; he had no real agenda to confer with Wilson or any particular desire to help with the prime minister's domestic difficulties.

An earlier draft of Wilson's message perhaps reveals Wilson's real thoughts on this issue. In this version the tone and content were much more forceful and assertive, particularly on the issue of British support on Vietnam, and on the role of SEATO.[128] Wilson acknowledged to Johnson that his problems on Vietnam must seem "relatively minor...compared with its all-pervading importance in your own case." However, referring to that morning's confrontation with the PLP he pointed out that "the whole complex of Far Eastern defence problems is becoming increasingly difficult and controversial here.... My concern is not to do anything which will reinforce the unnatural coalition, small in size but covering the whole spectrum of the Party, which we have for the time being totally deflated." The prime minister also attempted to assert some independence on the issue.

You point out in your message—and indeed ask us to admit publicly—that the fact of our not being militarily involved makes it difficult for us to comment authoritatively on the required military action. I know you will not mind my saying—indeed to say this to someone of your immense political experience is almost an impertinence—that we must equally be the best judges of what is politically possible for the Government if we are to maintain (as I am determined to do) our support for you in Vietnam and our continuing military involvement in South East Asia.

This draft version of Wilson's reply also commented on the issue of the SEATO request. "Of course we accept our obligations under the SEATO Treaty [including the obligation for consultation under paragraph 2 of article IV]. But these kinds of Treaty obligations cannot be isolated from the political context affecting them. As I said before, I believe that the relatively marginal military support you are asking us for here would threaten the policies I have referred to above."[129] The prime minister's anger at being dictated to by the president was evident in the unsent message. Wilson's decision to send instead a brief, dispassionate reply was therefore something of a triumph for the British and American embassies and the Foreign Office as they struggled to contain the emerging crisis over "dissociation" that continued over the following weeks.

In the weeks leading up to the POL bombing, despite the clarity of Wilson's position, the White House—more specifically, Walt Rostow—continued to put pressure on the British not to dissociate. While Patrick Dean was out of Washington on a visit to the Northwest, J. E. Killick deputized Dean and in this role engaged in communications with Murray Maclehose, a Foreign Office adviser in Downing Street. Despite Wilson's reply, Killick remained concerned about the president's message of June 14. He puzzled over the implications of the "SEATO ploy," wondering if it was

a serious attempt to put the Prime Minister on the spot (and if so, whether it presages an attempt to get British troops into Vietnam—which we rather doubt—or simply to hold the line on moral support from a vital SEATO ally in the suspicion that we are keen to write off SEATO—which is best guess), or whether it is no more than an attempt to pull out all the stops, which will have no particularly serious effect on relations between the two if it does not succeed.[130]

The following day, June 17, Killick talked to Walt Rostow on the telephone and gained further insight into the extent and nature of the president's displeasure:

Rostow said that Rusk and he had had to work very hard on the President to prevent the message of 14 June from being "something really bad." He was afraid that it was not fully appreciated in London that the President's state of mind was one of absolute determination to see Viet Nam through, come hell or high water. The Americans were being knocked "from hell to breakfast" on the ground over something which the President and Rusk saw in absolutely clear-cut terms as a matter involving SEATO no less than the Geneva Accord. The Asian Allies were all with the United States, the Europeans were not, and the President no longer attached any real importance to the co-chairmanship point in the case of the United Kingdom.[131]

Again, Killick thought Rostow's comments might be meant to push the British as far as possible:

It may, of course, be that much of this is a conscious ploy as part of an exercise to pull out all the stops...but I really do not think this can be wholly the case, and it will be wise to tread with the utmost caution in further exchanges in the foreseeable future. Although he has underlined his own internal difficulties in his message of 14 June, the President understands the Prime Minister's need to put a certain slant on anything he says publicly for home consumption over the next few weeks; but it would be no bad thing, if when this has to be, the President could be given some reassuring private warning and/or explanation.[132]

This Wilson would do. Johnson's retort that Wilson should visit only if he thought it "essential" was ignored by the Foreign Office, which thought it right to go ahead with such a visit. Maclehose told Killick that he thought this decision was "right" because "the damage that might have been expected from a suspended idea of a visit once it had been broached could have been greater than to go ahead and announce it as we have done. We all realised there were risks either way and that in any case we were dealing with an imponderable connected with the President's personality."[133] Maclehose understood the problem of reacting to gossip and rumor coming out of the White House, regardless of its source. He therefore advised Killick unofficially that not only could he see little chance of the terms of the announcement of dissociation being further revised, but thought Killick was "right not [to] try to extract from the White House indications of the President's reactions to these exchanges. We are very interested in the side effects and the noises off but what matters is the texts that passed; for the rest I suggest you play it cool."[134]

Johnson's anger became demonstrably apparent, however, in his obvious reluctance to receive Wilson in Washington. Having appeared to have agreed to the prime minister's visit, even if not a particular date for it, the president appears to have changed his mind shortly afterward. As Rostow put it to Rusk, "[A]s of the last moment the President became again deeply disturbed about the Wilson visit."[135] Johnson's initial doubts about the visit had now apparently crystallized into definite opposition. On the day the visit was made public in London, the British were perplexed to find that the announcement had not been made simultaneously in Washington as planned. Killick noted a few days later that "the handling of the announcement at this end was distinctly odd."[136] He outlined events as follows:

Although we know that the President himself, in an off-the-record talk with selected journalists the night before the announcement, made passing reference to Mr. Wilson in reply to a general question about visitors he expected during the coming weeks, the White House in fact did not itself formally make the announcement at all at the agreed time on the following morning. When our Information Department checked with the White House press people half an hour before the release was due, they were told enigmatically that there would be "no White House announcement at this stage" and that further enquiries should be directed to Rostow.[137]

Behind the scenes, the president was reconsidering. At 3:30 P.M. that afternoon Rostow sent a top-secret memorandum to the president summarizing the evolution of the visit's announcement as he saw it. Rostow explained that the change of date from "mid" to "mid or late July," cabled to Wilson on June 14, had been the president's idea. However, when Wilson replied accepting the suggested time frame on June 15, the president conveyed to Rostow his "deep and serious reservations about the visit as a whole" but "concluded . . . by observing reflectively that it would be difficult for us to turn down Wilson, having just agreed to Erhard." Then, according to Rostow's recollection, he had called Secretary Rusk, telling him of Johnson's "grave second thoughts about the visit" and urging him to talk to the president immediately. And as noted earlier, on June 16 the president had marked the prime minister's message with a grudging "OK if Rusk and you think necessary."[138] According to Rostow, Rusk had thought that it was "wise" to go ahead with the visit because of the commitment to see Chancellor Ludwig Erhard of West Germany and felt the announcement should be "as soon as possible before the week end so it would not be connected with decisions which might be made this week end." The British were informed that the announcement could go ahead for Friday, June 17, at 11:00 A.M. As Rostow put it, "[A]s of last night I thought we were all together."[139]

Rostow then outlined the position "as things stand."

I take it to be our task to make bloody clear to the British Embassy in Washington and the British government in London that (1) the visit must be very carefully prepared; (2) the Prime Minister, whatever his pressures at home, should not come unless what he says here in public and in private reinforces your position on Viet Nam; (3) if this is impossible for him, he must find an excuse for the visit not to take place.[140]

The president agreed that this was the position, and Rostow duly informed Rusk of the need to ensure that the relevant parties were informed.[141] The visit would go ahead, but Johnson obviously felt he had been pushed into it. The president now had no enthusiasm for a meeting with the British, especially if Wilson intended to criticize U.S. policy in Vietnam.

The Americans deliberated over the bombing of the POL targets for another two weeks. On June 17 the president acknowledged during National Security Council (NSC) meeting that one of the reasons for a delay in making a decision had been that Rusk had needed time to talk to some of the American's key allies, including Britain and Canada.[142] Rusk recognized that domestic and international opinion was trying to push the U.S. government in opposite directions. He explained that the American people "have a feeling of impatience and, over time, they may demand a quick end of the war as the price for their continued support. This restlessness is evident in the public opinion polls. Opinion abroad hopes that no larger military measures will be necessary . . . We are under constant observation by everyone abroad."[143] This fact was brought home later that month when a group of Democratic senators met with Senator Mike Mansfield to discuss Vietnam. The results of the discussion were forwarded to Johnson. The report was extremely negative, particularly in reference to the almost $2 billion per month cost of the war and the implications of that expenditure for Johnson's domestic policy. The senators were extremely concerned about the damage Vietnam was doing to the party: "Viet Nam is worse than Korea and remember what Eisenhower did with the latter." They also noted starkly that "the only major country supporting us is Britain which is totally dependent on us."[144] The Johnson administration was well aware, therefore, of the dangers posed by any weakening of Britain's public support for U.S. policy in Vietnam, however slight it might be. Despite the fact that British "dependency" gave the Johnson administration some leverage, in the days before the POL bombing the president was unwilling to force Wilson to go back on his Commons statement, and not dissociate. Discussions on sterling had revealed the risks involved in making Wilson cooperate on areas of foreign and defense policy. The British might just see devaluation of the pound as preferable to complete domination by their American cousins. That being said, Johnson was extremely angry at Wilson's plans to dissociate and would therefore not stop heavy hints being made about the potential impact of such an act on Anglo–American relations. For this reason, Dean Rusk and Walt Rostow both spoke to Patrick Dean about Wilson's forthcoming visit to Washington. As instructed, they were at pains to ensure that Wilson's visit did not cause Johnson further difficulties. On June 22 Dean informed Michael Palliser of the nature and content of his talks with Rostow and Rusk, noting that "both said very much the same things."[145] Palliser passed the details on to the prime minister.[146]

Rostow admitted that the president's first reaction to the idea of a visit by the prime minister had been "far from favourable." This was because the president was "under great domestic pressure and was, because of Vietnam, having to sit by and see his overwhelming political power fragmented."[147] In April 1965 Lester Pearson, Liberal prime minister of Canada, had angered Johnson by making a critical speech on Vietnam in Philadelphia. When Johnson met Pearson at Camp David, the president held the prime minister by the lapels, castigating him for adding to his problems. If it was not bad enough that some of his liberal friends at home were condemning him, he now had to contend with his allies abroad joining in.[148] Rostow warned that "if anything of this sort were to occur the damage to Anglo–American relations would be great and long-lasting." He also passed on the White House view that if Wilson "could not say helpful things about Vietnam both privately and publicly, i.e. to leading Senators and so on, when he was in Washington," then it would be best if he did not visit. Johnson was frustrated and annoyed by the disparity between the large amount of support he was getting privately on Vietnam and the minimal public expression of that support. Rostow said the president had received messages from Mrs. Gandhi, Lee Kuan Yew, and the Israeli government "urging him not to give way or abandon South Vietnam," yet they did not support him publicly.[149]

According to Rostow, the president wanted "practical help, not advice about how to run the war and conduct limited military operations from those who were taking no active part."[150] As a result of these feelings on the president's part, Rostow indicated that Johnson's first reaction to the prime minister's message of June 14 "had therefore been very strong, particularly to the implication that he was about to order the bombing of civilian centres when in fact all that the Americans intended to attack was oil installations and trucks." Moreover, the president "had very much admired the way in which the Prime Minister had stood his ground and given . . . such firm support when he had only a majority of three" but "could not understand why, when Mr. Wilson had a really big majority, he felt it necessary to dissociate himself much more than before from American action."[151] This indicates two errors in Johnson's understanding of the situation. First, in many ways the existence of a large majority allowed backbench opponents of the British stance on Vietnam the freedom to voice and act on their views in a way that was impossible when the government's tiny majority meant the life of the government might be jeopardized by internal dissent. And second, the president was ignoring the deepening unpopularity of U.S. action in Britain, particularly the military escalation. The numbers questioning the Labour government's support of U.S. policy in Vietnam had not remained the same.

The following day Dean conveyed yet more political gossip to Palliser. Francis Bator, who Dean felt was "friendly" to the British, had the previous night told an embassy officer much the same as Rostow had said to him. However, he said "specifically that if there is a row between the Prime Minister and the President over all this it will spill over into a lot of other matters." Dean suspected this meant "support for sterling." He therefore again suggested that Wilson rethink dissociation. "It does seem to me that if the bombing takes place and is successful in hitting the oil installations only and killing very few civilians, it would be well worthwhile if it were possible for the Prime Minister either not to make a public dissociation statement or to say the absolute minimum."[152] The same day (the 24th) the Foreign Office informed the prime minister that "even making allowance for some colourful reporting by Rusk and Rostow—I think we must take it that, whatever the President's present mood, he has been thinking and speaking privately pretty harshly about us during the past few days."[153]

London was aware that dissociation would be a gamble; no one could predict Johnson's response. To Wilson's credit, he resisted pressure from the president and his own civil servants and maintained his position on the POL bombings. Washington gave the prime minister advance warning of its decision to go ahead with the attack on the POL installations, and Wilson responded as predicted, saying he would dissociate the British from this action. However, he agreed to reaffirm support for the U.S. policy overall and would stress "that the onus for continuing the fighting and refusing a negotiation rests with Hanoi." He also promised to "do my best to include in the statement as many as possible of the points made in your personal message to me of June 14th."[154]

On the day of the POL bombings 10 Downing Street issued a carefully worded statement that Wilson later read out to the House. The Foreign Office apparently tried to water down the statement, offering Wilson an alternative, but Wilson refused. According to his memoirs, he "indicated to them into which part of their filing system they were free to put it."[155] The key sections of his statement were as follows:

It is difficult for the British Government, which is not involved in the fighting in Viet-Nam, to assess the importance of any particular action which the United States Government regards as militarily necessary in this conflict. Nevertheless, we have made it clear on many occasions that we could not support an extension of the bombing to such areas, even though we were confident that the United States forces would take every precaution, as always, to avoid civilian casualties. We believe that the value of each application of force must be judged not merely in terms of the military needs which it is designed to meet, but also in terms of the additional suffering and distress which it inflicts upon innocent people and the effect it can have on the prospects for an early move to a political solution.

For these reasons, when President Johnson informed me that the United States Government judged it necessary to attack targets touching on the populated areas of Hanoi and Haiphong, I told him that...we should...feel bound to reaffirm that we must dissociate ourselves from an action of this kind.[156]

Despite this dissociation, Wilson announced that Britain remained "convinced...that the United States are right to continue to assist the millions of South Vietnamese, who have no wish to live under Communist domination" and blamed the North Vietnamese refusal to talk for the continuation of fighting.[157] Wilson thus delivered his statement on the lines suggested by the White House, except for the exclusion of any reference to SEATO.

Wilson was criticized by the leader of the Opposition, Edward Heath, as holding "a completely untenable position" in generally supporting the U.S. policy in Vietnam while at the same time "dissociating himself from the implementation of that policy."[158] This was because, as the Economist later put it, Wilson had "alienated [the] US, and weakened the cardinal operating principle of Anglo–American alliance that UK generally goes along with US on big questions of foreign policy, while retaining useful 'nudging' function at times."[159] Wilson defended himself by arguing that it was "perfectly possible, reasonable and logical to support a general policy without committing oneself to every action taken in support of that policy. To assume in advance that one will support every action taken in support of a given policy might lead Her Majesty's Government, or even Her Majesty's Opposition, into a very difficult situation."[160]

Despite criticism from the official Opposition, most within his own party supported the dissociation, although some argued for a complete dissociation from U.S. policy in Vietnam. There was undoubtedly a fear that this latest action on the part of the Americans could trigger intervention by China or the Soviet Union and thus spark a third world war.[161] On the day of the bombing Barbara Castle noted in her diary, "What will Harold do now? None of us were consulted of course, but I was immensely relieved when he volunteered a statement to the House dissociating himself from it. It was a careful minimum of dissociation, however."[162] Wilson went to the cabinet the next day to ask for its approval of his dissociation statement. Richard Crossman noted that "we did so unenthusiastically because few of us, I think, felt it was more than a posture. We knew perfectly well that as soon as he got across the Atlantic and talked to Johnson, Harold would indicate to the President that there was nothing in what he had said or done which made his loyalty to the Vietnam policy less profound."[163]

British dissociation from the POL bombing was not the only negative reaction around the world. A number of nations voiced their objections to this latest escalation of the war. George Ball, acting secretary of state while Rusk was in Canberra at the SEATO meeting, was faced with responding to the criticisms.[164] During a meeting of the Senate Foreign Relations Committee, William Fulbright said that it was significant that none of America's NATO allies had given support for the raids. Defending U.S. action, Ball thought the British government's linkage between the POL targets and a loss of civilian life was a mistake.[165]

Wilson faced a double bind. Not only was he confronted with intense parliamentary pressure to extend his dissociation of the POL bombings to an outright dissociation of American policy, but he also knew that he had to prevent a full-scale rift with President Johnson. On July 1 Wilson sent a six-page telegram to Johnson in an attempt to justify his decision to dissociate, and as Crossman suspected, to assure the president of his continuing support of America's general policy in Vietnam. He began with a now familiar refrain: "[M]y thoughts have been very much with you during these past two exceptionally difficult days."[166] He then went on to outline the nature and extent of the negative criticism he had received over the POL bombing operation and castigated his critics for being "more vociferous in their criticism than fertile in providing any constructive alternative." He again explained the spread of opposition to the war. "Many of our more moderate British critics are gradually being maneouvred into taking their stand with extremists whose views as put forward they would probably, if challenged, repudiate. The fact that the British people are physically remote from the problem and, in particular, are not suffering the tragedy of the losses which your people are suffering serves to increase the lack of understanding of my full support for your basic policy."[167] He then progressed to the real reason for his telegram. "I know that you must feel that some actions and statements of ours in the past few days have not been helpful. And there are no doubt in both countries those ready to exploit those actions for the sake of sowing discord between the two governments or of pushing the two of us further apart, you in one direction me in another, from the position we have jointly held and still hold." He elaborated further:

I am being pressed to acknowledge that the logic of disagreeing with this particular operation would be a total denunciation of the whole of your Vietnam policy. This I have firmly rejected, not only because I distrust the motives of those who put this argument forward, but because their argument itself is balls...after the deepest heart searching...I cannot see that there is any change in your basic position that I could urge on you.[168]

Still, Wilson was assertive in defending his decision to dissociate:

I want you to realise that where we have differed in detail—but never in basic policy—and have had to express a different point of view, while we recognise that this can only add to your difficulties (and especially this time be more than a little hurtful), we believe that what we have done is right and necessary. I must be quite frank in saying that this is the price I have to pay for being able to hold the line in our own country where the public reaction is very widespread even if, as I have said, it stems from widely differing motives.[169]

After repeating his assurance that he was stoutly defending the U.S. record on peace moves, Wilson again put himself forward as a mediator. "But I wanted to make it absolutely clear that I would not contemplate taking any steps towards it unless I thought it had your agreement, not grudging or reluctant agreement, but wholehearted feeling that it was right and that it would not add to your difficulties."[170] He had one possibility in mind and that was trying a personal approach to Kosygin during his forthcoming visit to the British Trade Fair in Moscow.

The Johnson administration considered Wilson's telegram the following day. Patrick Dean spoke to Rostow and asked about the president's reaction to the message. Rostow related to Dean that once again Johnson felt that Wilson might use his forthcoming visit to Washington "for political purposes at home" and that the visit "must not be used in any way to undercut the President's position, particularly on American soil."[171] According to Rostow, Dean "valiantly defended the Prime Minister saying he was sure he knew very well what was in the President's mind and that the whole tone of his recent message showed how sympathetic he was to the President's difficulties. Moreover, the Prime Minister's statement had been very carefully worded and two thirds of it had been devoted to confirming the U.S. basic policy as regard Vietnam still had the support of the British Government." Rostow could not resist asking Dean to request that the prime minister say at some stage "that he had been worried over the risk of inflicting casualties among the civilian population if the bombing operation took place but that he was very pleased to hear that the casualties, if indeed there had been any, were extremely light."[172] Wilson did not change his position on this, and nothing of the sort was said during a debate in the House on July 7.

Despite Rostow's view that Johnson had "not gone up in smoke"[173] on receiving Wilson's message, the following day Johnson sent a terse, four-paragraph reply to Wilson's cable that demonstrates Johnson's continuing irritation on this matter. "Your message gave me the picture of your political problem and how you intend to deal with it. My problem is not merely political. I must also convince Hanoi that the will of the United States cannot be broken by debate or pressures—at home or from abroad."[174] On the proposal of another Wilson initiative, Johnson was noncommittal, although Rostow had in fact felt it would be useful:

We must and will continue to apply hard military pressure. There should be no ambiguity about this. It would be useful for the Soviets to be clear on this point. Yet it may give you some problems in connection with your trip to Moscow. If you do go to Moscow, I would hope you could canvass all useful possibilities with Kosygin and his colleagues and that your joint responsibilities as co-chairman might lead to some constructive initiative.

He also informed Wilson that "an acceptable date" for his visit would be July 29. The telegram ended abruptly, just with salutary "best wishes."[175] Rostow had suggested that Johnson conclude with the statement "I look forward to talking with you of these and other matters."[176] The president clearly did not look forward to such discussions. Moreover, he was unhappy with Wilson's use of the word "balls" in his message. Bruce felt responsible for the prime minister's use of the "rather colourful word."[177] Wilson intended to use the word "bull" but had asked Bruce if he thought the president "would be offended if he substituted balls." Bruce later noted that the latter term had greater currency in Britain than the former but at the time told Wilson "that the two words, and the physical juxtaposition of which they were expressive, were so intimately connected that I believed them equally apposite." Bruce had assured Wilson that Johnson "would not be disturbed by this picturesque description."[178] Bruce's explanation of events was not passed on to Johnson in that it was felt to be "chancy humor."[179] Again, Wilson overestimated the intimacy of his personal and working relationship with the president, and unfortunately for him, Bruce's usually sound judgment was on this occasion flawed.

Despite Wilson's lengthy and repeated explanations behind his decision to dissociate, Johnson remained puzzled over it and asked Bruce to comment on the reasons behind it, the position the administration should adopt during the forthcoming Washington visit, the agenda, and what Wilson himself was likely to say and do during the visit.[180] Bruce was sympathetic to Wilson's domestic political pressures on Vietnam and argued as much to Washington. He began by stating, yet again, that Wilson was "a political animal, highly skilled, intelligent, a master at infighting...and usually adept at making ambiguous public statements to serve his political aims." He explained that Wilson had "little or no room for maneuver" over the POL bombings because, in order to "meet tactical pressures from within his own party," he had in previous months frequently stated that there were limits on British support.[181] Though Wilson was committed to preserving friendly relations with the United States and was "prepared to cooperate with the United States on major American policies in ammeasure [sic] that would not always be popular here," in order "to counter the charge of being a mere puppet or satellite of the US, HMG would, from time to time, assert its independence by taking exception to certain details of policies to which he [*sic*] is ready to give general support."[182] Indeed, Bruce felt that Wilson regarded Vietnam "as posing in acute form the problem of defining acceptable limits of Anglo–American cooperation."[183]

Moreover, Bruce rightly acknowledged that Wilson's personal convictions on the war had also come into play: "[T]he military buildup apparently increased his fears of escalation and certainly cut against the grain of his belief that there could be no clear-cut military victory in Vietnam." Believing strongly in the need for a political settlement and increasingly frustrated by the lack of one, Wilson began to listen closely when "the dissidence over Vietnam widened to include a substantial number of Labor MPs in the center and on the right-wing," because party management was now at stake. According to Bruce, Wilson was also "influenced by an exaggerated idea of his possible effectiveness as a mediator with the Soviet authorities. He probably believes that had it not been for dissociation Kosygin would not now be about to receive him in Moscow."[184]

The ambassador, taking care not to sound too supportive of Wilson's decision, admitted that the prime minister "may have trapped himself...prematurely...by foreclosing the possibility of later differentiating between attacks successfully confined to military targets and those which have, in fact, consequences for civilian populations." He admitted, however, that it was doubtful Wilson could have sustained such a distinction within the Labour Party. He concluded by saying that "what saved him in domestic political terms was his not going...the whole hog with us."[185]

Bruce then went on to respond to the president's obvious fury over Wilson's statements and subsequent comments to the House. Johnson apparently expressed his firm opinion that British support for America's Vietnam policy should be complete.[186] Given what he had already said about Wilson's practical difficulties, Bruce suggested that the president "content himself with remarking on his disappointment in this connection, and say he expects continuing fidelity to the promises of adherence to our overall objectives in Vietnam." Having done that, Johnson could then "effectively add that after reviewing the debates in the House of Commons he had noticed that Heath, Douglas-Home and others of the opposition had been much stronger advocates for American policy in Vietnam" than Wilson's government.[187]

Bruce felt that he could not guarantee Wilson's silence over Vietnam during his trip to Washington. "Wilson is a cautious master of obfuscation. No one can guarantee in advance the conduct of another; the tongue is one of the least predictable of human organs. But given the overriding desire and necessity for the Prime Minister to remain on good terms with the President, or to restore any impairment of them, he will be doubly careful to try to avoid saying anything embarrassing to us."[188] At this stage the ambassador predicted that Wilson would "descant" upon British internal politics, Rhodesia, Vietnam, Europe, arms sales by Britain to the United States, East of Suez commitments, and the economic situation in Britain.

The following day Bruce attempted to analyze Wilson's decision making still further. In a question-and-answer exercise sent to Washington by cable, he asked why Wilson did not recognize that with the failure of Hanoi and Peking to talk "there would be progressive increase in the scale of U.S. military power" in Vietnam, since the president was determined to see the war through. He answered tentatively that "Wilson has never made that 'logical' jump. For political reasons he would not find it possible openly to endorse. He felt that he had to maintain posture that military victory in Vietnam not on cards, even though auspices for peace were so discouraging."[189] Washington, and the president in particular, had three major misgivings about the whole dissociation affair—first, why Wilson had gone to the "lengths of positive dissociation" from the bombings, "once it had been explained to him in advance that the sites selected were not near city centres" but legitimate military objectives that "could be taken out without substantial civilian losses"; second, why, given his now large majority, Wilson could not "more easily have controlled rebels than in last parliament"; and third, if the United States escalated its bombing campaign even further, whether Wilson would engage in other "dissociations."[190] Bruce admitted that he was not certain of the answer to the first question; he surmised that Wilson may have "felt trapped" by previous commitments; he may have felt that the bombings changed the situation psychologically and politically even if not necessarily militarily; and, of course, he had to manage his party. The second area of contention was easier to explain. Wilson could, and indeed had been able to, manage the hard left on Vietnam, but now the problem was more widespread and "it was because Wilson went part of [the] way through dissociation to dramatize [the] importance of 'independent' British position re. threat of expanding war...that he was able to avoid [a] wider pattern of revolt in party ranks." The last question surrounding the chances of further dissociations was, of course, unanswerable, but Bruce argued that Wilson "had made it...difficult for himself by taking this decision. He cannot 'reassociate' himself if bombing patterns develops [a] new turn."[191]

Without doubt, the dissociation episode had a detrimental impact on Anglo–American relations, particularly the personal relationship between Wilson and Johnson. Philip Kaiser, deputy U.S. ambassador to Great Britain, explained that "when we bombed Hanoi, Wilson felt compelled to criticize us, though he did so rather mildly. Johnson reacted with typical vehemence, sharply castigating the Prime Minister. As a consequence, relations between the two men, never too warm, deteriorated temporarily."[192] William Bundy agreed, stating that "the President just didn't trust Wilson" after dissociation. "He thought he was trying to make time politically.... [T]here's no doubt in the President's mind this established Wilson, as far as I know unchangingly, as a man not to go to the well with."[193]

On Thursday, July 14, the cabinet took note of a statement by the Foreign Secretary on the United States that read as follows:

[O]ur relations with the United States Government were passing through a difficult phase. They were for understandable reasons preoccupied with the conflict in Vietnam and, although our opposition to the bombing of the oil installations near Hanoi and Haiphong had been expected, there had been an adverse reaction to our public statement. Our position over the sale of arms which might be used in Vietnam had also been the cause of some friction. Although we must maintain our right to disagree from time to time with those aspects of United States policy of which we could not approve, it was important to our interests that there should be no major disagreement between us.[194]

Washington and London recognized that the summer of 1966 was the nadir in the Johnson–Wilson relationship so far, and probably the lowest point in Anglo–American relations since Suez. Attempts to repair the damage began right away.

WILSON'S TRIP TO MOSCOW, JULY 1966, AND THE STERLING CRISIS

In early July the British were faced with yet another crisis over sterling. Despite the chancellor's optimism over the state of the British economy, expressed at a meeting on July 1, the publication on July 4 of gold figures for June showed a further drain on sterling.[195] A number of factors were involved in this, not the least of which was the cost of a seven-week seaman's strike that began on May 16.

Rampant speculation ensued, and by July 14 the Labour government faced hard choices on how to deal with the crisis. At the cabinet meeting on that day Wilson, Callaghan, and George Brown were in agreement that "it was no answer just to go on borrowing," that there had to be "a fundamental appraisal of strategy."[196] They made a statement in the House that day announcing the government's decision that overseas spending would be cut by £100 million (in addition to previously announced defense cuts). In the course of the debate on this decision and in response to an attack by Michael Stewart, who felt this would have great effects on U.K. foreign relations and "ruin our influence," Wilson admitted it would mean "£50 million out of Germany and £50 million East of Suez."[197] A statement was duly delivered that announced a thorough review of Britain's financial position and the necessary measures needed to rectify the situation.[198] It did nothing to alleviate the pressure on sterling.

The cabinet also agreed that a fuller statement would be made the following Wednesday, July 20, announcing measures to compress internal demand. The Americans were eager to influence this particular statement. Secretary of the Treasury Henry Fowler telephoned Callaghan on the evening of July 14 to express his disappointment in the performance of the British economy in the last year and to urge the chancellor to take swift action to deal with the present crisis that "not only sounded adequate but would prove to be adequate." Callaghan outlined the program of measures to be undertaken and said he felt confident that it would be a success, although it would "comprise a very tough package for the country to swallow." He also said there was "no dissension in the Cabinet, except with respect to overseas expenditures, and the source of that problem really was in the United States."[199]

The U.S. contingency group that had been assembled the previous year to discuss sterling issues met again. The group acknowledged Wilson's difficulties in the long term and admitted that he still faced the prospect of saving money by cutting defense expenditures, both internally and externally. There was great domestic pressure for Wilson to do this. The U.S. position, however, remained opposed to the proposed British cure. McNamara in particular still believed it was "absolutely essential" that the United Kingdom remain in the Far East. Fowler informed the president of McNamara's views that "for the next year or two, he thinks anything which will smell of a British pull out will fatally undermine our domestic base on Viet Nam. Further, he believes that confrontation in Malaysia will, in fact, continue indefinitely and is determined that it remain a British responsibility."[200] Fowler admitted the United States faced some "critical choices" on this issue and informed the president that his advisors were "of two minds": some supported McNamara's view that Britain had to remain in the Far East at all costs, others believed devaluation of the pound should not be ruled out. Fowler personally believed that "if we adopt Bob's position—and Wilson goes alone—it will either cost us a weak Britain and a great deal of balance of payments money or, even more likely, a weak Britain and an eventual devaluation of sterling. Either would have disastrous consequences for the dollar—and for our international political position." Moreover, he did "not believe that this, or any other U.K. government, will be willing to maintain an overseas position in which it does not believe, for the sake of a friend—unless that friend is willing to pay for the favor."[201] Because Fowler felt the United States could not afford an open-ended financial commitment to the United Kingdom, he argued that "our first priority should be to move the United Kingdom to save its long-term economic and financial position and thereby to prevent potentially disastrous consequences for the United States, our over-all foreign policy, and the stability of the Free World financial system. A weak ally is of no use to us East of Suez, in Europe, in the international financial set-up, or anywhere else."[202] Despite Fowler's arguments, Johnson, a politician with an image to consider, particularly in the lead-up to congressional elections, favored McNamara's view that the United States could not afford to act alone as world police officer.

The White House was well aware that sterling would be on the agenda during Wilson's visit to Washington. In the middle of the sterling crisis, between July 16 and July 18, Wilson visited Moscow. The prime minister faced much criticism for leaving the country amid an economic crisis, and partly for this reason Wilson defended his decision in his memoirs, perhaps exaggerating the impact of his trip.[203] Though the trip was ostensibly arranged so that he could visit a British trade fair, the primary reason for his visit was to mediate over Vietnam. Although Wilson was genuine in his desire to encourage the Russians to intervene on Vietnam, he was once again primarily motivated by domestic considerations. After the prime minister's announcement of dissociation, Wilson faced calls from his left-wingers for complete dissociation from U.S. policy. On July 6 a petition signed by 100 M.P.s had called for a total condemnation of U.S. policy, and Wilson had had to intervene personally to prevent a PLP split. Before the visit to Moscow the U.S. Department of State felt "the subject matter and visibility of the trip are certainly designed to earn (and have already won) new political points for the Prime Minister on the domestic front in the UK, even if the gains in foreign relations terms turn out to be very minor."[204] It was also recognized that "coming less than two weeks before a Wilson visit to Washington to see President Johnson, the trip to the Soviet capital also gives Wilson the aura and glamor of confidante and go-between between East and West. This is a role which the British have long sought to play, while remaining closely linked to the US."[205] The Department of State also noted that Wilson's ploy had "effectively restored the situation among Labor Party MP's" when he was able to announce the visit to Moscow on July 7 during a Commons debate, "together with a Government motion that implied criticism of the bombings without directly expressing or withdrawing general support for U.S. policy in Vietnam." According to U.S. intelligence, "[I]n the division on the Government's motion some of the original rebels, such as Michael Foot, voted for the Government; none voted against; and only thirty-one chose to abstain. Many stated that the announcement of the Moscow visit had strongly influenced their ballot."[206] The Government won its motion.

Publicly Wilson made great play of the fact that his visit had Johnson's approval, although again the State Department held no great hopes for the visit in relation to Vietnam, believing correctly that the Russians would merely use Wilson to convey their belief that the dangers of escalation were great. However, in his memoirs Wilson emphasized what he called his "main point" in the discussions on Vietnam. The North Vietnamese had been threatening to put American POWs on trial in Hanoi, and it was hoped that Wilson could urge the Russians to intervene on this issue, particularly considering the probable U.S. repercussions should such trials go ahead. The Americans did not believe the Russians would want to discuss this.[207] However, Wilson claims that he "urged them as strongly as I could to bring home to Hanoi what this would mean. Clearly they were impressed; their fears of escalation were very real and I was left in no doubt... that they were going to act. They did."[208] He therefore judged his visit a success.

President Johnson later privately said, and Senator Mansfield, Senate majority leader, clearly on the President's briefing, publicly said that it was my intervention which had stopped the trials, and headed off the most dangerous situation in the war. Without doubt, US opinion, sharply divided on Vietnam, would have lurched violently to the side of the hawks if the pilots had been put on trial and I have little doubt, from all the President told me, that he would have had to respond.[209]

Wilson certainly voiced his belief that he had been vital in getting the North Vietnamese to rethink their plans for show trials. At their meeting in late July

1966, Wilson described to the president and his advisers how he had warned Kosygin "repeatedly and categorically of the reaction which the Soviet Government must expect if the Government of North Viet-Nam took exemplary action against the captured United States pilots; and he thought it reasonable to believe that it was as a result of Moscow's transmitting this warning to Hanoi that the Government of North Viet-Nam had subsequently adopted a more lenient attitude."[210] This partly explains Wilson's continuing belief that he was playing a vital role as a mediator between the United States and the Soviet Union/North Vietnam, despite that he had to conclude after his Moscow trip that there was "no give whatever" in the Soviets' position on Vietnam. He told President Johnson that Kosygin remained "bitter and tough," casting the U.S. president as "the bloodthirsty villain of the piece" and working for his "increasing isolation and friendlessness in the world."[211] Nevertheless, Wilson thought his visit had been worthwhile, believing the "unsensational relationship" that was developing between Kosygin and himself had "real—if still largely potential—value."[212]

During his visit to Moscow, Wilson was "kept in close touch with the situation in London."[213] After the financial measures announced by Callaghan on July 20, the U.S. government acknowledged that Wilson had "clearly swallowed the necessary economic medicine."[214] Indeed, the steps taken were extremely tough. Along with even more cuts in public investment and tighter controls on hire purchase and foreign exchange, the Labour government introduced a six-month freeze on pay and price increases, to be followed by a further six months of severe restraint. Not surprisingly, this package proved extremely unpopular with much of the Labour movement, including many within the PLP. Again, the U.S. Federal Reserve Bank helped coordinate a massive purchase of sterling to restore confidence.

It was at this time that the British embassy in Washington began to get the distinct impression that many U.S. officials were no longer terrified by the prospect of a British devaluation. Some of this feeling stemmed "from the D.O.D. [Department of Defense] who feel that continued United Kingdom psychological support of the United States in the Far East is of more importance than the sterling rate."[215] The Prime Minister would therefore have to raise the issue of further financial support, if needed, during his trip to Washington.

WILSON'S VISIT TO WASHINGTON, JULY 29, 1966

With the Wilson–LBJ relationship fraught over POL dissociation, the prime minister's plans to visit Washington proved predictably contentious. Wilson later admitted that "no overseas visit had a worse build-up."[216] The White House was well aware that Wilson's visit would be "big news" in Washington and anticipated several public relations problems. The prime minister's visit could stir up yet further reports on Hanoi's readiness for talks prior to the air attacks on the POLs and would reignite speculation that, despite Wilson's general statement of support, the British were really against the U.S. effort in South Vietnam.[217] Nevertheless, despite—or indeed, because of—the careful preparation that took place, the visit went remarkably well.

In the initial planning stages, the White House rightly surmised that one of the major reasons for Wilson's visit was "to reconfirm in public and private, the LBJ–Wilson friendship post 'dissociation.' "[218] Shortly before the prime minister's visit a member of the Foreign Office, J. A. Thomson, met with White House aides and State Department officials, concluding that most agreed with Rostow's view that the mood would be "tough" but "polite" when Wilson arrived in Washington.[219] Thomson reported back to London that many people spoke of "the President's adverse reaction to Her Majesty's Government's recent statements about the bombing and the sale of arms" and that Mr. Rostow had observed that the president "was hurt."[220] Reportedly Johnson wondered why the prime minister was coming. Thomson observed that "one implication of this remark was if the main reason for the visit lay in domestic political considerations in the United Kingdom the President would not be sympathetic." However, Thomson found evidence of a "deeper and more important implication" that was conveyed to him by Francis Bator, someone who did not always agree with Rostow. Thomson explained that Bator was Rostow's deputy on political matters but "is autonomous . . . in economic matters and has independent, direct access to the President." Apparently Bator was so concerned that Thomson knew the president's mind on the question of Wilson's visit that he concluded their interview in Washington on July 15 by driving Thomson to the railway station, talking as they went.[221] According to Bator, Johnson had two criteria for judging the worth of the visits:

(a) what effect will it have on his big problem, Viet Nam?

(b) how much confidence could he have in Britain controlling her affairs in such a way that she could play a useful and important role?[222]

This view is supported in the American documentation. The Americans' first requirement on a list of what they wanted from the Wilson trip was "support instead of trouble on Vietnam."[223] Overall, Thomson was left with the impression that it was hoped in the White House that the prime minister could "restore the President's shaken confidence in the reliability of Britain as an ally." This questioning of British trustworthiness as an ally was due to the government's statements on arms sales, the dissociation, yet another sterling crisis, and doubts in Washington that Britain could sustain the world role it had outlined for itself in the latest defense review. On Vietnam, Bator surmised that the president hoped Wilson's actions before and after the visit would reiterate general support for the president's policy; repeat that "the conflict and its continuance was the fault of Hanoi"; and completely refuse to say "anything substantive about the bombing of oil installations or the sale of arms," instead referring all questioners to Hansard. Overall, it would be considered a "disappointment" if the effect of Wilson's visit was "merely neutral" on Vietnam.[224]

But a few days later, the atmosphere in Washington appears to have changed. This was caused by the latest sterling crisis and the consequent announcement that Britain would be making stringent defense cuts. Now Washington was eager to talk to the British. Patrick Dean cabled London on July 22 to report on his latest talks with Rostow and Bator and wrote,

It is clear that the Prime Minister's announcement of the new economic measures has created a new situation and a much better climate here. It has removed previous doubts about the purpose and value of the Prime Minister's visit and has defined fairly clearly the main issues for discussion with the President. As Rostow put it "there are now very basic things for the President and the Prime Minister to discuss." All talk about "a laundry list" has disappeared.[225]

Wilson had stuck to the September 1965 "understanding." Monetary policy and Britain's world role would nevertheless be at the top of the agenda in Washington.

George Ball felt that Harold Wilson's visit offered an "opportunity for an act of statemanship" on the president's behalf. Perhaps sensing that Wilson might pull out of the "understanding" now that he had a new majority, Ball, in a lengthy memorandum, told the president that instead of following a "general line of short-term improvisation that has marked our relations with a succession of British Governments since the end of the war," the alternative would be "to look beyond the immediate present and to talk with Wilson in some depth about the longer-range relations between our two nations based on a clear understanding of the respective roles which each country should play in the development of a rational world system. This is a difficult and rigorous exercise. It requires that each of us clearly face reality."[226] Ball explained the reality of the situation as he saw it.

Britain must recognize that she is no longer the center of a world system but that she can nevertheless play a critical role by applying her talents and resources to the leadership of Western Europe. We, on our part, should face the fact that it is basically unhealthy to encourage the United Kingdom to continue as America's poor relation, living beyond her means by periodic American bailouts. We must, in other words, redefine the so-called "special relationship" in terms consistent with the longer-range interest of both our nations.[227]

The British in Washington got wind of these thoughts but were reassured that this was Ball experiencing "end-of-termism," and that there was no serious likelihood of the president or secretary of state approving this action. Nor did they approve it, not least because to have taken Ball seriously at the time would have been to broach a major realignment of the alliance system during an already difficult period for U.S. foreign policy.[228] More importantly, perhaps, was McNamara's fear of the signal such a pullout East of Suez would send to the rest of the world. In the end, the discussion between the president and the prime minister did not venture beyond short- and medium-term policies.

On the morning of Friday, July 29, Johnson and Wilson had a private talk for about one hour and 15 minutes. As was now usual, their talk included a discussion of their respective domestic concerns. Johnson reported to the other participants of the talks that "he felt that he now had a very good understanding and appreciation of the problems which faced the United Kingdom, and he hoped that the prime minister felt the same as regards the United States." The president also said the discussion had been "very interesting and most helpful" and that they discussed in detail the prime minister's trip to the Soviet Union and had exchanged views on their common problems, especially Vietnam, the British position East of Suez, the German situation, and the British economic measures.[229] The president said the purpose of the meeting "was to strengthen the ties which bound the two countries . . . in order that they might go forward in unity to deal with their common problems and to give the necessary leadership to their two peoples."[230]

The meeting adjourned for lunch, at which there were the usual toasts. The president began with a reference to recent events: "someone suggested, to-day, Mr. Prime Minister, that I begin by saying this toast: 'My good dis-associates.' But this is not the case at all. For 200 years the British and the Americans have had their differences but from them have emerged a strong bond, a hearty spirit, and a mutual respect that neither adversaries nor age can diminish." Later on in his toast, Johnson appeared to compare Wilson to Winston Churchill.

In World War II, Mr. Prime Minister, England saved herself by fortitude and the world by example. You personally are asking of the British people to-day the same fortitude— the same resolve—that turned the tide in those days.

I must say that England is blessed now, as it was blessed then, with gallant and hardy leadership. In you, Sir, she has a man of mettle. She is blessed with a leader whose own enterprise and courage will show the way. We believe your firmness and your leadership have impressed the people of the world deeply in the tradition of the great men of Britain.[231]

Wilson's response included his thanks that the president had rejected the "disassociates" theme, commenting, "[W]e are allies and not satellites and I think as long as we are allies and not satellites we are of more use to you, we are of more use to ourselves, and we are of more use to the world."[232] According to Wilson, the president's "gently ironic allusion" to British dissociation, as Wilson put it, did not detract from the warmth of the president's speech, which stressed the permanence of the bonds between Great Britain and the United States. Wilson was pleased that Johnson made no mention of the dissociation episode again during the talks, nor did he say anything about British arms supplies for use in Vietnam.[233] Of course, this may well have been a case of not opening old wounds.

When the meeting resumed at 2:30 P.M., the only commitment the prime minister made regarding the "joint effort" in Southeast Asia was to allow British army engineers to remain in Thailand for a further year to help with civil construction projects and to send specialist troops currently in Malaya to deal with communist guerrillas on the Thai border once the confrontation in Malaysia had ended.[234] At a later meeting between Rusk and Wilson, the secretary of state said he wondered if the recent episode with the captured U.S. airmen perhaps suggested that Hanoi was susceptible to pressure and consequently wondered if it was worth "trying to organise some kind of joint Parliamentary and Congressional *démarche* in relation to Hanoi to try to persuade the Government of North Viet-Nam to respond to the repeatedly declared willingness of the United States to start discussions for bringing the war to an end."[235] He suggested that the prime minister convey a message to Kosygin on those lines, emphasizing the U.S. interest in de-escalating, rather than escalating, the conflict. The United Kingdom might also approach the governments of nonaligned and Commonwealth countries to the same end. Rusk also suggested mobilizing the support of the pope and all living holders of the Nobel Peace Prize. In response to this, Wilson agreed that this might work but suggested "that any proposal of this kind might be combined with, or be an alternative to, the suggestion that the United States should now stabilise the level of their troops in Viet-Nam and abstain from any further build-up in return for an undertaking that the Ho Chi Minh trail would be effectively blocked."[236] Rusk said he would speak to the president and McNamara about this but could see no reason "to reject the idea out of hand." The prime minister felt "the first step might be to send two or three British Parliamentarians to Washington to discuss the project with such Congressional spokesman as the United States Government might suggest. Thereafter, the Commonwealth might be mobilised to support the initiative. And the process might culminate in a new international mission to Hanoi."[237] Yet again Wilson's need to appear active on the diplomatic front was given sanction by the Americans and, possibly in order to avoid further British dissociations, actively encouraged.[238]

Wilson returned to London in time for England's victory in the World Cup final and, as he himself admitted, "[T]he British reading and viewing public were not interested that weekend in international affairs."[239] Nevertheless, on Saturday *The Times* reported on Wilson's "pugilistic performance" and his "confident tone"[240] while in Washington, and the Sunday newspapers were, as Castle noted in her diary, "full of Harold's spectacular reception by Johnson in America." Henry Brandon in the *Sunday Times* described Wilson's public performance as "truly impressive."[241]

After the visit, Johnson sent a personal message to Wilson that was extremely warm in tone considering the previous month's difficulties.

Thank you for coming my friend. We had a good talk. As you know, our friendship is a source of comfort and strength to me. I very much enjoyed your toast—and I meant what I said in mine. And I look forward to meeting with you again. Best wishes to you and your colleagues for a safe journey home. I wish you well in the difficult task which you and your Government now face.[242]

Wilson reciprocated in equally friendly terms: "I find it difficult to say how much our talks together have heartened me at a time when life has not been altogether easy, there may still be rough weather ahead for both of us, but I have no doubt that, so long as we go on pulling together, it will work out all right in the end."[243]

The British were perplexed at the warmth of the reception Wilson had received in Washington. In the week following it, Patrick Dean reported that the general feeling in Washington was that the visit "was highly successful, certainly more so than people had expected."[244] He reported further that a number of people had said "how well the Prime Minister must have handled the President to have obtained such a satisfactory result and there is I think general pleasure on almost all sides that the close and friendly relations established during the Prime Minister's visit here last December have not only been preserved but strengthened."[245] During a brief conversation with the president at the diplomatic reception for Luci Johnson's wedding, Johnson told Bruce how much he had enjoyed seeing the prime minister and what a useful meeting it had been. And Jack Valenti, one of the president's closest advisers, also told Bruce that the president had said to him, "I really do like that man." Rusk admitted to Bruce after the visit that he had been very surprised at the warmth of the toast the president proposed at the lunch. Dean confided to Maclehose at the Foreign Office that Rusk's comments reflected "a report that the President's decision to line up so closely with the Prime Minister was only taken rather late in the day."[246]

Dean attempted to explain the success of the visit, particularly "why...the President deployed such an exceptional effort to turn the visit into a major political and personal event." First, the president's "instinctive friendliness" may have played a part.[247] Combined with this, Wilson had been wise to keep the visit short considering how busy the administration was. He believed "one of the reasons...the President likes doing business with the Prime Minister is that he can in a very short space of time talk to somebody who really knows his business and talks about what really matters."[248] Second, Dean surmised that for purely selfish reasons it made sense for the Americans to "reinforce international confidence in the Prime Minister and H.M.G. and, hence in sterling. When there are already so many problems and so many unfriendly 'allies' all over the world, there is no point in seeing them increased by the political or economic demise of the only other Western country which exercises genuine worldwide responsibility, whatever they may feel about the relationship between the pound and the dollar." Third, and directly related to the situation in Vietnam, Dean believed that

although the President must have known that he could not expect anything of major importance in the way of additional help or new commitments East of Suez, the negative aim of ensuring that H.M.G., whether now or later on, do not withdraw their general support for the United States over Vietnam and in relation to South East Asia generally, acquired an almost dramatic importance when the President began to reflect seriously upon the potential consequences of Britain drifting seriously out of line.

The reason that the president came to this viewpoint was also explained by Patrick Dean.

It may be that H.M.G.'s dissociation from the bombing of Hanoi and Haiphong and the position we took over arms supplies did more than just irritate the President at the time. Once the first annoyance had subsided they may actually have rattled him. On any careful calculation it is extremely important from the point of view of American standing with world opinion that the leading socialist-governed country in the world should support their objectives in South East Asia. The converse could be extremely damaging, not only internationally, but in domestic terms since American public opinion still has a latent sense of guilt which it is much easier to allay when the Administration can point to the moral and physical support of other countries for what the U.S. is trying to do in Vietnam.

This, of course, was received in London as evidence that Britain could influence Johnson and his policies. If Dean was right, and all the evidence seems to point that way, Britain still had some leverage in its relations with the United States.

And finally, Dean suggested that the Johnson administration might have had a fit of compassion for, and empathy with, the British government over its financial difficulties.

As is becoming more and more apparent, the Administration may be faced in the not-too-distant future with the need for fairly stringent economic measures to control the growing inflationary tendencies in the American economy stemming, in part, from the approach of full employment. The President may therefore see a strong vested interest in praising the Prime Minister's courage, in endorsing H.M.G.'s economic policies and, of course, in the success of a programme of retrenchment which is going to hurt quite a large section of the British public.[249]

Dean concluded that the only way to understand Johnson's change of heart was to recognize that

underneath all the President's fair words...there was a good deal of American self-interest in the whole exercise. Certainly the personal rapport between the President and the Prime Minister was reaffirmed and I have no doubt that the President genuinely enjoys seeing the Prime Minister and talking to him about their mutual problems. He also has admiration for the Prime Minister's power of exposition and conviction. In addition, the meeting brought out quite clearly that both the Americans and ourselves badly need each other.[250]

If it was essential that both Britain and the United States make their interests coincide, as the Foreign Office responded to Dean, then Wilson's July visit went as well as could be expected. The United States was reassured to hear that Wilson was being firm on economic issues and that Britain intended, for the time being at least, to continue the "joint effort" East of Suez. It was also relieved to hear that Wilson intended to continue to support the United States' general policy in Vietnam, even if he reserved the right to disagree with some of the specifics. The United States also believed that Britain could still increase its practical contribution to the fight in Southeast Asia. Wilson and his colleagues came away from Washington not only with pandered egos but also with the feeling that the Americans still needed them, particularly on Vietnam, and that that strengthened their position on sterling. The tensions in Anglo–American relations that had been so severe in June now appeared to have subsided. This was particularly timely because in the second half of 1966 events in Rhodesia preoccupied the British government's foreign policy, and London needed Washington's acquiescence and cooperation over this. At the same time, the United States continued its escalation of the war, and the unpopularity of the war continued to grow both at home and abroad. Consequently, although the Labour government had more pressing issues to deal with toward the end of 1966, plans for yet another peace initiative were under way.

NOTES

1. Sir Patrick Dean to Michael Stewart, United States of America: Annual Review for 1965, February 18, 1966, FO371/184995/AU1011/1, PRO.

2. Foreign Office Minute by G. C. Mayhew, Annual Review for 1965, February 22, 1966, FO371/184995/AU1011/1, PRO.

3. Sir Patrick Dean to Michael Stewart, United States of America: Annual Review for 1965, February 18, 1966, FO371/184995/AU1011/1, PRO.

4. Ibid.

5. Ibid.

6. Record of a Conversation over Lunch between the Foreign Secretary and Mr. Rusk at the State Department, January 27, 1966, PREM 13/1272, PRO.

7. Memorandum from Walt W. Rostow to Benjamin H. Read, Subject: North Vietnam Shipping—Prime Minister Wilson's Message of May 9 to the President, File: UK, vol. 8, Memos (2 of 2), 1/66–7/66, box 209, CF, UK, NSF, LBJL.

8. Chester Cooper, *The Lost Crusade: The Full Story of US Involvement in Vietnam from Roosevelt to Nixon* (London: MacGibbon and Kee, 1970), 492.

9. Robert S. McNamara, *In Retrospect: The Tragedy and Lessons of Vietnam* (New York: Random House, 1995), 221.

10. Telegram from Averell Harriman to President and Secretary of State, May 5, 1966, File: UK, Cables, vol. 8, 1/66–7/66, box 209 (2 of 2), CF, UK, NSF, LBJL.

11. McNamara, *Argument without End: In Search of Answers to the Vietnam Tragedy* (New York: Public Affairs, 1999), 276–78; and McNamara, *In Retrospect*, 207–31. At the same time, however, ground, air, and sea operations in South Vietnam and Laos not only resumed but actually increased (one reason that the North Vietnamese leadership did not take the bombing pause seriously).

12. McNamara, *In Retrospect*, 229.

13. *Times* (London), February 9, 1966, 12; Summary Notes of the 555th Meeting of the National Security Council, Washington, January 5, 1966, "Peace Offensive Regarding Vietnam," FRUS, Vietnam, vol. 4, 1966, 19.

14. Record of Conversation between the Prime Minister and the United States Ambassador at No. 10 Downing Street at 12:10 P.M., January 10, 1967, PREM 13/1917, PRO.

15. Telegram from Foreign Office to Patrick Dean, December 29, 1965, Vietnam, PREM 13/1271, PRO.

16. Code-named PINTA.

17. Telegram from Prime Minister to President, December 31, 1965, PREM 13/1196, PRO.

18. January 7–12, 1966.

19. Letter from Tom Bridges, Foreign Office, to Malcome Reid, 10 Downing Street, December 30, 1965, PREM 13/1271, PRO.

20. Notes of a Meeting, January 3, 1966, in FRUS, vol. 4, 7.

21. During the pause, DRV official representatives met directly with U.S. officials (Rangoon) and communicated officially to a friendly "neutral" (Vientiane). Washington suspected this move was made in an attempt to prevent a resumption of the bombing. There was also some indication that the North Vietnamese would free captured U.S. airmen. See Memo for Mr. Bundy from Chester L. Cooper, January 24, 1966, Declassified Document Series, Library of Congress. Wilson described the Vientiane approach as "dubious," and despite informing Moscow that the United States was prepared for any sort of confidential indication "that there was in fact any conscious change in the military pace," nothing came from Hanoi.

22. Telegram from the President to the Prime Minister, January 24, 1966, PREM 13/1196, PRO.

23. Telegram from the Prime Minister to the President, January 26, 1966, PREM 13/1196, PRO.

24. Memo from Bundy, "Diplomatic and Political Factors Affecting the Resumption of Bombing," January 28, 1966, in FRUS 1964–68, Vietnam, vol. 4, January 1–31, 1966, 153.

25. Notes of Meeting, January 29, 1966, in FRUS 1964–68, vol. 4, 182.

26. Notes of Meeting, "Resumption of Bombing," January 26, 1966, in FRUS 1964–68, Vietnam, vol. 4, January 1–31, 1966, 154; Telegram from the President to the Prime Minister, January 30, 1966, PREM 13/1196, PRO.

27. A by-election was also due to be held in Erith, so at the time of Solomons's death, Labour was faced with the prospect of having a majority of 2, 1, or 0 in the coming months.

28. Wilson, *The Labour Government 1964–70: A Personal Record* (London: Weidenfeld and Nicolson, 1979), 259.

29. Ibid., 266.

30. Benn, *Out of the Wilderness*, February 1, 1966, 381.

31. Telegram from Bruce, London, to Rusk, February 2, 1966, File: UK, vol. 8, Cables, 1/66–7/6, box 209, CF, UK, NSF, LBJL.

32. Richard Crossman, *The Crossman Diaries: Selections from the Diaries of a Cabinet Minister, 1964–70* (London: Mandarin, 1991), February 1, 1966, 175.

33. Telegram from Bruce, London, to Secretary of State, Washington, February 2, 1966, NSF, CF, UK, box 209, UK, vol. 8, Cables, 1/66–7/66, LBJL.

34. Wilson, *Labour Government*, 267.

35. Telegram from Prime Minister to President, February 9, 1966, PREM 13/1196, PRO.

36. Wilson, *Labour Government*, 267.

37. Telegram from Bruce to Rusk, February 2, 1966, File: UK, vol. 8, Cables, 1/66–7/66, box 209, CF, UK, NSF, LBJL.

38. Ibid.

39. Telegram from Prime Minister to President, February 9, 1966, PREM 13/1196, PRO.

40. Telegram from Bruce to Rusk, Washington, February 8, 1966, File: UK, vol. 8, Cables, 1/66–7/66, box 209, CF, UK, NSF, LBJL; *Hansard*, February 8, 1966, vol. 724, cols. 224–347.

41. Telegram from Bruce to Rusk, February 8, 1966, File: UK, vol. 8, Cables, 1/66–7/66, box 209, CF, UK, NSF, LBJL.

42. Telegram from Prime Minister to President, February 9, 1966, PREM 13/1196, PRO.

43. Barbara Castle, *The Barbara Castle Diaries 1964–76* (London: Papermac, 1990), February 3, 1966, 52.

44. Ibid.

45. Ibid.

46. Cabinet Minutes, February 3, 1966, CAB 128/41, PRO.

47. Wilson, *Labour Government*, 267.

48. Telegram from the Department of State to the Embassy in Vietnam, December 28, 1966, FRUS 1964–68, Vietnam, vol. 3, November–December 1965, 717.

49. Ibid. A Harris poll showed that 73 percent favored renewed effort for a cease-fire and 61 percent favored increased bombing if a pause failed to have any impact.

50. Telegram from Prime Minister to President, February 9, 1966, PREM 13/1196, PRO.

51. Cable, Harriman to President/Secretary of State, May 5, 1966, UK, Cables, VII, 1/66–7/66, box 209 (2 of 2), CF, UK, NSF, LBJL.

52. Cable from Arthur Goldberg, London, to President and Rusk, Washington, March 5, 1966, File: UK, vol. 8, Cables, 1/66–7/66, box 209, CF, UK, NSF, LBJL.

53. Cooper, *Lost Crusade*, 493.

54. Summary Notes of 555th Meeting of the National Security Council, January 5, 1966, "Peace Offensive Regarding Vietnam," FRUS, vol. 4, 19.

55. Text of message from Prime Minister Wilson to the President, February 14, 1966, PM Wilson Correspondence, August 30, 1965–February 27, 1966, Head of State Correspondence, UK, vol. 2 (1 of 2), box 9, NSF, LBJL.

56. Ibid.

57. Ibid.

58. Cable from the President to the Prime Minister, February 14, 1966, PREM 13/1196, PRO.

59. Cable from Prime Minister to President, no date, PREM 13/1196, PRO.

60. Wilson, *Labour Government*, 278.

61. Cable from the Prime Minister to President, no date, PREM 13/1196; Cabinet Minutes, February 24, 1966, CAB128/41, PRO.

62. Castle, *Barbara Castle Diaries*, 56.

63. Robert Jackson, *The Malayan Emergency: The Commonwealth's War 1948–1966* (London: Routledge, 1991), 139.

64. Record of a Conversation over Lunch between the Foreign Secretary and Mr. Rusk, the United States Secretary of State for Foreign Affairs, State Department, January 27, 1966, PREM 13/1272, PRO.

65. Ibid.

66. Foreign Office Minute, "End of Confrontation: Military Assistance to the United States," June 8, 1966, PREM 13/1890, PRO; and Cable from State to American Embassy London, May 20, 1966, NSF, CF, UK, box 209, vol. 8, Cables, 1/66–7/66, LBJL.

67. Cable from State to American Embassy London, May 20, 1966, NSF, CF, UK, box 209, vol. 8, Cables, 1/66–7/66, LBJL.

68. Telegram from Brussels to Foreign Office, June 6, 1965, PREM 13/1890, PRO.

69. Ibid.

70. Ibid.

71. *Hansard*, May 17, 1966, Oral Answers, vol. 728, col. 1119.

72. Ibid. It is also striking how British exports to the United States of pesticides and herbicides saw a 275 percent increase during the years from 1964 to 1967; chemical products saw an increase of 310 percent; and bombs, grenades, guided weapons, and ammunitions rose by 560 percent. U.S. Chamber of Commerce figures.

73. Memo of Conversation between Patrick Dean and Dean Rusk, June 22, 1965, File: UK, vol. 4, Memos (2 of 2), 7/65–9/65, box 208, CF, UK, NSF, LBJL.

74. Foreign Office Minute, South East Asia Department, "End of Confrontation: Military Assistance to the United States," June 8, 1966, PREM 13/1890, PRO.

75. Ibid.

76. Ibid.

77. Record of a Conversation between the Prime Minister and the U.S. Secretary of State at 10:00 A.M. at 10 Downing Street on Friday, June 10, 1966, PREM 13/1890, PRO.

78. Ibid.

79. Ibid.

80. Ibid.

81. Cable from Prime Minister to President, June 10, 1966, PREM 13/1808, PRO.

82. Foreign Office Minute, South East Asia Department, "End of Confrontation: Military Assistance to the United States," June 8, 1966, PREM 13/1890, PRO.

83. *Hansard*, June 23, 1966, vol. 730, cols. 918–22.

84. Ibid.

85. Telegram from Bruce to Rusk, June 25, 1966, File: UK, vol. 3, Cables, 1/66–7/66, box 209, CF, UK, NSF, LBJL.

86. Ibid.

87. Ibid.

88. Ibid.

89. *Hansard,* June 30, 1966, vol. 730, col. 324.

90. Memorandum to the President from Walt Rostow, July 14, 1966, File: UK, vol. 8, Memos (1 of 2), 1/66–7/66, CF, UK, NSF, LBJL.

91. Telegram from Bruce to Rusk, July 1, 1966, File: UK, vol. 8, Cables, 1/66–7/66, box 209, CF, UK, NSF, LBJL.

92. Memo to the President from Walt Rostow, July 14, 1966, File: UK, vol. 8, Memos (1 of 2), 1/66–7/66, CF, UK, NSF, LBJL.

93. Telegram from the President to the Prime Minister, May 27, 1966, PREM 13/1808, PRO.

94. Telegram from Bruce to Ball, Washington, July 11, 1966, NSF, Files of Walt Rostow, "Wilson Visit," box 12, LBJL.

95. Bruce to Acting Secretary of State Ball, June 2, 1966, UK, Cables, vol. 8, 1/66–7/66, box 209 (2 of 2), CF, UK, NSF, LBJL.

96. Telegram from the Prime Minister to the President, June 3, 1966, PREM 13/1808, PRO.

97. Telegram from Walt Rostow to the President, June 3, 1966, PM Wilson Correspondence, March 23, 1966–June 3, 1966, Head of State Correspondence File, UK, vol. 4, box 9, NSF, LBJL.

98. Summary Notes of the 559th NSC Meeting, Washington, June 17, 1966, in FRUS, 1964–68, vol. 4, Vietnam 1966, 438.

99. Telegram from Rusk to White House, June 7, 1966, File: UK, vol. 8, Memos, (1 of 2), 1/66/–7/66, box 209, CF, UK, NSF, LBJL.

100. Letter from A. M. Palliser to C. M. Maclehose, Foreign Office, June 10, 1966, PREM 13/1083.

101. Ibid.

102. Ibid.

103. Telegram to the President from Prime Minister Wilson, June 10, 1966, NSF, Files of Walt Rostow, "Wilson Visit," box 12, LBJL.

104. Telegram from Rusk to White House, June 2, 1966, File: UK, vol. 8, Cables, 1/66–7/66, box 209, CF, UK, NSF, LBJL.

105. Ibid.

106. Ibid.

107. Ibid.

108. Telegram from the Prime Minister to the President, June 10, 1966, PREM 13/1083, PRO.

109. Ibid.

110. Personal Cable to the Prime Minister from the President, June 14, 1966, File: Wilson Visit, Files of Walt W. Rostow, box 12, NSF, LBJL.

111. Ibid.

112. Ibid.

113. Telegram from Michael Stewart to Patrick Dean, June 14, 1966, PREM 13/1083, PRO.

114. Ibid.

115. Telegram from Patrick Dean to Michael Stewart, June 15, 1966, PREM 13/1083, PRO.

116. Robert Dallek, *Flawed Giant: Lyndon Johnson and His Times, 1961–1973* (Oxford: Oxford University Press, 1998), 364.

117. Ibid., 375.

118. Ibid., 356.

119. Telegram from Patrick Dean to Michael Stewart, June 15, 1965, PREM 13/1083, PRO.

120. Ibid.

121. Ibid.

122. Ibid.

123. Letter from Murray to A. M. Palliser, 10 Downing Street, June 15, 1966, PREM 13/1083, PRO.

124. Ibid.

125. Ibid.

126. Telegram from Prime Minister Wilson to the President, June 15, 1966, Files of Walt Rostow, "Wilson Visit," box 12, NSF, LBJL.

127. Ibid.

128. Draft Message from the Prime Minister to the President, June 15, 1966, PREM 13/1083, PRO.

129. Ibid.

130. Letter from J. E. Killick to C. M. Maclehose, June 16, 1966, PREM 13/1083, PRO.

131. Telegram from Killick to Maclehose, Foreign Office, June 17, 1966, PREM 13/1083, PRO.

132. Ibid.

133. Letter from Maclehose to Killick, June 17, 1966, PREM 13/1083, PRO.

134. Ibid.

135. Memorandum from Rostow to Rusk, June 18, 1966, Files of Walt Rostow, "Wilson Visit," box 12, NSF, LBJL.

136. Letter from J. E. Killick, British Embassy, Washington, to C. M. Macleshose, Foreign Office, June 20, 1966, PREM 13/1083, PRO.

137. Ibid.

138. Memorandum from Walt W. Rostow to the President, Friday, June 17, 1966, UK, vol. 8, Memos (1 of 2), 1/66–7/66, box 209, CF, UK, NSF, LBJL.

139. Ibid.

140. Ibid.

141. Memorandum from Rostow to Rusk, Files of Walt Rostow, "Wilson Visit," box 12, NSF, LBJL.

142. Summary Notes of 559th NSC Meeting, June 17, 6:05 P.M., NSC Meetings File, vol. 3, tab. 41, 6/17/66, Vietnam—POL, NSF, LBJL.

143. Ibid.

144. Discussion of Vietnam by Committee Chairmen or Designees, Washington, June 28, 1966, 12:30 P.M., FRUS, Vietnam, 1964–68, vol. 4, 465.

145. Letter from Patrick Dean to A. M. Palliser, June 22, 1966, PREM 13/1083, PRO.

146. Letter from A. M. Palliser to Patrick Dean, June 27, 1966, Top Secret and Personal, PREM 13/1083, PRO.

147. Letter from Patrick Dean to A. M. Palliser, June 22, 1966, PREM 13/1083, PRO.

148. Dallek, *Flawed Giant*, 258–59.

149. Letter from Patrick Dean to A. M. Palliser, June 22, 1966, PREM 13/1083, PRO.

150. Ibid.

151. Ibid.

152. Letter from Patrick Dean to A. M. Palliser, 10 Downing Street, June 23, 1966, PREM 13/1083, PRO.

153. Top Secret Minute to the Prime Minister from A. M. Palliser, "President Johnson," June 24, 1966, PREM 13/1083, PRO.

154. Telegram from Prime Minster to President, June 23, 1966, Head of State Correspondence File, UK, vol. 5 (1 of 2), PM Wilson Correspondence, June 10, 1966–December 5, 1966, box 10, NSF, LBJL.

155. Wilson, *Labour Government*, 320–21.

156. *Hansard*, June 29, 1966, vol. 730, col. 1796.

157. Ibid.

158. Ibid., col. 1797.

159. Telegram from Bruce to the President, July 12, 1966, Declassified Documents Series, Library of Congress.

160. *Hansard*, June 29, 1966, vol. 730, col. 1797.

161. For example, David Winnick, M.P., and Manny Shinwell, M.P.; *Hansard*, June 29, 1966, vol. 730, cols. 1806–7.

162. Castle, *Barbara Castle Diaries*, June 29, 1966, 72.

163. Crossman, *Crossman Diaries*, June 30, 1966, 214.

164. *Times* (London), July 1, 1966, 11.

165. Ibid.

166. From Prime Minister to President, July 1, 1966, NSF, Files of Walt Rostow, "Wilson Visit," box 12, LBJL; also PREM 13/1808.

167. Ibid.

168. Ibid.

169. Ibid.

170. Ibid.

171. Letter to Michael Palliser from Patrick Dean, July 2, 1966, PREM 13/1083, PRO.

172. Ibid.

173. Ibid.

174. From the President to the Prime Minister, July 2, 1966, NSF, Files of Walt W. Rostow, File, "Wilson Visit," box 12, LBJL; also PREM 13/1083.

175. Ibid.

176. No date, Files of Walt W. Rostow, File, "Wilson Visit," box 12, NSF, LBJL.

177. Telegram from Bruce to George Ball, July 4, 1966, Files of Walt W. Rostow, "Wilson Visit," box 12, NSF, LBJL.

178. Ibid.

179. Ibid.

180. Telegram from Bruce to Ball, July 11, 1966, Files of Walt Rostow, "Wilson Visit," box 12, NSF, LBJL.

181. Ibid.

182. Ibid.

183. Ibid.

184. Ibid.

185. Ibid.

186. Ibid.

187. Ibid.

188. Ibid.

189. Bruce to Secretary of State, Washington, July 12, 1966, UK, vol. 8, Cables, 1/66–7/66, box 209, CF, UK, NSF, LBJL.

190. Ibid.

191. Ibid.

192. Philip M. Kaiser, *Journeying Far and Wide: A Political and Diplomatic Memoir* (New York: Macmillan, 1992), 209.

193. Transcript, William Bundy oral history interview by Paige E. Mulholland, May 29, 1971, tape 4, 25, 36, LBJL.

194. Cabinet Minutes, July 14, 1966, CAB 128/41, PRO.

195. Wilson, *Labour Government*, 322.

196. Castle, *Diaries*, July 14, 1966, 73.

197. Ibid.

198. Wilson, *Labour Government*, 328.

199. Note of Telephone Conversation between Secretary of the Treasury Fowler and Chancellor of the Exchequer Callaghan at 6:30 P.M. on July 15, 1966, Files of Walt Rostow, "Wilson Visit," box 12, NSF, LBJL.

200. Memorandum for the President from Henry Fowler, July 18, 1966, Subject: The Sterling Crisis and the U.S. Bargaining Position vis-a-vis the UK, Files of Walt Rostow, "Wilson Visit," box 12, NSF, LBJL.

201. Ibid.

202. Ibid.

203. Wilson, *Labour Government*, 328–31.

204. Intelligence Note from Thomas L. Hughes to Rusk, July 15, 1966, UK, vol. 8, Memos (1 of 2), 1/66–7/66, box 209, CF, UK, NSF, LBJL.

205. Ibid.

206. Ibid.

207. Wilson, *Labour Government*, 329–30.

208. Ibid.

209. Ibid., 330.

210. Record of a Meeting between the Prime Minister and His Advisers and President Johnson and His Advisers at the White House on Friday, July 29, 1966, Visit of the Prime Minister to the United States and Canada, July 28–30, 1966, PREM 13/1083, PRO.

211. Telegram from Prime Minister to President, July 19, 1966, PREM 13/1262, PRO.

212. Ibid.

213. Wilson, *Labour Government*, 331.

214. Memo for the President from Francis M. Bator, Thursday, July 21, 1966, Files of Walt Rostow, "Wilson Visit," box 12, NSF, LBJL.

215. Telegram from Mr. Killock, British Embassy, Washington, to Foreign Office, July 27, 1966, PREM 13/1262, PRO.

216. Wilson, *Labour Government*, 341.

217. Robert E. Kinter, Memorandum for the President, July 7, 1966, WHCF, Confidential File, CO301, box 12, CO305, UK (1966), LBJL. Kintner recommended that Rusk hold background briefings or open press conferences a few days before Wilson's visit to put the British position into perspective.

218. Memo for the President from Francis M. Bator, Thursday, July 28, 1966, Memos, vol. 8 (1 of 3), 1/66–7/66, CF, UK, NSF, LBJL.

219. Report by J. A. Thomson on "The Prime Minister's Visit to Washington," July 18, 1966, PREM 13/126, PRO.

220. Ibid.

221. Ibid.

222. Ibid.

223. Memo for the President from Francis M. Bator, Thursday, July 28, 1966, Memos, vol. 8 (1 of 3), 1/66–7/66, CF, UK, NSF, LBJL.

224. Report by J. A. Thomson on "The Prime Minister's Visit to Washington," July 18, 1966, PREM 13/126, PRO.

225. Telegram from Sir Patrick Dean to Permanent Undersecretary, Foreign Office, July 21, 1966, PREM 13/1262, PRO.

226. Memorandum for the President from George Ball, "Subject: Harold Wilson's Visit—The Opportunity for an Act of Statesmanship," July 22, 1966, UK, vol. 8, Memos (2 of 2), 1/66–7/66, box 209, CF, UK, NSF, LBJL.

227. Ibid.

228. Memorandum of Conversation by J. E. Killick, the White House, July 27, 1966, PREM 13/1262, PRO.

229. Memorandum of Conversation, "General Remarks by the President," the White House, July 29, 1966, UK, PM Wilson Visit Briefing Book (1 of 2), 7/29/66, box 216, CF, UK, NSF, LBJL; Record of a Meeting between the Prime Minister and His Ad-

visers and President Johnson and His Advisers at the White House on Friday, July 29, 1966, Visit of the Prime Minister to the United States and Canada, July 28–30, 1966, PREM 13/1083, PRO.

230. Record of a Meeting between the Prime Minister and His Advisers and President Johnson and His Advisers at the White House on Friday, July 29, 1966, Visit of the Prime Minister to the United States and Canada, July 28–30, 1966, PREM 13/1083, PRO.

231. Ibid.

232. Ibid.

233. Telegram from Prime Minister Wilson to Holt/Holyoake, Canberra, August 3, 1966, PREM 13/1262, PRO.

234. Record of a Meeting between the Prime Minister and His Advisers and President Johnson and His Advisers at the White House on Friday, July 29, 1966, Visit of the Prime Minister to the United States and Canada, July 28–30, 1966, PREM 13/1083, PRO.

235. Record of a Discussion between the Prime Minister and Mr. Dean Rusk at the British Embassy, Washington, on July 29, 1966, PREM 13/1083, PRO.

236. Ibid.

237. Ibid.

238. Ibid.

239. Wilson, *Labour Government*, 344.

240. *Times* (London), July 30, 1966, 1; Castle, *Diaries*, July 31, 1966, 80.

241. Castle, *Diaries*, July 31, 1966, 80.

242. Personal Telegram from Johnson to Prime Minister Wilson, July 30, 1966, PREM 13/1262, PRO.

243. Personal Telegram from the Prime Minister to the President, July 30, 1966, PREM 13/1262, PRO.

244. Letter from Dean to Maclehose, August 3, 1966, PREM 13/1262, PRO.

245. Ibid.

246. Ibid.

247. Letter from Dean to Maclehose, August 6, 1966, PREM 13/1262, PRO.

248. Letter from Dean to Maclehose, August 3, 1966, PREM 13/1262, PRO.

249. Letter from Dean to Maclehose, August 6, 1966, PREM 13/1262, PRO.

250. Ibid.

Chapter 5

The Collapse of the Understanding:
August 1966–February 1968

With the Labour government's attention fixed on events in Rhodesia during the second half of 1966, very little of substance occurred in Anglo–American relations regarding Vietnam. The British used these months to prepare the ground for another peace initiative in February 1967 involving Premier Kosygin of the Soviet Union. This latest move would not only end in ignominious failure but would also test the so-called special relationship to the extreme. By early 1967 the Johnson administration was beginning to face the prospect of a military stalemate in Vietnam, yet the president still wanted a negotiated settlement without major concessions and only after some indication of military progress. Despite the problems associated with previous endeavors, the British were still keen to assess the sincerity of the U.S. desire for a diplomatic resolution of conflict and play the role of mediator.

GEORGE BROWN IN MOSCOW, NOVEMBER 1966

On Friday, August 12, George Brown, deputy leader of the Labour Party and former first secretary of state and minister of economic affairs, replaced Michael Stewart as Foreign Secretary. Despite his suspicion that Wilson had engaged in "unsavoury" deals with Johnson, he would nevertheless prove extremely sympathetic to the U.S. cause in Vietnam. At the time of his appointment David Bruce accurately portrayed him as a "staunch and useful supporter of major US policies" but admitted that "the Foreign Office has never before been headed by such an unorthodox diplomat." Brown's reputation as a maverick politician and a hard drinker was well known in Washington. By the end of September Bruce noted that "his abounding vitality, inquisitive absorption of briefs, informality, boisterousness, already amaze, inspire, or appall his staff, as they did those previously associated with him in official life."[1]

Brown was determined to make his mark in his new position and almost immediately turned his attention to a new initiative on Vietnam. During the foreign affairs debate at the Labour Party conference in Brighton on October 6, the Foreign Secretary announced a new plan for a negotiated settlement on Vietnam.[2] Brown announced that a conference of all interested parties should be called as soon as possible and suggested that the NLF or Vietcong could be represented at it. He argued that once the principle of a conference was established, the United States should cease bombing North Vietnam and stop introducing U.S. forces and military supplies into Vietnam, while the North Vietnamese should cease dispatching troops and military supplies to the south. He then put forward six main points for a negotiated political settlement that was based on free elections and the neutralization of North and South Vietnam.[3] This announcement was made partly to assuage the growing number of opponents of the government's policy on Vietnam who had put forward critical composite resolutions at the conference. The government's foreign policy motion, which was passed by a small margin, also stressed Britain's ability to act independently on Vietnam.

The Government have generally supported the American position because they believe quite simply, that so long as Hanoi refused to negotiate, the alternative to continuing the struggle is to abandon the South Vietnamese to aggression. On the other hand it has been made clear that we would not support every U.S. action regardless of its nature; the Government have dissociated themselves from the bombing of oil installations at Hanoi and Haiphong.[4]

The Americans were not given advance warning of the Brown plan.[5] However, they admitted it was "largely consistent" with their present position in that it allowed for "certain concessions to Hanoi to break the impasse," primarily the provision for the inclusion of the Vietcong in any talks.[6] Still, Washington felt it "regrettable" that Brown's formula had "surfaced publicly," as it was felt this reduced Hanoi's ability to respond favorably. North Vietnam did indeed reject the proposal immediately as "echoing previously discredited US 'peace tricks.' "[7]

Nevertheless, Brown hoped to discuss his plan further during his first trip to Washington as Foreign Secretary. The visit was scheduled for October 14, as part of a visit to the UN General Assembly, and once again Johnson had to be persuaded that it was worth cultivating a friendship with a senior British politician. Ambassador Bruce felt that Brown was worth the effort. He advised that it was "wise to consolidate the goodwill he has always manifested toward Americans," and he was "sure the President would enjoy the encounter with a politician so singular in deportment and speech."[8] Johnson agreed to meet Brown, and, as expected, Vietnam dominated the discussion between the president and the Foreign Secretary. As Gromyko, the Soviet foreign minister, was also in the United States for the session of the UN General Assembly and Brown was planning to visit Moscow at the end of November, the president stressed that in his talks with Gromyko, or with anyone else, Brown "was perfectly free to commit the President to meet anywhere at any time if there seemed to be a reasonable prospect of solving the Viet-Nam problem." Johnson also made it clear that although the United States could not abandon its commitments to South Vietnam, he personally was "most anxious" for the war to end in that it overshadowed everything else.[9] The major importance of the Washington visit, as Brown confirmed in his memoirs, was that Washington authorized him to take a secret proposal, known as the phase A/phase B formula, to the Russians on his forthcoming trip to Moscow.[10] This plan proposed secret measures of mutual de-escalation. The United States would stop bombing and then take additional steps to de-escalate, on the prior understanding that this would be followed by similar acts of de-escalation on the part of the North Vietnamese and the Vietcong.[11] We now know how hard Brown had to work to gain this concession. Henry Brandon recalls in his memoirs "the most turbulent dinner party" he had ever given. On October 15, Brandon entertained George Brown, Hubert Humphrey, Sir Patrick Dean, Robert McNamara, Bill Bundy, Senator Stuart Symington, and Bromley Smith of the National Security Council at a dinner at his home in Washington, D.C. The new Foreign Secretary soon got into an altercation with McNamara over Vietnam. According to Brandon, "[A]lmost from the start Brown tried to wheedle out of McNamara conditions for a reasonable basis for negotiations with Hanoi which he could put in his pocket to take to Moscow." Brown repeatedly asked what the United States' minimum terms were, only for McNamara and Bundy to answer with generalities. Brown—who Brandon says was not inebriated at the time—began to "get hotter and hotter under his collar." He finally exclaimed: "You, Bob, you don't speak with the same voice as the president [whom he had seen that morning]. Your president said quite different things to me. You sound as if you didn't want negotiations! The president does! Bob, you're protecting your ass when nobody is trying to bugger you!"[12] Brandon said he had never seen McNamara so enraged: "He was fuming, his eyes were rolling, and he jumped up and said: 'The president is now in the White House. I'll take you there right away and we'll see who is right!' " Brown also jumped up, "only too glad to have another go at the president." Bromley Smith and Brandon went after them and stopped them outside the front door. Smith said he thought the president was in Maryland making a speech somewhere, and Brandon suggested he ring the White House to check whether he was home or not, whispering to Smith to report that he was not, whatever the situation. Smith soon reported the truth of the matter, which was that Johnson was indeed making a speech outside Washington. He did not tell his fellow dinner guests, however, that he had asked that the chopper bringing LBJ back from Philadelphia "be delayed by a few minutes before landing at the White House to make sure that the presidential log did not contradict his report." At that point, the guests calmed down and returned to the dinner table, only for Brown to begin needling McNamara again. "He accused him of being inflexible to such an extent that he, Brown, was losing faith in the genuineness of the American readiness to negotiate." It was at that point that McNamara scribbled on an envelope next to his plate a set of conditions acceptable to the United States to get negotiations started.[13] Brandon characterized this as "the most blatant attempt by the British government to inject itself as a messenger between Washington and Moscow." Certainly, it is clear evidence of Brown's ebullience and determination. And, although McNamara claimed to have enjoyed the verbal badinage with Brown, the seriousness of some of Brown's accusations may well have tested his patience with the British somewhat.[14]

After meeting Gromyko in New York Brown reported back to the British cabinet that he sensed a softening of the Soviet position on a number of issues, "though not as yet on Vietnam."[15] Two weeks later the British acquired "additional examples of [the] more friendly Russian style first revealed by Gromyko in New York last month." Premier Kosygin confirmed that he would accept Wilson's invitation to visit London and agreed to a four- or five-day trip beginning February 5.[16] Brown's visit to Moscow was also brought forward to November 22.

On the evening of November 6, Averell Harriman, U.S. ambassador for peace, met the British Foreign Secretary to discuss his forthcoming talks with Gromyko in Moscow. This proved to be a very important meeting for Anglo–American relations, although not for reasons that were immediately apparent. Brown emphasized the role the British could play in influencing the Russians to mediate on Vietnam at a time when the Russians appeared to be signaling their intention to play a more active role on the negotiation front. The British Foreign Secretary was adamant that there was now "strong evidence" of a Soviet "desire to do business," quoting Kosygin's previous statement that he would not accept Wilson's invitation to come to London until such a visit would be "fruitful."[17] The British felt that they had managed to convince the Russians that the United States desired peace and that they could have a "critical influence" on the Russians in the next few months.

Brown's most "emphatic point" at this meeting was, however, as Bruce put it, "his desire for explicit, specific US guidance for use in Moscow." Brown wanted to know the U.S. position on such issues as the role of the NLF at any peace conference and the steps the United States would regard as "appropriate" from North Vietnam in response to a unilateral U.S. cessation of bombing. The president had apparently told Brown that he might settle for 40 percent reciprocity from North Vietnam rather than a 50/50 deal.[18] It was agreed that the Foreign Secretary should not urge the reconvening of the Geneva conference; instead he should "simply stress Soviet–UK responsibilities as co-Chairmen and explore . . . possible first steps toward de-escalation of hostilities and secret talks." Brown ended the meeting with Harriman by repeating his belief that he was going to Moscow for "a straight bit of negotiation on a specific topic." In what

Bruce felt was a "deliberate choice of words," Brown said any further escalation of bombing "might well lose you the support of all your friends in Europe like me, who are trying to help." Harriman said he would ensure that Washington provide Brown with "ammunition" for his trip and that this would include information on the U.S. congressional election results and Vietnam, and explicit guidance for his talks in Moscow.[19]

As it happened, the White House was not prepared to provide the British with full and advance notice of their own peace plans. At a meeting on November 10, State Department officials met with presidential advisers to consider what advice to give George Brown and Italian ambassador to South Vietnam Giovanni D'Orlandi. At the end of June 1966 a Polish representative of the ICC, Janus Lewandowski, contacted D'Orlandi to inform him that he had met with Ho Chi Minh, General Giap, and Premier Pham Van Dong and believed there was room for compromise in the North Vietnamese position. He believed Hanoi would begin negotiating if the United States suspended its bombing campaign and allowed the NLF to take some part in the proceedings.[20] The key individuals present at the meeting—William Bundy, Averell Harriman, and Chester Cooper—agreed that "Brown's talks in Moscow offered better immediate possibilities than the D'Orlandi channel."[21] At this stage the Americans were not convinced that D'Orlandi's contact was operating under instructions from his own government, and so those at the meeting decided to "concentrate on what we could give to Brown."[22] Harriman thought after material for Brown had been prepared, "[W]e should see what morsels could be given to D'Orlandi."[23] William Bundy's main concern was if phase A/phase B was accepted and "Hanoi took significant reciprocal action and we then suspended the bombing, pressures would quickly build up for us to stop troop re-inforcements as well." And, as Cooper reminded the meeting, Brown had publicly announced his own plan calling for "a bombing pause plus no-reinforcements in exchange for an end to infiltration." Bundy "agreed that ending U.S. troop re-inforcement seemed to figure prominently in Brown's thinking and came high on his timetable." For that reason Bundy observed that the United States "had to be careful about how far" it went with Brown; "[W]e would not want to make substantial concessions before Hanoi was even at the negotiating table."[24] Still, Bundy thought it right "to give Brown something to contribute to the value of his talks. Though he was not a discreet man he was well intentioned and capable and was a good friend to the US."[25] Although there was some skepticism regarding the Soviets' interest in a role as intermediary, Harriman concluded that they "might be interested in trying out some ideas in their talks with Brown" and therefore they "should not conclude in advance that nothing constructive would emerge." Noticeably, Harriman felt that "furthermore, our relations with the British would suffer a damaging blow if the British government were to conclude that we were not serious about reaching a negotiated settlement in Vietnam." It was agreed that the United States "should give Brown enough to work with to satisfy him but obviously should not give away our whole position."[26]

At this stage Chester Cooper, an NSC staff member, outlined U.S. plans for peace, and Brown's part in them, in a memo to Harriman a few days later.[27] The Americans clearly felt that Brown's visit to Moscow just one month before Christmas, when another bombing pause might take place, was significant, and a pause might be all-important in determining the success or failure of the visit. Moreover, their own ambassador in Moscow, Llewellyn Thompson, reported that the prospects for the Brown–Kosygin meeting were good as there was "some evidence that the Russians are concerned that the United States are getting together with Communist China."[28] However, at this stage they were not prepared to let the British know their definite plans regarding the prospects of a Christmas bombing pause. This may have been because they felt it was not worth risking a leak, but more likely they did not trust the British to represent them adequately. So Brown was advised to tell the Russians that a bombing pause was likely on the grounds of "precedent, rumor and reason" but that he had no advance knowledge of this. He was also to stress that if there was a pause, time was of the essence. The pause would be short due to Johnson's limited patience and would be the last one. Hanoi and Moscow ought to begin "contingency planning" immediately. In terms of what the United States would consider an appropriate response to U.S. cessation of bombing, the president would want "some credible and discernible reaction" in order to keep the pause going, such as "(1) an immediate stopping of southbound truck traffic..." and "(2) an immediate and substantial decline in the level of Communist military action and terror in the South." If this happened, the United States would be prepared to move to either public or private discussions with Hanoi, bilaterally or multilaterally. It was also prepared to do this at short notice, "perhaps during January *before Kosygin's visit to London and before Tet*."[29] It was envisaged that the Wilson–Kosygin talks could be used to set up a more formal Geneva-type conference.

Such plans proved precipitate. During Brown's visit to Moscow both Gromyko and Kosygin continued their hard line on Vietnam, stressing that any negotiations on Vietnam had to be understood and arranged in light of the U.S. position as the aggressor. Brown informed Rusk that he had a problem getting "Gromyko to lay off his gramophone record and get down to the question of issue."[30] And although Brown presented the phase A/phase B proposal to Gromyko, both verbally and on paper, the Soviets argued that there was "nothing new" in this and therefore they had "no new opinions" to express.[31] Nevertheless, Brown informed Rusk that Kosygin had characterized their discussions as "very useful" and told the secretary of state that he felt the meeting had still been worthwhile, not least because he had improved his "already sympathetic" relationship with Gromyko and "had established himself on amiable terms with Kosygin."[32] Also, although Brown had said he was acting in a personal capacity, without the authorization of the United States, he passed on to Kosygin Johnson's comment that if the Soviets could help, the British Foreign Secretary could say that he knew he could deliver his friend.[33] Brown reported back to the cabinet that the Soviet government "no longer maintained a wholly negative attitude on a number of major international issues" and that on Vietnam "the tone of the discussion was less harsh," even if the position was still the same.[34] The British would shortly discover why the Russians had not appeared interested in Brown's rendition of phase A/phase B.

CHRISTMAS TRUCE, 1966

From the end of November, Wilson had been under pressure at home to press Johnson for another bombing truce. The war in Vietnam continued unabated, and between December 2 and December 6 the United States carried out a series of bombing raids on military targets in the immediate vicinity of Hanoi, the first in the area since the POL installations were attacked in the summer. Although the Americans considered the targets to be legitimate military ones such as truck depots, rail yards, and fuel storage dumps, the possibility of mass civilian casualties alarmed much of world opinion. The air raids were further escalated on December 13 and 14 when U.S. bombers targeted the Hanoi area. The Soviet Union responded by accusing the United States of bombing residential sections of the city. Although Washington denied this, the suspicion remained that the likelihood of civilian casualties through stray missiles was high. The public outcry in Britain was greater than ever. Fifty-five members of Parliament sent a cable to Johnson expressing their grave concern at the successive bombing attacks on Hanoi and the "resultant loss of life among the civilian population" and asking that these attacks be stopped in the "interest of world peace."[35] Donald Murray of the British Foreign Office reported to the British embassy in Washington on December 16 that the "head of steam" over the Hanoi bombing had become "very serious indeed" and requested further information on the raids in order to prepare an official statement that Brown could deliver in the House of Commons.[36] Wilson was pressed to dissociate Britain from the American "bombing of schools, hospitals and population centers," as Labour M.P.s put it in the House.[37] Bruce suggested that Rusk, who was in Paris for the latest NATO meeting, do a background press briefing on the bombing to try to deal with the emerging public relations disaster. The original material the State Department sent to London, in the words of one U.S. official, had been "God-awful."[38] By refusing to provide a specific rationale for the attacks and not providing sufficient detail on the target areas, the Americans were not helping themselves, or their allies, to deal with the flak they would undoubtedly receive as a result of such incidents. Matters were made worse a few days later by the publication of reports by Harrison Salisbury in the *New York Times* describing civilian casualties in North Vietnam from the latest wave of U.S. air attacks. The official presentation of the air raids as surgical attacks on military targets was increasingly difficult to sustain as Salisbury reported at length that several towns and cities had been hit, with resultant civilian casualties.[39]

As it turned out, Brown had little choice but to respond to such criticism of the bombing of Hanoi with the now standard government response: he blamed the North Vietnamese for "prolonging the fighting," assured the House that the United States was attacking only military targets, and reiterated the urgent need to establish peace negotiations.[40] Bruce judged Brown's performance to be "smooth and authoritative" and credited the Foreign Secretary with effectively lessening the outcry over the bombing.[41] Wilson and Brown were also fortunate in that the parliamentary recess for Christmas was about to begin, and news of Rhodesian sanctions had hit the headlines.

Aware of the growing unrest in Britain over the bombing, Washington knew it was essential that the British government's resolve did not waver. Although not a priority issue, the White House and State Department worried about further British dissociations in light of the bombings. Strangely, members of the Johnson administration adopted a quixotic response to this concern. Rusk's patience with the British was running out, and the president obviously shared the same view. Reporting back on his NATO meeting, the secretary of state told the president that he had given the council some "old-time religion" on Vietnam and that this pressure might result in more allied assistance on a bilateral basis, particularly from Germany and the Netherlands. In relation to Britain, Rusk said he had hit George Brown "pretty hard" on their joint SEATO commitment in face of "the common danger" in Vietnam.[42] He further commented, "I intend to press them very hard for more participation but they will probably act like scared rabbits in the face of their domestic political situation."[43] Even at this late stage, Rusk remained dissatisfied with the British commitment on Vietnam.

The following day the president met at the ranch to discuss Vietnam with some of his key civilian advisers, including Secretary McNamara, Walt Rostow, Ambassador Harriman, and Ambassador Lodge. Lodge reported that progress had been made on third-country participation but more could be made. However, he thought the United States had "reached the limit of generating such assistance by exhortation." Again, Britain was specifically mentioned. Lodge said the United States could use the kind of British policemen who had worked in Kenya and suggested, provocatively, that "we ought to pressure the British to get some—perhaps by holding up shipments of scotch whiskey to the U.S."[44]

While Rusk and others were still determined to press the British toward a deeper involvement in Vietnam, they also recognized that Wilson needed to be encouraged to maintain his present level of support for the president. Patrick Dean had separate meetings with Dean Rusk, Walt Rostow, and Averell Harriman and reported their views back to the Foreign Office.[45] According to Dean, Rusk said that "it was highly unpopular for the Americans to have to go on alone and that was why the political support of the British Government was so valuable" and reiterated that "South East Asia and the attitude of foreign governments to the war in Vietnam mattered by far the most to the U.S. Government."[46] Ambassador Harriman also

wished to make it clear that if governments who were not directly engaged in Vietnam wished to retain influence with the President, who would be under continuous and increasing strain from the hawks to spread and intensify the war, it was most important that these governments should not "dissociate" themselves from the President. "Dissociation" was in any case an unfortunate word and had had an unfortunate effect. If outside governments felt that they could not approve any action the U.S. might take they should use expressions like "they did not see the necessity for such and such an action." Those who dissociated themselves from the President could not expect to have much influence with him.[47]

Harriman was aware that Johnson also faced his critics at home. Congressional disaffection had been evident since January 1966 when Senator William Fulbright presided over the Senate Foreign Relations Committee hearings on the war. However, Johnson not only faced criticism from opponents of the war; he also faced a small group of prowar critics centered around Senator John Stennis and the Senate Armed Services Committee. This group wanted to end the war by winning it through stronger action. Johnson continued to face countervailing pressures in Congress for the duration of the administration. Nevertheless, at this point, the hawks had the upper hand because of the approaching 1968 presidential election. Johnson was well aware that Democratic losses during the 1966 congressional elections were largely due to questions surrounding his own credibility with regard the war and his handling of it.[48] The president also knew that he would find it extremely difficult to achieve reelection without a satisfactory resolution of the war, or at the very least some indication that the war was being prosecuted successfully. Nevertheless, at this stage Harriman reassured Dean that there were "no signs at all the President was going to take any rash action in the near future. On the contrary, he would resist pressures for this for as long as he could, but he needed the support of world opinion and above all of the British government. This meant a very great deal both to the U.S. Administration and to the President personally."[49] But to complicate the picture, although probably reflecting Johnson's uncertainty about the best way forward, Rostow told Dean that the president was "personally disinclined to adopt a soft line toward the North Vietnamese." He also stressed that although the United States was still committed to the fight in Vietnam, it was also ready to find peace and was "encouraging all contenders for the Nobel Peace Prize."[50]

Fearing further parliamentary anger over U.S. bombings, Dean highlighted in his letters to London the fact that all three men—Rusk, Rostow, and Harriman—had expressed appreciation of the British support on Vietnam and hoped that "if the Prime Minister and the Secretary of State feel that they cannot actually continue to support U.S. policy, they will take account of Harriman's warning when formulating any statement."[51] The warnings were heeded; the British did not dissociate themselves from the bombing or make any criticisms of it.

PARALLEL PEACE EFFORTS: FROM MARIGOLD TO SUNFLOWER

According to William Bundy, assistant secretary of state for Far Eastern affairs, by the end of 1966 the Johnson administration, and in particular the president, had decided to take peace talks more seriously. If this was the case, then

LBJ and his staff mishandled many of the tentative contacts between their representatives and North Vietnamese officials.

On December 30 the British decided to try another tack on the peace front. Foreign Secretary George Brown came up with a new initiative, sent in a confidential cable simultaneously to the governments of the United States, North Vietnam, and South Vietnam. In it he proposed a three-way meeting to "arrange the cessation of hostilities."[52] Brown offered the services of Her Majesty's Government to facilitate such a meeting and said that, if desired, the meeting could take place on British territory. He suggested the facilities at Britain's base in Hong Kong. Hanoi rejected the proposal. This response was especially predictable considering that the Chinese had two days earlier charged that Hong Kong was being used as a base for aircraft carriers whose planes were bombing North Vietnam. American journalist Harrison Salisbury put this down to either "incredible bumbling" on Brown's part or suggested that it was a measure aimed at appeasing those baying for the Labour Party to take action to end the war.[53] It could have been both. The Americans formally welcomed Brown's proposal, and Johnson repeated his position that the United States was "ready to meet anywhere, any time that Hanoi is willing to come to a conference table."[54]

Just a few days after Brown's proposal was made, the British heard some disturbing news from the Americans. Rusk informed London on January 4 that during the previous six months, the Poles had been negotiating with the North Vietnamese with the agreement of the U.S. government. Rusk had been forced into this admission by the fact that Harrison Salisbury had had discussions with Britain's consul in Hanoi, John Colvin, about his exchanges with North Vietnamese ministers.[55] Salisbury told Colvin that from his discussions with the prime minister of North Vietnam, Pham Van Dong, he thought the North Vietnamese "had gone further than ever before, and that if there were any receptivity in United States Administration there were grounds for further exploration."[56]

Not surprisingly, the British were alarmed and disheartened by this revelation. It told Wilson, Brown, and the Foreign Office three things: first, that the Americans were being far from frank with them regarding their attempts to find peace; second, that Washington had been prepared to let Brown go to Moscow ill informed; and third, that the chances of the latest discussions with Hanoi coming to anything were compromised by the fact that the latest intermediary was a journalist whose temptation would be to publish an account of his discussions with Premier Pham Van Dong rather than maintain the required silence.

Still, the Polish peace effort, code-named Marigold, did suggest that the North Vietnamese were looking to negotiate. The Marigold affair still remains a "murky episode," but it appears that it was made up of a series of secret indirect contacts between the U.S. government and the North Vietnamese authorities brokered by the Poles. The episode reveals a great deal about the negotiating stance of the United States and its apparent ineptitude in diplomacy with regard to Vietnam.[57]

In November the United States showed serious interest in the D'Orlandi/Lewandowski channel, at which point Ambassador Lodge allowed the Polish diplomat to pass on the U.S. position regarding a final solution to the current stalemate to the authorities in Hanoi. This included Rusk's 14 points, the statement of the Manila conference (October 24–25, 1966) that American troops would withdraw from Vietnam within six months of a peace settlement (on the condition that the North Vietnamese would also withdraw from the south), and the phase A/phase B formula that Brown had also taken to Moscow in November. On November 30 Lewandowski returned to Saigon from Hanoi to report to Lodge on his meeting with the North Vietnamese. On December 1 he told the U.S. ambassador that he was authorized to tell the American government, "If the U.S. is really of the view which I have presented, it would be advisable to confirm them directly by conversation with the North Vietnamese ambassador in Warsaw."[58] A direct contact was in the cards. However, the State Department scrutinized Lewandowski's version of the American position presented to Hanoi, only to find that he had neglected to include the details of the de-escalatory phase A/phase B formula. Lewandowski said that it had been presented orally. Washington decided to pursue this lead, telling Lewandowski that the U.S. ambassador in Warsaw, Gronouski, would be in contact with the North Vietnamese embassy on December 6 or soon after. At the same time, however, Lodge added that the 10 points Lewandowski had presented only broadly reflected the U.S. position and that "several specific points were subject to important differences of interpretation."[59] Adam Rapacki, the Polish foreign minister, intervened at this point and warned that any American intensification of the bombing campaign would destroy the possibility of a contact through Warsaw, expressing deep concern at any reinterpretation of the 10 points. The Polish attempt at mediation ended when the United States stepped up its bombing campaign on December 13, attacking a railroad yard and vehicle depot near Hanoi for the second time in 10 days.[60] Four days later, Wilfred Burchett, an Australian Communist journalist with close ties to the North Vietnamese leadership, told U.S. officials in Paris that the DRV had had an official en route to Warsaw "when the US resumed bombing Hanoi."[61] Rapacki informed Gronouski that Hanoi had requested that the Poles end their mediation to arrange a direct contact between the governments of North Vietnam and the United States and said that "the whole responsibility for losing this chance of a peaceful solution to the Vietnam War rested on the United States government."[62] The United States tried one desperate attempt to restart the exchanges by stopping the bombing within a 10-mile radius of Hanoi. The Poles again contacted Hanoi but to no avail. Despite U.S. protestations that the Hanoi bombing targets had been decided upon months before, Moscow, Poland, and Hanoi were left with the impression that Washington preferred a military solution to the war. At the very least, the Johnson administration had mishandled the Marigold affair.

Brown was furious at Rusk's cable telling of the Polish peace efforts. In a cable designated "flash" traffic, Brown replied tersely: "Thank you for this information. But, though I realise your difficulties, I must say I wish you had told me of this before I went to Moscow. To put it mildly a very valuable opportunity may have been lost. It is not surprising that the Russians were so puzzled... If a further opportunity arises I am sure you will keep me fully in the picture."[63]

Not surprisingly, this latest news also prompted a flurry of discussion in Downing Street and the Foreign Office. Reporting on the matter to the prime minister on January 4, 1967, Michael Palliser commented that Rusk's telegram was "disheartening" in that it revealed "a disconcerting lack of frankness with us by the Americans." Moreover, Palliser felt "the gravity of this failure by the Americans to keep us informed (however valid the reasons given by Rusk, and the validity seems at best questionable) is compounded by the fact that they let the Foreign Secretary go to Moscow from November 22–25 without knowing what was going on between them and the Poles." He elaborated further on the perception the Russians may have received during Brown's visit and hinted that this had been a lost opportunity:

Since the Polish representative in Saigon (Lewandowski) got the message wrong and was in fact conveying to Hanoi an inaccurate summary of the American position (omitting in particular the two-phase agreement under which U.S. bombing would have stopped provided there was clear advance agreement about subsequent action by Hanoi) at precisely the same time as the Foreign Secretary was in Moscow giving the Russians an accurate account of the American position, it is not surprising the Russians (who pretty clearly *had* been informed of what was going on) seemed puzzled by the Foreign Secretary's exposition and pressed him very closely on it. Since it did not correspond with what Lewandowski was explaining to Hanoi they may have concluded that the Foreign Secretary did not, despite what he said, enjoy full American confidence—which seems regrettably to have been true—or alternatively that the two-phase agreement was his own bright idea and had no American backing.[64]

Washington's decision to keep the British deliberately in the dark on this matter was probably made in the genuine belief that the less third parties knew about the Polish contact, the less would be the likelihood of leaks and therefore failure. Certainly Hanoi and the Polish government had requested absolute secrecy.[65] If this was the case, however, the Americans would have saved British blushes had they not given Brown the phase A/phase B proposal.

Wilson asked to see Bruce to discuss the exchanges between Rusk and Brown over the Polish contact. According to the record of conversation the prime minister spoke firmly on the matter, saying that it "raised a major issue of confidence in relations between the Foreign Secretary and himself and the President and Mr. Rusk." The prime minister said he had been "disturbed" at what had happened, that Brown had been "placed in an impossible situation for his talks in Moscow," and that those talks may have proved "counter-productive" with the Russians. Wilson expressed his dissatisfaction not only that the Poles knew what was going on and Brown did not, but also that he thought it "even more unacceptable" that the Italians also "knew the facts" when they had no "need to know," whereas the Foreign Secretary, "who had to deal with 'some of the toughest eggs in the business' did not."[66] He felt that the Foreign Secretary's message to Rusk over this had in fact been "relatively temperate," and things were more serious than this implied. Wilson was keen to ensure that this not happen again, especially given Kosygin's planned visit to London early in February, arguing that "it was essential, before he came, the United States Government should have put the British Government completely in the picture without holding anything back."[67] To this end, the prime minister requested that Chester Cooper be sent to London to fully brief himself and the Foreign Secretary. Cooper's experience with Asia and Vietnam was, as Averell Harriman later put it, "long and unique."[68] Cooper was a member of the U.S. delegation to the 1954 Geneva conference on Indochina, the 1954 conference in Manila that established SEATO, the 1961–62 Geneva conference on Laos, and the 1966 summit conference in Manila.[69] In 1964 he had been asked to serve as the assistant for Asian affairs on the White House staff and in 1966 became assistant to Averell Harriman on Vietnam. Despite his expertise on Vietnam, his public profile was such that he was considered someone who would not attract too much media attention and thus lead to speculation that the British government was being briefed or indeed being given instructions before the visit.[70]

Bruce gallantly tried to defend the U.S. position, stressing that he had not known what was happening with the Poles and that this in itself was proof that "this was all being kept very close." The prime minister reminded Bruce that the situation was "similar" to one that happened the previous year, when it was only as a result of his own pressure that Arthur Goldberg, U.S. ambassador to the United Nations, had sent to London to brief Wilson on the "peace offensive" and that "without that exchange, the British Government would not have been as well informed as they should be."[71]

Wilson was not content to leave things at that; instead, he told Bruce that "the broader question of confidence must be raised with the President at some point." Wilson emphasized the serious pressure he would be under once Parliament reassembled but said that "there was no question of this affecting the Government's general attitude" and assured Brown that they had no intention of dissociating from the U.S. government on Vietnam. He did admit, however, that Harrison Salisbury's articles had made a big impact and that public opinion in Britain generally was growing ever more critical of the U.S. government. For this reason, although he felt he "could hold the position," he believed that "the general Anglo–American relationship was bound to come under greater strain and this made even more intolerable the American failure to keep us in the picture over the Vietnam exchanges with the Poles." As was now usual, Wilson discussed with Bruce the merits of sending a personal message to the president. At first Bruce suggested he "get some illumination" on the Polish discussions before Wilson did this and obviously inferred that it might even be best if the prime minister left such a discussion until their next face-to-face meeting. Bruce emphasized the president's many difficulties at home. Wilson replied that although he recognized that Johnson was "going through a tough period and he would not let a friend down at such a time," their working relationship must become more of a partnership "in things that mattered." Indeed, he threatened that "this kind of thing must not happen again or he would go personally direct to the President." At this point Bruce said he thought Wilson should contact the president via a short message expressing how seriously he took the matter.[72]

Wilson's advisers worked on a draft message later that day. In it Wilson repeated his serious concern over the Polish discussions and Brown's "equivocal position" while in Moscow, expressing his doubts that Britain would have been informed at all had it not been for Harrison Salisbury. He repeated that it was essential that there be "complete frankness" before Kosygin's visit.[73] The draft went further, talking of "the key" to their "whole relationship" being "mutual support and counsel" and a "concept of partnership" based on "total confidence between us. I am bound in all honesty to say that, in the present case, this confidence seems to me to have been lacking: and I wanted you to know how gravely I view such a situation."[74] As with previous angry draft messages, Wilson changed his mind and two days later sent a brief and somewhat mellower message to the president, stating that, as he had told David Bruce privately, he was "seriously concerned at a matter which is, I think, pretty fundamental to our relationship."[75] This did not mean, however, that London had relaxed over the issue. On the contrary, a reply from Rusk to Brown's cable had inflamed British sensitivities still further. The secretary of state argued that

there was nothing on which we could have informed you prior to your visit to Moscow. Your visit came at the time of Lewandowski's visit to Hanoi but before we had any information whatever from him on his visit...In fact, we gave you for your trip a major concession to the other side in the form of a two-phased proposal in which we would stop the bombing if they would agree that subsequently there could be a de-escalation of the violence. I am sorry if there has been any mis-understanding on this point.[76]

Brown found this statement "disappointingly disingenuous," and although he decided not to continue the exchange with Rusk, he did ask Murray Maclehose to write to Patrick Dean explaining the nature of his grievance. Dean could then pass this on to Bill Bundy.[77] Maclehose explained that the British did "not want an argument, but the State Department must not be allowed to pass off the impropriety of this action in this way. They must realise that the Secretary of State's message to Rusk was based on very serious considerations."[78] Maclehose privately hoped that the Russians had understood what had happened in November.

In the long run, and after they had time to check it all up (and no doubt to grill Lewandowski) they have probably got it all straight now, and realised that Lewandowski muffed it, and the Secretary of State got it right. Perhaps as a result of this belated realisation the Secretary of State's stock may even have risen rather than the reverse in Moscow, and the extent of the generous U.S. concession which he conveyed may have got through.

Notwithstanding this glimmer of hope, Maclehose concluded that "the risk which the Americans ran, both to their own interests and to the Secretary of State's reputation, by their lack of frankness, strikes us as amazing."[79]

The following day, when Brown addressed the British cabinet, he reported that the chances of resolving the conflict in Vietnam were "slightly more hopeful than hitherto," even if they remained "confused and uncertain." He reassured his colleagues that the government was continuing to "promote some form of mediation between the parties to the dispute" via both public and private discussions. Perhaps bending to pressure from within the party, Brown admitted that the British government "must continue to deplore the United States bombing of North Vietnam" but argued, as the Americans had pressed him to, that it would be "impolitic to dissociate ourselves from United States policy, especially since we had reason to believe that the United States President, although determined not to expose United States prestige to a rebuff, was continuing to resist pressure within his Administration for the adoption of more extreme military measures against North Vietnam."[80]

In an attempt to smooth the troubled transatlantic waters, Chester Cooper was dispatched to London to brief the prime minister on the latest developments on Vietnam. When he met with Brown and Wilson on January 18, the prime minister's sensitivities regarding the Polish affair were all too apparent. Cooper tried to appease him over this, explaining that "the President was in a 'psychotic' state about leaks not only in regard to top secret matters such as these but over anything that he wished to keep confidential; this was why there had been a 'clamp-down' on security about the exchanges."[81] Wilson and Cooper then concentrated on the Kosygin visit. Cooper elaborated on the latest contacts with the Russians and reported that Washington now understood that if there was to be a settlement, the leadership in Hanoi wanted advance notice of what "package" would be available before committing themselves to talks. The American ambassador in Moscow, Llewellyn Thompson, would soon be informing the Russians of this change in the U.S. position and would also confirm that Washington accepted that the NLF could be involved in any discussions. Cooper also confirmed that a draft "package settlement" had now been written and that it was envisaged that Hanoi and Washington agree on a basic understanding before holding an international conference to ratify the secret agreement. Cooper presented this information as top secret, noting that because only four people in the State Department knew of it, "[T]here were now more people on this side of the Atlantic who were fully in the picture of the current United States approach to Vietnam than in the United States itself."[82] This emphasis on absolute secrecy was, of course, necessary to preserve the chances of a private deal being negotiated. It was also, as Cooper had stressed regarding the Polish affair, the result of Johnson's growing paranoia.

Wilson pressed Cooper to emphasize to Washington not only the desirability of a Tet truce but also that the pause in the bombing of North Vietnam should last for the duration of the entire Kosygin visit. Again, Wilson suggested reinforcing Cooper's points by sending a message to the president. When Cooper said it was best to wait and see whether Washington was amenable to the prime minister's views, Wilson said he would not send an immediate message.[83] In the end, Wilson trusted Cooper to do the job and merely responded to Johnson's reply to Wilson's telegram on the Polish affair. Wilson thanked the president for the "admirably full briefing" he and George Brown had received from Cooper, and said he felt they were "now fully in possession of the facts."[84] He also asked that Cooper pay another visit, immediately prior to the Kosygin visit.

KOSYGIN'S VISIT TO LONDON, FEBRUARY 6–13, 1967

By the end of January, the United States suspected Hanoi was seeking a settlement in Vietnam. In addition to the United States' coming close to establishing direct contact with North Vietnam during the Polish affair, a number of indirect contacts indicated some movement in North Vietnam. By the beginning of February, three journalists had had separate interviews with senior North Vietnamese officials that suggested Hanoi had changed its formula for establishing peace. Harrison Salisbury's interview with Pham Van Dong had been followed on January 28 by an interview between William Burchett, an experienced Australian Communist journalist, and the foreign minister of North Vietnam, Nguyen Duy Trinh, during which Trinh appeared to abandon the four points as a prerequisite of any peace settlement, instead indicating that there "could" be talks if the United States stopped bombing. This statement marked the first time that Hanoi had "directly addressed the possibility of an official dialogue between North Vietnamese and Americans." Moreover, Trinh had modified the condition that a bombing halt should be "final and unconditional" to "unconditional" only.[85] A meeting between Robert Kennedy and officials of the French Foreign Office on January 31 seemed to confirm that this was Hanoi's official policy.[86] This movement in Hanoi's position was underscored by the publication of Trinh's interview in North Vietnamese newspapers, including the party journal, *Nhan Dan*, indicating that Hanoi was preparing its own public for talks of some kind.[87] These private contacts appeared more portentous in light of recent statements on North Vietnamese radio indicating that there might be a willingness in Hanoi to negotiate.

Also, on January 20 an interview between Gloria Stewart and Nguyen Van Hieu, the NLF's foreign minister, was published in the *New Statesman*.[88] The Vietcong's settlement aims appeared to differ from North Vietnam's four points. Apparently, Hieu said to Stewart that the NLF was willing to "begin preliminary talks directly with America—without conditions" and argued that the NLF was not wedded to the idea of establishing the same political system as the north.[89] It appeared, at the very least, that discussions on possible peace terms were taking place among the Vietnamese nationalists.

In the lead-up to the Wilson–Kosygin talks, the British Foreign Office established a close liaison with the British embassy in Washington and with Chester Cooper to ensure that the U.S. government kept Wilson and Brown fully abreast of the latest developments.[90] The British would not be "put into bat" a second time without adequate protection and without knowing the score.[91] By the end of January, less than a week before Kosygin was due to arrive in London, Brown was pressing Cooper for "any additional information on American thinking on Vietnam."[92] He was particularly concerned to learn whether Thompson had spoken to the leadership in Moscow about the latest U.S. position, and whether the Americans could comment on the conversation between the journalist William Burchett and Pham Van Dong. As already noted, Burchett's report of the talk indicated that the North Vietnamese might be trying to make contact via a Communist country.[93] Three days before Kosygin's visit, Chester Cooper arrived in London in response to Wilson's request to be fully briefed on these latest developments in Vietnam diplomacy. Although Cooper had originally intended to return to Washington before Wilson's talks with Kosygin began, the prime minister asked that Cooper remain in England so that he could "serve as link between London and Washington in the event there were substantive discussions on Vietnam." As Cooper put it, "[I]t was by no means clear that such discussions were likely," but he stayed on just the same.[94] Cooper, representing Washington's views, told Wilson that these latest contacts

sounded rather less forthcoming than what tended to be read into the public statements of the North Vietnamese. Their present line was not apparently that, if the Americans would stop bombing, they would then be willing to talk seriously about negotiation; but simply that, if this happened, they would be prepared to listen to what the Americans thereafter had to propose; which implied that stopping the bombing would not be enough in itself to produce a real dialogue.[95]

Nevertheless, Wilson and the Americans believed Hanoi was now sending signals to the Americans. The State Department was certainly "disposed" to treat the Stewart and Burchett interviews seriously. Goldberg believed that the various approaches from Hanoi represented either

(A) A sign of serious interest on Hanoi's part in beginning process toward reaching settlement or toward mutual abatement of the conflict; or

(B) Part of an intensified propaganda effort to increase pressure of world and domestic opinion on Us to end bombing.

He suggested to Rusk that Washington follow a course that did not exclude either possibility.[96]

For this reason, the Americans decided to pursue parallel peace efforts. In addition to allowing Wilson to pursue peace talks with Alexei Kosygin during his visit to London beginning on February 6, the president agreed to a direct American approach to Hanoi via Moscow. According to Cooper, in early January the Russians had informed the U.S. embassy in Moscow that if the Americans "made an effort to see the chargé d'affaires of the North Vietnamese Embassy, preliminary exchanges might take place which could lead to serious talks."[97] The Americans decided to go along with the suggestion, and on January 10 John Guthrie, the senior embassy officer in Moscow, called at the North Vietnamese embassy. The embassy was not expecting Guthrie, and after a long delay he met with a North Vietnamese official, La Chang. Guthrie followed his brief and told the shocked official that the U.S. government was prepared to engage in direct talks with the North Vietnamese government.[98]

The Wilson–Kosygin peace initiative and the United States' direct approach to the North Vietnamese, code-named Sunflower, began separately but eventually became interrelated. The Sunflower effort was "enormously complex and confusing" but also offered "further evidence of American diplomatic ineptitude." The Pentagon Papers also noted that this episode "aroused heated controversy"[99] between the United States and Great Britain. This was clearly the case. A detailed analysis of the evolution of the Wilson–Kosygin peace initiative illuminates the sources of the disagreement between Washington and London and the reasons for the intensity of the feelings on both sides of the Atlantic.

Of course, neither the British nor the Americans were sure that Moscow was interested in acting as an intermediary. Although Brown had felt there was some movement in the Soviet position, and Wilson was convinced that Kosygin's decision to come to London during the Tet truce was a hopeful sign, before the actual visit there was no clear evidence that the Russians would play "go-between" on Vietnam. They might just decide to leave Hanoi to make a direct contact themselves. Brown was worried this was the case when it was announced that the entourage Kosygin would bring with him to London was relatively low-level.

Unlike the Marigold peace effort, which focused on the terms of a final peace settlement, Sunflower focused on mutual de-escalation as a way of establishing the right atmosphere in which to discuss a final settlement. The impasse at this stage was still as follows: the United States required some kind of mutual de-escalation; the North Vietnamese demanded that the United States stop the bombing unconditionally.

THE PHASE A/PHASE B FORMULA: THE CONFUSION OVER TENSES

Wilson felt optimistic about a positive outcome from his talks with Kosygin. Cooper describes the prime minister as being in "high spirits" about meeting the Russian premier at the London airport and escorting him to Claridge's Hotel. The American representative admitted later that Wilson might not have been so enthusiastic had he known how Washington viewed his plans to talk to Kosygin about Vietnam. According to Cooper, the president, Walt Rostow, and some within the State Department "took a rather dim view" of Wilson's eagerness to play a part in Vietnam diplomacy:

There was a sense that the British Government was pushing hard, perhaps too hard, to undertake the role of mediator. To be sure the British could claim both a right and responsibility to assume such a role; they and the Russians were Co-chairmen of the 1954 Geneva Conference and of the 1961–62 Laos Conference. But some of Wilson's American cousins felt his underlying motivation was to bolster his own and England's prestige... that both Wilson and Brown were having happy dreams of being in the spotlight of a major international conference.[100]

Available records appear to verify Cooper's beliefs. Clearly there was deep suspicion about the "eagerness of the British leaders to participate with maximum personal visibility in bringing peace to Vietnam."[101] Wilson certainly would have experienced a great deal of domestic relief from backbench pressures had he pulled off such a coup and would have welcomed the recognition that went along with it. However, it is difficult to believe that Wilson and Brown were primarily concerned with their chances of receiving the Nobel Peace Prize. It must be remembered that Wilson was simply not convinced that a military victory was possible and that he had openly questioned U.S. military tactics. His desire for peace in Vietnam appears to have been genuine, and one must credit him with some humanitarian, as well as political, motives. That is not to argue, however, that domestic, political concerns or international prestige factors were not spurring Wilson and Brown on; rather, it is to affirm that there were other, important motives at work here too.

Cooper admits, however, that Washington held another "less articulated but more deeply felt attitude" about Wilson's talks with Kosygin.[102] Johnson was not about to let the British prime minister get credit for pulling off peace talks after all the work the Americans had recently put in through the Polish contact and Guthrie's meetings with La Chang. In this sense, any form of third-party mediation was not particularly welcomed. If Hanoi was ready to talk, then the president was determined to reap the political benefits. There was also a third factor involved in the president's lack of enthusiasm for the Wilson–Kosygin talks: Johnson did not trust Wilson in negotiations. The Americans generally preferred direct talks, but they were particularly worried that the prime minister might trap them into terms that would prove unpalatable to them.

Despite American reservations about the desirability of the prime minister's conducting peace talks, Washington had little choice but to support the Wilson–Kosygin talks. The Johnson administration still wanted British support on Vietnam and was well aware that the price they paid for it was condoning Wilson's peace efforts. There was also a recognition that the Soviets might be able to apply pressure on the North Vietnamese on the negotiation front. The State Department later judged this matter in the following terms:

Kosygin's visit to London in early February made British participation inevitable. Kosygin and Wilson would discuss Vietnam and issue statements on it with or without a US input. If we stood aloof from it, the results could be harmful to the US. And the possibility that Kosygin could use Soviet influence in Hanoi introduced an element of potential value, not available in direct US–DRV exchanges... Looking back on it, there seems little doubt that bringing the British in was to US advantage.[103]

However, this did not mean that Washington was going to be fully open with the British. President Johnson had since the end of January been working on a draft letter to Ho Chi Minh appealing for peace. Early drafts apparently included the now standard phase A/phase B formula but also included talk of an unspecified time lag between the cessation of U.S. bombing and the ending of North Vietnamese infiltration of the South. When the letter was finally delivered via Moscow on February 8 the terms had changed. The letter, published in full in Johnson's memoirs, set out the following offer: "I am prepared to order a cessation of bombing against your country and the stopping of further augmentation of U.S. forces in South Vietnam as soon as I am assured that infiltration into South Vietnam by land and by sea has stopped."[104] The operative words were "has stopped." Unfortunately for the Wilson–Kosygin talks, the British were not made aware of this letter to Ho or its content. Nor, as far as we know, were the U.S. representatives in London told of this development.[105]

Kosygin arrived at the London airport on February 6, having been diverted from Gatwick because of fog. Wilson's first session of private talks with Kosygin was at 3:30 P.M. on the day of Kosygin's arrival in London, and the two statesmen got straight down to business on Vietnam. Wilson reviewed the U.S. position as he knew it and referred to the apparent change of position in Hanoi that the Trinh interview seemed to indicate. He also reminded Kosygin of the phase A/phase B proposal that Brown had delivered in Moscow the previous November and emphasized the nature of the opportunity offered by the fact that current talks coincided with the Tet truce. According to the British record, Wilson presented his interpretation of this formula as

a two-phased agreement designed to meet the situation in which North Viet-Nam required an unconditional cessation of bombing while the United States needed an assurance that some measure of de-escalation would follow if the bombing stopped. Assuming that an agreement could be reached secretly on such an arrangement, it would result in two things happening—first there would be overt action in the cessation of bombing, and secondly there would be further action in de-escalation by the United States side to which North Viet-Nam and the Liberation Front would respond by similar acts of de-escalation.[106]

This outline of the formula "got no flicker of interest," as Cooper quickly reported back to Rusk in Washington.[107] Wilson was also eager to arrange a Geneva-type conference to arbitrate over Vietnam, but Kosygin felt that this was a premature suggestion, as did the Americans.[108]

At this stage Wilson was "holding back on US refinements" on the mutual de-escalation formula, particularly the nature of the further acts of U.S. de-escalation that would comprise phase B.[109] He nevertheless stressed the hope that Kosygin could encourage the North Vietnamese to give the Americans "a firm sign, during Tet, of a readiness to make a positive and visible response to a cessation of bombing."[110] According to Wilson, for the first time Kosygin seemed ready to talk about this issue. Although denying that he was speaking for the North Vietnamese, or that he knew any more about their position than had been publicly stated, Kosygin did say that Trinh's statement should be endorsed by Britain and the Soviet Union in a public or private statement to the president as a basis for direct talks between the United States and North Vietnam. This was "unacceptable" to the British but was considered to be merely Kosygin's "opening move" and therefore not taken too seriously.[111]

Little more was agreed on at this first meeting, but the British were not discouraged. Indeed, Donald Murray of the Foreign Office concluded that Kosygin was getting over four points, all of which were new. Kosygin agreed that there was a sense of urgency over the situation in Vietnam and the need to encourage peace talks; he acknowledged that the Tet truce provided an opportunity to begin the process of establishing contact between the United States and North Vietnam; he accepted that Russia and Britain had a part to play in assisting such talks; and he acknowledged that the North Vietnamese appeared ready to consider settling by negotiation.[112]

The next meeting between Kosygin and Wilson was to be at an informal dinner given by the prime minister at No. 10 Downing Street at 8:00 P.M. that night. In the meantime, as Wilson put it, both sides were "busy."[113] The prime minister had further talks with Bruce and Cooper, and Kosygin was in touch with Hanoi.[114] Wilson attempted to telephone Johnson but, having failed to reach him, sent a telegram reporting on his talks with Kosygin and asking for further clarification of the U.S. position, especially regarding the Trinh formula.[115] He specifically asked "whether the U.S. could stop the bombing of North Vietnam in exchange for an indication that Hanoi would enter into talks without any military acts of de-escalation on their side."[116] Johnson was clearly annoyed by this message. In a lengthy reply the president reminded Wilson that the United States had refrained from bombing within a 10-mile radius of Hanoi because this had been given as the reason for Hanoi's termination of discussions with the Poles. Despite the continuation of this restriction, Hanoi had not offered any corresponding action. Moreover, given that Hanoi insisted on a permanent end to the bombing rather than a suspension, Johnson felt it "all the more necessary to know what military action Hanoi would take" if the United States stopped bombing. The Americans feared the North Vietnamese would use an end to the bombing to their military advantage by introducing even more troops and supplies into the south in order to strengthen their position during negotiations. Johnson explained his version of phase A/phase B to Wilson as follows: "[W]e are prepared to and plan, through established channels, to inform Hanoi that if they will agree to an assured stoppage of infiltration into South Viet Nam, we will stop the bombing of North Viet Nam and stop further augmentation of U.S. forces in South Viet Nam. We would welcome your joint advocacy of this position."[117] Wilson was, therefore, well aware of the United States' continuing approaches to Hanoi but did not realize that the wording of this communication would differ from Johnson's final draft letter to Ho Chi Minh. It would change from "if they will agree to an assured stoppage" to "as soon as I am assured that infiltration...has stopped." It was a subtle difference but an important one.

Johnson also expressed his skepticism regarding Hanoi's willingness to begin talks and urged Wilson "to separate the political processes of discussion from military action...We are prepared to move immediately on major steps of mutual de-escalation...What we cannot accept is the exchange of guarantee of a safe haven for North Viet Nam merely for discussions which thus far have no form or content, during which they could continue to expand their military operations without limit." The president was annoyed at Wilson's pushiness on this issue, saying he doubted that Kosygin "expected to resolve this matter on his first evening in London"; he strongly urged the two cochairmen not to send a joint message to him "suggesting a stoppage of the bombing in exchange merely for talks" but instead to explore additional leads.[118] Johnson's frustration with Wilson can, perhaps, be explained by a meeting the president had had earlier in the day with Robert Kennedy.[119] Johnson invited Kennedy to the White House at 4 P.M. to discuss a *Newsweek* report that, during Kennedy's 10-day trip to Europe, the French had given him a "message" from Hanoi indicating a willingness to negotiate a three-stage settlement, with the first stage being a U.S. bombing pause. Fearing that Kennedy had leaked this story to the press in order to maintain pressure on the president to seek peace, Johnson accused Kennedy of doing so. When Kennedy protested his innocence, Johnson angrily responded, "It's not *my* State Department, God damn it. It's *your* State Department." When Johnson further accused Kennedy of aiding the enemy and thereby killing American soldiers, Kennedy left around 6 P.M., stating, "I don't have to take that from you."[120] Wilson attempted to call the president at 7:30 P.M.[121] Given Johnson's well-documented paranoia regarding anything to do with Robert Kennedy, we can assume that the president's anger toward critics of his war policy was still in play when he met with Rostow later that night to discuss the situation in London and pen a reply.

The Foreign Office and Downing Street were alarmed by the strident and dismissive tone of this presidential message. However, Cooper soon explained to the prime minister that the message was "pure Rostow" and that had the message originated in the State Department, then the tone would have been "substantially different."[122] Either way, this brief from LBJ was "tougher" than Wilson wanted it to be.[123] Cooper believed that, after discussions with the prime minister and his advisers, he would be able to get "something rather more forthcoming out of Washington."[124] Wilson, well aware that the Tet pause would begin the next day, was not prepared to wait for Washington's tone to change; instead he decided to maintain the momentum of the previous day's talks by putting Vietnam on the afternoon's agenda.[125]

At that meeting on February 7, the prime minister informed Kosygin that the Americans wanted to stop the bombing but "needed an assurance that could be kept secret." Then, North Vietnamese acts of reciprocation "would not be presented as having been taken in response to the stopping of the bombing, which would be presented as unconditional."[126] The consequential actions were spelled out to Kosygin:

The United States were willing to stop the build-up of their forces in the South if they were assured that the movement of North Viet-Namese forces from the North to the South would stop at the same time. Essentially, therefore, the two stages were kept apart. But because the United States Government would know that the second stage would follow, they would therefore be able first to stop the bombing, even if there was a short period between the first stage and the actions to be taken by both sides in the second stage. There would be balanced concessions at the second stage; the first stage would be carried out by the United States alone; but the United States would only carry out the first stage because they would know that the second stage would follow within a short period of time.[127]

Wilson also informed Kosygin that the United States was now seeking to get word directly to Hanoi along similar lines. Indeed, Wilson and Brown expected that the "palm-tree" discussions were set for the following day.[128] While Kosygin welcomed the fact that Washington was about to contact North Vietnam directly, he argued that he could not praise a decision to stop the bombing because the bombing had been wrong in the first place. He also thought it unrealistic to expect "North Vietnam to stop the guerrillas and the NLF from further hostilities." Wilson assured him that this "was not in the package."[129] After further clarification from Wilson, Kosygin asked for the proposal to be put in writing to him. When Bruce visited 10 Downing Street after the talks to hear a "resumé" of Wilson's discussions with Kosygin, he got the impression that things had gone "unexpectedly well." He admitted in his diaries: "I have begun at last to feel a moderate optimism about the possibilities of at least initiating talks with Hanoi."[130]

After speaking with Wilson, Cooper was also reasonably confident about the portents coming from Kosygin. Later that night Cooper cabled Rusk and Harriman to outline the day's events, particularly the offer made by Wilson that phases A and B were to be "kept apart." He reported that Kosygin had shown "considerable interest in this formulation."[131] He also noted that if a direct approach was made to Hanoi, the British hoped that "if any questions arise as to differences in the formulation of Phase A and Phase B as worked out today in London, and the formulation forwarded to Hanoi by Washington, Hanoi be told that the British text was authoritative in substance, although there may be stylistic or translation differences from the U.S. version."[132]

The same day Wilson attended question time in the House, where he mishandled a reply to a supplementary question referring to "some tentative peace reports that Hanoi was willing to start negotiations but called them off when the Americans started bombing again last December." His reply was a little too unguarded:

I do not think that during this week it would be helpful to comment on a number of important points about Vietnam, but, as my Hon. Friend has referred to the discussions in December, of which I have all the details, perhaps I might tell him it is my view that what happened then was based on a very considerable two-way misunderstanding, and that is why I think certain events in December occurred. If my Hon. Friend is referring to the Polish discussions in anything that has happened since then, I do not think that it would be very helpful for me to offer comments this afternoon.[133]

Wilson's response, with its tacit acceptance of the questioner's premise that secret peace negotiations had indeed been attempted in December 1966, caused consternation in the White House. Rostow cabled his friend and British counterpart, Michael Palliser, saying that the prime minister's answer had "greatly distressed" Washington, which had "held the facts tightly" and "severely avoided any response, analysis, or explanation of that series of exchanges." Moreover, Rostow (and his colleagues at the White House) disagreed with Wilson's analysis of events, saying, "[W]e are by no means convinced that there was a mis-understanding. Other explanations better fit the facts as we know them."[134]

Given the prime minister's hopes for the Wilson–Kosygin talks, Palliser felt it necessary to reply at length to Rostow's cable in the hope that the matter would be laid to rest. He pointed out that the British Sunday papers had run with stories from Rostow himself that peace moves were under way behind the scenes and that "an extremely interesting and delicate phase" in diplomatic probing had opened in an effort to find out whether the Communists were really interested in cease-fire talks. This revelation had been linked to the disclosure in the *Washington Post* that Lewandowski had been involved in talks in Hanoi. Palliser went on with admitted "frankness" to say that the prime minister would find it ironic to be charged with leaking information on this subject, when it would not have been possible for the supplementary question to be asked had Washington not given the British press enough details already.[135] Indeed, Palliser argued that taking Wilson's political problems into consideration, the prime minister could not have said less without "exposing himself to heavy pressure to say a great deal more. As it was the Prime Minister had refused to comment on the Polish discussions, was in no way critical of the US Government, had merely revealed that he had knowledge of the events, and his answer had disposed of the matter."[136] Also, by talking of a "two-way misunderstanding," the prime minister was letting Kosygin know that he did not necessarily believe Hanoi's version of events.[137]

Clearly, Washington, or at least Rostow and Johnson, overreacted to Wilson's comments in the House, possibly because they were not fully aware of the background as Palliser explained it, but probably because by now they no longer trusted Wilson to maintain a dignified silence on such issues. Rostow expressed his gratitude for Palliser's explanation but replied that Rusk's rule on peace moves was "no substantive comment on any single channel." At this stage, Rostow was content to say that the damaging part of Wilson's answer in the House was the expression "two-way misunderstanding" and that they would have to deal with that "sometime." He also accepted "full opprobrium" for his own lapse in this respect when he used the words "interesting and delicate" to describe private peace moves.[138] The incident may partially explain why the White House had failed to inform London of the revisions to the letter to Ho Chi Minh.

While this spat between London and Washington was simmering in the background, diplomatic wrangling over Sunflower was heating up. On February 8, LBJ sent his letter to Ho Chi Minh.[139] Back in London, Kosygin attended a number of business and civic engagements. During one of these, a luncheon given by the Lord Mayor at the Guildhall, Kosygin gave a speech in which he referred to the possibility of reconvening the Geneva conference under UK–USSR chairmanship.[140] Given the British preference for such a move, this speech prompted a flurry of activity on both sides of the Atlantic. Cooper remembered how Kosygin's "cryptic comment" "interrupted the first proper dinner I had had in several days, kept me up most of the night, threw parts of Whitehall into disarray, gave Mrs. George Brown a pounding headache, and complicated Washington's instructions to me." Cooper was called to George Brown's flat after an "excited call" from the Foreign Secretary. Apparently, Brown "was convinced that he and Wilson were on the right track in proposing another Geneva Conference—Kosygin's remarks suggested that the Russians were anxious to take this route."[141] Brown, and a reluctant Foreign Office, came up with the suggestion that as well as pursuing peace talks privately (phase A/phase B), a public route should also be taken. Brown asked for a written draft proposal to be ready for the next day's meeting with Kosygin. Gore-Booth, Murray Maclehose, and Cooper returned to the Foreign Office and prepared the following draft:

The two cochairmen will announce immediately that they:

   A.   Invite the US to assure them that the bombing of North Vietnam will stop;

   B.   Invite the North Vietnamese to assure the cochairmen that infiltration into South Vietnam will stop and invite the US to assure the cochairmen that they will stop further augmentation of US forces in South Vietnam.[142]

Should both parties agree to this, the cochairmen would invite members of the 1954 Geneva conference to reconvene on February 15 to work out a settlement of the present conflict.[143] Should the Soviets dissent from this public approach, Brown would press them to endorse the phase A/phase B formula in private instead. Cooper cabled the State Department after midnight to report Brown's plans; the reply confirmed his belief that Washington "was unenthusiastic about the Geneva track."[144]

At the same time that Cooper had been summoned by Brown, Bruce had been called by Michael Palliser, just as he was about to go to bed, asking him to go to Downing Street. Bruce remembered that his chauffeur deposited him "in the lee of the Foreign Office, whence I circuited around to the postern gate in Whitehall. It seemed conspiratorial." There he met the prime minister, Michael Palliser, Burke Trend, Michael Halls, and Lord Chalfont, who were discussing Kosygin's speech and the "possible ploys" they might use in tomorrow's meeting. Bruce noted that all present looked tired. No one got to bed before 2:30 A.M.[145]

The late night was used constructively. Despite Washington's preference for a private approach, Wilson arranged with Brown that, on cue, the Foreign Secretary would probe Kosygin about his Geneva comments at the following morning's meeting with the premier. During the discussion, on February 9, Brown asked if Kosygin's references to collaboration between the Soviet Union and Britain on Vietnam, and subsequent reference to the Geneva agreement, signaled a Russian willingness to reconvene the conference, even if the Chinese refused to attend. According to notes taken by Murray Maclehose of the Foreign Office, Kosygin replied that this was "not exactly" what he had meant to imply, rather that he had "proceeded upon the assumption that the main thing was for the UK and the Soviet Union to assist the two sides to meet together after the bombing stopped." He suggested that after this had been done, "[T]here may be various proposals for moving further ahead, including the reconvening of the Geneva Conference." He also pointed out that he "could not speak for Hanoi at this point" and that it was important to "do first things first."[146] Brown then read orally from the draft public announcement formulated in the early hours, asking if he would agree to it reconvening on February 15 if the two-phase acts of de-escalation were agreed upon.[147] According to Cooper, again "Kosygin gave the idea short shrift," although he did inquire whether this proposal had been discussed with the Americans.[148] Although the British answered that the formula did not have the approval of the U.S. government, Brown later said that if Kosygin could deliver his friends in Hanoi, the British would try to "deliver the Americans." Kosygin said that he would need to know Hanoi's views first and that, in any case, a Geneva conference would be "a complicated issue."[149] Kosygin did, however, ask for a copy of the British text.

Before Washington received news of these latest developments, Rusk and Johnson discussed events in London on the telephone. Rusk expressed his concern that the British proposal to the Russians was "not good enough" and that State would be suggesting a reply to it. He thought the "trouble" was with the second point about augmentation, which was not adequate "as a substitute for infiltration because that would mean that the other side would be free to go ahead with a rotation and sending arms and re-supply and all that kind of thing." He told Johnson that "our original formulation—stopping infiltration—is the one we ought to stay with."[150] On hearing news of the latest developments in London, the U.S. State Department decided it was time to make its views more explicit. Rusk cabled Bruce to express his doubts that Hanoi would accept a public announcement of its acceptance of mutual de-escalation, even if it could be persuaded by the Soviets to go for such a deal. Russian involvement in the brokerage of the deal might make it particularly difficult for the North Vietnamese in light of their concerns over Chinese Communist reactions, and the Russians themselves might be concerned about appearing to be working so closely with the Americans. Rusk's skepticism about the possibility of a public deal led him to inform Bruce that the "British should be left in no doubt that, while we are most grateful for their serious considered efforts, they may well have to accept results rather than overt British participation in them."[151] Wilson might have to settle for less of a public profile in the resolution of the conflict, in the background helping to secure a private settlement rather than being the orchestrator of a public, Geneva-type conference. The British were told formally that they wanted Kosygin to know, and to pass on to Hanoi, their willingness to go along with either proposal. They did not "at any cost want to appear to be pressing Hanoi to accept publicly any commitment which they might think would involve them in a loss of face."[152]

The same day, February 9, Secretary of Defense McNamara telephoned Johnson to report that the U.S. Joint Chiefs of Staff were requesting a resumption of military activity during the remainder of Tet. McNamara explained that this recommendation, which was "almost impossible for us to accept," had come because U.S. intelligence sources indicated increased waterborne activity by the North Vietnamese along the coastal area north of the demilitarized zone. McNamara acknowledged that Johnson could easily counter the Joint Chiefs' concerns about these movements because the movements were confined to a "limited area" and admitted, "[W]e're reinforcing our forces just as North Vietnam is reinforcing theirs, and in the remaining period of the truce, 2 or 3 days, this just can't penalize us in any important way." Moreover, he advised Johnson that "beyond all that, you're engaged in a very delicate set of relationships here between the Pope and Kosygin and Wilson and the American people and the international community," and breaking the truce was thus almost impossible. McNamara did remind the president, however, that the Joint Chiefs had opposed the truce from the start, and the relationship with military commanders was "a serious problem."[153] Johnson, McNamara, and Rusk met with General Wheeler later that afternoon, but no decision to resume air bombardments was made. Washington cabled London on the movement of troops and equipment from North Vietnam heading toward the South. Wilson had mentioned this to Kosygin at their Thursday morning meeting, explaining that this did not help in the call for an end to U.S. bombing.[154] According to Wilson, Kosygin "took the figures seriously."[155] Further messages were sent from Washington on this issue, and these were passed on to Kosygin. In the meantime, however, Rusk cabled the U.S. embassy in London to ask for an amendment to the British proposal—replacing the words "augmentation of forces" with "infiltration into South Vietnam will stop."[156]

The following morning, Friday, February 10, two days after LBJ's letter to Ho Chi Minh, Wilson met with Kosygin and summarized the current position. There were now two propositions on the table, both based on mutual de-escalation: a public one that would result in a Geneva-type conference, and a private one based on phase A/phase B. Kosygin asked to hear the phase A/phase B proposal again. Wilson outlined it again. According to Wilson, "Mr. Kosygin suddenly looked interested. It seemed that the way I had put it was in some way more attractive than what had been said earlier in the week."[157] At this stage, Kosygin said he would like to think about the proposal. Wilson and the Foreign Office felt that Kosygin's response "was sufficiently forthcoming" to warrant the prime minister's promise to provide the proposition in writing later that day.[158] Kosygin wanted it before leaving for Scotland that evening.[159]

Late on Thursday afternoon, February 9, Chester Cooper, Murray, and Gore-Booth had begun work on the written version of phase A/phase B to be delivered to Kosygin. Wilson recorded that he "wanted to make absolutely certain that the text was approved by the Americans."[160] Wilson insisted that he was assured the text had been confirmed as the American position and that he had been "assured that there had been the fullest consultation with the State Department at top level" about the text. The Americans, as we shall see, viewed the situation differently.[161] When drafting the letter to Kosygin, Cooper and Murray clearly had America's 14 points in mind. The points, which had been publicly issued on January 7 and further elaborated upon as recently as January 27, contained the following as part of the 14th point: "We are prepared to order a cessation of all bombing of North Viet-Nam, the moment we are assured—privately or otherwise—that this step will be answered promptly by a corresponding and appropriate deescalation of the other side."[162] Cooper thought the draft also "seemed fully consistent" with the text of Johnson's cable to Wilson of February 7.[163] The draft version read:

(a) the United States will stop bombing North Vietnam as soon as they are assured that the infiltration from North Vietnam to South Vietnam will stop...

(b) within a few days (with the period to be agreed between the two sides before the bombing stops) the United States will stop further augmenting their forces in South Vietnam and North Vietnam will stop infiltration and movement of forces into the South.[164]

The authors of the text therefore felt that they were clear on America's terms for phase A/phase B. Consequently Cooper "cabled the statement to Washington, confident that it required little more than pro forma approval."[165]

Cooper recorded that he felt happy that Washington should receive his cable by around 6:30 P.M. Washington time on Thursday, February 9, and that this allowed plenty of time for the State Department to reply before Kosygin's scheduled departure for Scotland on Friday evening at 10:30 P.M. However, the only cable Cooper had received by Friday morning was one reminding him to tell Wilson of the State Department's concern that North Vietnamese troops continued to move southward. He thought, however, that "the Department might have taken a dim view of my troubling busy people with such a simple question. But, I thought, they could at least send a terse 'O.K.' "[166] Cooper informed Wilson about the cable regarding the continuing flow of North Vietnamese troops, but that he had heard nothing back on the phase A/phase B message. By late afternoon there was still no reply, so a repeat message was sent. The cable merely said, "[H]ere is text of Phase A–Phase B formula which is to be sent to Kosygin at his request ASAP. Need guidance urgently," and then outlined the steps involved.[167]

We now know that on the afternoon of February 10, Rostow wrote a memorandum to the president, raising "some of the questions we ought to answer in our minds before we flash London." The first question raised, and answered, by Rostow was as follows:

How do we assure ourselves that infiltration has stopped? (The exact language of your letter to Ho is "I am assured.")

   Possible answer: We stand down our bombing in the short run when we have Ho's word backed by the UK/USSR. We do not move to the next step, however—"stop augmenting our forces"—until unilateral U.S. military surveillance and Westy's judgement tell us infiltration has, in fact, stopped.[168]

This document makes it clear that Washington was working on a different version of phase A/phase B than the people in London were.[169]

Apparently Wilson was "restless" about Washington's lack of feedback given that Kosygin had pressed the British for the written version earlier in the day.[170] But Cooper remembered that by "7 o'clock I was convinced there would be no reply—and that silence meant consent."[171] By that time, Wilson had left for a reception given by the Soviet ambassador, and Cooper felt able to go to the theater to watch a production of *Fiddler on the Roof*. He left word that he could be contacted there and informed the ushers where he was seated. At around 9 o'clock, Cooper received a telephone call from Rostow asking him to return to the embassy, which he did. At 9:30 P.M. he received a message saying there had been a "complete revision" of the proposal to be handed to Kosygin.[172] Although Cooper had telephoned Walt Rostow on his return to Grosvenor Square and had told him that there was a possibility that the written version of phase A/phase B had already been passed to Kosygin, he did not think "it registered."[173] Cooper was told to meet Wilson and Brown at 10 Downing Street, where the revised message would come through on teletype.

The prime minister had returned from the reception and private dinner at the Soviet embassy at Kensington Palace Garden, where at around 7 P.M. he had handed Kosygin a document outlining "almost word for word" what Wilson had said in their morning meeting.[174] According to Wilson, "Mr Kosygin was taking the day's developments very seriously and clearly with some hope."[175] On returning to Downing Street, Wilson recalled, he found Bruce and Cooper waiting for him. According to Wilson, after telling them of the latest talks with Kosygin, Bruce said, "Prime Minister, I think you've made it. This is going to be the biggest diplomatic coup of this century." Wilson claimed he "demurred," arguing that Hanoi and China's reactions were not yet known.[176] Bruce later denied that he had said Wilson "had it in the bag." He believes "that was hyperbolic. I was skeptical about achieving a result. I was in favor of his taking a try at it. I think that's the distinction."[177] Either way, Wilson was soon deflated when Cooper informed the prime minister that a message was about to come through from the White House. It arrived at about 10:30 P.M., and according to Cooper, "My heart fell as I saw it. We were in a brand new ballgame."[178]

The key aspect of the original phase A/phase B proposal was the U.S. agreement to stop bombing first; the new terms reversed the order of events—now the North Vietnamese had to stop infiltration first and then the United States would stop bombing. As Cooper later put it:

The sequence of Phase A and Phase B had been reversed, and the whole formula had been distorted. In short what we would be saying to the North Vietnamese was that a bombing cessation would be directly conditional on their stopping infiltration—a proposition Hanoi had thrown back to us time and time again, and one that was completely inconsistent with Rusk's elaboration of his "Fourteen Points," as publicly released only a few days before. It was hard to believe that the Washington draftsmen realised the implications of their new formula.[179]

In addition to the change in tenses, the new text also included an additional change. Despite having assured the British that Washington would be happy with a private arrangement with Hanoi, the new package insisted on a public commitment. The text included the following (emphasis added):

A.   The United States will order a cessation of bombing of North Vietnam as soon as they are assured that infiltration from North Vietnam to South Vietnam *has stopped*. This assurance can be communicated in secret if North Vietnam so wishes.

B.   Within a few days (with the period to be agreed with the two sides before the bombing stops) the United States will stop further augmenting their force in South Vietnam. The cessation of bombing of North Vietnam is an action which will be immediately apparent. This requires that the stoppage of infiltration becomes public very quickly thereafter. If Hanoi is unwilling to announce the stoppage of infiltration, the United States must do so at the time it stops augmentation of U.S. forces. In that case, Hanoi must not deny it.

C.   Any assurances from Hanoi can reach the United States direct, or through Soviet channels, or through the Soviet and British Governments. This is for North Vietnam to decide.[180]

Cooper double-checked with Rostow that Washington understood that this was not just a change of tense, it was a complete reversal of the terms, and that if Wilson had already delivered a text to Kosygin, the new version should be substituted for it. Apparently by now both men had nearly lost their "cool," and Cooper was informed that the change in terms had come from the president, largely as a result of the North Vietnamese troop movements over the past few days.[181] Cooper admitted that when he called Rostow he was "sore as hell" and said, "Well, Jesus, how can you do this! You kept telling me to press the Phase A–Phase B, that is what Wilson was doing, the only Phase A–Phase B I knew was the one that was current." Rostow replied that he did not "give a Goddamn" about either Cooper or Wilson; "[Y]ou damn well change it."[182] According to Cooper, Wilson and Brown were "incredulous and irate."[183] This action placed the British in a most embarrassing situation with Kosygin. Wilson had already delivered the written statement and was now in the position of having to hand Kosygin a revised text before he boarded his overnight train to Scotland, which was due to depart at 11:35 P.M. from Euston station. Because Kosygin had already left Claridge's Hotel and was on his way to the station, Wilson's private secretary, Michael Halls, was dispatched to the station and duly delivered the letter to Kosygin as he boarded the train. The letter included an introductory sentence that stated this was a message received direct from the White House and could be taken now as "the authentic United States position on the subject."[184]

Cooper was left to pick up the pieces. He describes the atmosphere at Downing Street that night as "gloomy and hostile." As those assembled struggled to explain what had happened, Wilson and Brown turned their anger on one another. Cooper remembered that they "just went at each other, it was just terrible. Brown accused Wilson of being too premature; and that time and time again during these discussions Wilson didn't inform Brown as to what was going on; Brown on at least three occasions that night resigned as Foreign Minister."[185] When Wilson took Brown into a private room to straighten things out, Cooper was asked to accompany them, almost as a witness.[186] The day's events had descended into farce. Brown later claimed that he thought it was a mistake to deliver the new version of phase A/phase B to Kosygin before he arrived in Scotland; after all, there was nothing Kosygin could do with the message while he was on a train. Instead, he thought they should have used Kosygin's journey time to Edinburgh to try to persuade the Americans to change their minds.[187]

Wilson could not contain himself. He called the White House and spoke to Walt Rostow. Cooper said that in the two decades of his diplomatic career he "had never seen anyone quite so angry" but that "Wilson kept himself very much under control as he explained how embarrassing and damaging the Washington message was."[188] Cooper felt partly responsible for events, feeling that he had "somehow...led Wilson astray." He considered that his career might come to an end as a result of the day's events.[189] "They were all mad at Washington; they were mad at each other; they were angry at me; and I was angry at them; and I was angry at Washington—more angry at Washington than anybody. It was a pretty rough night."[190] Cooper called it "Black Friday."[191] Bruce remembered that after the revised version had been delivered to Kosygin, Wilson "dictated and discussed with us a series of four telegrams" he proposed sending to the president. One of the telegrams concerned "his now settled wish to go, with or without Kosygin, to Hanoi, if the discussions break down on Sunday." Bruce predicted this would "cause a violently unfavourable reaction in Washington." The prime minister asked Bruce and Cooper to explain his arguments for such a visit.[192]

The following morning, Saturday, February 11, Wilson and Brown endeav-
ored to keep the peace initiative going. Cooper received a telegram from the
White House explaining in more detail the reasoning behind the change in
tenses. He later described this rationale as "contrived."[193] The cable argued that
the revised phase A/phase B was consistent with the details in Johnson's letter
to Ho Chi Minh, dated February 8, which of course neither Cooper nor Wilson
was aware of. The telegram stressed the warnings Washington had delivered
regarding North Vietnam's violation of the Tet truce. Cooper judged the
telegram to be "a very tortured ex post facto rationalization" that was "drafted
by Bill Bundy, who was attempting to pick up the pieces, not having been at the
meeting on Friday night."[194] Washington also forwarded the latest figures on
the North Vietnamese troop movements. During the truce, up to 6 P.M. on Friday, more than 2,050 trucks had been spotted heading south, as compared to a
daily average of 100 trucks in the pretruce period.[195]

This telegram inflamed the situation in London. Wilson, Brown, Cooper, and
Bruce were all outraged at events. With Kosygin in Scotland, they had all day to
reflect on matters and decide on a course of action for the final day of talks with
the Russians at Chequers on Sunday. Wilson had had high hopes for the talks;
they now looked to be in ruin. He was convinced the Soviets would no longer believe he was in the confidence of the Americans and could certainly not "deliver"
them to the negotiating table. Bruce recalls that Wilson instructed Paul Gore-
Booth at the Foreign Office "to chew us up" on the shift in American policy. Wilson also began using the "dissociation" word again, this time in relation to U.S.
plans to renew bombing in Vietnam while Kosygin was still in Britain. Once back
at Grosvenor Square, Bruce and Cooper "indulged in an orgy of telephone conversations."[196] Rusk rang twice regarding the bombing renewal decision and Rostow once "to deliver a lecture in defence of the controversial paper."[197]

More worrying as far as Bruce was concerned was a call he took from Burke
Trend. The prime minister was considering making a trip to Washington on
Monday after his talk with Kosygin. Bruce did "not think well" of this proposal.[198] Bruce also received a telephone call from George Brown "to report he
was most unhappy over recent events, and intimated, to use his favourite word,
the US had made a 'bloody' mess of things." Bruce sent a telegram to Dean and
McNamara expressing his personal opinion that the political effects of a renewal of bombing before Kosygin left London would be severe, particularly the
risk of alienating the Soviets. The experts in Washington discussed Wilson's request that the United States defer the resumption of military action against
North Vietnam until after Kosygin's departure from Britain. After much discussion the president agreed to extend the pause, although the decision would
not be made public until Kosygin had left London.[199] At this stage, Rostow
judged the chances of Kosygin's and Wilson's "developing anything" between
then and Sunday night as a 5 percent chance.[200]

Later that evening, Wilson and Brown, and three advisers, met with Bruce
and Cooper to discuss in detail what had happened, to consider the latest

telegrams from Washington, and to decide on the best way forward. This proved to be yet another stormy session; indeed, Cooper recalled that he thought they would be lucky to "finish the night's work without some very ugly scenes between the British and the Americans, or among the British themselves. Ten years before, during the Suez crisis, I had had a ringside seat at a major Washington–London squabble. Once again I sensed Anglo–American relations dissolving before my eyes."[201] Bruce remembered that he and Cooper "had two and a half hours of rather rough handling."[202] He also noted in his diary that Brown was more "vehement" than Wilson in his criticism of the United States but thought that "he was fatigued and perhaps somewhat inebriated."[203]

The meeting was indeed lengthy, lasting just over three hours. Both parties outlined their version of events, and Wilson and Bruce expressed three immediate concerns. First, the British were worried that the change in the text signaled a harder line from the United States. Second, they thought a resumption of U.S. bombing would shock world opinion and further increase the British government's domestic difficulties. Wilson was worried that the Soviets might leak the news of what happened and argued that "the Soviet Government would thereby make the British look fools and not knaves and make the Americans look knaves and not fools."[204] And finally, the British were extremely angry that the United States had allowed them to misrepresent themselves to the Russians as being in the confidence of the Americans. Wilson stressed that he thought he had been operating with the full cooperation and encouragement of the Americans and had had Cooper's approval for the version of phase A/phase B that he had delivered to Kosygin. Since the events of the previous day, "[T]here was now a very serious implication in the fact that if we failed to deliver our friend, i.e., the United States, we would lose credibility and hence influence with the Russians."[205]

The British also informed the Americans of the implications of these latest developments. One possible consequence might be partial or even total British dissociation from U.S. policy in Vietnam. Brown was equally candid with Bruce and Cooper and admitted that although he was "very anxious" that the word dissociation not be repeated, American action was pushing the British government in that direction. Wilson agreed, admitting that if the United States had decided to resume bombing before Kosygin left London, "[H]e would have been forced to dissociate." He also revealed that before the Americans had arrived

he had been discussing the possible direction of British policy with the Foreign Secretary. At that point he thought he had known where his duty lay. If the message which he knew was coming from Washington was not going to give him anything on Phase A of the two-phase package, and of course nothing on Phase B, he thought that the British would have to distance themselves somewhat from the United States and manifestly take a line more independent of their policy. He wondered whether the line to take with Mr. Kosygin was to advise him not to assume that the British always agreed with United States policy.[206]

The prime minister stressed on a number of occasions that the British should probably take a more independent line in that this would help stabilize British public opinion. Either way Wilson believed that "things might not ever be the same again. Trust had been broken. Naturally, even if there were an act of dissociation... Anglo–American relations would recover. Nevertheless, neither side wanted another Suez. It was essential for the United States to put matters back on an even keel again." Moreover, Wilson would "stand by" the first letter he had given Kosygin on Friday evening.

In terms of peace negotiations, the prime minister pointed out that another consequence of the U.S. change of mind might well be a loss of Russia's credibility with Hanoi. He also gave his frank opinion of the three choices he had available to him. He could say to Kosygin that he was after all not in the president's confidence, or he could tell him that the change was due to the Tet violations, or "he could say American policy was confused and that one member of the Administration was saying one thing and another was saying another thing."

Bruce and Cooper did their best to take the heat out of the situation at the same time as defending the U.S. position. This was particularly difficult given that neither approved of the White House's actions. Cooper valiantly put forward the line Washington expected of him and suggested he thought it credible that Kosygin would believe the change in tenses was due to North Vietnamese troop activity. He did, however, reveal that he personally thought that "the United States Administration had not kept the Prime Minister as fully and as rapidly informed as he would have hoped."[207] Bruce tried to calm Wilson down by suggesting that Kosygin's reaction might not be as bad as the prime minister feared. However, when the ambassador wondered whether the difference between the two proposals was "very great," Wilson replied that if that was the case, "he was inclined to try to get Mr. Kosygin to accept the original text and then to press the American Administration to accept it as their policy."[208]

They moved on to discuss the tactics for the final day's meeting with Kosygin on Sunday. Brown and Wilson agreed that the best way forward was to raise the discrepancies in the various messages with Kosygin, stress that the U.S. change in policy had been brought on by the Tet violations but then "press hard for the Prime Minister's (7 P.M.) version of the letter to Mr. Kosygin; if Mr. Kosygin accepted it, then to undertake to seek American acceptance of it." In response to a question from Brown, Chester Cooper said it might be possible to secure a further suspension of the bombing if there was a "glimmer of hope" in the discussions. Wilson decided he would after all send a message to the president.[209]

The meeting ended at 1:45 A.M., and Wilson did not leave for Chequers until 3:15 A.M. Nevertheless, he apparently woke "fresh and with a clear view."[210] "If I could get nothing more reasonable to offer than the existing US attitude, I would put my own views as the British view and attempt to sell it to the US on the one hand and Mr. Kosygin on the other. Thereafter that would be the British Government's definite proposal for the ending of the war."[211] Wilson also suggested on Saturday that Chester Cooper go out to Chequers where a direct telephone link to the White House and Bruce at the embassy would allow the Americans to be kept fully up-to-date with developments during the final day of the talks. The Americans agreed to this request.

In Washington, Johnson and his military and civilian advisers considered Wilson's request, sent via Bruce, for an extension to the Tet pause and assessed the situation in the diplomatic ballgame in London.[212] Not surprisingly, Earle Wheeler felt that a decision to delay the resumption of bombing would endanger U.S. forces in Vietnam and that it "subverted the U.S. Government policy that we will not suspend our air campaign against North Vietnam in return for a promise to engage in talks." He also characterized Wilson as "operating...from a narrow objective of obtaining importance and prestige in the British domestic political scene," stressed that Britain was no longer a first-class power and would dearly desire to be a leading player on the world stage, and reminded the president that the British government would "not have to bear the onus of losses" that the United States would by the unimpeded buildup of North Vietnamese forces.[213] Rusk supported Bruce's judgment that if the United States resumed action before Kosygin left London, then "we shall inevitably be charged with having broken up a major possibility of peace."[214] Although doubting that Hanoi would accept the proposal made, he judged that an immediate end of the bombing pause "would prevent Kosygin from dealing" at the final day of the talks and the United States "could be losing a serious, though small, chance of progress." Moreover, a resumption of military action "could do really significant harm to our relations with the British and the Soviets. Unlike the December case with the Poles, we are dealing with two key and generally responsible nations." Rostow also felt that it was worth holding up the bombing until Kosygin had left London; the president joked, "[H]e's not afraid of getting hit in London, is he?"[215] Rusk quickly reassured the British that no military action against North Vietnam would be taken until Kosygin had left.[216]

The same day, Rostow informed the president that, in effect, there was now "not an A-B proposal but an A-B-C-D proposal": Hanoi informs Washington that infiltration has stopped, the United States stops bombing, Saigon confirms that infiltration has ceased, Washington announces that there will be no further augmentation of U.S. forces.[217] Rusk made it clear to Bruce and Cooper that the United States could not prolong the suspension of bombing in the absence of a firm word on infiltration. Wilson "should also know that when we say 'stop infiltration' we mean 'stop infiltration.' We cannot trade a horse for a rabbit and will react to bad faith on this point."[218]

Washington also responded sharply to the suggestion that Wilson travel to Hanoi, expressing "appreciation" of the offer but noting that "such a trip, in the light of the present situation, would not be desirable."[219] Privately, they told Bruce that they saw "little point in it" and through the two cochairmen had concluded that the best prospects for peace lay in bilateral contact between the United States and Hanoi.[220]

Having had some time to digest and reflect on Friday evening's events, Wilson finally sent the president two messages by private wire. The first one outlined the "hell of a situation" he was in for the final day of talks with Kosygin.[221] He expressed his anguish over the change of tenses in the new text and reiterated his view that his own credibility with the Russians had been compromised and that Kosygin may have lost the confidence of Hanoi as a result of the switch. He also informed Johnson that he intended to pursue the softer version, the one he had originally handed to Kosygin, and if it was accepted, he would try to press the president on the matter. He then said he hoped to get to a position where he and Kosygin, knowing the views of their respective friends, could find a solution to the conflict that they could then recommend, "like two solicitors seeking to settle a matter out of court, ad referendum to the two clients."[222] Wilson's second message contained his version of the "misunderstanding" that had taken place over the tenses, which was basically a defense of British actions.

Johnson replied almost immediately. Wilson described the president's cable as "warm." However, as Wilson himself admitted in his memoirs, there was some doubt over who drafted such memos.[223] Often, it was Bundy or Nicholas Katzenbach, undersecretary of state from 1966 to 1969, so there was probably little genuine sentiment in this. Most space was dedicated to refuting many of Wilson's allegations and gently refusing his suggestions. In particular, Johnson did not believe that "the matter hangs on the tenses of verbs," given that the phase A/phase B proposal had been on the table since November and Hanoi had "shown no flicker of interest" in it. At the same time, the North Vietnamese had continued their military buildup. Neither did the president accept Wilson's view that the U.S. position on phase A/phase B was inconsistent: "We asked on February 7 for an 'assured stoppage' of infiltration. In your version...it was transmuted to an assurance that infiltration 'will stop.' This, in our view, is a quite different matter."[224] Johnson informed Wilson that Hanoi was likely to get in touch regarding the president's message to Ho Chi Minh at the conclusion of the present talks in London and suggested that "there is importance...in our staying together. We must not let them play one position off against another." Wilson's notion of following his own line was not welcome, and therefore the president concluded, "I'm always glad to know that you are in my corner but I would have some difficulty, in view of my responsibilities and problems here, in giving anyone a power of attorney."[225] Wilson vehemently denied that he wanted "a power of attorney" and pointed to the wording of his message, which had been "ad referendum."[226]

One of the main purposes of the final meeting between Wilson and Kosygin was to agree on the wording of a communiqué on the visit. Wilson hoped, however, that his last try at proposing de-escalation would prove successful. To meet the president's fear that the U.S. cessation of bombing would be used by the North Vietnamese to rush troops into the demilitarized zone, he would propose that the "two-way assurance" contain a specific timetable for the ending of DRV infiltration into the South.[227] Wilson was not asking for permission to put this plan forward to Kosygin, as he would take sole responsibility for it, but he would ask the president for his view if the Russian premier appeared interested. In the hope that the president would reply almost immediately to any such request, Cooper was duly ensconced in a private bedroom at Chequers shortly after lunch. An attic room that had in 1465 been used as a prison for Lady Mary Grey, sister of Jane, the room was ideal for Cooper's purposes in that it was well away from the main proceedings and had a window that overlooked the courtyard to the front. Cooper would be able to see the comings and goings at Chequers. Washington was in emergency session on and off throughout the day and into the evening. But although it was earlier in Washington than in London, as time wore on, Bruce remembered, "[W]e found the officials at home becoming testier and testier."[228] The stage was now set for Act II of the farce.

By Sunday afternoon Wilson was reportedly in a calmer frame of mind, having played a round of golf. Kosygin also apparently arrived in a relaxed mood after his visit to Scotland. During their first afternoon meeting the Soviet premier made no mention of the change in text that had occurred on Friday night, but he made it clear that he saw no point in pursuing the Trinh formula. A discussion of the communiqué brought some tension to the proceedings as Kosygin was loath to have any mention of Anglo–Soviet joint peace efforts; he was adamant that there be no publicity. The final signed statement was rather lengthy, covering the broad spectrum of the talks. However, it remained vague on Vietnam, acknowledging "a prolonged exchange of views" on the subject and agreeing that "it was essential to achieve the earliest possible end" of the war.[229] Washington quickly gave its approval to the communiqué, which was issued on February 13 following Kosygin's departure.

At around 5 P.M., having sat around for hours thinking, Cooper had a "brainstorm." When Burke Trend came up to Cooper's room for a chat and a drink, Cooper tried his plans out on him. Cooper felt that as the day's events were going "reasonably well" it was worth trying to "salvage something of value."[230] It was felt that the White House's concern about North Vietnamese troop movements could be dealt with by an assurance from Hanoi that it would keep its forces north of the 17th parallel in exchange for an extension of the current bombing pause. Once that commitment was in place, "[T]here would be diplomatic elbowroom to explore further steps that might lead to talks, even negotiations." Trend thought the proposal was worth trying and took it down to Wilson, who was still in talks with Kosygin. Having learned a lesson from Friday's events, the note stressed that the prime minister should not mention it to Kosygin before Washington had approved the idea. Wilson agreed to it. Cooper was quickly in contact by phone to Benjamin Read at the State Department, who thought the proposal "sounded eminently reasonable."[231] He agreed to forward it to Walt Rostow at the White House and let Cooper know the White House's decision as soon as possible.

Cooper, well aware that Kosygin would leave Chequers shortly after dinner, became impatient as hours went by with no response from Washington. He made two further calls to Ben Read and one to Walt Rostow and was assured that the president and members of the National Security Council were examining the proposal carefully and would let him know the outcome shortly. Wilson, in the meantime, was sending notes to Cooper asking for the approval so that he could present the new proposal to Kosygin before he left. Wilson recalls that he tried to stall Kosygin's departure by engaging him in a filibuster conversation on subjects ranging from the Common Market to geology, a subject in which Kosygin had a personal interest.[232]

It was now after 10 o'clock; Cooper was told to expect an answer shortly and that the prime minister was to try to delay Kosygin's departure. Still no answer came. Cooper tried one last-ditch attempt to get an answer out of the White House by telephoning Rostow. To prove that he was not lying when he said Kosygin was about to leave, Cooper took drastic action: "In utter desperation I...dangled the telephone as far out of the window as I could get it so that he could hear the sound of the roaring motors."[233] Rostow then told Cooper that Wilson should inform Kosygin that an important message may come through after he had returned to Claridge's. At this point, the American and British delegations thought they were "in the clover." According to Cooper, "Wilson came up, Brown came up; there was a lot of hooch. And it was great—we thought we'd really pulled a rabbit out of the hat."[234]

Once back at Downing Street, a message came through from the president to the prime minister. The Americans had agreed that they would not resume the bombing of North Vietnam, if before 10 A.M. Monday morning (London time) the North Vietnamese had given an assurance (directly or through the Russians) that they would stop the movement of troops and supplies into South Vietnam from that time.[235] As Cooper said, "[I]t was an impossible deadline. Wilson would have to discuss the proposition with Kosygin, Kosygin would have to send the message to Hanoi, Hanoi would have to consider it and then transmit a reply. It seemed inconceivable, however efficient and well-intentioned all parties involved were, that a response could be received within the ten hours at our disposal."[236] By the time Wilson had received the message, had the proposal typed up on Downing Street paper, and got over to Claridge's to deliver it to Kosygin, it was 1:00 A.M., so in effect there were only nine hours in which to respond. To justify the imminent resumption of bombing, the president stressed that the phase A/phase B offer had been outstanding for three months and there had as yet been no reply, and reminded the prime minister that as president he had responsibilities to U.S. troops, to South Vietnam, and to the allies.[237]

Cooper immediately got on the phone to Rostow to complain about the tightness of the deadline. Rostow was "by no means friendly" and commented to the effect that "we've had about enough out of you guys."[238] At the same time, Wilson raced over to Claridge's to pass the message on to Kosygin. Not surprisingly, the Russian premier was alarmed at the American ultimatum. After a few minutes of arguing about the nature of the message and the unreasonable deadline, Kosygin said he would pass the message on to Moscow to pass to Hanoi. According to Wilson, Kosygin had begun writing the draft in his presence. American intelligence confirmed that Kosygin had indeed transmitted the proposal via Moscow almost as soon as Wilson left. Wilson also told Kosygin that he would request more time from the Americans, and indeed, on returning to Downing Street he cabled a request that the bombing suspension be extended for a further 24 hours.[239] After "an awful lot of expenditure of energy" from the Americans and British in London, Washington relented and added an extra six hours to the deadline, extending it to 1600 hours (London time). The president informed the prime minister of this news and again stressed that

in making this decision I bore in mind Moscow's and Hanoi's problems of transmittal two ways. But I also was conscious of the fact that they have had the possibility of responding to essentially this message for the 3 months since we gave it to the Poles and you gave it to the Russians; and the 5 days since it was transmitted direct to Hanoi and also given by you to Kosygin.... If there is any interest in some such A-B proposition, there had—and still is—been ample time for them either to agree or come back with a counter-proposal.

Johnson acknowledged Wilson's "gallant last minute effort."[240] The discussions in Washington regarding these additional few hours are particularly revelatory. Wilson was correct in his assessment of the hawks and doves. McNamara was against extending the deadline, arguing that Wilson had already had two bombing extensions and that to "give them" a third was volunteering something for no obvious reason. Vice President Hubert Humphrey disagreed with the hawks, believing it was worth the risk because this was the first time the Soviets had "been in like this." It was also acknowledged that any short-term extension was in fact a political decision, and that a few hours' difference would not make much difference militarily. Bundy felt that the United States had "gone more notches." Rostow believed there was "danger" in the Russians coming back with something concrete—that is, what if the Russians came back with a "modified" no from Hanoi? Would the United States be put in a position of having to compromise its position further?[241]

On the way to Gatwick airport, where Kosygin was due to depart for Moscow at 11:15 A.M., the Russian premier informed Wilson that he had passed on the message to Hanoi. Wilson told him of the six-hour extension, but Kosygin was not impressed. There was no official reply from Hanoi by 4:00 P.M. (London time), and a few hours later bombing resumed. Hanoi Radio did, however, broadcast a reply to a message to Ho Chi Minh from Pope Paul VI expressing the hope for an early, peaceful solution to the war in Vietnam. The reply came just 30 minutes before the end of the U.S. deadline and as usual castigated U.S. imperialists and demanded an end to their aggression.[242]

By the time Kosygin left London, Anglo–American relations were in a parlous state. Not surprisingly, a postmortem was necessary to discover what had
gone wrong and why. Not surprisingly, Wilson was incensed at Washington's
change in tenses at the last moment. He later wrote in his memoirs:

We were staggered...No one could understand what had happened. I said that there
could be only three explanations....One, which I was reluctant to believe, that the
White House had taken me—and hence Mr. Kosygin—for a ride. Two...that the Washington hawks had staged a successful take-over. Three...that the authorities were suffering from a degree of confusion about a possible and unfortunate juxtaposition of
certain parts of their anatomy, one of which was their elbow.[243]

The prime minister later put it in more diplomatic terms, suggesting that
"there was a state of unutterable, anatomical confusion in the higher part of the
Administration."[244] Cooper later learned that the advisers who met to discuss
his telegram were not Vietnam experts. Bill Bundy, the specialist on Far Eastern
affairs, was not in attendance. Instead, it appears the decision was made by LBJ,
Dean Rusk, and Walt Rostow.[245] "They were addressing my draft as something
that was kind of invented apparently in London, instead of being something
that had been developed and manicured for about five months," Cooper explained.[246] Bruce's favored hypothesis was also that there had been a breakdown of communication not only between London and Washington but also
between key foreign policy advisers at the White House.

Privately, Wilson believed there had been deliberate sabotage and clearly favored his second possible explanation of events. He later commented that "no
degree of mental confusion in Washington...could possibly be adduced in defence of such a fundamental change. It was a reversal of policy, and it had been
deliberately taken just when there was a real chance—one thinks of Ambassador Bruce's words earlier that evening—of a settlement based on the prolon-
gation of the Tet truce from the end of the week when it was due to end."[247]
Twenty years later Cooper himself still felt unable to defend the United States
in relation to changing the conditions for talks.[248]

Johnson, in his memoirs, insisted that Wilson had not received specific approval from Washington to deliver the first draft.[249] This was, strictly speaking,
true. This does not, however, explain the textual change. Noticeably, in a meeting
with Wilson during the prime minister's visit to Washington in June 1967, Johnson "did not try to deny" Wilson's belief that "there had been a change of policy
under pressure by their hawks."[250] Rostow was labeled the chief culprit. Wilson
noted that "in terms of influence on his master, the more I saw of certain White
House advisers the more I thought that Rasputin was a much-maligned man."[251]
Brown also agreed that Rostow was the major problem in Washington:

There were doveish officials in Washington who were trying to help, and hawkish officials, mostly nearer to the scene of events, who were trying to prevent the doves from
helping. The Prime Minister's hot line to President Johnson was not as reliable as it

ought to have been. I think that the fact of the matter was that Mr. Johnson didn't really like the Prime Minister much, and the hot line from No. 10 that went allegedly directly to the President was inclined to go instead to Mr. Rostow.[252]

Rostow may well have encouraged Johnson to take a harder line with North Vietnam. As already noted, the White House had only reluctantly agreed to sanction Wilson's peace initiative with Kosygin. Moreover, by early 1967 the president was being given relentlessly optimistic assessments of the state of the military campaign in Vietnam. Despite the appearance of a stalemate, the CIA reassured Johnson that U.S. bombing was now having an effect on the North Vietnamese economy; the agency was convinced that no serious concessions should be given to Hanoi because military pressure would shortly push them toward negotiations. This was, according to Brigham, a stage when both sides in the conflict were "fighting while talking," and both were unwilling to make the concessions necessary to make negotiations a reality.[253] And although the president was desperate for an end to the war, he genuinely felt the United States had responded positively to every indication that the North Vietnamese were seeking peace, to no effect. As far as he was concerned, the Wilson–Kosygin talks might be good for America's image as peace seeker, but they did not appear to offer a realistic chance for peace.

Of course, Wilson and Brown were unaware of Johnson's true feelings on the war and were, as far as they were concerned, receiving decidedly mixed signals from Washington. The prime minister was wrong, however, to discount entirely his unpalatable theory that he might have been taken for a ride by the White House. Wilson had not been part of the loop; he had not been kept fully up-to-date on latest developments, particularly the change in tenses contained in Johnson's letter to Ho Chi Minh. The Americans, especially the president, were not fully behind his efforts. Johnson's antipathy for Robert Kennedy may well have played a part here. During a telephone call with Rostow on February 11 (the day after the change of tense), Johnson admitted that he would "just as soon not have a damn bit of connection to London...because the first thing you'll have, Bobby will have arranged the thing in London. I wouldn't be a bit surprised to see that leak tomorrow—that he worked this all out with Wilson."[254] It is entirely possible, therefore, that the change of tense in the phase A/phase B proposal occurred partly because there had been some confusion in the White House caused by the absence of Bill Bundy over the detail of previous texts, and that this coincided with a hardening of attitude toward the North Vietnamese (and London) by Johnson, who felt his own politically risky gesture of initiating a bombing pause had been abused by Hanoi. Because Washington was making no special efforts to cooperate with British peace initiatives and had its own peace feelers out to Hanoi, Johnson and his advisers were not particularly worried if Wilson was temporarily embarrassed in front of the Russians.

The failure of the Wilson–Kosygin initiative raised a number of questions. Did Wilson exaggerate how "close" they came to peace? In his memoirs Wilson wrote that "a historic opportunity had been missed."[255] He also said this during a television interview some two years after the event: "I believe, we got very near . . . then the whole thing was dashed away." He believed that a further 48-hour suspension of the bombing might have been crucial in encouraging a response from Hanoi.[256] This judgment is difficult to argue with; an extension *might* have been crucial. As we have seen, the British were convinced that the Soviets were willing to play the role of mediator and remained so, even after the failure of the Wilson–Kosygin peace initiative.[257] However, there were clear limits on how far they would go in this respect. Moscow wanted peace in Vietnam but not at the risk of being portrayed as a tool of the United States. It is much more difficult to ascertain whether Hanoi was receptive to either Soviet mediation, the proposal, or both, although in recent years members of the Vietnamese leadership have indicated that Sunflower was a "near miss."[258] The National Security Agency reported that on February 13 the North Vietnamese transmitted two messages from Hanoi to Moscow. It is highly unlikely, however, that Hanoi would have accepted the amended phase A/phase B proposal due to its conditional nature. What is important here, however, is that Wilson "felt" that Washington had bungled a unique opportunity and had made the British, and more particularly himself, look foolish in the bargain.

If it is difficult to draw any firm conclusions about the potential success of the phase A/phase B proposal as a catalyst for peace, what does the Wilson–Kosygin episode tell us about Anglo–American relations by early 1967? The most obvious conclusion is that relations at the highest levels were nowhere near as intimate as Wilson liked to claim or, indeed, believed. Johnson admitted that although he was in touch with Wilson by cable and via third parties, he did not speak to Wilson on the telephone at any point during the Wilson–Kosygin talks.[259] And as William Bundy argued, the failure of this peace initiative had "great significance as a source of lasting distrust and feeling of misunderstanding on both sides, between the President and Wilson. If they were not too well off before, they were infinitely worse after this."[260]

THE AFTERMATH OF SUNFLOWER

The immediate concern in the days after the Kosygin visit was secrecy. By early on February 13 the press on both sides of the Atlantic were running speculative news stories on the reasons behind the bombing extension. Not surprisingly, Kosygin's presence in London led journalists to link the two events, but the extension of the bombing pause was explained as being connected to Kosygin's presence in London and no other reason. The Americans were once more worried that the Wilson government might not keep quiet. For a number of reasons, the peace proposals had to be kept secret. The Americans stressed to their ambassadors in Britain and the Soviet Union that the "British must realize that [the] Soviets went out on a very long limb, and that any exposure of

[the] serious discussions in fact carried on could do serious and indeed ir-reparable harm to [a] future Soviet role." The State Department added that "it goes without saying that British silence is imperative whatever they think of [the] positions we put forward or [the] timing of our resumption."[261]

They were right to be worried. Wilson was not yet able to contain his anger and disappointment at the failure to establish talks. On February 13 he ad-dressed the House of Commons on the Kosygin visit.[262] The following day he faced questions in the House and clarified the previous day's comments.[263] He said he believed there were moments when the conditions to secure a peace set-tlement "could have been very near."[264] He also revealed that there had been a plan to end the war, saying that "there is an initiative, there is a plan—that I can't tell the House about—which could bring peace tomorrow and requires a very, very small movement to activate all the complicated machinery which would bring us to peace negotiations."[265] He explained the failure to secure such a plan in terms of a lack of trust and confidence on the part of both the Americans and the North Vietnamese in relation to one another. He did, how-ever, place particular emphasis on the activities of North Vietnamese troops during the Tet truce. This criticism drew a sharp response from Wilson's left-wing opponents. They demanded to know who had provided information on the southward movement of North Vietnamese troops and supplies. When the prime minister refused to reveal his sources, cries of "Was it the Americans?" were heard. As the *New York Times* commented, this implied that Washington could not be trusted.[266] On the resumption of bombing, nearly 50 Labour M.P.s signed a telegram to President Johnson deploring his decision.[267] Shortly after-ward 100 M.P.s signed a petition condemning the renewal of bombing.

Despite Wilson's comments being interpreted in his own country as pro-American, Washington felt, with some justification, that Wilson was in fact re-ferring unfavorably to American intransigence when he spoke of the need for "a very, very small movement" to bring about peace. Journalists and M.P.s were intrigued by Wilson's comments on machinery and plans. Wilson also made a ministerial broadcast on television on the evening of February 14 in which he repeated that peace in Vietnam "was almost within our grasp" the preceding weekend. He explained that "one single, simple act of trust could have achieved it."[268]

Wilson's statements caused much annoyance in Washington. Philip Kaiser at the American embassy in London met with Michael Palliser on February 17 to voice the administration's "gravest concern." Kaiser told Palliser that the telegram instructing him to speak on this issue "had been couched in very tough language indeed."[269] The suggestion that peace was "very near" and that there was a "secret plan" upset Washington for two reasons. First, the Johnson administration did not believe such comments were accurate given that Hanoi had not shown the slight-est interest in this approach or other approaches to them. Second, "whatever the facts," such public discussions put the Americans "on the spot" with their allies and were causing them "considerable embarrassment at home."[270]

In the United States it encouraged the "doves" to step up pressure on the Administration to stop the bombing, and generally to get out of the war; while it brought all the "hawks" circling in with cries of outrage at the prospect of a negotiation and demands for a full revelation of what the Administration was up to. The whole debate became thereby impassioned and the President's task of steering a judicious middle course—already appallingly difficult—was made even more so. Moreover, your remarks had caused the Ambassadors of all America's allies in the war...to ask in peremptory fashion what the US Government was doing behind their backs.[271]

Palliser defended the British position. He understood the U.S. anxiety on this issue but felt the prime minister would have found it difficult "to make so effective a case for the U.S. and British positions without saying the things he did in public." He also pointed out that the prime minister's "backgrounder" to the newspaper correspondents on Monday evening had helped to secure positive press coverage for the United States on Tuesday.[272] He also told Kaiser—and later reported back to Wilson—that in his opinion, "[H]owever inconvenient this fact might be for the Administration, they must accept that the British Government could not best help them simply by an absolute toeing of the American line; the political pressures were too strong for this, even if it otherwise seemed right, which in present circumstances I thought it did not."[273] Palliser also made it clear that the tone of the prime minister's instructions had also been very firm, and he was to leave Kaiser "in no doubt of the strength" of Wilson's "feelings about the conduct of last week's affairs," especially his "dissatisfaction at the way in which virtually three days had been lost through what seemed, on the most charitable interpretation, inexplicable muddle and confusion." Palliser nevertheless reassured Kaiser that the prime minister had no intention of embarrassing the president, but that "there could of course be no question" of the prime minister's retracting anything he had already said. The prime minister endorsed Palliser's comments in private.[274]

Kaiser reported back to Rusk that

while Palliser was obviously genuine in expressing his understanding of the nature of our problems, he also made it clear that the PM was more bullish about the significance of last week than we were. Palliser stressed on several occasions the "dramatic" change in Kosygin's attitude in contrast to last July when the PM visited Moscow and even as late as November when Brown was there.... It is also the firm conviction of the British that Kosygin did transmit our last proposal to Hanoi and very possibly with the recommendations that "they give it serious consideration."[275]

London and Washington therefore interpreted the actions of the Russians and North Vietnamese differently. Palliser argued that rather than taking such a negative stance on any public discussions of the possibilities for peace, it might be desirable to allow a "ray of hope to pierce the otherwise gloomy scene."[276]

It was now clear that the Kosygin episode required delicate handling if a full-blown rift between London and Washington was not to develop. The British could not easily forget the events that occurred during Kosygin's visit. The prime minister, in particular, was not able to move on; relations with the Johnson administration had been irrevocably damaged. The prime minister suggested he visit Washington to discuss matters personally with the president. Over a month later, Kaiser was still reporting back to Washington that it was "apparent that Wilson and Brown do a lot of churning over the Kosygin visit and may still have some scars from our having given the Phase A/Phase B formula to the Poles in November without telling Brown."[277]

Walt Rostow was dispatched later in the month to try to smooth over the difficulties caused by the breakdown in communications between the transatlantic partners.[278] Given his prominent role in events, however, he was probably not the most appropriate person for this task. He was also of the opinion that in many ways the Americans had been too cooperative with Wilson, considering that the prime minister had explored the phase A/phase B formula verbally on his own.[279] Prior to the meeting, Rostow had been informed by Palliser that the prime minister would "wish to explore pretty firmly...the apparent inconsistencies and fumblings during the Kosygin visit."[280] Rostow said that he would welcome the chance to discuss this. He also reported that the president had wanted to support Wilson throughout the Kosygin visit because he believed in the sincerity of the prime minister's hopes for the peace, not because he believed there would be a successful outcome. "Indeed, the President was coming increasingly to feel that mediation in the conflict, whether between the United States and North Vietnam, or between the United States and the Soviet Union (acting as agent for North Vietnam) was becoming counter-productive." Not only was there little sign that Hanoi was interested in negotiating, but the various mediation efforts "tended to create confusion and misunderstanding amongst world opinion."[281] Bill Jordan, a senior staff member of the National Security Council, also told Rostow that if Wilson returned to his idea of coming to Washington, then he knew how to handle it.[282] This meant "[N]ot now Harold."

On February 25 Rostow met with the prime minister and Foreign Secretary. It soon became clear to Rostow that, as expected, "[T]he main point of his interview with me was to get off his chest his [Wilson's] frustrations with the week with Kosygin." The prime minister argued that there had been a "breakdown in communications," that the Americans had not objected to his formulation of the phase A/phase B formula on Tuesday but then "overtook" his Friday proposal. He also felt that the "final effort to redress the situation inevitably assumed the form of an ultimatum." Wilson was adamant that the problem of communication be cleared up.

According to Rostow, he did not argue with Wilson in any real sense, except to say that Washington had not expected the message to be delivered on Friday until the prime minister had heard from the Americans. As Rostow put it, "I let him use my presence to unload his feelings rather than put them on paper to

Washington."[283] Rostow commented that "beneath it all was a rankling that we did not cut him in fully on the direct channel."[284] Although Wilson agreed with Rostow that Hanoi appeared to regard negotiations as "defeat," he stressed that the importance of Kosygin's visit was that this was the first time the Soviets had been "ready to move."[285] Rostow summarized Wilson's position. "His problem with Viet-Nam is clear: he has a quite strong anti-Viet-Nam wing in the Labor Party; bombing the North is more widely unpopular in Britain; and Wilson feels he must keep moving in a peace posture or the basis for over-all support of the U.S. position will slip away from him. We shall be hearing from him about his problems with 'escalation,' I would guess."[286] Rostow told the president that he left "pretty indelibly" three points—first, that the president had responsibilities to more than 500,000 U.S. servicemen and to "our fighting allies"; second, that there was a danger to the Johnson administration's political base at home from pursuing peace moves that failed; and finally, that there was also a danger from "panmunjom-type" negotiations, that is, engaging in point-less talk for talk's sake, if the other side was not interested in ending the war by nonmilitary means and U.S. soldiers were dying in the meantime.[287]

The British record of this meeting paints a somewhat different picture. Ros-tow, according to this record, said that although he was grateful for Wilson's frankness, "[H]e was inclined to question the extent of misunderstanding or breakdown in communications suggested by the Prime Minister" and "in any case President Johnson was becoming increasingly sceptical of the possibilities of effective mediation" and felt the "best prospect for the future might well lie more in direct contacts" with Hanoi. Rostow thought that "opinion in Wash-ington was now fairly firmly that progress by mutual de-escalation was un-likely and that they would have to concentrate on 'looking towards the end of the road.' "[288] This comment infuriated Wilson, who saw it as affirmation that "he and the Foreign Secretary had been allowed to discuss the problem with Mr. Kosygin on a somewhat false premise—since all the propositions they had put to Kosygin with the approval and encouragement, as they understood it, of the U.S. Government, had hinged around the prospect of mutual de-escalation. If this was not to be the American policy he found it difficult to see why he had not been told so before."[289] Rostow vehemently denied that Washington had been insincere on this point. He did, however, go on to explain in detail John-son's main concerns over his presidency. Internally, the war on poverty and the struggle for black civil rights dominated his objectives; externally, resistance to aggression in Vietnam was his main consideration. He explained that the pres-ident was aware that neither of his campaigns "was likely to yield an early div-idend of political popularity; and he was facing up realistically to the possibility of a defeat in the 1968 election." However, believing he could still win, the pres-ident "recognised that his handling of the Vietnam war could be a crucial fac-tor." Recent opinion polls had convinced the president that "if he were to handle the war in such a way as to retain the confidence of the middle of the road majority of American opinion, his public position had to achieve a balance between readiness to negotiate and determination to prosecute the war with firmness but moderation."[290] Wilson commented that although he supported Johnson personally and understood his preoccupation with Vietnam, too much reliance should not be placed on such polls, because "they tended to fluctuate; and in any case a Government had to base its policies on something more solid than the polls."[291] To illustrate his point, he said that even though a majority of the British public opposed the war in Vietnam and the British government's support for the Americans, there would be no change of policy on their part. He did, however, expect domestic pressure to increase if the hawks in Washington had their way and the war was further intensified.

Wilson said that "he could not conceal...that during the weekend February 11/12 he had been gravely concerned about the future relationship between London and Washington." He thought that this should have been made clear from his messages to Washington and Bruce's reports, and would have been even more apparent had he not refrained from sending a third message that he had drafted. He also admitted that the present meeting had done little to reassure him. He then reminded Rostow that "on a previous occasion, where there had been a similar and apparently major failure of communications between London and Washington, President Kennedy had arranged for a detailed inquiry to be made." He was talking about the 1962 Skybolt affair, but Rostow was "non-committal" on the idea of an investigation. Wilson then pressed for another meeting with the president "fairly soon." Rostow said that he had been instructed to invite Wilson to Washington just before his visit in June to Expo 67 in Canada. Wilson said he would have preferred an earlier meeting but understood the scheduling difficulties.[292]

The meeting with Rostow had done little to heal the wounds. A few days later, the prime minister cabled Johnson to say that although he had found the meeting with Rostow "very helpful," it did not resolve his "anxieties" about the problems they had discussed. To avoid any more misunderstandings before his next visit to Washington, Wilson requested that the president meet with Patrick Dean on his return to Washington later that month.[293] Rostow, who received the incoming cable, told Johnson that what Wilson wanted was "full and complete information about negotiations" as well as confirmation that the United States' final formulation at the end of Kosygin week still stood.[294] Despite being briefed further on "the essence of the breakdown in communications," the president was still not prepared to accede to Wilson's request to have an insider's access to U.S. diplomacy on Vietnam.[295]

As the United States escalated the war further, British domestic difficulties did indeed increase. The British public and press continued to turn against the war. As a consequence, the British government asked Rusk if a prominent American, possibly Vice President Humphrey or Ambassador Goldberg, might visit the United Kingdom to help fight the propaganda battle.[296] It was proposed that a U.S. delegation could come under the cover of other business, and then present the U.S. case before small groups of journalists, politicians, and academics. Although the United States was at first worried that the British request and subterfuge might come to light, and therefore the impact of such a visit would be substantially weakened, Rusk eventually agreed that Bill Bundy could visit later in the month.[297] Bundy visited London between March 20 and March 22 and "completed...the most effective and useful job of expounding" American policy in Vietnam. He met with M.P.s, newspapers editors and journalists, the Foreign Secretary and other Foreign Office officials, trade union leaders, and the head of BBC public affairs. Kaiser reported back to Rusk that Bundy had done "a superb job...he has been candid, eloquent, and persuasive. I am sure that he has shaken a lot of the critics and persuaded a lot of the doubtful." The British were "extremely pleased" with Bundy's performance. [298]

Another visitor was Hubert Humphrey, who saw Wilson at Chequers on Sunday, April 2, on his way back from a tour of Europe. After dinner, the prime minister raised the issue of Vietnam. Wilson continued to worry the Americans, especially as he told Humphrey that

he thought the key to peace lay through the Soviet Union and the key to the Soviet Union lay with Britain. He felt that he had a real opportunity to act as middleman between the US and USSR to reach a negotiated settlement. In fact, he had been considering the possibility of moving more toward the middle, between the two nations, on Vietnamese policy. If he did this, he wanted us to understand that he was doing so in the interests of peace and not because of any lack of friendship or loyalty to the US.[299]

Not surprisingly, Humphrey said that this change by Wilson would be misunderstood in the United States and that "it might result in increased pressure from 'hawks' for unilateral and strong US action to crush North Vietnam."[300]

In the meantime, the diplomatic arguments over the Kosygin visit continued at the highest level. Wilson continued to pursue the matter via a stream of cables to the president. He was encouraged in this by the publication of President Johnson's exchanges with Ho Chi Minh.[301] By early April, however, Patrick Dean, the British ambassador in Washington, felt the matter should not be pushed further as it was unlikely to pay dividends.[302] Washington did, nevertheless, take heed of Humphrey's report that the British might move away from a close alliance with the Americans on Vietnam. As George Brown was about to go to Moscow, planning to discuss a revised version of his November 1966 suggestion for peace in Vietnam, on May 18 the State Department asked David Bruce to give Wilson or Brown warning that a military attack against Hanoi's power station would take place that night, and to explain this action fully. Rusk acknowledged to Bruce the "major purpose in informing them is...to forestall any drastic reaction by Wilson or Brown, either in the form of some public adverse comment or in the form of private recrimination that we have sabotaged Brown's mission in any fashion." Although not knowing "how serious" the dangers of a "significant" reaction by the British were, it was thought wise to at least "reduce the possibilities" of such a response.[303]

THE UNDERSTANDINGS COLLAPSE

Despite the February setback, the Wilson government continued to work toward peace. In June 1967 Wilson visited Washington again. Although the fallout from the Kosygin visit overshadowed proceedings, this did not prevent Wilson from being "formally" received, including a welcoming ceremony with military honors. This led one of Wilson's critics, Tony Benn, to describe the prime minister as being received "with all the trumpets appropriate for a weak foreign head of state who has to be buttered up so that he can carry the can for American foreign policy."[304]

Although this trip was largely concerned with Britain's role East of Suez, Wilson remained preoccupied with Vietnam due to increasingly vociferous attacks on his government's still broadly pro-American policy on that issue. Washington remained concerned that Wilson might indeed distance himself from the United States on Vietnam. By this stage, Wilson' main concern was the possibility that the United States might escalate the war even further, and perhaps even invade the north. In April, Johnson had authorized bombing raids against power transformers, ammunition dumps, and other targets near Hanoi and Haiphong. And, as many outside of Washington suspected, Walt Rostow was now advocating a full-scale invasion of the north. Johnson had taken a middle course between the advocates of increased air action and those who argued for a reduction in the bombing to the south only. Instead, the president ordered a halt to air attacks on targets within 10 miles of Hanoi. More importantly, as far as Wilson was concerned, LBJ gave the impression that he hoped to shift bombing away from "strategic targets" to supply lines in the southern parts of North Vietnam and South Vietnam itself.[305]

When Wilson met with Johnson on the morning of June 2 the president categorically denied the rumors of an invasion. The prime minister was reassured to hear this, quoting Kosygin on the dangers of Chinese intervention should America go this far. Johnson said he was well aware of this risk and had no intention of courting a third world war by invading the north.[306] Little more of substance was said on Vietnam, apart from Wilson's repetition of his belief that there had been "a serious failure of communication between the British and American Government" and that the Soviets had claimed to have been in touch with Hanoi.[307] Johnson repeated that neither Kosygin nor Gromyko had "delivered" the North Vietnamese, and doubted they ever had the power to do so. The prime minister said the lesson to be learned "appeared to be that, if any other chance of establishing contact with Hanoi occurred, the American Government should deal direct with the Soviet Government or invoke our [British] assistance rather than using Poles, Hungarians or other unreliable intermediaries."[308] Ironically, Wilson still saw himself as a possible honest broker. Still, once more, the British prime minister realized that the White House was not being candid on Vietnam, and by August, Wilson concluded that he had lost touch with the president's thinking on the war.[309]

DEVALUATION OF THE POUND, NOVEMBER 1967

Having still not recovered from the Kosygin episode and British talks of dissociation, Anglo–American relations faced another, more fundamental crisis point in November 1967. Sterling was in trouble again, but this time the Americans were not prepared to bail it out. On November 8 the governor of the Bank of England informed the Americans that massive U.S. financial help was required to save the pound. Although both James Callaghan, chancellor of the exchequer, and Roy Jenkins, home secretary, were resigned to devaluation, Wilson still believed he could rescue the situation with another trip to Washington and a personal appeal to the president. He could now play hardball with Johnson, arguing that if Britain did not receive financial assistance to help the pound, he would have to withdraw British forces from East of Suez immediately. When Wilson suggested via David Bruce that he should visit the president two days later, however, he had little choice but to mask the real reason for his visit, instead saying he wanted to discuss Vietnam, among other things.[310]

Though sterling was uppermost in Wilson's mind, the Vietnam excuse was not entirely fabrication. The Labour government's difficulties went from bad to worse. At the Labour Party conference in Scarborough October 2–6, the government was defeated on a resolution on Vietnam.[311] Wilson personally felt the brunt of the growing opposition to the Vietnam War at the end of October when he was in Cambridge speaking to a Labour Party meeting. His car was stopped and badly damaged by egg-throwing, chanting antiwar demonstrators. Wilson and his wife, Mary, were jostled and manhandled by the crowd and a policeman was seriously injured.[312] Johnson offered his sympathies to Wilson and his Foreign Secretary: "I want you both to know how heartened I was by your success in holding the line so well at Scarborough. With what I confront every day, it wasn't hard for me to reconstruct what you faced. I think you understand how much it matters that the government of the country which means most to me, aside from my own, is lending its support for what we all know is right, despite the storms around us."[313] On November 8, Wilson had met with a Parliamentary Labour Party that was extremely angry over Vietnam, particularly the government's failure to dissociate itself from the latest waves of bombing of civilian parts of Hanoi and Haiphong. Bruce told Rusk, acting on material from an important Labour Party informant, that the opposition to the prime minister's policy on Vietnam now came from all sections of the party, including the right and center.[314]

Johnson, however, was not prepared to receive Wilson on this pretext lest there be yet more speculation regarding possible peace moves or further rifts between Britain and America on the subject. Instead, Sir Patrick Dean, the British ambassador, delivered Wilson's appeal for financial help. By November 13, the Americans had replied in the negative, as Wilson put it, "with reluctance they would have to see us go down."[315] Despite some last-minute signs that Washington was wavering, on November 15 it was recognized that there were "no serious signs of a cheque book" from the Americans.[316] The decision to devalue was then taken. On November 18 the pound sterling was devalued from $2.80 to $2.40. Although it was a substantial devaluation, the Americans correctly judged that it was not large enough to have a serious impact on the dollar.

Although prepared to offer limited financial aid, Washington was now prepared to "think the unthinkable." It had its own financial problems. The Vietnam War was costing $20 billion per year by 1967, and the budget deficit had reach $10 billion for that fiscal year.[317] To help deal with this burden, Johnson had reluctantly acknowledged that the United States could not afford guns *and* butter and had introduced a 10 percent surcharge on individual and corporate taxes. This contributed to Johnson's difficulties in securing favorable public opinion. Those regarding the commitment to Vietnam as a "mistake" rose to 46 percent.[318] Johnson's own popularity rating decreased as the antiwar movement continued to grow in numbers and public visibility. In addition to continuing congressional pressure, elements of the media also began to question U.S. involvement in Vietnam, most noticeably *Life* magazine, whose chief editor, Hedley Donovan, argued that the conflict was no longer "worth winning."[319] Even worse, as far as Johnson was concerned, there was increasing dissent within his own cabinet. Robert McNamara increasingly questioned the validity of the American's military campaign, particularly the effectiveness of bombing North Vietnam. In May McNamara and Assistant Secretary of Defense John McNaughton challenged National Security Action Memorandum 288, which authorized McNamara's recommendation in March 1964 to increase U.S. military support to South Vietnam and provided the justification for the American war in Vietnam: "[W]e seek an independent non-Communist South Vietnam." They argued that U.S. war aims should be more limited—"only to see that the people of South Vietnam are permitted to determine their own future." Johnson and the Joint Chiefs of Staff were outraged at the proposed softening in America's position. The president believed McNamara had turned "dovish" on him, and by November McNamara had resigned as secretary of defense and been appointed president of the World Bank.[320]

THE EAST OF SUEZ DECISION, JANUARY 1968

After devaluation came the most damaging blow to the "special relationship." On January 10, 1968, George Brown met with Dean Rusk and informed him that on Tuesday, January 16, Her Majesty's Government would announce its plans to withdraw all forces from the Far East (except Hong Kong) by March 31, 1971, and to withdraw all forces from the Persian Gulf by the same date.[321] The decision was made to ensure the success of the devaluation of the pound. Although Brown admitted that the decision had for all practical purposes been made, it still had to be confirmed by the cabinet on January 12, and he said he would report the views of the U.S. government. Rusk engaged in some last-minute statecraft, using both emotive and strategic arguments to try to influence the British.

Rusk's entreaties were quickly followed by a last-minute personal appeal from the president. Johnson flattered Wilson for his courage in bearing the financial burdens so far but continued, "I cannot conceal from you my deep dismay upon learning this profoundly discouraging news. If these steps are taken, they will be tantamount to British withdrawal from world affairs, with all that means for the future safety and health of the free world. The structure of peacekeeping will be shaken to its foundations. Our own capability and political will could be gravely weakened if we have to man the ramparts alone." He urged Wilson and his colleagues to review the alternatives before taking such "irrevocable steps."[322] Johnson knew, however, that his efforts were futile. The announcement to withdraw East of Suez was made as part of a January 16, 1968, statement on sizable budget cuts in government spending and was endorsed by the cabinet and Parliament. The military cuts resulted in a reduction of 75,000 military personnel and 80,000 civilians. Britain also canceled its order for 50 U.S. long-range reconnaissance aircraft, the F-111s. As the CIA put it: "By making such defense cuts, Britain has underlined the fact that it now considers itself a European rather than a world power."[323] British newspapers were quick to recognize that the military retrenchment was "a blow to the Americans, morally if not materially, to the US at a time when its troops were fighting in Asia." And they speculated that although Johnson probably had "great sympathy for Wilson's grave dilemma," the United States resented the timing and extent of the withdrawal. This was an accurate reading of the situation.

On January 18 *The Times* summed up the unraveling of the tacit agreements that had been the feature of Anglo–American relations over the last two-and-a-half years: "[T]he basis of Wilson's foreign policy was an understanding with the U.S. that Britain supported American actions in Viet-Nam and maintained troops in the Far East in return for a close relationship with the U.S. and American support for the pound. That world commitment has now been dropped; the one element that remains is British support for the U.S. on Viet-Nam. That support is purely diplomatic and probably hypocritical."[324]

Despite the fact that the war became more unpopular in Britain, Wilson continued his support for the United States in Vietnam until he left office. In early February 1968 Wilson arrived at the Johnson White House for the final time. When the prime minister had expressed his desire to see Johnson the previous December for a "short communication," Johnson had scribbled his response on a memorandum informing him of the request: "I'll see Wilson if he can keep shut up about Cuba and Viet Nam."[325] On his arrival the band played "The Road to Mandalay." The prime minister masked his embarrassment at this ironic choice of welcoming music by later saying that he liked the tune.[326] It was probably no mistake that it was played. The Johnson White House used this visit to reiterate "distress at the UK's accelerated withdrawal from Southeast Asia and the Persian Gulf" and urged in the case of Southeast Asia "that the UK concert with the countries of the area to promote regional security arrangements prior to the British departure."[327]

Wilson, still with an eye on his domestic audience, also made comments regarding Vietnam that must have finally consigned him to the growing ranks of opponents of the war, whom Johnson now saw as traitors. In response to upbeat and supportive comments from the president, including the phrase "The American people are backing Britain," Wilson launched into a lengthy speech on Vietnam. The Tet offensive, a mighty blow to all those who believed in the war effort, had been under way since January 31. Although couching his feelings in ostensibly friendly and supportive language, Wilson warned, "I have said a hundred times that this problem will never be solved by a military solution, which I see is one of the lessons of the last few days—a determined resistance to see that a military solution is not imposed on the people of Vietnam."[328] He then talked about calls for "dissociation" in his own country and explained that he would have dissociated had he thought it would result in peace. He had, however, been "in a position to know a good deal about the history of negotiations and consultations," and these had all resulted in failure. But this did not mean that "we were wrong, all of us here, to try, and to go on trying."[329] With the president desperately trying to rally support for the redoubled U.S. military action in the wake of the Tet setback, Johnson must have found it intolerable to listen to Wilson's final effort to cast himself as a peace broker.

THE END OF THE SPECIAL RELATIONSHIP?

In May 1967 the U.S. embassy in Britain judged the "special relationship" to be "little more than sentimental terminology."[330] At a meeting of the National Security Council a year later, Rusk concluded that "the special relationship the UK has with us is less important to them now because the British have less interest in maintaining a world role. Operationally, the U.S. and U.K. are working on fewer real problems. The concept of Atlantic cooperation could replace the special relationship. Close bilateral relations with the British, however, will certainly continue."[331] Clark Clifford, the new secretary of defense, put it more bluntly, saying the British "are no longer a powerful ally of ours because they cannot afford the costs of an adequate defense effort."[332] At the same time Bruce argued that "Britain's future role is almost surely that of a middle sized though outward looking European power."[333] He judged that "while the special U.S.–UK relationship is diminishing, no early dramatic changes are likely, and a substantial relationship will endure based on the practical recognition of mutual interest."[334] Despite everything that had happened over the last few years, Bruce was still wise enough to recognize that

[i]t would be a mistake to over react to these changed circumstances and write off the UK as a US ally and a significant force in the world. Even in her reduced circumstances, Britain remains the European power most engaged in world affairs...Britain has, therefore, international prestige and influence which, though diminished, still matter. The fact is, wherever one strikes the balance on this arrangement of tangible and intangible assets, Britain remains the most likeminded and most useful of US allies in world affairs.

By June 1970 both Wilson and Johnson had left high office, their reputations forever stained by their involvement with Vietnam, and yet the two remained in contact with each other. Their relationship, much like the Anglo–American relationship during this period, was damaged but not destroyed.

NOTES

1. Telegram from Bruce to Rusk, September 26, 1966, "Subject: When George Brown Comes to Washington," Declassified Document Series, Library of Congress.

2. Report of the 65th Annual Conference of the Labour Party, Brighton, October 3–7, 1966, Transport House, Smith Square, London, SW1.

3. Ibid.

4. Ibid. Carried 3,470,000 to 2,932,000 against.

5. Handwritten Note on Telegram from Bruce to Harriman, October 6, 1966, File: UK, vol. 9, Cables, 8/66–1/67, box 210, CF, UK, NSF, LBJL.

6. Background Paper "The Brown Proposal for a Negotiated Settlement On Vietnam," Visit of UK Foreign Secretary, George Brown, October 12, 1966, Visit of UK Foreign Secretary George Brown (1 of 2), 10/14/66, box 216, CF, UK, NSF, LBJL.

7. Ibid.

8. Memo from Rusk to the President, October 13, 1966, File: UK, Visit of UK Foreign Secretary George Brown (1 of 2), 10/14/66, box 216, CF, UK, NSF, LBJL.

9. Draft Memorandum of Conversation: President, Bruce, Brown, and Dean, Subject: US–Soviet Relations; Viet-Nam, October 14, 1966, Declassified Document Series, Library of Congress.

10. George Brown, *In My Way: The Political Memoirs of Lord George-Brown* (London: Victor Gollancz Ltd., 1971), 142.

11. Ibid.

12. Henry Brandon, *Special Relationships: A Foreign Correspondent's Memoirs from Roosevelt to Reagan* (London: Macmillan, 1988), 212–13.

13. Ibid.

14. Ibid.

15. Cabinet Minutes, October 20, 1966, CAB 128/41, PRO.

16. Telegram from Bruce to Secretary of State, November 4, 1966, File: UK, vol. 9, Cables, 8/66–1/67, box 210, CF, UK, NSF, LBJL.

17. Telegram from Harriman to Rusk, November 7, 1966, File: UK, vol. 9, Cables, 8/66–1/67, box 210, CF, UK, NSF, LBJL.

18. Ibid.

19. Ibid.

20. János Radványi, *Delusion and Reality: Gambits, Hoaxes, and Diplomatic One-Upmanship in Vietnam* (South Bend, Ind.: Gateway Editions Limited, 1978), 193.

21. Memorandum of Meeting in Washington, November 10, 1966, 3 P.M., in FRUS, vol. 4, 822.

22. Ibid., 821.

23. Ibid., 824.

24. Ibid., 822.

25. Ibid., 822–23.

26. Ibid., 823.

27. Memorandum from Governor Harriman to Chester Cooper, November 10, 1966, File: UK, vol. 9, Memos, 8/66–1/67, box 210, CF, UK, NSF, LBJL.

28. Memorandum of Conversation (Dean–Stewart–Thompson), November 16, 1966, Memos 8/66–1/67, box 210, CF, UK, NSF, LBJL.

29. Ibid.; Memorandum from Governor Harriman to Chester Cooper, November 10, 1966, File: UK, vol. 9, Memos, 8/66–1/67, box 210, CF, UK, NSF, LBJL.

30. Telegram from Brown to Rusk, November 25, 1966, Memos, 8/66–1/67, box 210, CF, UK, NSF, LBJL.

31. Record of a Meeting between the Foreign Secretary and the Chairman of the Council of Ministers of the USSR in the Kremlin, Moscow, at 10:30 A.M., on November 25, 1966, Visit of the Foreign Secretary to the Soviet Union, November 22–25, 1966, Annex, PREM 13/1917, PRO.

32. Telegram from Brown to Rusk, November 25, 1966, File: UK, vol. 9, Memos, 8/66–1/67, box 210, CF, UK, NSF, LBJL; From Bruce to Rusk, November 27, 1966, File: UK, vol. 9, Cables, 8/66–1/67, box 210, CF, UK, NSF, LBJL.

33. Record of a Meeting between the Foreign Secretary and the Chairman of the Council of Ministers of the USSR in the Kremlin, Moscow, at 10:30 A.M., on November 25, 1966, Visit of the Foreign Secretary to the Soviet Union, November 22–25, 1966, Annex, PREM 13/1917, PRO.

34. Cabinet Minutes, December 1, 1966, CAB 128/41, PRO.

35. Telegram to the President, December 15, 1966, EXCO305, United Kingdom 1/1/65, box 76, CO305, 11/4/66–6/14/67, LBJL.

36. Telegram from Bruce to Rusk, December 16, 1966, File: UK, vol. 9, Cables, 8/66–1/67, box 210, CF, UK, NSF, LBJL.

37. *Hansard*, House of Commons Debate, 5th series, February 19, 1965, vol. 706, col. 254.

38. Memorandum, Richard M. Moose to Walt Rostow, December 16, 1966, File: UK, vol. 9, Memos, 8/66–1/67, CF, UK, NSF, LBJL.

39. Letter to Paul Gore-Booth from Pat Dean, December 29, 1966, PREM 13/1917, PRO.

40. Telegram from Bruce to Rusk, December 20, 1966, File: UK, vol. 9, Cables, 8/66–1/67, box 210, CF, UK, NSF, LBJL.

41. Ibid.

42. Personal Telegram from Rusk to the President, December 16, 1966, Declassified Document Series, Library of Congress.

43. Ibid.

44. Meeting with the President, December 17, 1966, Files of Walt Rostow, box 3, NSF, LBJL.

45. Letter from Sir Patrick Dean to Sir Paul Gore-Booth, December 28, 1966, PREM 13/1917; Two Letters from Sir Patrick Dean to Sir Paul Gore-Booth, December 29, 1966, PREM 13/1917, PRO.

46. Letter from Sir Patrick Dean to Sir Paul Gore-Booth, December 28, 1966, PREM 13/1917, PRO.

47. Letter from Sir Patrick Dean to Sir Paul Gore-Booth, December 29, 1966, PREM 13/1917, PRO.

48. Although the Democrats retained a large majority in both the House of Representatives and the Senate, the party had sustained 47 losses in the House and three in the Senate. Before the 1966 elections the position had been 295–140 in the House and 68–32 in the Senate; after, the majority was reduced to 248–187 and 64–36. See Robert Dallek, *Flawed Giant: Lyndon Johnson and His Times 1961–1973* (Oxford: Oxford University Press, 1998), 338–39.

49. Letter from Sir Patrick Dean to Sir Paul Gore-Booth, December 29, 1966, PREM 13/1917, PRO.

50. Ibid.

51. Ibid.

52. Telegram from Foreign Office to British Embassy, Hanoi, December 30, 1966, PREM 13/1917, PRO.

53. Harrison Salisbury, *Behind the Lines—Hanoi* (New York: Harper and Row, 1967), 230.

54. Telegram from Rusk to Bruce, January 13, 1967, File: UK, vol. 9, Cables, 8/66–1/67, box 210, CF, UK, NSF, LBJL.

55. Top Secret Report on Vietnam for the Prime Minister, January 4, 1967, PREM 13/1917, PRO.

56. Telegram from British Embassy, Hanoi to Foreign Office, January 4, 1967, PREM 13/1917.

57. For a full discussion of the Marigold episode see James G. Hershberg, "Who Murdered 'Marigold'?—New Evidence on the Mysterious Failure of Poland's Secret Initiative to Start U.S.–North Vietnamese Peace Talks, 1966," Cold War International History Project, Working Paper no. 27, http://cwihp.si.edu/cwihplib.nsf.

58. Telegram from Lodge, American Embassy in Vietnam, to Rusk, December 1, 1966, in FRUS, vol. 4, 893.

59. Radványi, *Delusion and Reality*, 197.

60. Ibid., 198.

61. George C. Herring (ed.), *The Secret Diplomacy of the Vietnam War: The Negotiating Volumes of the Pentagon Papers* (Austin: University of Texas Press, 1983), 370.

62. Radványi, *Delusion and Reality*, 198–99.

63. Flash Telegram from Foreign Office to Dean, January 4, 1967, PREM 13/1917, PRO.

64. Top Secret Report from Michael Palliser to Prime Minister, January 4, 1967, PREM 13/1917, PRO.

65. Telegram from the Embassy in Vietnam to the Department of State, December 1, 1966, FRUS, vol. 4, 891.

66. Record of Conversation between the Prime Minister and the United States Ambassador at No. 10 Downing Street at 12:10 P.M. on Tuesday, January 10, 1967, PREM 13/1917, PRO.

67. Ibid.

68. Averell Harriman in Chester L. Cooper, *The Lost Crusade: The Full Story of US Involvement in Vietnam from Roosevelt to Nixon* (London: MacGibbon and Kee, 1970), ix.

69. Ibid.

70. Record of Conversation between the Prime Minister and the United States Ambassador at No. 10 Downing Street at 12:10 P.M. on Tuesday, January 10, 1967, PREM 13/1917, PRO.

71. Ibid.

72. Ibid.

73. Secret and Personal. Draft Message to the President from the Prime Minister. 2nd Draft. January 10, 1967, PREM 13/1917, PRO.

74. Ibid.

75. Immediate Foreign Office to Dean, January 12, 1967, PREM 13/1917, PRO.

76. Letter from Dean Rusk to George Brown, no date, PREM 13/1917, PRO.

77. Top Secret Letter from C. M. Maclehose to Sir Patrick Dean, January 11, 1967, PREM 13/1917, PRO.

78. Ibid.

79. Ibid.

80. Cabinet Minutes, January 12, 1967, CAB 128/42, part 1.

81. Secret. Record of a Conversation between the Prime Minister and Mr. Chester Cooper in the Prime Minister's Room in the House of Commons at 6:00 P.M. on January 18, 1967, PREM 13/1917, PRO.

82. Ibid.

83. Ibid.

84. Top Secret. Telegram from the Prime Minister to the President, January 21, 1967, PREM 13/1917, PRO.

85. Chester Cooper, *The Lost Crusade: America in Vietnam* (London: MacGibbon and Kee, 1990), 351.

86. Memo from D. F. Murray to M. Palliser, "Vietnam, Mr Kosygin's Visit," February 6, 1967, PREM 13/1917, PRO; Cooper, *Lost Crusade*, 352.

87. Record of First Formal Meeting Held at 10 Downing Street at 4:30 P.M. on Monday, February 6, 1967, PREM 13/1840, PRO.

88. Gloria Stewart, "What the Vietcong Really Want," *New Statesman*, January 20, 1967, 69–70.

89. Ibid.

90. For a more detailed examination of the Wilson–Kosygin talks, see John Dumbrell and Sylvia Ellis, "British Involvement in Vietnam Peace Initiatives, 1966–1967: Marigolds, Sunflowers, and 'Kosygin Week,' " *Diplomatic History* 27, no. 1 (January 2003): 113–49.

91. Top Secret Letter from C. M. Maclehose to Sir Patrick Dean, January 11, 1967, PREM 13/1917, PRO.

92. Immediate Telegram from Brown to Cooper, January 31, 1967, PREM 13/1917, PRO.

93. Ibid.

94. Cooper, *Lost Crusade*, 354 (1970).

95. Secret. Record of a Meeting at No. 10 Downing Street at 10:00 A.M. on Saturday, February 4, 1967, PREM 13/1917, PRO.

96. Telegram from Goldberg to President and Secretary Rusk, February 2, 1967 in Herring, *Secret Diplomacy*, 428.

97. Cooper, *Lost Crusade*, 346 (1970).

98. Ibid.

99. Herring, *Secret Diplomacy*, 373.

100. Cooper, *Lost Crusade*, 355–56 (1970).

101. Herring, *Secret Diplomacy*, 396.

102. Cooper, *Lost Crusade*, 356 (1970).

103. Herring, *Secret Diplomacy*, 396.

104. Letter to Ho Chi Minh from President Johnson, February 8, 1967, in Lyndon B. Johnson, *The Vantage Point: Perspectives of the Presidency 1963–1969* (New York: Holt, Rinehart and Winston, 1971), 592.

105. Herring, *Secret Diplomacy*, 397.

106. Record of First Formal Meeting between Harold Wilson and Alexei N. Kosygin, held at 10 Downing Street at 4:30 P.M. on Monday, February 6, 1967, PREM 13/1840, PRO.

107. Telegram from Cooper to Rusk, February 6, 1967, in Herring, *Secret Diplomacy*, 434.

108. Record of First Formal Meeting Held at 10 Downing Street at 4:30 P.M. on February 6, 1967, PREM 13/1840, PRO.

109. Wilson, *The Labour Government 1964–70: A Personal Record* (London: Weidenfeld and Nicolson, 1971), 445.

110. Ibid.

111. Secret memorandum from D. F. Murray to George Brown, "Kosygin," February 6, 1967, PREM 13/1917, PRO.

112. Ibid.

113. Wilson, *Labour Government*, 447.

114. Ibid.

115. Note from Walt Rostow to the President, February 6, 1967, File: PM Wilson (2/67), Files of Walt W. Rostow, box 9, NSF, LBJL.

116. Telegram from the President to the Prime Minister, February 7, 1967, in Herring, *Secret Diplomacy*, 436.

117. Ibid.

118. Ibid., 436–38.

119. Lloyd C. Gardner, *Pay Any Price: Lyndon Johnson and the Wars for Vietnam* (Chicago: Ivan R. Dee, 1995), 345–46; Evan Thomas, *Robert Kennedy: His Life* (New York: Simon and Schuster, 2000), 332–33.

120. Ibid.

121. Note from Walt Rostow to the President, February 6, 1967, Files of Walt W. Rostow, File: PM Wilson (2/97), box 9, NSF, LBJL.

122. Message from Michael Palliser to Prime Minister, Secret, "Vietnam," February 7, 1967, PREM 13/1917, PRO.

123. Secret Note from Oliver Wright, "Agenda for this PM," February 7, 1967, PREM 13/1917, PRO.

124. Message from Michael Palliser to Prime Minister, Secret, "Vietnam," February 7, 1967, PREM 13/1917, PRO.

125. Secret Note from Oliver Wright, "Agenda for this PM," February 7, 1967, PREM 13/1917, PRO. The bombing pause was scheduled to last from February 8 to February 12 (starting at 7 A.M. Wednesday, February 8, Vietnam time, and scheduled to end 7 A.M. Sunday, February 12, Vietnam time).

126. Visit of Mr. Kosygin to London: Record of a Meeting Held at 10 Downing Street at 4:30 P.M., Tuesday, February 7, 1967, PREM 13/1840, PRO; Wilson, *Labour Government*, 449.

127. Visit of Mr. Kosygin to London, Record of a Meeting at 10 Downing Street, February 7, 1967, PREM 13/1840, PRO.

128. Wilson, *Labour Government*, 449.

129. Ibid., 450.

130. Bruce diaries, February 7, 1967.

131. Telegram from Cooper to Rusk, February 7, 1967, in Herring, *Secret Diplomacy*, 439.

132. Telegram from Cooper to Rusk and Harriman, February 7, 1967, Files of Walt W. Rostow, Marigold-Sunflower, box 9, NSF, LBJL.

133. Personal Telegram from Michael Palliser to Walt Rostow, February 9, 1967, PREM 13/1917, PRO.

134. Personal Telegram from Walt Rostow to Michael Palliser, February 8, 1967, File: (2/8/67 Wilson Kosygin), Files of Walt W. Rostow, box 9, NSF, LBJL.

135. Personal Telegram from Michael Palliser to Walt Rostow, February 9, 1967, PREM 13/1917, PRO.

136. Ibid.

137. Ibid.

138. Telegram from Walt Rostow to Michael Palliser, February 10, 1967, PREM 13/1918, PRO.

139. Herring, *Secret Diplomacy*, 441.

140. London BBC Television Service in English, Kosygin Speech at Lord Mayor's luncheon at the Guildhall in London on February 8 in Herring, *Secret Diplomacy*, 442.

141. Cooper, *Lost Crusade*, 358.

142. Telegram from Rusk to Bruce, February 9, 1967, in Herring, *Secret Diplomacy*, 446.

143. Ibid.

144. Cooper, *Lost Crusade*, 358.

145. Bruce diaries, February 8, 1967.

146. Telegram from Bruce to Rusk, February 9, 1967, in Herring, *Secret Diplomacy*, 444–45.

147. Secret Note on Mr. Kosygin's Visit—Vietnam, February 9, 1967, PREM 13/1917, PRO; and Telegram from Bruce to Rusk, February 9, 1967, in Herring, *Secret Diplomacy*, 447.

148. Cooper, *Lost Crusade*, 358.

149. Telegram from Bruce to Rusk, February 9, 1967, in Herring, *Secret Diplomacy*, 445.

150. Telephone Conversation between President Johnson and Secretary of State Rusk, February 9, 1967, 9:07 A.M., tape F67.05, side A, PNO 5 in FRUS, 1964–68, vol. 5, Vietnam 1967, doc. 48.

151. Rusk to Bruce, February 9, 1967, in Herring, *Secret Diplomacy*, 446.

152. Note, February 10, 1967, PREM 13/1918, PRO.

153. Telephone Conversation between President Johnson and Secretary of Defense McNamara, February 9, 1967, 8:29 A.M., tape F67.05, side A, PNO 4 in FRUS, 1965–68, vol. 5, Vietnam 1967, doc. 47.

154. Cooper, *Lost Crusade*, 357.

155. Wilson, *Labour Government*, 455.

156. Telegram from Rusk to Bruce and Cooper, February 9, 1967, 1:45 P.M., in FRUS, 1964–68, vol. 5, Vietnam 1967, doc. 50; also Herring, *Secret Diplomacy*, 446.

157. Wilson, *Labour Government*, 455.

158. Telegram from Cooper to Rusk and Harriman, February 9, in Herring, *Secret Diplomacy*, 444.

159. Cooper, *Lost Crusade*, 359.

160. Wilson, *Labour Government*, 456.

161. Ibid.

162. Department of State, Public Information Bulletin, February 13, 1967, in Herring, *Secret Diplomacy*, 450.

163. Cooper, *Lost Crusade*, 359.

164. The text was repeated the next day in Telegram from Bruce to Rusk, February 10, in Herring, *Secret Diplomacy*, 453.

165. Cooper, *Lost Crusade*, 359.

166. Ibid.

167. Telegram from Bruce to Rusk, February 10, in Herring, *Secret Diplomacy*, 453.

168. Rostow to LBJ, February 10, 1967, "Sunflower, vol. 1," box 256, CF, Vietnam, NSF, LBJL.

169. Ibid.

170. Transcript, Chester Cooper oral history interview by Paige E. Mulhollan, August 7, 1969, interview 3, 16, LBJL.

171. Cooper, *Lost Crusade*, 360.

172. Transcript, Chester Cooper oral history interview by Paige E. Mulhollan, August 7, 1969, interview 3, 17, LBJL; and Chester Cooper, *Lost Crusade*, 360.

173. Ibid.

174. Wilson, *Labour Government*, 456.

175. Ibid., 456–57.

176. Ibid., 457.

177. Transcript, David K. E. Bruce oral history interview by Thomas H. Baker, December 9, 1971, tape no. 2, LBJL.

178. Cooper, *Lost Crusade*, 361.

179. Ibid.

180. Cable from Rostow to Bruce and Cooper, February 10, 1967, PREM 13/1918, PRO.

181. Cooper, *Lost Crusade*, 361–62.

182. Transcript, Chester Cooper oral history interview by Paige E. Mulhollan, August 7, 1969, interview 3, 19, LBJL.

183. Cooper, *Lost Crusade*, 362.

184. Letter from Harold Wilson to His Excellency Mr. A. N. Kosygin, February 10, 1967, Secret, PREM 13/1918, PRO.

185. Transcript, Chester Cooper oral history interview by Paige E. Mulhollan, August 7, 1969, interview 3, 21, LBJL.

186. Ibid.

187. George Brown, *In My Way*, 146.

188. Cooper, *Lost Crusade*, 362.

189. Ibid.

190. Transcript, Chester Cooper oral history interview by Paige E. Mulhollan, August 7, 1969, interview 3, 21, LBJL.

191. Ibid.

192. Bruce diaries, February 10, 1967.

193. Transcript, Chester Cooper oral history interview by Paige E. Mulhollan, August 7, 1969, interview 3, 21, LBJL.

194. Transcript, Chester Cooper oral history interview by Paige E. Mulhollan, August 7, 1969, interview 3, 21–22, LBJL.

195. Secret. Record of a Meeting at 10 Downing Street at 10:40 P.M. on Saturday, February 11, PREM 13/1918, PRO.

196. Bruce diaries, February 11, 1967.

197. Ibid.

198. Bruce diaries, February 11, 1967.

199. Ibid.

200. Telephone Conversation between President Johnson and Walt Rostow, February 11, 1967, 9:15 A.M., tape F67.05, side B, PNO 1, in FRUS 1964–68, vol. 5, Vietnam 1967, doc. 55.

201. Cooper, *Lost Crusade*, 363.

202. Bruce diaries, February 11, 1967.

203. Ibid.

204. Record of a Meeting at 10 Downing Street at 10:40 P.M. on Saturday, February 11, 1965, PREM 13/1918, PRO.

205. Ibid.

206. Ibid.

207. Ibid.

208. Ibid.

209. Ibid.

210. Wilson, *Labour Government*, 461.

211. Ibid.

212. See Telephone Conversation between President Johnson and Walt Rostow, February 11, 1967, 9:49 A.M., in FRUS 1964–68, vol. 5, Vietnam 1967, doc. 57.

213. Memorandum from the Chairman of the Joint Chiefs of Staff (Wheeler) to Secretary of Defense McNamara, February 11, 1967, in FRUS 1964–68, vol. 5, Vietnam 1967, doc. 62.

214. Memorandum from Rusk to Johnson, February 11, 1967, in FRUS, 1964–68, vol. 5, Vietnam 1967, doc. 58.

215. Telephone Conversation between President Johnson and Rostow, February 11, 1967, 9:49 A.M., in FRUS, 1964–68, vol. 5, Vietnam 1967, doc. 57.

216. Telegram from Rusk to Bruce, February 11, 1967, 2:08 P.M., in FRUS, 1964–68, vol. 5, Vietnam 1967, doc. 59.

217. Memorandum from Rostow to Johnson, February 11, 1965, 8:35 A.M., Sunflower 1, box 255, CF, Vietnam, NSF, LBJL.

218. Telegram from Rusk to Bruce/Cooper, February 11, 1967, 2:08 P.M., in FRUS, 1964–68, vol. 5, Vietnam 1967, doc. 59.

219. Top Secret Note to Wilson, February 12, 1967, PREM 13/1918, PRO.

220. Telegram from Rusk to Bruce/Cooper, February 11, 1967, 2:08 P.M., in FRUS, 1964–68, vol. 5, Vietnam 1967, doc. 59.

221. Wilson, *Labour Government*, 459; Herring, *Secret Diplomacy*, 460–61.

222. Herring, *Secret Diplomacy*, 461, 844 n; Wilson, *Labour Government*, 461.

223. Wilson, *Labour Government*, 461.

224. Telegram from President to Prime Minister, February 12, 1967, in Herring, *Secret Diplomacy*, 463.

225. Ibid.

226. Herring, *Secret Diplomacy*, 462.

227. Wilson, *Labour Government*, 461–62.

228. Bruce diaries, 12 February 1967.

229. Telegram from Kaiser to Rusk, 13 February 1967, File: UK, Vol. X, Memos, 1/67–4/67, box 210, CF, UK, NSF, LBJL.

230. Transcript, Chester Cooper oral history interview by Paige E. Mulhollan, August 7, 1969, interview 3, 26–27, LBJL.; Cooper, *Lost Crusade*, 365.

231. Cooper, *Lost Crusade*, 365.

232. Wilson, *Labour Government*, 464.

233. Cooper, *Lost Crusade*, 365.

234. Transcript, Chester Cooper oral history interview by Paige E. Mulhollan, August 7, 1969, interview 3, 28–29, LBJL.

235. U.S. Formula, February 12, 1967, Files of Walt W. Rostow, Marigold-Sunflower, box 9, NSF, LBJL.

236. Cooper, *Lost Crusade*, 366.

237. Telegram from President to Prime Minister, February 13, 1967, in Herring, *Secret Diplomacy*, 467.

238. Transcript, Chester Cooper oral history interview by Paige E. Mulhollan, August 7, 1969, interview 3, 28–29, LBJL.

239. Wilson, *Labour Government*, 466–67.

240. Telegram from Rostow to Bruce, February 13, 1967, in Herring, *Secret Diplomacy*, 469.

241. "Meeting on Vietnam," February 13, 1967, Tom Johnson's Notes of Meeting, box 1, set II, LBJL.

242. Telegram from Katzenbach to American Embassy Saigon, TS/Nodis, sent 2258, February 13, 1967, in Herring, *Secret Diplomacy*, 473.

243. Wilson, *Labour Government*, 457–58.

244. Record of a conversation between the Prime Minister and the President of the United States of America at the White House on the morning of Friday, June 2, 1967, Confidential Annex to the Visit of the Prime Minister to Canada and the United States, June 1–3, 1967, PREM 13/1919, PRO.

245. David Kraslow and Stuart H. Loory, *The Secret Search for Peace in Vietnam* (New York: Vintage, 1968), 194.

246. Transcript, Chester Cooper oral history interview by Paige E. Mulhollan, August 7, 1969, 3, 20, LBJL.

247. Wilson, *Labour Government*, 458–59.

248. Robert S. McNamara et al., *Argument without End: In Search of Answers to the Vietnam Tragedy* (New York: Public Affairs, 1999), 291.

249. Johnson, *Vantage Point*, 254.

250. Record of a conversation between the Prime Minister and the President of the United States of America at the White House on the morning of Friday, June 2, 1967, Confidential Annex to the Visit of the Prime Minister to Canada and the United States, June 1–3, 1967, PREM 13/1919, PRO.

251. Wilson, *Labour Government*, 468.

252. Brown, *In My Way*, 145.

253. This view is discussed in more detail in George Herring, *America's Longest War: The United States and Vietnam 1950–1975* (New York: McGraw-Hill, 1986), and

Robert K. Brigham, *Guerrilla Diplomacy: The NLF's Foreign Relations and the Vietnam War* (Ithaca: Cornell University Press, 1999).

254. Telephone Conversation between President Johnson and Walt Rostow, February 11, 1967, 9.15 A.M., tape F67.05, side B, PNO 1 in FRUS, 1964–68, vol. 5, Vietnam 1967, doc. 55.

255. Wilson, *Labour Government*, 468.

256. *Washington Post,* July 29, 1969, in Cooper, *Lost Crusade,* 367.

257. Secret, Vietnam, Talking Points, no date, FCO 7/777, PRO.

258. McNamara et al., *Argument without End,* 284–91, 308.

259. Confidential memo from Walt Rostow to the President, March 3, 1967, File: UK, vol. 10, Memos, 1/67–4/67, box 210, CF, UK, NSF, LBJL.

260. Transcript, William Bundy oral history interview with Paige E. Mulhollan, tape 4, February 6, 1969, 27, LBJL.

261. Cable from Katzenbach to American embassies in London and Saigon, February 13, 1967, in Herring, *Secret Diplomacy,* 471.

262. *Hansard,* February 13, 1967, vol. 741, col. 109.

263. *Hansard,* February 14, 1967, vol. 741, cols. 345–54.

264. *Hansard,* February 14, 1967, vol. 741, col. 346; *New York Times,* February 15, 1967, 1.

265. *Hansard,* House of Commons Debates, 5th series, February 14, 1967, vol. 740, col. 350.

266. Ibid., col. 351; *New York Times,* February 15, 1967, 4.

267. *Times* (London), February 14, 1967, 1.

268. *New York Times,* Wednesday February 15, 1967, 1.

269. Michael Palliser, Minute on Anglo American Relations over Vietnam, February 17, 1967, PREM 13/1918. PRO.

270. Telegram from Kaiser to Rusk, February 17, 1967, in Herring, *Secret Diplomacy,* 481; Michael Palliser, Minute on Anglo American Relations over Vietnam, February 17, 1967, PREM 13/1918, PRO.

271. Palliser, Minute on Anglo American Relations over Vietnam, Secret, February 17, 1967, PREM 13/1918, PRO.

272. Telegram from Kaiser to Rusk, February 17, 1967, in Herring, *Secret Diplomacy,* 481.

273. Palliser to Prime Minister, February 17, 1967, "Anglo-American Relations over Vietnam" PREM 13/1918, PRO.

274. Ibid.

275. Telegram from Kaiser to Rusk, February 17, 1967, in Herring, *Secret Diplomacy,* 481.

276. Palliser to Prime Minister, Secret, February 17, 1967, "Anglo-American Relations over Vietnam," PREM 13/1918, PRO.

277. Telegram from Kaiser to Rusk, March 21, 1967, in Herring, *Secret Diplomacy,* 502.

278. Interview of Walt Rostow, September 8, 1994, LBJL.

279. Top Secret, Report by Walt Rostow on "The Essence of the Breakdown in Communications," Files of Walt W. Rostow, Marigold-Sunflower, box 9, NSF, LBJL.

280. Extract from a Minute from M. Palliser to Prime Minister, February 23, 1967, PREM 13/1918, PRO.

281. Ibid.

282. Telegram from Bill Jorden to Walt Rostow, American Embassy, London, no date, File: UKI, vol. 10, Memos, 1/67–4/67, box 210, NSF, LBJL.

283. Telegram from Walt Rostow to President/Rusk, February 25, 1967, Files of Walt W. Rostow, Marigold-Sunflower, box 9, NSF, LBJL.

284. Ibid.

285. Ibid.

286. Ibid.

287. Ibid. Talks to end the Korean War began in July 1951 at the village of Panmunjom. Talks dragged on for two years until an armistice agreement was signed on July 27, 1953.

288. Secret. Record of a Conversation between the Prime Minister and Mr. Walt W. Rostow at No. 10 Downing Street at 5:30 P.M. on Friday, February 24, 1967, PREM 13/1918, PRO.

289. Ibid.

290. Ibid.

291. Ibid.

292. Ibid.

293. Message from the Prime Minister to the President, March 16, 1967, Head of State Correspondence File, box 10, UK, vol. 5 (1 of 2), PM Wilson Correspondence, June 10, 1966–December 5, 1966.

294. Note from W. W. Rostow to the President, March 16, 1967, Files of W. Rostow, Marigold-Sunflower, box 9, NSF, LBJL.

295. Ibid.

296. Telegram from Rusk to Bruce, March 13, 1967, File: UK, vol. 10, Cables, 1/67–4/67, box 210, CF, UK, NSF, LBJL.

297. Ibid.

298. Telegram from Kaiser to Rusk, March 22, 1967, NSF, CF, UK, box 210, File: UK, vol. 10, Memos, 1/67–4/67, LBJL.

299. Telegram from Humphrey to Johnson and Rusk, April 4, 1967, "Subject: Meeting with Prime Minister Wilson, Chequers, Sunday 2 April 1967," Memos, vol. 9, 4/67–6/67, box 211, CF, UK, NSF, LBJL. See also Confidential Record of a Conversation between the Prime Minister and the Vice President of the United States at Chequers, April 2, 1967, PREM 13/1919, PRO.

300. Ibid.

301. Note from Michael Palliser to Prime Minister, Secret, President Johnson's Exchanges with Ho, March 23, 1967, PREM 13/1919, PRO.

302. Memo from Walt Rostow to the President, April 7, 1967, Files of Walt W. Rostow, Marigold-Sunflower, box 9, NSF, LBJL.

303. Telegram from Dean Rusk to Bruce, May 18, 1967, File: Memos, vol. 9, 4/67–6/67, box 211, CF, UK, NSF, LBJL.

304. Benn, *Out of the Wilderness,* June 1, 1967, 501.

305. Cable, Kaiser to Rusk, August 15, 1967, Memos, vol. 7, 7–12/67, box 211, CF, UK, NSF, LBJL.

306. Record of Conversation between the Prime Minister and the President of the United States of America at the White House on the Morning of Friday, June 2, 1967, Confidential Annex, Visit of the Prime Minister to Canada and the United States, June 1–3, 1967, PREM 13/1919, PRO.

307. Record of a Meeting between the Prime Minister and His Advisers and the President of the United States and His Advisers at the White House at 3 P.M. on Friday, June 2, 1967, PREM 13/1906, PRO.

308. Ibid.

309. Ibid.

310. Wilson, *Labour Government,* 574.

311. Report of the 66th Annual Conference of the Labour Party, Scarborough, October 2–6, 1967, Transport House, Smith Square, London, SW1.

312. Wilson, *Labour Government,* 567.

313. Message from the President to the Prime Minister, October 5, 1967, Special Head of State Correspondence, UK (3 of 4), box 56, NSF, LBJL.

314. Cable from Bruce to Rusk, November 8, 1967, in Bruce diaries.

315. Ben Pimlott, *Harold Wilson* (London: HarperCollins, 1993), 481.

316. Ibid.; Wilson, *Labour Government,* 579.

317. Karnow, *Vietnam: A History* (New York: Penguin, 1991), 502.

318. Ibid.

319. Ibid., 503.

320. Marilyn Young, *The Vietnam Wars, 1945–1990* (New York: HarperCollins Publishers, 1991), 207–8.

321. Meeting between Secretary Rusk and Foreign Secretary Brown, January 12, 1968, Bruce diaries.

322. Telegram from President to Prime Minister, January 12, 1968, Bruce diaries.

323. CIA Intelligence Memorandum: Britain Begins Implementation of Budget Cuts, February 6, 1968, File: UK, vol. 8, Memos, 1/67–7/69, box 212, CF, UK, NSF, LBJL.

324. *Times* (London), January 18, 1968.

325. Memorandum from Walt W. Rostow to the President, November 16, 1967, File: UK, vol. 7, Cables, 7–12/67, box 211, CF, UK, NSF, LBJL.

326. Exchange of Toasts between the President and Prime Minister Wilson of Great Britain, 8 February 1968, File: UK, Visit of PM, 2/7–9/68, box 216, CF, UK, NSF, LBJL.

327. Memorandum for the President from Rusk, February 3, 1968, Subject: Your Talks with British Prime Minister Harold Wilson on Thursday, February 8, 1968, File: UK, vol. 8, Memos, 1/68–7/69, box 212, CF, UK, NSF, LBJL.

328. Exchange of Toasts between the President and Prime Minister Wilson of Great Britain, February 8, 1968, File: UK, Visit of PM, 2/7–9/68, box 216, CF, UK, NSF, LBJL.

329. Ibid.

330. Telegram from Bruce to Rusk, May 8, 1967, File: UK, vol. 9, Memos, 4/67–6/67, box 211, CF, UK, NSF, LBJL.

331. Summary Notes of the 587th NSC Meeting, June 5, 1968, NSC Meetings File, vol. 5, tab. 69, 6/5/68, box 2, Current Issues Affecting US/UK Relations, NSF, LBJL.

332. Ibid.

333. Telegram from Bruce to Rusk, Annual Assessment on Britain, Spring 1968, June 1, 1968, File: vol. 8, Memos, 1/68–7/69, box 211, CF, UK, NSF, LBJL.

334. Ibid.

Conclusion

The "more flags" program failed miserably. The Johnson administration's most obvious failure was its inability to persuade its partner in the Anglo–American relationship to commit fully to the anti-Communist crusade in Vietnam. The United States' closest ally was not willing to send its troops to South Vietnam, damaging U.S. efforts to portray the war as an allied anti-Communist crusade and, inevitably, raising questions about the rationale behind the war. Critics of Washington's policy in Vietnam could ask why the free world was not showing solidarity on this issue. If South Vietnam was worth saving, why was Britain not willing to get heavily involved in the rescue effort as it had done in Korea?

First Kennedy and then Johnson had hoped London would join in a multilateral force that would aid South Vietnam. During the Kennedy years, the British government did not think a negotiated settlement on the lines of the Laos settlement was desirable or attainable, was prepared to back the United States fully on the diplomatic front, and was willing to consider a military involvement in Vietnam.[1] So when Lyndon Johnson came to power, he found the British had supported Kennedy's Vietnam policy and had even established the British Advisory Mission in Saigon in 1961. However, when J. E. Cable became head of the South East Asia department of the British Foreign Office late in 1963, a new assessment of the situation in Vietnam was made. The department became convinced that a military solution to the Vietnam War was impossible without risking a confrontation with either the Soviets or the Chinese, and that the United States would ultimately face ignominious defeat. As a result, the British government was encouraged to promote peace negotiations on the grounds that a compromise settlement ought to be preferable to the risks involved in escalation. If the British did not offer an alternative to a military solution in Vietnam at this stage, the Labour government elected in October 1964 could have changed policy on Vietnam and advocated alternatives. In the lead-up to, and the immediate aftermath of, the 1964 presidential election, the Wilson government could have taken the opportunity to indicate a change of view. As large-scale U.S. military intervention looked increasingly likely, and with a social democratic Labour Party in charge, could London have changed tack on Vietnam, possibly even indicating that it could not support an Americanization of the war? Certainly Harold Wilson, many within the Labour Party, and a large part of the Foreign Office had concluded by late 1964 that a U.S. military involvement would only complicate matters and was unlikely to succeed in solving the political problems in South Vietnam. The British government could have provided a lead to other dissenting voices, particularly in Europe, by indicating, publicly and privately, its misgivings about U.S. intervention in Vietnam. But the obstacles in its way were not easily surmountable, even if the Labour leadership was convinced it should not encourage U.S. military intervention in Vietnam. The new Labour government—out of office for 13 years—was shackled by a small parliamentary majority and by a financial crisis that was truly apparent to the prime minister only on the day he entered 10 Downing Street. The balance-of-payments deficit threatened sterling and British overseas defense capabilities. Prime Minister Wilson and his cabinet understood immediately that the new government was likely to need American support for the pound at some stage in the near future. Moreover, the Labour leadership had inherited foreign policy commitments that affected its thinking on Vietnam. First, Great Britain was a charter member of the South East Asia Treaty Organization (SEATO) and as such was committed to the defense of Vietnam, a protocol state. Any abandonment of SEATO—or condemnation of fellow members—would have significantly decreased British influence in the region and would have weakened its status within the Western alliance. Second, the British were protecting Malaysia from pro-Communist Indonesian forces. Any distancing from the United States in Vietnam might have weakened Johnson's diplomatic support for the military action taken by Britain in Malaysia. And finally, the new government received cautionary advice from the Foreign Office and from the British ambassador in Washington, feeling it would be too risky to jeopardize other areas of close cooperation with the United States by being too honest over Vietnam. A breach in Anglo–American relations shortly after Wilson took office would have been an extremely risky proposition, particularly given that Wilson had spent the previous year courting Washington and had long indicated his intention to keep the Anglo–American relationship at the center of British foreign policy. Significantly, Her Majesty's Opposition had not indicated that there would be any significant change of policy on Vietnam. The new British government judged that it could not afford rifts between itself and the Johnson administration over Southeast Asia. And it must be remembered that although the portents for an American war in Vietnam were there, especially after the Gulf of Tonkin incident in August, Johnson had campaigned in 1964 promising to let Saigon win its own war. To threaten to dissociate from the Americans on arriving in office was something the new prime minister did not even consider, possibly because Wilson was aware that the large-scale military commitment in Malaysia—which by 1964 was over-stretching British defenses—provided the perfect excuse not to get involved to any great extent in Vietnam. The Foreign Office advised, and the beleaguered prime minister concurred, that the British should "hope for the best" in Vietnam; continue with a policy of a small counterinsurgency advisory role; and attempt to mediate for peace by advocating a return to Geneva, although organizing a conference only if the United States permitted it. Nevertheless, Wilson attempted to keep Britain's options open on Vietnam, indicating early on that he would not sanction U.S. policy ahead of time. And, of course, Wilson expected to be able to use his interpersonal skills to influence Johnson from the sidelines.

We know, of course, that the American government was extremely unhappy with limited support from the British. But how far did the Johnson administration pressure the British government to send troops and to stay loyal on Vietnam? The Labour government's refusal to send even token military support to Vietnam angered President Johnson and members of his administration, most notably Dean Rusk and Robert McNamara, but most scholars have agreed that Washington put only limited pressure on London to change its mind. This appears to be the case. However, if the pressure was limited, it was also persistent and ill-tempered. In December 1964, the first Washington summit meeting between Wilson and Johnson saw the first, and only, formal inquiry about the possibility of a specific British troop contribution of around 100 men. After Wilson's refusal to consider this, it is evident that the Johnson administration understood the limits of British support in Vietnam. On a practical level, the White House appears to have valued Britain's role in Malaysia; was prepared to accept that this precluded a military involvement in Vietnam; and was happy to receive the public, political support of the British as the second-best option. And yet, although Johnson did not make further specific requests for British troops, the administration tried on a number of occasions—and in a number of ways—to encourage such action. This was revealed on the night of February 10, 1965, when Wilson telephoned LBJ to ask whether he should fly over to Washington to discuss the United States' response to the attack on the U.S. barracks at Qui Nhon. The president fumed at the prime minister, asking him to "send us some men" if he wanted to help. Johnson and his aides also tried indirect means of putting pressure on London. In early April 1965, after LBJ's Baltimore speech at Johns Hopkins, Patrick Dean reported back to London that the president was indicating his desire for British troops. Wilson was thus given advance warning of the possibility that he might be approached on this during his next trip to Washington. Consequently, on April 14, 1965, the British prime minister forestalled such a request by playing the Malaysia card. Then, in May 1965, the Americans attempted to engage the British more fully through SEATO. In early July, as Washington moved toward its decision to Americanize the war in

Vietnam, Rusk indirectly asked for a British contribution via the Australian foreign minister, Hanluck, and this was followed shortly afterward by LBJ's cable asking for increased third-party assistance. And in July and August 1965 members of the Johnson administration, including McGeorge Bundy, Robert McNamara, and Dean Rusk, were very tempted during discussions on the pound to introduce a formal quid pro quo linking U.S. financial help to a British troop commitment in Vietnam. President Johnson's intervention prevented the British from being asked to become "Hessians" in Vietnam. Though LBJ would have dearly loved a British presence in Vietnam, there was always the risk that the Wilson government would call the American bluff, devalue, and take an independent line on Vietnam. But when the situation in Malaysia improved in June 1966 Rusk put pressure on Michael Stewart, at a meeting of NATO, to redeploy troops or equipment (trucks and helicopters), or both, to other parts of Southeast Asia, including Vietnam. And as late as April 1967, at the funeral of former West German chancellor Konrad Adenauer, Johnson could not resist disarming Wilson—and preventing more criticism of U.S. bombing—by asking the prime minister when he was going to send his two brigades of troops to Vietnam.[2] And these were just the more obvious forms of pressure on Britain. It is clear that almost every time the British were discussed in Washington in relation to Vietnam, their lack of troops in the field was the most telling undercurrent in the conversation. On an emotional level, the Americans expected better of the British. This was largely due to Washington's perception of the role that a valued ally should play, but there was also a personal dimension to this inability to accept British noninvolvement. It seems that only a British deployment would have convinced Johnson of British loyalty and reliability. But Wilson resisted the Johnson administration's pressure—subtle and otherwise—to introduce ground troops. And, in the process, he did, in a sense, indicate to the rest of the world that the British government was providing what Wilson later characterized as "negative support."[3] Despite public, political backing for U.S. intervention, it was clear that the British were not wholeheartedly supporting the effort.

London's steadfast determination to avoid a military involvement in Vietnam could easily have caused serious problems between the United States and Great Britain. But Wilson was well aware that despite the disappointment over the lack of troops in Vietnam, it was extremely important to the Johnson administration that London support its aims and actions in Vietnam firmly in public. Congress and U.S. public opinion expected this sort of response from their ally across the Atlantic; Johnson demanded it. But Wilson's public support of U.S. intervention came at a high price at home and abroad. It complicated London's relationship with members of the Commonwealth, most of whom were either opposed to the war or neutral, and no doubt played a part in establishing the British as too pro-American in the eyes of General de Gaulle of France, thus contributing to the delay in Britain's entry into the European Economic Community. Wilson's support for Johnson came at an even higher price domestically. Once the United States began its bombing campaign and introduced ground troops, the unpopularity of the war grew in Britain, and Wilson faced increasing pressure from Labour backbenchers to take action for peace. His government's small working majority meant that internal rebellion had to be taken seriously, especially as opposition to the war became more widespread. Prior to February 1965 the Wilson government asked for only one consideration from the United States over Vietnam: that the British be consulted about steps the United States might take in Vietnam, so that they could support the U.S. effort effectively and not face awkward questions in the House of Commons. The Johnson administration understood Wilson's domestic political difficulties over Vietnam and made some effort to allow the prime minister to portray his relations with the Americans as closer, or at least more significant, than they actually were. This explains Johnson's indulgence of Wilson's need to visit the White House on a regular basis, six times in less than four years (although Johnson might have been persuaded to visit the United Kingdom had the British been fighting side by side with the Americans in Vietnam). And, on several occasions, the United States did use the British as a sounding board, trying ideas out on them during meetings and private discussions. For example, Walt Rostow traveled to London in January 1965 to discuss the possibility of selective bombing of North Vietnam, for which he received no encouragement from Wilson. But the British never received "consultations" in the strictest sense of the word. The Johnson administration was not seeking advice from the British but was willing to see what their reaction to proposed action might be. In other words, The United States wanted to assess how critics of the war might respond in reaction to further military escalation. More often than not, the British were told that an action was about to take place very shortly before it did, and then often only after Wilson forced the issue. This was seen in February 1965 when the prime minister's late-night telephone call to the president led to a cable sent by McGeorge Bundy outlining plans to bomb an army barracks in North Vietnam. But the British were not always extended the courtesy of prior notice of military escalation or changes of tactics. When, in March 1965, the news broke that the United States was using gas in Vietnam, the Labour government resented not being kept fully informed of events when its support of U.S. policy in Vietnam was so politically sensitive at home. The "gas incident" led to the first major, open, face-to-face disagreement between the president and a member of the Wilson government, in this case Michael Stewart, who was in Washington at the time. Britain increasingly felt it was being asked to support an unpopular war without being fully convinced of either the justification for U.S. involvement in Vietnam or the military strategy and tactics employed by the Americans. The "fuss," as Bundy put it, made by the British over this episode, which threatened to become public, perhaps persuaded Washington that it might be worthwhile to brief London more often about the military campaign, especially if there was a danger that the British might withdraw its support for American action. Consequently, Britain did receive a month's notice that the United States would bomb POL targets in Hanoi and Haiphong in June 1966. But although the United States was prepared to provide advance notice of military action, however grudgingly, the British, along with most of the rest of the world, were forced to almost beg Washington for an explanation of U.S. aims and future strategy in Southeast Asia. This led to fears on the part of London that Washington was not taking the issue of negotiations seriously enough.

By April 1965 the Anglo–American relationship had begun to suffer because of Vietnam. London was beginning to protest privately about the methods the United States was employing in Vietnam, most notably during the gas episode, and was also threatening to take unilateral action for peace in the role of Geneva cochair. Friction had surfaced at the highest level, not only during Michael Stewart's trip to Washington but also through third parties—ambassadors and personal advisers—when the United States attempted to dictate the terms of the prime minister's response to questions in the House of Commons on Vietnam in the aftermath of the war's escalation throughout March. The United States was concerned that British behind-the-scenes criticism of its actions in Vietnam might spill over into the public arena and clearly considered the possibility that the British might join forces with the French in mischief making. There was a danger that Wilson might openly criticize U.S. policy in Vietnam and call for a negotiated settlement, possibly even neutralization. The Labour government and the Johnson administration were able to avoid a direct, and possibly public, confrontation with each other by agreeing to endorse a series of "understandings" on Vietnam. Though the nature of these understandings is open to dispute—certainly they were unofficial and tacit—they are discussed in governmental papers and political memoirs and clearly shaped attitudes and policies on both sides of the Atlantic. The first understanding was reached not in December 1964 as many members of the Labour Party suspected, but in April 1965 during Wilson's second summit meeting in Washington. The British government understood that the United States would pursue its military war in Vietnam, and that Britain would support this effort wholeheartedly in public. In return, Washington would endorse, in public if appropriate, any British peace initiative that stood a chance of establishing talks. Only days after the Baltimore speech, during which President Johnson indicated the United States' readiness for unconditional discussions for peace, the Johnson administration was forced to recognize that Harold Wilson took them at their word and duly accepted that the cost of British approval of their Vietnam policy was to support the British prime minister's attempt to play the role of peace broker. And the prime minister soon got to work on this, partly, as the White House suspected, to appease his domestic critics, but also through a genuine desire to see an end to a war that could have proliferated into a third world war. The peace initiatives that the British government embarked upon between 1965 and 1968—attempts to revitalize the role of Geneva cochair, the Gordon-Walker peace mission, the Commonwealth peace mission, the Harold Davies visit to Hanoi, the Wilson–Kosygin peace initiative—have in the past been viewed as driven primarily by Wilson's need to deal with his political problems at home. Consequently, many of the efforts have been seen as peace "gimmicks." This is too harsh an assessment. This work has demonstrated that although Prime Minister Wilson was, at times, prone to exaggerating his role in influencing the Americans and overplaying the role of world statesman, his government invested a great deal of time, energy, and commitment to mediating for peace. And although some of the efforts for peace became public, and thereby eased Wilson's parliamentary difficulties, some did not. Wilson's efforts to engage the Russians in a variety of different roles as cochairs of the Geneva conference were carried out discreetly and tirelessly, including the attempt to establish a conference on Cambodia in April 1965. Details of diplomatic activity with the Russians, in addition to meetings with North Vietnamese diplomatic staff, were not revealed to the Parliament or the British public through the media. This is not to deny Harold Wilson's Walter Mitty tendencies but to suggest that the British government and Foreign Office were keen to help facilitate peace talks in whatever way possible, and if such efforts could be made public without endangering their chances of success, and in the process assuage Wilson's critics at home, then all the better. The growing opposition to the war in Britain drove Wilson to pursue behind-the-scenes peace efforts with vigor, but it is likely that Britain, due to its worldwide commitments and role as Geneva cochair, would have sought peace regardless of the war's unpopularity. The pressure placed on the Wilson government by backbench revolts, antiwar demonstrations, and poor ratings in the public opinion polls encouraged the prime minister to be persistent and imaginative in his approach to peace.

What is equally notable is how much the British peace gambits irritated the White House. Although Washington usually sanctioned British peace efforts, the record shows it did so reluctantly. President Johnson and his closest advisers did not trust the British government to represent American wishes adequately during talks and were convinced that Wilson might be tempted to leak information about possible talks to help him handle his recalcitrant backbenchers. This is demonstrated most palpably by the fact that the U.S. government was not prepared to take the British into its confidence over behind-the-scenes negotiations. Most damagingly, the White House did not inform the British government of the parallel peace tracks under way in late 1966 and early 1967, culminating in the fiasco that transpired during Premier Kosygin's visit to London in February 1967. Washington's lack of candor on the negotiation front indicated its preference not to deal through third parties if at all possible and, in relation to Britain, a great deal of insensitivity to the embarrassing position in which it placed the British government with regard to the Russians.

Vietnam also played a major part in the second, wider "understanding" that was reached in September 1965, linking the maintenance of British defense commitments around the world to the American effort to relieve pressure on sterling. The United States, expecting a decreasing commitment, wanted the British to understand how much Washington valued their worldwide commitments. Though Wilson kept Vietnam out of this tacit understanding, insisting that the British would not make a contribution to Vietnam, the war was part of the reason for the White House's strong desire not to be left alone in the role of world policeman. Essentially, both countries understood that the Anglo–American relationship had to be viewed in its totality, and Washington was determined to ensure that the British government did not withdraw from its commitments East of Suez while the United States was fighting in Southeast Asia. There was, however, no explicit quid pro quo, but instead a recognition that both countries had worldwide commitments and an assurance by the British that they would consult with the Americans in the course of the defense review. The implied, and somewhat vague, nature of this verbal agreement meant that Britain and America had different expectations of each other. Washington believed it had received a firm commitment from London that it would be consulted fully before any decision was made regarding the withdrawal of troops from East of Suez and felt that a decision would not be made that would damage U.S. interests in Vietnam. Whitehall felt the British government had committed themselves to consulting the Americans but reserved the right to make hard decisions on defense in its own best interests.

The two "understandings" reached in 1965 did not stay intact for very long, and almost immediately the United States began to question the British commitment to them. Johnson still had to be persuaded that Wilson provided staunch public support for the United States on Vietnam, despite the fact that the British government was providing the firmest verbal backing of all the major allies. The prime minister regularly condemned Vietcong and NLF attacks on the Americans, denounced Hanoi for its intransigence, praised Johnson for his attempts to find peace and his moderation in the military war, and consistently supported U.S. objectives in Vietnam. This did not stop Johnson, as early as December 1965, from trying to prevent Wilson's mentioning Vietnam during a speech to the United Nations. Johnson felt that the British prime minister might make political capital out of him by publicly emphasizing the need for negotiations. And, of course, Wilson had begun to distinguish between the ends and the means in this war, between its goals and its military methods.

But what led the prime minister to move away from the understandings on Vietnam and British defense commitments was a mixture of internal politics, a growing frustration with the United States on Vietnam, and the ending of the confrontation in Malaysia. Despite the victory in the March 1966 general election, Harold Wilson's position at home became increasingly stressful as opposition to the war widened. By 1966 Wilson's parliamentary critics were no longer left-wing ones. The government was being pressed to distance itself from American action in Vietnam. This clearly contributed to Wilson's decision to dissociate from the bombings of oil installations in Hanoi and Haiphong in

June 1966. The public act of dissociation condemned Wilson to the ranks of other critics in LBJ's mind; Wilson was now a suspicious and unreliable character. And, as the prime minister and his closest advisers suspected, this act of independence severely undermined London's influence in Washington. After dissociation, even Wilson later acknowledged, the British failed to have any influence on the Johnson administration. Before making that decision, Wilson could rightly claim that U.S. decision making on Vietnam had been affected by the British periodically. The prime minister claimed some responsibility for President Johnson's peace offensive that included the Baltimore speech in April 1965, and the record shows that there was some veracity to this. The White House felt pressure from international critics, as well as domestic ones, to pursue a carrot-and-stick approach to the conflict in Vietnam. Likewise, British encouragement of bombing pauses had to be taken seriously by Washington, especially when these were combined with wider international pressure to give Hanoi a chance to respond to peace initiatives. World opinion was important in the propaganda war, and as such, the Johnson administration had to appear to be making strenuous efforts toward a peaceful solution to the Vietnam conflict.

By late 1967 the "understandings" had been breached by both sides. Although the POL dissociation by the British had been a qualified act, after which they continued to support U.S. objectives in Vietnam, this public act of betrayal probably contributed to the Johnson administration's impatience and lack of candor during the Wilson–Kosygin talks in February 1967. And with the end of the Malaysian confrontation in August 1966 the British government was under pressure from Parliament to make savings in defense by withdrawing from East of Suez. Britain's economic situation dictated that eventually sterling had to be devalued, and Britain's role East of Suez ended. Through the "understandings" reached with the Americans during 1965 Wilson was able to postpone the inevitable, particularly where the defense review was concerned. His achievement was to avoid both decisions until he was in a strong enough domestic position to take them and weather the political fallout.

So how are we to assess Harold Wilson's performance with regard to both Vietnam and the broader issue of Anglo–American foreign policy of which Vietnam was such an integral part? However much Wilson felt humiliated by the Americans' lack of trust and candor and frustrated by the war, ultimately he survived the balancing act on Vietnam and managed to avoid devaluation until a more propitious time. He was a skillful pragmatist; Johnson and many of his advisers may well have felt that Wilson got the better of them. Wilson, who suffered castigation at the time—and indeed, since—for his support of America's war in Vietnam, has to be given some credit for his skillful handling of persistent U.S. pressure for a deeper British involvement, particularly a token military force. And the prime minister did offer more advice and criticism of American tactics in private than many of his critics suspected. The advice was, however, circumspect, the criticism muted. Perhaps, ultimately, Wilson had a failure of courage where Vietnam was concerned. He was probably unwise to have firmly fixed his colors to the Vietnam mast so early on in his tenure in office. On coming to office in October, just one month before the Johnson presidential landslide, the British prime minister could have signaled a change in Vietnam policy from that of his predecessors without necessarily jeopardizing wider relations with the Americans. At this stage, there were no U.S. ground troops in Vietnam, the president had not yet fully committed himself to the fight, and Britain could have taken a more neutral stance on the conflict. That is not to deny, however, that the stakes were high; clearly, this would have been a gamble. Johnson was notoriously unpredictable and could have reacted so badly to such an act of perceived disloyalty that he might have taken extreme steps, particularly relating to financial help to Britain, although given the obvious links between sterling and the dollar, America's own vital interests would probably have dictated against such action. What was more likely, and perhaps to Wilson even more frightening, was a public presidential snub to the British. Johnson may not have received Wilson at the White House so often, and thus jeopardized the image of Britain as a world power whose opinion still counted, and Wilson's own self-image as a statesman whose counsel mattered. Wilson never considered such an alternative; perhaps he was unable to contemplate risking such a breach. Instead, he conducted, very skillfully, the balancing act of doing the minimum to keep the Americans on Britain's side, but at the same time managing to keep his own backbenchers just about at bay. Wilson walked a political tightrope on Vietnam successfully, although he did wobble once or twice along the way. Nevertheless, Wilson's exaggerated public claims for his role as "honest broker" meant he faced humiliation at the hands of the Americans. His support for an unpopular and cruel war left his personal reputation tarnished and the Labour government's morally suspect. The prime minister certainly lost credibility and respect in many liberal and left-wing circles, and this betrayal of democratic socialism, as many saw it, may have combined with other events to create the circumstances for his shock defeat in the 1970 general election.

Ultimately the British can be criticized for not being forceful enough soon enough on Vietnam, but as Logevall suggests, the Johnson administration was not open to unwarranted advice and, at least during the first year of the Wilson government, preferred a military solution to a political one. Moreover, it is clear that the White House, through its embassies and intelligence, was well aware of the Labour leadership's feelings on Vietnam. It did not necessarily need an open rift with the British government to know that it harbored serious doubts about the wisdom of the U.S. effort in Vietnam and most definitely preferred a negotiated settlement to the risks of military escalation. Was London like the dog that did not bark, as Logevall suggests—important for what it did not do? Certainly, to extend the metaphor, the British government barked too late and too quietly. This was not the bark of a Doberman but more the constant yapping of a toy dog, with the occasional snarl. But, in some ways more importantly, a deaf owner will never hear the dogs, however loudly they bark. Ultimately the British may well have been too timid on Vietnam, but the American government did not really need the support of its allies to continue the fight in Vietnam and could act alone if it needed to. In the final analysis Vietnam affected Johnson's judgment in most matters, and Anglo–American relations were no exception. Lyndon Johnson's personal obsession with the war is starkly apparent in the communications between Great Britain and the United States. The president and his close advisers regularly stressed the personal commitment to the battle, and the domestic ramifications of it, especially after the July 1965 decision to Americanize the conflict. This personal dimension inevitably led to difficulties in the personal and working relationship between Wilson and Johnson. Given the nature and difficulty of understanding any relationship between human beings—never mind between politicians of such complexity as Wilson and Johnson—it is difficult to comment on the relationship between the two statesmen with any certainty, let alone evaluate its impact on policy decisions. The evidence at times appears contradictory, but in many ways it merely reflects the fact that the relationship between the president and the prime minister was neither simple nor static, but was multidimensional, with distinct peaks and troughs. There were periods, usually after one of Wilson's visits to Washington, when the relationship seemed to flourish, but the possibility of a close, working relationship developing into a cordial personal one ended in June 1966 with Wilson's dissociation decision. The president was convinced that the prime minister acted purely out of domestic concerns and firmly believed that Britain had reneged on its SEATO commitments; and Wilson was beginning to question LBJ's conduct of the Vietnam war. Philip Kaiser observed that the relationship between President Johnson and Prime Minister Wilson "had its ups and downs" and that, at best, they developed a "shaky rapport."[4] This appears to be the most accurate assessment of an ambiguous partnership.

There was no personal chemistry or ideological common ground between Wilson and Johnson. Those who served in both the Kennedy and the Johnson administrations acknowledged that the special relationship lost its emotional charge during the Johnson years. If compared with the earlier relationships between the heads of the United States and the United Kingdom, with, say, Roosevelt and Churchill, Eisenhower and Macmillan, and Kennedy and Macmillan, and with the later relationships between Reagan and Thatcher and Clinton and Blair, the Wilson–Johnson relationship was indeed cool. Given Johnson's obsession with Vietnam, it could be argued that any British prime minister who took such unpopular decisions as staying out of Vietnam and reducing Britain's defense role would have had difficulty establishing a close personal relationship with any American president. Moreover, Johnson's own problems of paranoia and self-esteem—his fixation over leaks and his demands for complete loyalty from colleagues and allies—would equally have caused problems for any prime minister. And, with Wilson's domestic difficulties over sterling and Vietnam, it is hard to see how he could have done more to ensure a close personal relationship. He could have stayed out of peace negotiations and could have said less on the whole issue of Vietnam, but in so doing he would have risked an internal split in his own party. And, while never explicitly linked, Wilson was aware that his diplomatic support on Vietnam helped in negotiations over sterling.

Rifts in the Anglo–American relationship were often prevented by skills of mediation, and the wise guidance of key officials was also vital in preventing a breakdown in the relationship between the president and the prime minister. Michael Palliser and Walt Rostow would probably take much of the credit, but the fact that disputes on Vietnam did not lead to a lasting breach in Anglo–American relations is also partly testimony to the decisive role of the two ambassadors. Both David Bruce in London and Patrick Dean in Washington helped establish the spring 1965 understanding that remained firmly in place until the late summer of 1966 and were generally instrumental in maintaining cordiality and cooperation at most levels of diplomacy. Both men were respected, and their advice heeded, by Johnson and Wilson. They may have helped Wilson achieve something approximating his vision of a "close" relationship with Americans, for the Wilson/Johnson years could hardly be deemed "special."

NOTES

1. Peter Busch, *All the Way with JFK? Britain, the US, and the Vietnam War* (Oxford: Oxford University Press, 2003). Busch argues that the Macmillan government's policy toward SEATO shows there is evidence to suggest that Britain would have taken part in a SEATO intervention in Vietnam if the United States had insisted.

2. President Johnson's Daily diary, April 23, 1967, LBJL.

3. Caroline Page, *U.S. Official Propaganda during the Vietnam War, 1965–1973* (Leicester: Leicester University Press, 1996), 109.

4. Philip M. Kaiser, *Journeying Far and Wide: A Political and Diplomatic Memoir* (New York: Macmillan, 1992), 209, 230.

Bibliography

UNPUBLISHED DOCUMENTS

Lyndon Baines Johnson Library (Austin, Texas)

National Security File, 1963–69
    Country File
    Memos to the President, McGeorge Bundy and Walt Rostow
    Files of McGeorge Bundy
    Files of Walt W. Rostow
    Name File
Oral History Collection
    George W. Ball
    David K. E. Bruce
    McGeorge Bundy
    William P. Bundy
    Harlan Cleveland
    Chester L. Cooper
    Thomas K. Finletter
    Lyndon Baines Johnson
    Nicholas Katzenbach
    Benjamin H. Read
    Walt W. Rostow
    Dean Rusk
    Harrison Salisbury
Papers of Francis Bator
Papers of Gardner Ackley
Special Files, 1927–73
    Tom Johnson's Notes of Meetings
White House Central File
    Subject File

White House Tapes and Transcripts
  TAPE WH6402.15—February 11–12, 1964
  TAPE WH6411.12—November 6–7, 1964
  TAPE WH6411.13—November 8–9, 1964
  TAPE WH6411.24—November 18–19, 1964
  TAPE WH6411.12—November 22, 1964
  TAPE WH6411.29—November 24–25, 1964
  TAPE WH6503.11—March 23–24, 1965
  TAPE WH6504.06—April 27–29, 1965
  TAPE WH6503.06—March 11 and 13, 1965
  TAPE WH6506.03—June 10–15, 1965
  TAPE WH6506.03—June 10–15, 1965
  TAPE WH6506.04—June 15–17, 1965
  TAPE WH6506.03—June 17–21, 1965

John F. Kennedy Library (Boston, Massachusetts)

Oral History Interviews
  Henry Brandon
  David Bruce
  McGeorge Bundy
  Chester Cooper
  Sir Alec Douglas-Home
  Lord Paul Gore-Booth
  Averell Harriman
  Louis Heren
  Roger Hilsman
  Henry Cabot Lodge
  James Reston
  Dean Rusk
  Sir Humphrey Trevelyan
Presidential Papers, 1961–63
  National Security Files
  President's Office Files
  White House Central Files

Library of Congress (Washington, D.C.)

Declassified Documents Series

Virginia Historical Society (Richmond, Virginia)

David Bruce diaries

Public Record Office (Kew, Richmond, Surrey)

CAB 128 Cabinet Minutes

CAB 129   Cabinet Memoranda
FO 371   Foreign Office, General Political Correspondence
PREM 11   Prime Minister's Office, Correspondence and Papers
PREM 13   Prime Minister's Office, Correspondence and Papers

Modern Records Centre (Warwick University)

I.C.D.P. MSS 181/6
J. Askins MSS 189/V(1–6)

Brynmor Jones Library (Hull University)

Papers of David Winnick, M.P.
Papers of Kevin McNamara, M.P.

Churchill Archives Centre (Cambridge)

Papers of Patrick Gordon-Walker

National Museum of Labour History (Manchester)

The Parliamentary Labour Party Minutes
Tribune

Fabian Society Archives (Oxford)

International and Commonwealth Bureau
Venture

Bodleian Library (Oxford)

Papers of George Brown

Marx Memorial Library (London)

Daily Herald
Pamphlets of British Vietnam Committee, Vietnam Solidarity Campaign, and Stop It

INTERVIEWS

Baroness Castle of Blackburn, April 28, 1993
Lord Ennals of Norwich, April 26, 1993
Baron Glenamara (Edward Short), January 12, 1994
Sir Michael Palliser, November 9, 1993
Walt W. Rostow, September 8, 1994

Peter Shore, M.P., November 8, 1993
Sir Oliver Wright, April 27, 1993

CORRESPONDENCE

Tony Benn
James Callaghan
Sir Patrick Dean
Marcia Falkender
Joe Haines
Ian Mikardo

PUBLISHED DOCUMENTS AND OFFICIAL
PUBLICATIONS

United States

Clafin, Edward B., ed. *JFK Wants to Know: Memos from the President's Office, 1961–63*.
New York: William Morris and Co. Inc., 1991.
Glennon, John P., ed. *Foreign Relations of the United States, 1961–1963*. Vols. 1–3, *Vietnam 1961–63*. Washington, D.C.: United States Government Printing Office,
1991.
———. ed. *Foreign Relations of the United States (FRUS) 1964–1968*. Vol. 1. *Vietnam 1964*. Washington, D.C.: United States Government Printing Office, 1992.
Herring, George C., ed. *The Secret Diplomacy of the Vietnam War: The Negotiating Volumes of the Pentagon Papers*. Austin: University of Texas Press, 1983.
Humphrey, David C., ed. *Foreign Relations of the United States, 1964–1968*. Vol. 4,
Vietnam 1966. Washington, D.C.: United States Government Printing Office,
1998.
Humphrey, David C., Ronald D. Landa, and Louis J. Smith, eds. *Foreign Relations of the United States, 1964–1968*. Vol. 2, *Vietnam January–June 1965*. Washington,
D.C.: United States Government Printing Office, 1996.
Humphrey, David C., Edward C. Keefer, and Louis J. Smith, eds. *Foreign Relations of the United States, 1964–1968*. Vol. 3, *Vietnam June–December 1965*. Washington,
D.C.: United States Government Printing Office, 1996.
Porter, Gareth. *Vietnam: A History in Documents*. New York: New American Library,
1981.
Public Papers of the Presidents of the United States: Lyndon B. Johnson 1963–1964.
Washington, D.C.: United States Government Printing Office, 1965.
Public Papers of the Presidents of the United States: Lyndon B. Johnson 1965. Washington, D.C.: United States Government Printing Office, 1966.
Public Papers of the Presidents of the United States: Lyndon B. Johnson 1966. 2 vols.
Washington, D.C.: United States Government Printing Office, 1967.
Public Papers of the Presidents of the United States: Lyndon B. Johnson 1967. 2 vols.
Washington, D.C.: United States Government Printing Office, 1968.

Great Britain

Command Paper 2834, *Documents Relating to British Involvement in the Indo-China Conflict 1945–1965.* London: Her Majesty's Stationery Office, 1965.

Hansard: House of Commons Debate, Fifth Series. London: Her Majesty's Stationery Office.

Keesing's Contemporary Archives. Keynsham, Bristol: Keesing's Publications.

Labour Party Conferences, Transport House, Smith Square, London.

Newspapers and Journals

New Statesman
New York Times
The Times (London)
Tribune
Venture

Memoirs, Diaries, and Autobiographies

Ball, George. *The Past Has Another Pattern: Memoirs.* New York: W. W. Norton and Company, 1982.

Benn, Tony. *Office without Power: Diaries 1968–72.* London: Arrow Books, 1989.

———. *Out of the Wilderness: Diaries 1963–67.* London: Arrow Books, 1991.

Brandon, Henry. *Special Relationships: A Foreign Correspondent's Memoirs from Roosevelt to Reagan.* London: Macmillan, 1988.

Brown, George. *In My Way: The Political Memoirs of Lord George-Brown.* London: Victor Gollancz Ltd., 1971.

Callaghan, James. *Time and Chance.* London: Collins, 1987.

Castle, Barbara. *The Barbara Castle Diaries 1964–76.* London: Papermac, 1990.

———. *Fighting All the Way.* London: Macmillan, 1993.

Cooper, Chester L. *The Lost Crusade: The Full Story of U.S. Involvement in Vietnam from Roosevelt to Nixon.* London: MacGibbon and Kee, 1970.

Coopey, R., S. Fielding, and H. Tiratsoo, eds. *The Wilson Governments 1964–1970.* London: Pinter, 1993.

Crossman, Richard. *The Crossman Diaries: Selections from the Diaries of a Cabinet Minister 1964–70.* London: Mandarin, 1991.

Falkender, Marcia. *Downing Street in Perspective.* London: Weidenfeld and Nicolson, 1983.

Gore-Booth, Paul. *With Great Truth and Respect.* London: Constable, 1974.

Healey, Denis. *The Time of My Life.* London: Penguin, 1989.

Heren, Louis. *No Hail, No Farewell.* Harper and Row, 1970.

Johnson, Lady Bird. *A White House Diary.* London: Weidenfeld and Nicolson, 1970.

Johnson, Lyndon B. *The Vantage Point: Perspectives of the Presidency, 1963–69.* New York: Holt, Rinehart and Winston, 1971.

Kaiser, Philip M. *Journeying Far and Wide: A Political and Diplomatic Memoir.* New York: Macmillan, 1992.

McNamara, Robert S. *In Retrospect: The Tragedy and Lessons of Vietnam.* New York: Random House, 1995.

Pearce, R., ed. *Patrick Gordon Walker: Political Diaries 1932–1971.* London: The Historians' Press, 1991.

Reedy, George. *Lyndon Johnson: A Memoir.* New York: Andrews and McNeal, Inc., 1982.

Short, Edward. *Whip to Wilson.* London: Macdonald and Co., 1989.

Stewart, Michael. *Life and Labour: An Autobiography.* London: Sidgwick and Jackson, 1980.

Williams, Marcia. *Inside Number 10.* London: Weidenfeld and Nicolson, 1972.

Wilson, Harold. *The Labour Government 1964–70: A Personal Record.* Harmondsworth: Penguin, 1974.

Wilson, Harold. *Final Term: The Labour Government 1974–1976.* London: Weidenfeld and Nicolson and Michael Joseph, 1979.

Wright, Peter. *Spycatcher: The Candid Autobiography of a Senior Intelligence Officer.* Victoria, Australia: William Heinemann, 1987.

BOOKS AND DISSERTATIONS

Allen, H. C. *Great Britain and the United States: A History of Anglo-American Relations 1783–1952.* London: Odhams Press Limited, 1954.

Amis, Kingsley, ed. *Harold's Years: Impressions from the New Statesman and the Spectator.* London: Quartet Books, 1977.

Ashmore, Harry S., and William C. Baggs. *Mission to Hanoi: A Chronicle of Double-Dealing in High Places.* New York: G. P. Putman's Sons, 1969.

Barber, David. *The Presidential Character: Predicting Performance in the White House.* Englewood Cliffs, N.J.: Prentice-Hall, 1992.

Bartlett, C. J. *"The Special Relationship": A Political History of Anglo-American Relations since 1945.* London: Longman, 1992.

Baylis, John. *Anglo-American Defence Relations, 1939–80: The Special Relationship.* Basingstoke: Macmillan, 1981.

Berman, Larry. *Lyndon Johnson's War: The Road to Stalemate in Vietnam.* New York: Norton, 1989.

———. *Planning a Tragedy: The Americanization of the War in Vietnam.* New York: W. W. Norton and Company, 1982.

Beschloss, Michael, ed. *Taking Charge: The Johnson White House Tapes, 1963–1964.* New York: Simon and Schuster, 1997.

———, ed. *Reaching for Glory: Lyndon Johnson's Secret White House Tapes, 1964–1965.* New York: Simon and Schuster, 2001.

Bird, Kai. *The Color of Truth: McGeorge Bundy and William Bundy: Brothers in Arms.* New York: Touchstone, 1998.

Blackburn, Robert M. *Mercenaries and Lyndon Johnson's "More Flags": The Hiring of Korean, Filipino and Thai Soldiers in the Vietnam War.* Jefferson, N.C.: McFarland, 1994.

Blang, Eugenie Margareta. *To Urge Common Sense on the Americans: United States' Relations with France, Great Britain and the Federal Republic of Germany in the Context of the Vietnam War, 1961–1968.* DA 9989342, William and Mary College, April 2001.

Bransby, Guy. *Her Majesty's Vietnam Soldier.* Hanley Swan, Worcestershire: Self Publication Association, 1992.

Bridge, Carl, ed. *Munich to Vietnam: Australia's Relations with Britain and the United States since the 1930's.* Melbourne: Melbourne University Press, 1992.

Brigham, Robert K. *Guerrilla Diplomacy: The NLF's Foreign Relations and the Vietnam War.* Ithaca, N.Y.: Cornell University Press, 1999.

Burke, John P., and Fred I. Greenstein. *How Presidents Test Reality: Decisions on Vietnam, 1954 and 1965.* New York: Russell Sage Foundation, 1989.

Busch, Peter. *All the Way with JFK? Britain, the US, and the Vietnam War.* Oxford: Oxford University Press, 2003.

Campbell, Duncan. *The Unsinkable Aircraft Carrier: American Military Power in Britain.* London: Michael Joseph, 1984.

Clark, Ian. *Nuclear Diplomacy and the Special Relationship: Britain's Deterrent and America, 1957–1962.* Oxford: Clarendon Press, 1994.

Coates, Ken. *Mr Wilson Speaks Frankly and Fearlessly on Vietnam to Bertrand Russell.* London: Bertrand Russell Peace Foundation, 1968.

Cohen, Warren I., and Nancy Bernkopf Tucker, eds. *Lyndon Johnson Confronts the World: American Foreign Policy 1963–1968.* Cambridge: Cambridge University Press, 1994.

Commager, Henry Steel, ed. *Britain through American Eyes.* New York: McGraw-Hill, 1974.

Conkin, Paul K. *Big Daddy from the Pedernales: Lyndon Baines Johnson.* Boston: Tawyne, 1986.

Cormier, Frank. *The Way He Was.* New York: Doubleday and Co. Inc., 1977.

Dallek, Robert. *Lone Star Rising: Lyndon Johnson and His Times 1908–1960.* Oxford: Oxford University Press, 1991.

———. *Flawed Giant: Lyndon Johnson and His Times 1961–1973.* Oxford: Oxford University Press, 1998.

Debenedetti, Charles. *An American Ordeal: The Antiwar Movement of the Vietnam Era.* Syracuse, N.Y.: Syracuse University Press, 1990.

Dickie, John. *"Special" No More. Anglo-American Relations: Rhetoric and Reality.* London: Weidenfeld and Nicholson, 1994.

Dimbleby, David, and David Reynolds. *An Ocean Apart: The Relationship between Britain and America in the Twentieth Century.* London: Guild Publishing, 1988.

Divine, Robert, ed. *The Johnson Years, Volume 3: LBJ at Home and Abroad.* Lawrence: University of Kansas Press, 1994.

Dobson, Alan P. *Anglo-American Relations in the Twentieth Century.* London: Routledge, 1995.

Dockrill, Saki. *Britain's Retreat from East of Suez: The Choice between Europe and the World?* Basingstoke: Palgrave, 2002.

Donovan, Hedley. *Roosevelt to Reagan: A Reporter's Encounters with Nine Presidents.* New York: Harper and Row, 1985.

Dorril, Stephen, and Robin Ramsay. *Smear! Wilson and the Secret State.* London: Grafton, 1992.

Dumbrell, John. *A Special Relationship: Anglo-American Relations in the Cold War and After.* Basingstoke: Macmillan, 2001.

Englander, David, ed. *Britain and America: Studies in Comparative History, 1760–1970.* New Haven: Yale University Press, 1997.

Epstein, L. *Britain—Uneasy Ally.* Chicago: University of Chicago Press, 1954.

Evans, Rowland, and Robert Novak. *Lyndon B. Johnson: The Exercise of Power.* New York: Signet Books, 1966.

Foot, Paul. *The Politics of Harold Wilson.* Harmondsworth: Penguin, 1968.

Frankel, Joseph. *British Foreign Policy, 1945–1973.* London: Open University Press for the Royal Institute of International Affairs, 1975.

Friedrich, Alexandra M. *Awakenings: The Impact of the Vietnam War on West German-American Relations in the 1960s.* DA 9990315, Temple University, April 2001.

Gallup, George H. *The Gallup Poll—Public Opinion, 1935–71.* Vol. 3, *1959–71.* New York: Random House, 1971.

Gardner, Lloyd C. *Pay Any Price: Lyndon Johnson and the Wars for Vietnam.* Chicago: Ivan R. Dee, 1995.

Gardner, Lloyd C., and Ted Gittinger, eds. *International Perspectives on Vietnam.* College Station: Texas A&M University Press, 2000.

Gelb, Leslie, and Richard K. Betts. *The Irony of Vietnam: The System Worked.* Washington. D.C.: The Brookings Institution, 1979.

Gelber, L. *America in Britain's Place: The Leadership of the West and Anglo-American Unity.* New York: Frederick I. Praeger, 1961.

Gittinger, Ted, ed. *The Johnson Years: A Vietnam Roundtable.* Austin: University of Texas, 1993.

Goldman, Eric F. *The Tragedy of Lyndon Johnson.* New York: Dell, 1969.

Goodman, Allen E. *The Long Peace: America's Search for a Negotiated Settlement of the Vietnam War.* Berkeley: University of California, 1986.

Gordon, Michael. *Conflict and Consensus in Labour's Foreign Policy, 1914–65.* Stanford: Stanford University Press, 1969.

Grosser, Alfred. *The Western Alliance: European-American Relations Since 1945.* New York: Continuum, 1980.

Halberstam, David. *The Best and the Brightest.* New York: Fawcett Crest Books, 1972.

Hammond, Paul Y. *LBJ and the Presidential Management of Foreign Relations.* Austin: University of Texas, 1992.

Hatcher, Patrick Lloyd. *Suicide of an Elite: American Internationalists and Vietnam.* Stanford, Calif.: Stanford University Press, 1990.

Hathaway, Robert M. *Great Britain and the United States: Special Relations since World War II.* Boston: Twayne, 1990.

Herring, George C. *America's Longest War: The United States and Vietnam 1950–1975.* New York: McGraw-Hill, 1986.

———. *LBJ and Vietnam: A Different Kind of War.* Austin: University of Texas Press, 1994.

Hitchens, Christopher. *Blood, Class and Nostalgia.* London: Chatto and Windus, 1990.

Hogan, Michael J., ed. *America in the World: The Historiography of American Foreign Relations since 1941.* Cambridge: Cambridge University Press, 1995.

Hollander, Paul. *Anti-Americanism: Critiques at Home and Abroad 1964–1990.* New York: Oxford University Press, 1992.

Jackson, Robert. *The Malayan Emergency: The Commonwealth's War 1948–1966.* London: Routledge, 1991.

Jones, Matthew. *Conflict and Confrontation in South East Asia, 1961–65.* Cambridge: Cambridge University Press, 2001.

Karnow, Stanley. *Vietnam: A History.* New York: Penguin Books, 1991.

Kaufman, Victor S. *Confronting Communism: U.S. and British Policies toward China.* Columbia: University of Missouri Press, 2001.

Kearns, Doris. *Lyndon Johnson and the American Dream.* New York: Signet, 1976.

King, Cecil. *Cecil King Diary 1965–70.* London: Jonathan Cape, 1972.

Kraslow, David, and Stuart H. Loory. *The Secret Search for Peace in Vietnam.* New York: Vintage, 1968.

Langguth, A. J. *Our Vietnam: The War 1954–1975.* New York: Simon and Schuster, 2000.

Lankford, Nelson. *The Last American Aristocrat: The Biography of Ambassador David K. E. Bruce.* Boston: Little, Brown and Co., 1996.

Lapping, Brian. *The Labour Government 1964–70.* London: Penguin, 1970.

Larsen, Stanley Robert, and James Lawton Collins Jr. *Allied Participation in Vietnam.* Washington, D.C.: Department of the Army, U.S. Government Printing Office, 1975.

Leigh, David. *The Wilson Plot: How the Spycatchers and Their American Allies Tried to Overthrow the British Government.* New York: Pantheon, 1988.

Logevall, Fredrik. *Choosing War: The Lost Chance for Peace and the Escalation of War in Vietnam.* Berkeley: University of California Press, 1999.

Louis, William Roger, and Hedley Bull, eds. *The Special Relationship: Anglo-American Relations since 1945.* Oxford: Oxford University Press, 1986.

Lowe, Peter. *Britain in the Far East: A Survey from 1819 to the Present.* London: Longman, 1981.

Mander, John. *Great Britain or Little England?* London: Penguin, 1963.

McDonald, Ian S. *Anglo-American Relations since the Second World War.* New York: St. Martin's Press, 1974.

McNamara, Robert S., James Blight, Robert Brigham, Thomas Biersteker, and Col. Herbert Schandler. *Argument without End: In Search of Answers to the Vietnam Tragedy.* New York: Public Affairs, 1999.

Miller, Merle. *Lyndon: An Oral Biography.* New York: G. P. Putnams and Sons, 1980.

Moïse, Edwin E. *Tonkin Gulf and the Escalation of the Vietnam War.* Chapel Hill: University of North Carolina Press, 1996.

Neustadt, Richard E. *Alliance Politics.* London: Columbia University Press, 1970.

Nicholas, H. G. *Britain and the United States.* Baltimore: Johns Hopkins University Press, 1963.

———. *The United States and Britain.* Chicago: University of Chicago Press, 1975.

Nunnerly, David. *President Kennedy and Britain.* London: Bodley Head, 1972.

Olson, James. *Where the Domino Fell.* New York: St. Martin's Press, 1991.

Page, Caroline. "The Strategic Manipulation of American Official Propaganda during the Vietnam War, 1965–1966, and British Opinion on the War." Ph.D. dissertation, University of Reading, 1989.

———. *U.S. Official Propaganda during the Vietnam War, 1965–73: The Limits of Persuasion.* Leicester: Leicester University Press, 1994.

Painter, David S., and Sally G. Irvine. "The Geneva Conference of 1954: Indochina." Washington, D.C.: Pew Case Studies in International Affairs, 1988.

Pathak, Archana. "British Foreign Policy towards Malaysia, 1957–1967." Ph.D. dissertation, University of Hull, 1988.

Pelling, Henry. *America and the British Left: From Bright to Bevan.* London: Adam and Charles Black, 1956.

Pimlott, Ben. *Harold Wilson*. London: Harper Collins, 1993.

Ponting, Clive. *Breach of Promise: Labour in Power 1964–1970*. London: Penguin, 1990.

Preston, Thomas. *The President and His Inner Circle: Leadership Style and the Advisory Process in Foreign Affairs*. New York: Colombia University Press, 2001.

Radványi, János. *Delusion and Reality: Gambits, Hoaxes, and Diplomatic Oneupmanship in Vietnam*. South Bend, Ind.: Gateway Editions Limited, 1978.

Renwick Robin. *Fighting With Allies: America and Britain in Peace and War*. Basingstoke: Macmillan, 1996.

Richardson, George G. "George Ball's Grand Design, 1961–1966." Ph.D. dissertation, University of South Carolina, 1992.

Richardson, Louise. *When Allies Differ: Anglo-American Relations During the Suez and Falklands Crisis*. New York: St. Martin's Press, 1996.

Richelson, Jeffrey T., and Desmond Ball. *The Ties That Bind: Intelligence Cooperation between the UKUSA Countries—the United Kingdom, the United States of America, Canada, Australia and New Zealand*. Hemel Hempstead: Allen and Unwin, 1985.

Rosie, George. *The British in Vietnam: How the Twenty Five Year War Began*. London: Panther Book, 1970.

Rostow, Walt W. *Diffusion of Power: An Essay in Recent History*. New York: Macmillan, 1972.

Roth, Andrew. *Sir Harold Wilson: Yorkshire Walter Mitty*. London: Macdonald and Jane's, 1977.

Rowan, Randy. "A Foreign Policy in Opposition: The British Labour Party and the Far East, 1951–1964." Ph.D. dissertation, Texas Tech University, 1992.

Ruane, Kevin. *War and Revolution in Vietnam, 1930–1975*. London: UCL Press, 1998.

Salisbury, Harrison. *Behind the Lines—Hanoi*. New York: Harper and Row, 1967.

Sanders, David. *British Foreign Policy since 1945*. London: Macmillan, 1990.

Schulzinger, Robert D. *A Time for War: The United States and Vietnam 1941–1975*. Oxford: Oxford University Press, 1997.

Shesol, Jeff. *Mutual Contempt: Lyndon Johnson, Robert Kennedy, and the Feud That Defined a Decade*. New York: W. W. Norton, 1997.

Smith, Geoffrey. *Reagan and Thatcher*. London: Bodley Head, 1990.

Smith, R. B. *An International History of the Vietnam War*. Vol. 2. *The Struggle for South East Asia 1961–65*. London: Macmillan, 1985.

Stone, Gary Steven. *The Senate and the Vietnam War, 1964–1968*. DA 9970290, Columbia University, October 2000.

Thies, Wallace J. *When Governments Collide: Coercion and Diplomacy in the Vietnam Conflict 1964–68*. Berkeley, CA: University of California Press, 1982.

Thomas, Evan. *Robert Kennedy: His Life*. New York: Simon and Schuster, 2000.

Thompson, Robert. *Defeating Communist Insurgency: Experiences from Malaya and Vietnam*. London: Chatto and Windus, 1974.

———. *Make for the Hills. Memories of Far Eastern Wars*. London: Leo Cooper, 1989.

Thorne, Christopher. *Allies of a Kind*. London: Hamish Hamilton, 1978.

VanDeMark, Brian. *Into the Quagmire: Lyndon Johnson and the Escalation of the Vietnam War*. New York: Oxford University Press, 1991.

Warbey, William. *Vietnam: The Truth*. London: Merlin Press, 1965.

Watt, D. C. *Succeeding John Bull: America in Britain's Place*. Cambridge: Cambridge University Press, 1984.

White, Brian. *Britain, Détente and Changing East-West Relations.* London: Routledge, 1992.

Widgery, David. *The Left in Britain.* London: Penguin, 1976.

Wyn Rees, G. *Anglo-American Approaches to Alliance Security, 1955–60.* Basingstoke: Macmillan, 1996.

Young, Marilyn. *The Vietnam Wars, 1945–1990.* New York: HarperCollins Publishers, 1991.

Ziegler, Philip. *Wilson: The Authorized Life of Lord Wilson of Rievaulx.* London: Weidenfeld and Nicolson, 1993.

ARTICLES

Ball, Moya Ann. "The Phantom of the Oval Office: The John F. Kennedy Assassination's Symbolic Impact on Lyndon B. Johnson, His Key Advisers, and the Vietnam Decision-Making Process," *Presidential Studies Quarterly* 24 (1994): 105–19.

Barrett, David M. "Doing Tuesday Lunch at Lyndon Johnson's White House," *Political Science and Politics* (December 1991): 676–79.

———. "The Mythology Surrounding Lyndon Johnson, His Advisers, and the 1965 Decision to Escalate the Vietnam War," *Political Science Quarterly* 103 (Winter 1988–89): 637–63.

———. "Secrecy and Openness in Lyndon Johnson's White House: Political Style, Pluralism and the Presidency," *Review of Politics* (1992): 72–111.

Beckett, Ian F. W. "Robert Thompson and the British Advisory Mission to South Vietnam, 1961–1965," *Small Wars and Insurgencies* 8, no. 3 (1997): 41–63.

Cable, James. "Interdependence: A Drug of Addiction?" *International Affairs* 59 (1983): 365–79.

Catterall, Peter, ed. "Witness Seminar: The East of Suez Decision," *Contemporary Record* 7, no. 3 (Winter 1993): 612–53.

Clutterbuck, Richard. "Sir Robert Thompson: A Lifetime of Counterinsurgency," *Army Quarterly and Defence Journal* 120, part 2 (1990): 140–45.

Combs, Arthur. "The Path Not Taken: The British Alternative to U.S. Policy in Vietnam, 1954–1956," *Diplomatic History* 19, no. 1 (1995): 33–57.

Conkin, Paul K. "The Johnson Years: An Essay Review," *Wisconsin Magazine of History* 56 (Autumn 1972): 59–64.

Crawford, Kenneth. "LBJ: Who's That?" *Newsweek,* February 11, 1963, 39.

Dallek, Robert. "Lyndon Johnson and Vietnam: The Making of a Tragedy," *Diplomatic History* 20, no. 2 (Spring 1996): 147–62.

———. "Labour or Conservative: Does It Matter in Anglo-American Relations?" *Journal of Contemporary History* 25 (1990): 387–407.

Dobson, Alan P. "The Years of Transition: Anglo-American Relations 1961–1967," *Review of International Studies* 16 (1990): 239–58.

Dockrill, Saki. "Forging the Anglo-American Global Defence Partnership: Harold Wilson, Lyndon Johnson and the Washington Summit, December 1964," *Journal of Strategic Studies* 23, no. 4 (December 2000): 107–29.

Dumbrell, John. "The Johnson Administration and the British Labour Government: Vietnam, the Pound and East of Suez," *Journal of American Studies* 30, part 2 (August 1996): 111–231.

Dumbrell, John, and Sylvia Ellis. "British Involvement in Vietnam Peace Initiatives, 1966–1867: Marigolds, Sunflowers, and 'Kosygin Week,' " *Diplomatic History* 27, no. 1 (January 2003): 113–49.

Etheredge, Lloyd S. "Personality Effects on American Foreign Policy, 1898–1968," *American Political Science Review* 72 (June 1978): 434–51.

Fielding, Jeremy. "Coping with Decline: U.S. Policy Towards the British Defence Reviews of 1966," *Diplomatic History* 23, no. 4 (Fall 1999): 633–56.

Hack, Karl. "The Limits of British Influence in Asia," *20th Century British History* 6, no. 1 (1995): 101–5.

Herring, George C., and Richard H. Immerman. "Eisenhower, Dulles and Dienbienphu: 'The Day We Didn't Go to War' Revisited," *Journal of American History* 71 (September 1984): 343–63.

Hershberg, James G. "Who Murdered 'Marigold'?—New Evidence on the Mysterious Failure of Poland's Secret Initiative to Start U.S.-North Vietnamese Peace Talks, 1966," Working Paper no. 27, *Cold War International History Project*, http://cwihp.si.edu/cwihplib.nsf.

Jones, Matthew. "U.S. Relations with Indonesia, the Kennedy-Johnson Transition, and the Vietnam Connection, 1963–1965," *Diplomatic History* 26, no. 2 (Spring 2002): 249–81.

Kearns, Doris. "Lyndon Johnson's Political Personality," *Political Science Quarterly* 91 (Fall 1976): 385–409.

Kunz, Diane. "Lyndon Johnson's Dollar Diplomacy," *History Today* 42 (April 1992): 45–51.

Kunz, Diane B. " 'Somewhat Mixed Up Together': Anglo-American Defence and Financial Policy during the 1960s," *Journal of Imperial and Commonwealth History* 27, no. 2 (1999): 213–32.

Miliband, Ralph. "Vietnam and Western Socialism," *Socialist Register* (1967): 11–25.

Nicholas, H.G. "Britain After Labour's First Year," *Modern Age* 10 (Winter 1966): 21–29.

Reynolds, David. "A 'Special Relationship'? America, Britain and the International Order since the Second World War," *International Affairs* 62 (Winter 1985): 1–20.

———. "Rethinking Anglo-American Relations," *International Affairs* (1989): 89–111.

Ruane, Kevin. "Anthony Eden, British Diplomacy and the Origins of the Geneva Conference of 1954," *History Journal* 37, no. 1 (1994): 153–72.

———. " 'Containing America': Aspects of British Foreign Policy and the Cold War in South-East Asia, 1951–1954," *Diplomacy and Statecraft* 7, no. 1 (March 1996): 141–74.

———. "Refusing to Pay the Price: British Foreign Policy and the Pursuit of Victory in Vietnam, 1952–1954," *Economic History Review* 435 (1995): 70–92.

Small, Melvyn. "The Impact of the Anti-War Movement on Lyndon Johnson 1965–68," *Peace and Change* (Spring 1984): 1–22.

Steininger, Rolf. " 'The Americans Are in a Hopeless Position': Great Britain and the War in Vietnam, 1964–65," *Diplomacy and Statecraft* 8, no. 3 (November 1997): 237–85.

Thorne, Christopher. "After the Europeans: American Designs for the Remaking of Southeast Asia," *Diplomatic History* 12 (Spring 1988): 201–8.

—————. "Indochina and Anglo-American Relations," *Pacific Historical Review* 45 (February 1976): 73–96.

Turnbull, C. Mary. "Britain and Vietnam 1948–1955," *War and Society* 6, no. 2 (September 1988): 104–24.

Warner, Geoffrey. "The Anglo-American Special Relationship," *Diplomatic History* 13 (1989): 479–99.

—————. "The United States and Vietnam 1945–65: Part II: 1954–65," *International Affairs* 4 (October 1972): 593–613.

Weddernburn, K. W. "The British Government and Vietnam," *Listener,* March 18, 1965, 393–95.

Wilson, Craig. "Rhetoric, Reality and Dissent: The Vietnam Policy of the British Labour Government, 1964–1970," *Social Science Journal* 23, no. 1 (1986): 17–31.

Wright, Esmond. "The Special Relationship," *History Today* (April 1991): 53–57.

Young, John W. "The Wilson Government and the Davies Peace Mission to North Vietnam, July 1965," *Review of International Studies* 24 (1998): 545–62.

POPULAR MAGAZINES

Alsop, Stewart. "The Interesting Mr Wilson," *Economist,* December 1964, 14.

Freeman, John. *New Statesman,* December 11, 1964, 916.

Stewart, Gloria. "What the Vietcong Really Want," *New Statesman,* January 20, 1967, 69–70.

"Vietnam—What's Wilson Waiting For?" (editorial), *New Statesman,* March 12, 1965, 1.

CHAPTERS IN EDITED BOOKS

Costigliola, Frank. "LBJ, Germany and the 'End of the Cold War.' " In *Lyndon Johnson Confronts the World: American Foreign Policy 1963–1968,* edited by Warren I. Cohen and Nancy Bernkopf Tucker. Cambridge: Cambridge University Press, 1994.

McDougall, Derek. "The Malayan Emergency and Confrontation." In *Munich to Vietnam: Australia's Relations with Britain and the United States since the 1930s,* edited by Carl Bridge. Melbourne: Melbourne University Press, 1992.

Toynbee, P. "Dictators, Demagogues or Prigs?" *New Statesman,* January 5, 1965. In *Harold's Years: Impressions from the New Statesman and the Spectator,"* edited by Kingsley Amis. London: Quartet Books, 1977.

Woodward, Nicholas. "Labour's Economic Performance, 1964–70." In *The Wilson Governments 1964–70,* edited by R. Coopey, S. Fielding, and N. Tiratsoo. London: Pinter, 1993.

Index

About the Author

SYLVIA ELLIS is Senior Lecturer in History at the University of Northumbria at Newcastle, England. She received her Ph.D. from the University of Newcastle and has published several articles and book chapters on Anglo-American relations in the 1960s.